D0350010

THE TEN
YEAR WAR

ALSO BY JONATHAN COHN

Sick:

The Untold Story of America's Health Care Crisis—
and the People Who Pay the Price

THE TEN YEAR WAR

Obamacare and the
Unfinished Crusade for
Universal Coverage

JONATHAN COHN

ST. MARTIN'S PRESS NEW YORK

First published in the United States by St. Martin's Press, an imprint of St. Martin's Publishing Group

THE TEN YEAR WAR. Copyright © 2021 by Jonathan Cohn. All rights reserved. Printed in the United States of America. For information, address St. Martin's Publishing Group, 120 Broadway, New York, NY 10271.

www.stmartins.com

Design by Meryl Sussman Levavi

The Library of Congress Cataloging-in-Publication Data is available upon request.

ISBN 978-1-250-27093-1 (hardcover)

ISBN 978-1-250-27094-8 (ebook)

Our books may be purchased in bulk for promotional, educational, or business use. Please contact your local bookseller or the Macmillan Corporate and Premium Sales Department at 1-800-221-7945, extension 5442, or by email at MacmillanSpecialMarkets@macmillan.com.

First Edition: 2021

10 9 8 7 6 5 4 3 2 1

For Mom and Dad

Contents

Part III: 2010–2018

THE TEN
YEAR WAR

Introduction

The Ten Year War

1.

John McCain stood on the Senate floor, an outstretched arm signaling for the clerk's attention, as his colleagues and a nation watched to see what he would do.

It was about an hour and a half past midnight on Friday, July 28, 2017—the culmination of a debate that had begun some six months before, when Donald Trump had become president. Republicans were finally in a position to repeal the Affordable Care Act, the 2010 law that had transformed American health care.

"Obamacare" represented everything conservatives hated about big government. They saw it as a sprawling amalgam of taxes, spending, and regulation that interfered with the workings of the free market and forcibly redistributed money from one group in society to another. But in the years since the law's enactment, repeal had become more than another agenda item. It had turned into the party's defining cause, the rallying cry that brought its different factions together and animated its most passionate supporters.

And now it was on the verge of happening. The House had already passed a repeal bill of its own. If the Senate did the same, it would only be a matter of time before the two chambers worked out a compromise and sent legislation to the White House for presidential signature.

Trump was plainly eager to secure his own place in the history books and, perhaps more importantly, to scratch out Obama's—so much so that it wasn't clear whether he grasped, or cared, about repeal's impact. But that impact promised to be enormous.

More than twenty million people relied on the Affordable Care Act for their health coverage. The number of Americans without insurance had plummeted to less than 10 percent of the population, the lowest rate ever recorded. And the lives of real people were changing for the better. More were seeing the doctor and getting the tests they needed. Fewer were going bankrupt because of hospital bills. They were hotel housekeepers and cancer survivors, retail workers and parents of children with rare diseases—all of them with security they had never known before, security that was suddenly in jeopardy.[1]

Still, even with the law in place, "universal health care" remained an aspiration. Millions had no insurance, and millions more still struggled with medical bills. Some had cheaper insurance before the Affordable Care Act took effect, only to see carriers cancel those plans—and they remembered, bitterly, Obama's promise that they would be able to keep their old coverage if they liked it. Their anger at Obama and the Democrats was one reason that Republicans had gained control of Congress and taken back the White House, putting repeal within reach.

Republicans had moved swiftly, using a special parliamentary procedure that allowed the Senate to pass legislation with just fifty votes, instead of the customary sixty. Whip counts showed that forty-nine of the chamber's fifty-two Republicans were already on board. But two relatively moderate Republicans, Susan Collins of Maine and Lisa Murkowski of Alaska, were voting no. Too many of their constituents would suffer, they said. McCain's would be the decisive vote.

His instincts on domestic policy were mostly conservative, making him skeptical of the taxes and regulations that the law had fostered, and he sounded like his more strident colleagues when he said the Affordable Care Act was a "disaster" that was "failing" his constituents. Arizona's experience with the law had been among the rockiest, with premiums skyrocketing and insurers leaving the state because they were losing so much money. Those problems were the focus of McCain's very first 2016 campaign ad, which trumpeted that "John McCain is leading the fight to stop Obamacare."[2]

But McCain had been making Republican leaders nervous all week, ever since his dramatic flight back from Arizona, where he was undergoing treatment for the brain tumor that would soon take his life. A war hero and former presidential candidate, McCain was notoriously unpredictable and had a history of bucking the party leadership. He was one of the few remaining institutionalists in the Senate, somebody who took words like "deliberation" and "bipartisanship" seriously. Among his proudest accomplishments was a major reform of campaign finance laws he had cosponsored with Russ Feingold, a liberal Democrat from Wisconsin.

Repeal, by contrast, was a purely partisan project, one that GOP leaders were trying to ram through the chamber as quickly as possible. The usual committees weren't holding hearings, and members were being asked to vote before they even understood the basics of what they were considering. McCain had made his most explicit warning a few days earlier as debate began. Standing in the well of the Senate, a long scar from the recent medical work visible across his lower temple, McCain vowed, "I will not vote for the bill as it is today."

Most Republican leaders found it difficult to believe McCain would fly back from Arizona, in the middle of life-sustaining cancer treatment, to cast a vote that would alienate so many of his colleagues and supporters—to say nothing of rescuing a program signed into law by the man who once vanquished him in a presidential election. On Wednesday, the day before the final vote, he told administration officials he was a likely yes on repeal. But he had been having misgivings for weeks. Just before returning to Washington from Arizona, he had confided by phone to his old friend, former senator Joe Lieberman of Connecticut, that he was thinking seriously of voting no.[3]

In the evening, as the moment approached, Vice President Mike Pence, on hand as the administration's chief lobbyist and potential tie-breaking vote in the Senate, pulled McCain aside for a conversation. Pence left with a conspicuously grim look on his face. A few minutes later, McCain was standing on the floor and joking with Democrats while Mitch McConnell, leader of the Senate Republicans, huddled with several of his lieutenants a few feet away. Trump called by phone, and McCain listened, according to multiple accounts, without saying much.[4]

The GOP leaders were still standing there when the roll call got underway. McCain, who had left the floor, walked back through the chamber doors and stopped in front of the podium. He was unable to lift his arms above his shoulders, a result of torture during the five years he spent as a prisoner of war in Vietnam. All he could do was to hold his right hand outward, stiffly, while he waited for the clerk's attention. For a second, he looked like a Roman emperor waiting to rule on a gladiator—until the clerk looked up, and McCain turned his thumb down in a quick, jerky move. "No," he said.

One Democratic senator gasped audibly, another pumped her fist in the air. Way in the back, beneath the overhang of the visitors' gallery, two more Democratic senators cheered until minority leader Chuck Schumer frantically waved at them to stop.[5]

At the front of the chamber, McConnell stood motionless, hands across his chest while he stared down at his feet. McCain walked away, taking his usual seat a few rows up on the Republican side of the chamber. Not once did he look in McConnell's direction.

2.

It was the most dramatic moment the Senate chamber had seen in a generation and surely among the most consequential. A year and a half later, Republicans lost control of the House in a devastating midterm election and, with it, their ability to pass repeal legislation—bringing to a close a fight over policy and politics that had officially started ten years earlier, the day Obama won the 2008 presidential election.

When Obama as a presidential candidate had vowed to sign a universal health care bill, achieving a goal Democrats had pursued since Harry Truman's day, it felt like just another empty political promise. The idea that Obama would become president still seemed hard to believe, and the prospect of a forty-seven-year-old novice at national politics achieving something so big and controversial as universal health care was downright preposterous. But Obama would go on to win the election, and despite pressure from outside and inside his inner circle to abandon his pledge, he committed to pursuing major health care reform right away.

He got plenty of help. Advocates for reform had spent years preparing quietly for the moment, developing both a detailed policy proposal and a strategy for getting it through Congress. Many were veterans of past efforts, and they were determined not to make the same mistakes. So were their allies in Congress, especially one, Massachusetts senator Ted Kennedy, who was battling the same kind of brain tumor that would later afflict McCain. He knew this chance at reform was his last.

The ensuing political fight was brutal and dragged on for longer than anybody had anticipated, stretching through and then beyond Obama's first year in office. Democratic leaders had to satisfy caucus members who wanted legislation to do more without losing the ones who insisted that it do less, while addressing frequently conflicting demands of organizations representing patients, unions, employers, and the health care industry itself.

Democratic leaders also had to contend with relentless, unyielding opposition from Republicans, whose power was magnified by funders like the Koch brothers, loyal media outlets like Fox News, and an apportionment system in the U.S. Senate that gave Wyoming the same number of votes as New York. On multiple occasions, the effort seemed to falter, with even enthusiastic champions ready to accept defeat. But Obama didn't give up, and neither did his partners, and late in the evening of March 21, 2010, the House gave final approval to the legislation.

Two days later, as triumphant Democrats gathered in the East Room of the White House for a signing ceremony, Obama reminded them why the law was so important—the many decades they'd spent trying to create a program like this, the many people who so desperately needed the help. "We have now just enshrined, as soon as I sign this bill, the core principle that everybody should have some basic security when it comes to their health care," Obama said. Joe Biden was vice president then, and he embraced Obama, telling him the legislation was a "big fucking deal."

Nobody questioned that assessment. But the debate in Congress had exposed deep new ruptures between the two parties. Democrats believed that health care should be a right. Republicans didn't. That was a change from the recent past, when large numbers of Republicans at least paid lip service to the idea of universal coverage. It was a sign of how much the party's ideological and strategic moorings had changed.

And Republicans weren't about to give up. They committed themselves to undoing what Democrats had done and spent the next few years trying—by challenging the law's constitutionality in federal courts, turning its shortcomings into a political cudgel, and using leverage in Congress and state capitals to undermine implementation.

Many of these endeavors succeeded, even though repeal legislation failed, and Republicans didn't stop even after they lost their House majority. In the latter years of the Trump presidency, they rewrote insurance rules, slashed funds for outreach, and looked for ways to reduce enrollment in Medicaid.

Also, they filed another lawsuit.

3.

I decided to write this book in 2019, following the midterms, thinking the public's decisive verdict on Republican control of Congress had put to rest, finally, existential questions about the Affordable Care Act. I was wrong. As this book goes to press, the justices of the Supreme Court are weighing a new lawsuit that alleges the program now contains a fatal constitutional flaw.

Odds of the case succeeding increased with the September 2020 death of Justice Ruth Bader Ginsburg, a liberal and reliable vote to defend the program. Virtually any outcome now seems plausible, including a ruling that wipes the Affordable Care Act off the books. But legal experts, including architects of previous challenges to the Affordable Care Act, think this latest case has no merit. Even some of the conservative justices seemed skeptical during oral arguments in November. And a decision to invalidate the law would risk a severe political backlash, because the majority of Americans don't want to give up the law's key features.

Probably the best proof is the way Republicans have behaved in the past two elections. After hammering away at Obamacare and promising to abolish it for so many years, in both 2018 and 2020 they did everything they could to avoid the subject. And when they couldn't dodge questions, they furiously denied that their repeal efforts would have deprived millions of coverage or taken away the law's protections for preexisting conditions. Some pledged to support those provisions so emphatically and so repeatedly that they started to sound like Obama.

But the 2020 campaign also took place against the backdrop of the COVID-19 pandemic. For all the millions who now had health security from the Affordable Care Act, many millions still did not. At a time when affordable medical care was more important than ever, large numbers of people couldn't find it.

Joe Biden won the election by promising to keep pushing toward universal coverage. It's a goal that Democrats continue to share, although there's a divide within the party over how to do it. Some want to build on the Affordable Care Act, while others want to replace it with a government-run insurance program that would cover everybody.

"Medicare for All," as advocates call it, is not a new concept. It dates back to the 1930s and '40s, when national health insurance first got serious attention in American politics. The idea fell out of fashion, politically and intellectually, starting in the 1960s. But its potential to make health care simple, to control health care prices through brute government force, and, finally, to guarantee coverage for all has won it newfound attention.

Republicans have responded by warning that Medicare for All would lead to rationing, higher taxes, and too much government control. These are the very same arguments about "socialized medicine" that critics have deployed against every major health care reform, going back almost a century.

It is a reminder that a great deal about the health care debate has changed over the years, but not everything—and that, to chart a course for the future, it would help to learn from the past.

4.

This book is an attempt to do just that—an effort to look back at the Affordable Care Act, arguably the most important and controversial piece of legislation in the last few decades, and learn from it. What led to its passage? Why did it end up looking like it did? What worked and what didn't? Why did it generate such intense debate for so long? And what does it tell us about our governing institutions?

The Ten Year War is a reference to the decade from November 2008 and the election of Obama to November 2018 and the defeat of the House Republican majority. But the book reaches back much further into history, because it's impossible to answer all those questions about the Affordable Care Act without understanding the political, economic, and psychological circumstances that led to it.

The book draws on my experience as a journalist writing about health care, which also goes back more than a decade—all the way to the late 1990s, when I first started covering the issue from Washington, D.C. Especially in the early years, the focus of my reporting was people who could not afford their care, because they didn't have insurance or the insurance they had didn't cover what they needed.

My reporting soon took me outside the capital and across the country. In Chicago, I met an uninsured former nun being sued by a Catholic hospital over unpaid emergency room bills. In Los Angeles, I met a security guard whose eye problems went untreated until he could no longer see. There was the Florida realtor with diabetes who couldn't get insurance because of her preexisting condition. Eventually, she found coverage, but it was through a sham program that left her on the hook for thousands of dollars in expenses. And there was the retiree in rural Tennessee who couldn't afford his medications, because the state had cut funding to the program that once paid for them. He died from a preventable heart attack.

One story in particular always stuck with me. It was about Gary Rotzler, who lived with his wife, Betsy, and their three young children in a bucolic New York village nestled in the Catskill Mountains. After he lost his job at a defense contracting firm in a round of layoffs, he and Betsy cobbled together part-time work but could never get insurance—not even when he got his old job back, because when he returned, the employer classified him as a contractor rather than a full-time employee. Betsy started feeling weak and experiencing severe back pain, but held off getting exams because she thought she might need some kind of intensive, expensive treatment and wanted to wait until either she or Gary found a job with coverage. Eventually, the pain became too much, and she found a free clinic. They diagnosed her with metastatic cancer that soon took her life—and left Gary with such massive hospital bills he had to declare bankruptcy.

I put some of these stories into a book called *Sick,* and used them to make an argument for universal coverage, ideally something that looked like one of the more high-performing programs in Europe. The book came out in the spring of 2007, right as the Democratic presidential campaign was getting underway and the candidates, including Obama, were laying out their plans. I was able to cover the debate that ensued on the campaign trail and then after Obama took office.

I was there in the East Room when Obama hosted congressional leaders, activists, and health industry officials at a summit, making the case for a broadly supported, bipartisan reform. I was back there a year later to watch Obama at the signing ceremony. I was on Capitol Hill for committee markups and floor debates, and at the Supreme Court for the first two cases challenging the law's constitutionality. Before and after, I was all over the country—California and Iowa, Florida and Idaho, North Carolina and my home state of Michigan—listening to people talk about how the law had affected them for better, worse, or both.

This book combines what I learned over those years with new reporting, including interviews with dozens of figures who shaped the Affordable Care Act and its aftermath in one way or another. The list includes officials at the very highest levels of power, including Obama, as well as influential staff, advisers, and advocates who have been largely invisible to the public—and whose contributions to public policy frequently fall out of historical narratives. I made my best attempt to collect multiple viewpoints and speak with representatives from both political parties. Trump did not grant an official interview, but Republicans who worked for and closely with him did.

One of my goals was to produce a chronicle that future researchers would find valuable. I have tried to be as transparent as possible about where I obtained information, both in the endnotes and, sometimes, in the text itself. Where I have relied on an individual's recollection of a statement or event, I have stated so clearly; where accounts differed, I have so indicated. When I have relied on unnamed sources, I have provided what identifying details I can, so that readers can at least know the sources' general perspectives and judge statements or recollections accordingly.

That's important, because the stories people tell don't always provide an accurate or full picture of what actually happened. This isn't because sources are being intentionally deceptive or manipulative, although sometimes that's the case. It's because human memory is fallible, people see or hear what they want, and even the most disinterested observers have only limited perspective. This is true for what officials tell reporters, and even what they write in their diaries or memos. There's always some bias.

And that goes for journalists too. Just as my previous book made explicit my belief in universal coverage, my past writings made clear that I thought the Affordable Care Act was a worthwhile piece of legislation—flawed, yes, but on balance something that would do a lot more good than harm. In my reporting for this text, I frequently asked sources to reckon with their own misconceptions and mistakes; with my writing, I have tried to hold myself accountable in the same way. Pretty much everybody who was a part of this debate got things wrong, and I am certainly no exception. The willingness of people from so many perspectives to speak with me is, I hope, a sign of their trust in my ability to navigate these questions with honesty and an open mind.

5.

Understanding the successes and failures of the Affordable Care Act is essential to addressing the maddening and, sometimes, tragic shortcomings of American health care. But *The Ten Year War* is not simply a book about policy. It's also a book about our political system and how it has changed.

Congress and the courts, interest groups and the media, the Democrats and the Republicans—they all operate differently from how they did two or three decades ago. The electorate is different, as well.

Figuring out how to fix American health care has never been entirely, or even primarily, about what kind of system would work best. It's also been about what kind of changes can actually survive the political process. And if the story of the Affordable Care Act has shown anything, it's that the process doesn't stop simply because a bill becomes a law. A political fight can last a lot longer than the congressional debate, shaping a program just as surely as the authorizing language in the federal code.

In 2009 and 2010, President Obama liked to say that the health care reform effort was really a test of whether America could still face up to its most serious problems. At the signing ceremony, as he prepared to affix his signature to the law with twenty-two ceremonial pens, he returned to that theme. "It's been easy at times to doubt our ability to do such a big thing, such a complicated thing," he said. "But today, we are affirming that essential truth . . . that we are not a nation that scales back its aspirations. . . . We are a nation that faces its challenges and accepts its responsibilities. We are a nation that does what is hard. What is necessary."

It's time to look back and decide whether Obama was right.

Part I

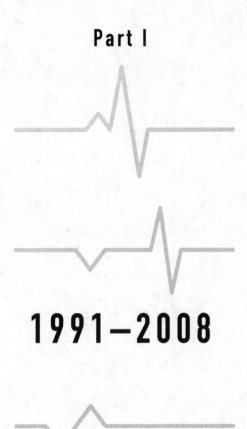

1991–2008

One

The Last Failure

Another year, another president, another address to Congress calling for a national health care program. It was a familiar scene, one that had played out pretty much the same way since Harry Truman's day, with an enthusiastic launch giving way to shambolic negotiations and then, inevitably, catastrophic failure. Still, something about this time felt different, with the public desperate for action and a young, newly elected president on the scene to deliver it.[1]

He was cool and confident, maybe even a little cocky, and understood better than most the audacity of what he and his allies were about to attempt. But this president also believed that common values could transcend partisan disagreement, so that someday Americans would "find it unthinkable that there was a time in this country when hard-working families lost their homes, their savings, their businesses—lost everything simply because their children got sick or because they had to change jobs."

The president's effortless, engaging delivery belied what was transpiring behind the scenes. Staff had been furiously entering last-minute edits en route from the White House and, with one errant keystroke, the aide operating the teleprompter accidentally loaded the new speech below a previous one. Nobody had noticed until the president was standing at the rostrum and saw the old text. While the aide hurriedly scrolled down to the new speech, causing a blur of prose to whoosh by on the display, the president spoke from memory.[2]

The speech went on for more than an hour and was full of policy detail, which was asking a lot of a viewing audience that would otherwise be watching sitcoms or football. But this president had a special gift for making his case in a way the average American could grasp. He talked about what his reform plan would mean for somebody who couldn't afford coverage on his own, or for a small business owner worried about her employees, or for a doctor who just wanted to do right by patients. The earnest focus on substance, sprinkled with invocations of American idealism, was a hit, as even some Republicans conceded. "It's a great start on a long, tough journey," one GOP senator said afterward. "He'll get the public on our backs to get the job done."[3]

Alas, it was not to be. It was September 1993, and the president was William Jefferson Clinton. One year later, in a nondescript part of the Capitol not far from where Clinton had given his address, Senate majority leader George Mitchell would tell a gaggle of reporters that he was giving up on reform for the session. The factions of liberal Democrats, moderate Democrats, and moderate Republicans who had spent the spring and summer negotiating were moving further apart from one another. With the midterms weeks away, no bill had a chance of passing.[4]

"We are going to keep up the fight," Clinton said afterward. But on Election Day, Democrats lost their majorities in both chambers. Although health care wasn't the only reason for the drubbing, one in three voters said it was their most important issue, according to a postelection poll from the Henry J. Kaiser Family Foundation. And while the public hadn't completely given up, polling director Robert Blendon explained, "what the public means by health reform now comes closest to a more moderate vision: one which is more limited in scope, incremental, and that involves a much more limited role for government."[5]

Democrats took the lesson to heart—and then some. It would be years before party leaders would even talk about pursuing a health care initiative on Clinton's scale, let alone make a serious effort to pass one. But reform advocates understood that another chance would come eventually, because the diseased U.S. health care system wasn't going to heal on its own. Rising costs would keep putting bigger strains on government and employers, while the rickety, gap-filled insurance system would be leaving more and more people unable to pay medical bills—and suffering grievous harm because of it.

When the public once again looked to politicians for help, Democrats and their supporters were determined to be ready. At conferences and private dinners, on chat boards and in academic journals, they analyzed and then reanalyzed what had gone wrong and why—not just in 1993 and 1994 but in the many efforts at universal coverage that had come before.

They hadn't been the first to succeed. But maybe, just maybe, they would be the last to fail.

Two

America's Path

1.

American politicians had been arguing about health care policy for nearly 70 years by the time of Clinton's presidency.

The debate had started in the 1920s, as medicine was entering the modern era. Before that, going to the doctor was mainly a way to get comfort and spiritual help on the way to death. All of that changed with the development of anesthesia and better understanding of how to prevent infection. Medical professionals were performing appendectomies and tonsillectomies, and repairing fractures too.

But newly capable doctors required more training. Hospitals needed new facilities. It took money, and the providers passed that cost along to patients. Previously, illness or injury had meant missing work and pay. Now there was a new concern: medical bills that, as one New York philanthropist observed in 1929, were "beyond the reach of the great majority of people."[1]

They were going bankrupt and losing homes, or simply going without the care they needed, as a groundbreaking series of reports from a group called the Committee on the Costs of Medical Care made clear. It was an early version of the very same crisis that Bill Clinton would describe. But there was a solution, the committee explained. Insurance could solve the medical cost problem because of the way health care spending was distributed back then—and is still distributed today.[2]

It turns out that, within any large and relatively random group of people, a small minority are responsible for the vast majority of medical care. It's the people suffering serious injuries and heart attacks and those dealing with chronic conditions. If everybody in the group makes small payments into a common fund, then there will be enough money to cover all the expenses. At any given time, it might seem like a bad deal to some people who are healthy. But anybody can get sick or injured; over time, most people will.[3]

The distribution of medical expenses is the same everywhere: At any one time, about 80 percent of costs come from just 20 percent of the people. The 80–20 rule, as it has come to be known, is as fundamental to health economics as $E=mc^2$ is to physics. And over the course of the twentieth century, every other developed country on the planet has dealt with it in the same way: by creating some kind of national health system.

Each country's system evolved in a different way and at a different pace. Today some, like Sweden, have one government program that insures people directly, covering the vast majority of their medical bills. Systems like this are known as *single-payer*. Other countries, like France, have hybrids with government-run insurance programs as well as private supplemental policies. Still others, like the Netherlands, rely exclusively on private insurance, although the insurers operate under such strict regulation that they are more like public utilities than private enterprises.

These arrangements have a few traits in common. Governments are firmly in charge, using some form of taxes or mandatory premiums to finance benefits. Governments also dictate how much money goes to the providers and producers of health care—that is, the doctors, the drugmakers, and so on. Most importantly, everybody pays into these systems, and everybody gets coverage from them, so that money from the young and healthy effectively covers bills for the old and sick.[4]

The United States had its first and possibly best opportunity to create a similar system in the 1930s, when some of Franklin Roosevelt's advisers urged him to make medical insurance part of the New Deal. FDR of all people understood the importance of medical care because of the polio that had left him paralyzed. The idea of national health insurance fit neatly into his basic philosophy—that a primary purpose of government is to help people at moments of need, that some parts of the economy simply won't work for most Americans without extensive public oversight, and that everybody benefits when they band together to protect themselves from common vulnerabilities.

But Roosevelt was also a pragmatist. Progressive Era flirtations with the idea of "compulsory medical insurance" had aroused the ire of state medical societies that feared it would eventually mean government interference with autonomy and incomes. Rather than jeopardize Social Security or other proposals by provoking similar opposition, FDR put health care aside.[5]

In the absence of government action, the private sector took matters into its own hands. It was the Great Depression, after all, and all those newly built and outfitted hospitals were now full of patients who couldn't pay their bills.

Among the facilities in deep financial trouble was Baylor Hospital in Dallas, Texas, where a new administrator who had worked previously as superintendent of the city's schools offered a deal to the teachers he'd once supervised: up to twenty-one days of medical care annually, with most services covered fully, for any teacher willing to pay fifty cents a month. Teachers signed up, and on Christmas Day 1929, Baylor physicians set the ankle of one who had slipped on the ice. They charged her nothing for the treatment, making her, quite possibly, the first American to pay her medical bills with modern health insurance.[6]

Other hospitals copied Baylor, and in 1934, a Minnesota executive with a flair for creativity advertised the new plans with posters showing a blue cross like the kind nurses frequently had on their uniforms. An icon was born.[7] The Blue Cross employer-based arrangements caught on partly because the math worked and partly because the federal government made it extra appealing—initially, by exempting employer health insurance from World War II wage and price controls, so that employers could use health benefits to lure workers. Unions later won the right to bargain for insurance, giving organized labor a stake in the system.[8]

By the late 1940s, about half the population had private insurance, mostly through employers, and the number was rising. The United States was now on its own, separate path for organizing health care. With each passing year, deviating from that path would get harder.[9]

2.

Harry Truman was the first president to try. As a soldier in World War I, he'd been shocked at the poor health of recruits. As a county judge in Missouri, he'd been alarmed at how many constituents couldn't afford care. He proposed to create a new government program that would pay everybody's medical bills—in other words, an American version of a single-payer program.

Truman, like FDR, saw his proposal as an analogue to Social Security. "I just don't understand how anyone can be against my health program," he said at one point. But the majority of Republicans, even those who had made their peace with the New Deal, opposed creating yet another new government program. Southern Democrats feared national health insurance would force their states to integrate racially segregated hospitals. And then there were the interest groups, led by the American Medical Association (AMA), which warned that Truman's plan would give socialism a foothold in the United States. It was an especially potent charge against the backdrop of the Cold War.[10]

Public support wasn't strong enough to overcome these obstacles; the emerging private insurance system was working just well enough for just enough people to sustain it. But it had some big gaps that were becoming more conspicuous with each passing year, thanks in part to a transformation in private insurance that was simultaneously underway.

Once Blue Cross plans had enough business from employers, they began selling policies directly to individuals. And they sold to anybody, regardless of age or medical status, at the same premium—or, as it came to be known, a *community rate*. But their growth attracted the attention of commercial insurers, who had briefly experimented with medical coverage in the 1920s by offering it as a supplement to life insurance plans. The only people who signed up were people who already had medical problems or were likely to get them. That drove up expenses, forcing the carriers to raise prices, and it was difficult to make money that way. This pattern of *adverse selection* convinced the commercial carriers that the medical business was a loser—that is, until they saw a business opportunity in the success of Blue Cross.

The insurers understood that, in a given year, the risk of medical problems varies from individual to individual. A diabetic or somebody diagnosed with cancer is likely to have high medical bills. The same goes for somebody working in a physically hazardous job. Young people tend to stay healthy, and at older ages, women are healthier than men—though at younger ages they require more care on average because of reproductive health and pregnancy. The tendencies apply to groups too. A company with an older workforce will reliably generate more bills than one where most employees are in their twenties.

The whole point of the community rate was to treat everyone the same, and functionally it meant that individual Blue Cross plans operated by the same egalitarian ethos as national health systems abroad. The healthy subsidized the sick, the young subsidized the old. Insurers like Aetna and Prudential, on the other hand, were out to make money. They targeted companies with younger, healthier workers and, taking into account their predictably lower expenses, offered lower premiums than Blue Cross. They got a lot of business that way.[11]

Commercial insurers also had a very different approach to insuring individuals buying coverage directly, rather than through employers. They would check for preexisting medical conditions and risk factors like working in a coal mine or a family history of cancer. Then they would charge those customers more or deny coverage altogether, effectively leaving them to Blue Cross plans—which, in turn, had to raise premiums because they were losing their healthiest beneficiaries. As Blue Cross premiums went up, more customers fled for the cheaper commercial alternatives. Eventually, most of the Blues had to abandon their old way of doing business, ditching community rating and the promise of insurance to all who could buy it.[12]

By the late 1950s, in large swaths of the country, people at high risk of medical expenses had no realistic way to get comprehensive insurance. One of those groups was especially sympathetic politically, and that's where veterans of the Truman effort decided to focus their efforts.

3.

In May 1962, another Democratic president gave a speech on health care. Imagine, he said, a man who "has worked hard all his life and he is retired. He might have been a clerk or a salesman or on the road or worked in a factory, stores, or whatever. He's always wanted to pay his own way. He does not ask anyone to care for him; he wants to care for himself." Then the man's wife gets sick, and the hospital bills start. "First goes the twenty-five hundred dollars—that's gone. Next he mortgages his house, even though he may have some difficulty making the payments out of his social security. Then he goes to his children . . . now, what is he going to do? His savings are gone—his children's savings, they're contributing though they have responsibilities of their own—and he finally goes in and signs a petition saying he's broke and needs assistance."[13]

The president was John Kennedy, and he was making a case for universal coverage of the elderly—Medicare, as advocates were calling it. Like Truman, he envisioned a single-payer program that operated through Social Security. Like Truman, he couldn't get a bill out of committee.

Then came Kennedy's assassination and the 1964 election, which kept Lyndon Johnson in the White House and increased Democratic majorities in Congress. Even with that mandate, it took all of Johnson's formidable legislative skills and some shrewd maneuvering by his congressional allies to pass Medicare. Among their decisions: They co-opted the AMA's preferred alternative, a government program that would limit itself to the lowest-income seniors, and turned it into a program called Medicaid that would operate alongside Medicare.[14]

The law's architects decided that the model for Medicare would be the old Blue Cross plans, which had paid whatever hospitals charged. This secured the hospital industry's support. It also meant the program had no control over spending, creating a fiscal problem that, as critics warned, future generations of lawmakers would have to address.[15]

But that debate would come later. Following the 1965 signing ceremony, which LBJ held in Truman's hometown and with an aging Truman at his side, the political conversation moved to exactly where the architects of Medicare had hoped it would: extending the program to everybody else. The goal became "Medicare for All," although nobody really called it that back then, and its most visible champion was JFK's youngest brother, Edward, who had taken Jack's seat in the Senate.[16]

In the early 1970s, Kennedy's promotion of national health insurance prompted a reaction from President Richard Nixon, as anything associated with the Kennedys did. But that reaction was not hostility. Nixon had lost two brothers to tuberculosis and likely had a milder case himself when he was a child, as the scholars David Blumenthal and James Morone chronicled in their book on presidential health and its effect on policy. When Nixon was an adult, he would reflect frequently about the affliction's impact, including his family's difficulty with medical bills. He pledged his support for universal coverage and, in 1974, formally introduced a counterproposal that left employer plans in place but included a new government program for the uninsured. The insurance benefit itself would be less generous than what liberal Democrats preferred, and participation would be voluntary. But the hope was that it would make insurance available to nearly everybody.[17]

Nixon's posture was not unusual for Republicans of the era. Although the majority of Republican lawmakers had opposed Medicare, a minority had supported it all along—and in the final floor votes, when passage was inevitable, half of House Republicans and nearly half of their Senate counterparts voted yes. Although Nixon warned against placing "the entire health care system under the dominion of social planners in Washington," he sounded a lot like Johnson, Kennedy, and Truman when he talked about the virtues of his approach. "Without adequate health care, no one can make full use of his or her talents and opportunities," Nixon said in an address to Congress.[18]

Back-channel discussions followed. At one point, Kennedy and Nixon staff met secretly in a Washington church, trying to hammer out a deal. But Nixon had made his public pitch in February 1974, and by then, with Watergate escalating, Democrats and their allies could sense a big midterm win. Labor pressured Democrats to hold off, figuring the extra leverage would lead to a better overall package.[19]

It didn't. Divisions within the pro-reform coalition, an economy racked by inflation, and a career-wrecking scandal for a congressional leader conspired to make legislating difficult during Gerald Ford's brief presidency. Jimmy Carter's one, belated reform effort was a proposal to control hospital prices that the industry defeated handily. It left Carter with little to show for his efforts and gave voters in 1980 one more reason to think about his Republican opponent.[20]

4.

Ronald Reagan's rise heralded a broader political shift that would make universal coverage an even more difficult cause to pursue.

Back in the early 1960s, Reagan had served as the AMA's front man in its campaign against Medicare, recording a message that the organization distributed to women's coffee groups. "One of the traditional methods of imposing statism or socialism on a people has been by way of medicine," Reagan said. And if Medicare became law, Reagan predicted, "behind it will come other federal programs that will invade every area of freedom as we have known it in this country. . . . [O]ne of these days you and I are going to spend our sunset years telling our children, and our children's children, what it once was like in America when men were free."[21]

Although Reagan failed to stop Medicare, by the 1970s, his views about government were ascendant in both the GOP and the country. One reason was a methodical campaign to build a case against the public sector through think tanks, advocacy groups, and campus networks. The money to support these efforts came from tycoons and business leaders eager to shake off the yoke of regulations and taxes. The intellectual force of the anti-government movement came from figures like William Buckley, founding editor of *National Review* magazine. He and other conservatives argued that large public programs were both inefficient, because they stifled the effects of market competition, and unjust, because they robbed people of money they'd earned through hard work.[22]

These arguments resonated with a public that, following Vietnam and Watergate, was rapidly losing faith in the federal government. In late 1964, on the eve of Medicare's enactment, 77 percent of Americans trusted officials in Washington to do the right thing most of the time, according to polling by Pew Research. In late 1979, just before Reagan's election, just 28 percent did. Anti-government ideology also resonated with a large swath of white voters who were angry over federal interventions on behalf of African Americans. These efforts included everything from court-ordered school integration to the creation of Great Society programs focusing on the poor.[23]

Reagan tapped into this anger, most famously when he railed against "welfare queens" who were supposedly collecting government checks when they could have been working, and it was among the reasons he won in 1980. As president, Reagan slashed taxes while cutting funding for food stamps, public housing, and Medicaid. He also kept up his rhetorical attacks on the government—like in 1986, during a press conference, when he said, "The nine most terrifying words in the English language are: 'I'm from the Government, and I'm here to help.'"[24]

Ironically, the one big program Reagan avoided attacking was Medicare, quite possibly because polls showed that between 70 and 80 percent of Americans supported it. In 1988, Reagan even signed the Medicare Catastrophic Coverage Act, a bipartisan bill to fill in benefit gaps that had left seniors on the hook for prescription drugs and other major expenses. The same law created a commission, named for Claude Pepper, a Florida Democratic congressman and champion of the elderly, with a charge to recommend a new approach to universal coverage.[25]

Neither of the law's elements amounted to much. Congress repealed the Medicare benefit enhancements before they took effect, following a backlash to its financing scheme. And the Pepper Commission's recommendation for a universal coverage system similar to what Nixon had once proposed got little attention. Although Medicare was safe, there was little pressure to go beyond that—until, two years after Reagan left office, a tragedy in Pennsylvania thrust universal coverage back onto the national agenda.[26]

Three

A Right to Health Care

1.

It was a little after noon on April 4, 1991, when the pilots of a twin-propeller charter flight approaching Northeast Philadelphia Airport noticed a light indicating its nose gear had not deployed. After they aborted the landing, the pilot of a nearby helicopter offered to make a visual inspection. As the two craft approached each other, the plane's wing smacked into a helicopter rotor—or maybe a rotor smacked into the wing, investigators were never quite sure—and the two craft exploded, raining fiery debris on a school-yard below. Among the seven who perished was the plane's lone passenger: Senator John Heinz.[1]

Heinz, fifty-two, had first won election to the Senate in 1976, following three terms in the U.S. House. A popular, widely respected figure, he was a Republican in good standing who had once led the GOP's Senate campaign committee. But he was not a Reagan revolutionary, and he worked frequently with Democrats on programs that helped people get medical care. At his memorial, Senator Tim Wirth, a Colorado Democrat and close friend, remarked that "the cause of decent health care has not had a fiercer advocate."[2]

Pennsylvania's governor, Democrat Robert Casey, had to name an interim senator who could then run in the special election to fill out Heinz's term. But the state's voters had not elected a Democratic senator in nearly three decades and the likely GOP candidate was the politically formidable Richard Thornburgh, the former two-term governor serving as attorney general in the George H. W. Bush administration. After failing to recruit a series of high-profile challengers, Casey turned to one of his cabinet officials, Labor and Industry secretary Harris Wofford.[3]

A lawyer by training who had spent his early career in academia, Wofford had been active in the civil rights movement and advised Martin Luther King Jr. before joining the Kennedy campaign in 1960. Afterward, Wofford joined the new administration and stayed on through LBJ's early years, helping to establish the Peace Corps. In 1966, he returned to academic life, eventually becoming president of Bryn Mawr College before joining Casey's administration in 1988.[4]

To manage Wofford's campaign, Casey recruited Paul Begala and James Carville, a pair of consultants who had engineered Democratic victories in a handful of difficult congressional and state races. Their specialty was an especially pugnacious brand of populism that attacked Republicans as defenders of corporations and the rich while everybody else was struggling to keep food on the table. With unemployment rising, as a recession set in, their approach seemed like one way to put the Pennsylvania Senate race in play. It also lined up nicely with Wofford's instincts on policies, which included support for unions, a higher minimum wage, and infrastructure projects to create jobs.[5]

Public polls in the first few weeks showed Wofford, relatively unknown outside of political circles, trailing by thirty to forty points. One internal survey put the deficit at forty-nine. Then Wofford encountered an old friend, an ophthalmologist, during a fundraiser at a Philadelphia hospital. Americans have a right to a lawyer when they are charged with a crime, the ophthalmologist said, so why don't they have a right to a doctor when they are sick? On a phone call afterward, Begala was disappointed to hear the haul from the fundraiser was small. But Wofford brushed right past that, excitedly relating the ophthalmologist's line. It became a staple of his speeches, and Wofford started surging in the polls.[6]

Thornburgh responded with the usual attack on national health insurance, calling it "a massive federal bureaucracy to run a centrally directed health-care system out of Washington, D.C." But this time, it wasn't working. With health care more and more expensive, and employment a less reliable source of coverage, anxiety was spreading from the poor to the middle class.[7]

Among the first to notice this shift was Paul Starr, a sociologist at Princeton and author of a Pulitzer Prize–winning history of American medicine. Starr had recently cofounded a liberal policy journal called *The American*

Prospect, and in one of its inaugural issues, he'd written an essay, "The Middle Class and National Health Reform," arguing that the cause had greater potential to succeed because so many more people needed help. When Carville read an excerpt of the essay, he arranged for Starr to visit Wofford's home outside Philadelphia, where they spoke about policy for several hours.[8]

On Election Day, Wofford prevailed with 55 percent of the vote and the political class took notice. "This sends a very dramatic message," public opinion expert Daniel Yankelovich told *The New York Times.* "Health care is one of the cutting edge issues of the 1992 elections."[9]

2.

Bill Clinton becoming president was, in retrospect, even more improbable than Harris Wofford becoming senator. In fact, the idea of any Democrat winning the White House in 1992 seemed hard to fathom given that the party's candidates had lost five of the past six elections. Reagan's victory in 1980 and then his sweeping reelection in 1984, when he won forty-nine states, seemed to confirm that Carter's 1980 win was a fluke, although for Democrats, it was Bush's 1988 triumph that may have been the most dispiriting.

The once-promising candidacy of Michael Dukakis had withered in the face of Republican attacks that the Massachusetts governor was a "card-carrying liberal"—which, in practice, meant that he was insufficiently patriotic, too eager to raise taxes, and too soft on crime. Like Reagan, Bush claimed Democratic plans for new spending and regulation would stifle business and, thus, the economy. And like Reagan, Bush exploited white racial feelings, only instead of focusing on "welfare queens," he attacked Dukakis for approving a prison furlough program that, allegedly, allowed a convicted black criminal to commit rape. On Election Day, Dukakis carried just ten states, struggling especially with white, working-class voters, who had once been the foundation of FDR's New Deal coalition. The devastation gave new credence to arguments that the party's survival depended on distancing itself from "liberal fundamentalism" and embracing a "New Democrat" way of thinking.[10]

Exactly what that approach should entail depended on which New Democrat was talking. But frequently, it meant explicitly repudiating traditional liberal positions and embracing more conservative ones, whether it was requiring tougher sentences for convicted criminals or requiring that people

receiving public assistance find work. New Democrats said they weren't simply thinking about politics—that, on the merits, it was time to move away
from the big-government approach of the New Deal and the Great Society.
When it came to helping people with health care, New Democrats wanted to
channel coverage through private insurance rather than public programs.[11]

A big focus of the New Democrats was on winning back the Southern
states that had been trending Republican since the 1960s, and so it was
not surprising that Clinton, the governor of Arkansas, would become the
movement's standard-bearer. He had spent his first term trying to overhaul
the public schools and restructure the state's regressive tax code, alienating the state's more conservative voters and running afoul of Little Rock's
corporate lobbyists. After losing reelection, he won the seat back and then
won three more terms by pursuing an agenda that deferred to industry and
didn't push voters outside of their comfort zones.[12]

As a presidential candidate in 1992, Clinton promoted work requirements for welfare and touted his support for the death penalty, returning
to Arkansas to sign the execution warrant of a convicted African American
murderer who, after killing a police officer, had lobotomized himself in a
suicide attempt. Clinton also assured voters he'd be a prudent steward of the
federal treasury by wringing existing programs for waste, getting budget
deficits under control, and leaning more heavily on business than government to create wealth—an approach he described as "no more trickle-down
economics but not tax-and-spend economics."[13]

But there was a part of the traditional Democratic Party identity Clinton didn't want to shed. "Putting People First" was his campaign mantra;
the populist Begala and Carville were his strategists. And he was struck
by the same kinds of health care stories that Wofford had encountered in
Pennsylvania—especially one from an uninsured New Hampshire small
businessman, Ron Machos Jr., who couldn't pay for his son's heart surgery.

Machos, Clinton said later, was "the symbol of what my efforts in 1992
were all about."[14]

3.

Wofford's election had guaranteed that health care would be a big part of
the 1992 campaign, and early on, one of Clinton's rivals staked out a familiar position.

The candidate was Bob Kerrey, a Nebraska senator and veteran of the

Vietnam War, where he had lost his lower leg and won the Congressional Medal of Honor. That made him an especially formidable opponent for Clinton, who faced accusations of draft dodging. Kerrey wanted to achieve universal coverage with a system that featured both a public program and private insurance alternatives, but with the federal government setting budgets and regulating prices in the way a single-payer plan would—in other words, not quite Trumanesque but not that far off either.[15]

Clinton also called for universal coverage, but said he preferred an approach that relied more heavily on private insurance. Initially, he endorsed an idea called *pay or play,* in which businesses could cover their employees' coverage (*play*) or contribute to a fund that would cover the uninsured (*pay*). It was basically a version of what both Nixon and the Pepper Commission had proposed. But Clinton avoided committing to details until after he got the Democratic nomination, when his lack of specificity drew criticism from Bush.[16]

That is when Clinton settled on a concept called *managed competition,* which was the latest effort to blend the liberal goal of universal coverage with the conservative principle of relying on the free market. The idea was to have all individuals shop for policies, giving insurers incentives to compete on price and quality. People who worked for the largest companies would shop through their employers, which would select a group of plans to offer. Everybody else would shop through new marketplaces that either governments or independent third-party organizations would set up and operate.

In either instance, the government would regulate insurance companies, so that everybody could get coverage regardless of preexisting condition, and it would subsidize coverage for the poor, so that everybody could afford coverage regardless of income. But the idea was to provide an alternative to single-payer reforms, on the theory that so much government control would misallocate spending, leading to waste, rationing, or both. Consumers, according to the theory of managed competition, would make better decisions than politicians and career bureaucrats.

"The current unregulated markets allow insurers to discriminate against the chronically ill," Michael Weinstein, an influential opinion writer for *The New York Times,* explained in one of several editorials he wrote on the subject. "And full-scale government regulation would require Washington to run a huge market, nearly the size of Britain's, with thousands of price controls; that's bureaucratic folly."[17]

Managed competition, like any broad concept for public policy, came in a few varieties. The original iterations, which grew out of discussions among business leaders and health industry executives who gathered regularly in Jackson Hole, Wyoming, envisioned only modest regulation and government spending. They were really trusting the free market to do the heavy lifting of making America's health care system work better. Although they would talk about universal coverage, the goal was clearly secondary.

In California, a pair of Democratic state officials, insurance commissioner John Garamendi and policy deputy Walter Zelman, weren't prepared to give the private sector so much leeway. Their plan for refashioning the state's insurance system featured tighter rules for insurers, more generous subsidies for consumers, and, critically, an overall cap on spending—an analogue, roughly, to the national budgets most European nations used. If for some reason competition didn't restrain spending in the way free market enthusiasts hoped, then the cap would control it the old-fashioned way: by government fiat. That budget backstop, anathema to the more conservative Jackson Hole crowd and its allies in the business community, appealed to longtime universal coverage advocates like Paul Starr. He ended up collaborating with Zelman on a national version of the proposal, calling it "competition under a cap."[18]

Their fusion of new and old, right and left, mirrored Clinton's sensibilities, and he embraced the model, formally introducing a version of the Starr-Zelman proposal in a September speech. At times, Clinton channeled Truman's spirit, decrying the American system for its arbitrary cruelty: "We are the only advanced nation in the world that does not provide basic health care to all its citizens." But when Clinton pivoted to his plan, he sounded almost Reaganesque: "We've got to quit having the Federal Government try to micromanage health care and instead set up incentives for the private sector to manage the costs."[19]

4.

Clinton's victory in the November election was an exhilarating moment for Democrats. Still just forty-six, Clinton was the third-youngest president ever to take office. The Clinton campaign had done everything it could to make him seem like the next generation's John Kennedy. They even found footage of Clinton, as a teenager, shaking hands with JFK during a student trip to Washington.

When it came to governing, Clinton's model was a different Democratic icon: FDR. Clinton may have committed himself to a New Democratic strategy that scorned big government, but he did so in the service of an ambitious social and economic agenda, very much including health care. Even for liberals wary of managed competition, Clinton's triumph and the opportunity for a breakthrough on health care was a moment to savor. "There was no one who had been involved in health policy who did not want to be involved in it," Chris Jennings, a veteran Capitol Hill staffer who had gone to work for Clinton, later remembered.[20]

But Clinton was in a much weaker political position than FDR had been, having won only 43 percent of the popular vote. Ross Perot, the billionaire third-party candidate, had won 19 percent, and he had done so by campaigning on the need to reduce, not expand, government spending.

Clinton proceeded anyway, tapping First Lady Hillary Clinton to lead a task force that would craft his proposal. Health care had come up frequently in her work as a children's legal advocate and in her husband's political work. After the 1992 presidential campaign, she would speak frequently about the people she heard telling stories of health care hardship, saying they played over and over in her head like a movie. To manage the task force on a day-to-day basis, Clinton deputized another trusted aide, Ira Magaziner. A Rhode Island–based management consultant, Magaziner's penchant for big, complex solutions to big, complex problems stretched back to his days as an undergraduate at Brown, where he had written a four-hundred-page memo urging the university administration to let students design their own curricula.[21]

More recently, Magaziner had led working groups that produced reports on how to restructure Rhode Island's health care system—although, notably, his effort to convince politically connected hospitals they could live with less revenue proved a lot more difficult than persuading Brown administrators to junk math, science, and writing requirements. Nobody questioned Magaziner's brilliance, but even some of his colleagues wondered how it would translate into policy. Among them was former partner and future Massachusetts governor Mitt Romney, who recalled that "Ira generated lots of ideas, but he had no sense of which ones were usable and which ones were not."[22]

To craft a solution to the problems of U.S. health care, Magaziner set up the kind of process he would use to reconstruct a corporation. He staffed the task force with a combination of experts, officials, and advocates, eventually numbering more than five hundred, and divided them into subgroups that would drill down on specific problems. Writing the plan would require making more than one thousand individual decisions, Magaziner warned Clinton in a memo. But by the time they were done, they would have thought up every possible policy challenge and devised a way to overcome it.[23]

Or at least that was the plan. Things went awry pretty quickly, as David Broder and Haynes Johnson later recounted in *The System*, their history of the Clinton health care fight. A primary goal of Magaziner's process was to come up with more creative ways of thinking. That necessarily meant pushing past objections of veterans who would reject new ideas as impractical. Magaziner had started doing that during the campaign, when he vied for influence with advisers like Judy Feder, a Georgetown public policy professor. She had helped develop the Pepper Commission's pay-or-play proposal and had urged Clinton to stick with that model, in part because it would be a less radical break with the status quo.

Magaziner had included congressional staff representatives on the task force, but they, like Feder and other more experienced hands, said they felt more like observers than contributors. Many had been working on health care issues for years, some for decades. Whether that experience was ultimately a plus or a minus, or a bit of both, their support for the proposal was essential because they would ultimately be the ones advising their bosses on how to vote. And while Magaziner believed he was bringing them into the process by including them in task force discussions, they felt excluded because he didn't seem to listen to them.[24]

The task force drew a lawsuit, which claimed that the private meetings violated federal transparency laws. It also generated lots of criticism from Republicans, who said that the administration was trying to hatch its plan in secret. The attack was silly. Officials and lawmakers always craft proposals privately before introducing them, and in any event, with so many people attending the task force meetings, nothing of consequence remained confidential for long. ("The worst of all worlds—the perception of secrecy with no actual secrecy," Chris Jennings later quipped.) But the arguments resonated. Clinton disbanded the group, leaving a small group of key advisers to write the bill, and by the fall, the whole effort was in deep peril.[25]

Clinton seemed to revive his plan's prospects with that triumphant address to Congress in September 1993. A week after the speech, Hillary Clinton testified about the plan on Capitol Hill. Lawmakers thought she was even more impressive than Bill, with members of Ways and Means applauding her at the end of her appearance—"a virtually unheard-of trib- ute," as *The Times* put it.[26]

"We thought we were on the launching pad, that we were about to soar," Len Nichols, a White House economist working on the health care effort, remembered years later. "It was only in retrospect we realized her testimony was as high as we were going to get."[27]

Four

Harry and Louise

1.

The drafters of the U.S. Constitution were trying to balance competing impulses. They wanted to create a government nimbler than the post-Revolution confederacy of states, but they wanted to prevent the new government from acting hastily. They wanted a representative democracy, but they had to accommodate small states fearful that big states would dominate, especially on the issue of slavery. One of their solutions was to create a legislature with two houses and then make sure every state had two seats in the "upper" body, the Senate, regardless of population size. This structure, James Madison argued in *The Federalist,* would provide "impediment . . . against improper acts of legislation."[1]

More than two centuries later, the practical effect of the Senate's design was to give Republicans disproportionate power, because they were more likely to represent states with smaller populations. This effect was enhanced by a parliamentary tool adopted in 1805, the filibuster, which effectively allowed groups of senators, or even one individual senator, to block legislation by refusing to yield the floor and consent to a vote. Senate leaders of the time had not intended to give Senate minorities the power to block legislation, according to historian Sarah Binder. And it didn't work out that way until the later parts of the twentieth century, when Southern senators deployed filibusters to block civil rights legislation. By the time Clinton took office, opposition parties were using it to stop bills on a regular basis.[2]

He and his allies knew this was a problem, because the Senate had fifty-seven Democrats, three shy of the sixty that it took to break a filibuster. Their first thought was to try moving health care reform through the "budget reconciliation" process, a special legislative track where filibusters couldn't block a bill. But Senate rules dictated that reconciliation was only for certain kinds of fiscal legislation, and the senator who wrote those rules, Democrat Robert Byrd of West Virginia, said that health care legislation did not qualify. Daniel Patrick Moynihan, the New York Democrat and chairman of the powerful Finance Committee, had objections of his own. Going through reconciliation would require a majority vote, and with Byrd and Moynihan refusing to budge, Democratic leaders told the White House, Democrats would join Republicans in sufficient numbers to block the move.[3]

That left just one option: winning over a handful of Republicans to get their support for legislation or at least to keep them from supporting a filibuster. Neither goal seemed outlandish. The Senate GOP caucus in 1993 and 1994 still included a large number of members who were accustomed to working with Democrats and were open to the possibility of substantially more government involvement in health care.

John Chafee of Rhode Island was one of them. During the 1980s, Chafee was among the architects of laws that dramatically expanded eligibility for Medicaid to children and pregnant women. When Clinton won, Chafee saw it as a defeat for his party but also an opportunity, according to former aides. Christine Ferguson, who was Chafee's chief of staff, recalled many years later that he and his like-minded colleagues were "eager and excited" to meet and work with the new president.[4]

In late 1993, Chafee introduced a bill that got widespread support in the GOP caucus and that he hoped would become the basis of a deal with Clinton. A big difference between his plan and Clinton's was that Clinton's bill required employers to contribute money in the form of a payroll tax. Chafee's plan didn't. Instead, it had an *individual mandate*, a requirement that people get coverage or pay a penalty. But Chafee could imagine a workable deal on that and other unresolved issues, like how to finance a massive expansion of coverage, according to Ferguson.[5]

2.

Twenty or even maybe ten years before, such a compromise would have seemed unremarkable. Philosophically, Clinton's reform wasn't that different from Richard Nixon's. But Republicans weren't the party of Nixon anymore. They were increasingly the party of Reagan, with his extreme hostility to government programs.

Republicans were also in the process of becoming more of a regional party, representing the Great Plains and Deep South, while Democrats were becoming the party of the Northeast, Upper Midwest, and West Coast. Within the GOP Senate caucus, power was shifting away from the moderates, all of whom came from states that were either strongly Democratic or moving in that direction. Two of these moderates, James Jeffords from Vermont and Arlen Specter from Pennsylvania, would eventually leave the GOP, as would Chafee's son Lincoln, who in 1999 took over his father's Senate seat from Rhode Island.

As the moderate Republicans lost influence within their own party, their way of doing business also fell out of favor. And not just in the Senate. Over in the House, a Georgia congressman named Newt Gingrich had been gaining power and, in the process, remaking the GOP into a party that was both more doctrinaire and more combative.

Unlike his immediate predecessors in GOP leadership, who struck something of a balance between attacking Democrats and making deals with them, Gingrich was on the attack constantly and urged his colleagues to do the same. In one memo, called "Language: A Key Mechanism of Control," Gingrich suggested fellow Republicans use words like "sick," "traitors," and "shame" when describing Democrats. Gingrich also urged Republicans to block Democratic legislation however and whenever possible, on the theory that, as the party in power, Democrats would take the blame and lose seats in the next election. Among those who took notice was a (then) newish senator named Mitch McConnell. The Gingrich strategy, he quipped, "gives gridlock a good name."[6]

Gingrich wasn't the only one urging total opposition. In November 1993, political strategist William Kristol, who had served in the Bush White House, established a small conservative think tank. One month later, he was out with a memo on health care: "Defeating the Clinton plan outright . . . must be our goal," he wrote, warning specifically that "any Republican urge to negotiate a 'least bad' compromise with the Democrats . . . should also be resisted."[7]

The memo raised objections to Clintoncare as policy, warning that its limits on spending would undermine the quality of medical care and lead to rationing. But its most powerful passages were about the long-term impact on politics: "Passage of the Clinton health care plan, in any form, would guarantee and likely make permanent an unprecedented federal intrusion into and disruption of the American economy—and the establishment of the largest federal entitlement program since Social Security. Its success would signal a rebirth of centralized welfare-state policy at the very moment we have begun rolling back that idea in other areas." This would be tragic for America, Kristol said, and it would be tragic for the Republican Party, because it would "revive the reputation of the party that spends and regulates, the Democrats, as the generous protector of middle-class interests."[8]

When Kristol made his case at a GOP Senate retreat, he drew a rebuke from Utah senator Robert Bennett. Bennett was not a moderate in the way that Chafee and Jeffords were. But he had his own history of cooperation with Democrats, sometimes on health care. "That's just politics," Kristol would later remember hearing from Bennett, "and I'm an American and I want to do what's good for the country." Kristol responded that he too wanted what was good for the country, only Kristol thought even a compromise with Clinton would produce legislation that would undermine American medical care and freedom more generally.[9]

But the argument played better with some other GOP senators, including majority leader Robert Dole of Kansas. Health care was a personal issue for Dole. After being shot in the back while serving in Italy during World War II, he spent three years in a hospital recuperating. An athlete in high school, he wasted away to ninety pounds and could barely move. He had grown up poor, living in the basement of a home so that his parents could rent out the upstairs; after the war, neighbors collected money in a cigar box to pay for his treatment, including surgery that enabled him to walk again. Years later, as a senator, he kept the box on display in his office as a way to show thanks and to remind himself of what he owed his community.[10]

Dole spoke frequently about how his hospital experience taught him the importance of "compassion" and "sensitivity" to the sick, and in Congress, that frequently made him a friend of government-administered health care programs. In the late 1970s, he was an early advocate for strengthening Medicare benefits so that they would include prescription drugs and protect senior citizens from excessive costs. In the early 1980s, he worked with the Children's Defense Fund, the group with all those ties to Hillary Clinton, to exempt pregnant women from out-of-pocket costs that the Reagan administration was trying to introduce to Medicaid.[11]

Dole's chief adviser on health care issues was Sheila Burke, a registered nurse. She was a Democrat and the child of a union family, two facts she made sure Dole knew when he first interviewed her for a junior policy position. Dole said he didn't care. He wanted somebody with clinical experience, so that he could make policy decisions with patient well-being in mind. By 1993, she had become his chief of staff—and he had become the minority leader.[12]

Dole had cosponsored Chafee's bill, and later, he cosponsored yet another relatively moderate Republican proposal, this one from Oregon senator Bob Packwood. But there was tension within the Senate Republican caucus from the get-go. Tuesday policy meetings would get testy, sometimes uncomfortably, with more conservative members like Phil Gramm, newly elected from Texas, berating leadership and the moderates for even contemplating a compromise. Chafee didn't waver. But with each passing week, more and more Republicans were lining up with Gramm—and soon Dole was moving in that direction too.[13]

In January 1994, during the official State of the Union response, Dole launched an all-out attack on the Clinton plan. He even brought a prop: a poster board chart full of boxes and crisscrossing arrows depicting the tangle of money and regulations in the Clinton plan. "The president's idea is to put a mountain of bureaucrats between you and your doctor," Dole said. By this time, Dole wasn't just attacking the Clinton proposal. He was attacking its very rationale. "Our country has health care problems, but not a health care crisis," Dole said in a major break with Republican rhetoric to that point.[14]

In the coming months, Dole would abandon the Chafee bill and, in due time, the Packwood bill as well. "Too much government," he said.[15]

3.

The lasting image of the Clinton health care fight for many of the people who lived through it wasn't Bill Clinton giving his speech, Hillary Clinton testifying before Congress, or Bob Dole pointing to his chart of legislative spaghetti. Instead, it was a white, presumably middle-class couple from "the future" sitting at their kitchen table, sifting through medical bills and bemoaning what the Clinton health plan had done to them. The couple was the star in an advertising campaign from the Health Insurance Association of America. The names of the actors were Harry Johnson and

Louise Caire Clark, which is how the spots came to be known as the Harry and Louise ads.

In that first installment, Louise discovers a medical bill that the new government health care plan isn't covering. "But this was covered under our old plan," she says, dumbfounded. "Yeah, that was a good one," Harry responds, at which point a narrator breaks in to explain that "things are changing, and not all for the better. The government may force us to pick from a few health care plans designed by government bureaucrats." The rest of the ad goes back to the couple, still in distress over what's happened to their insurance. Louise: "Having choices we don't like is no choice at all." Harry: "They choose." Louise: "We lose."[16]

The argument about restricting choice had become one of the primary lines of attack against the Clinton plan. It was a genuine point of ideological objection for Republicans, who even in prior, less politically polarized eras were wary of government setting rules for how businesses should work. It also drew on an actual feature of the Clinton plan. If enacted, the government would define a benefit standard that all insurers would have to meet.

But the ads never mentioned why the plan included such requirements: to upgrade coverage for the tens of millions whose insurance left out key benefits like mental health or prescription drugs. Coverage under the Clinton plan would have become more comprehensive, not less, for the vast majority of Americans. And although most people under the Clinton plan would be shopping from a relatively small number of insurance policies, as the ad claimed, that was still more choice than most people had already.[17]

One reason that Harry and Louise–style attacks resonated was that the vast majority of Americans had private insurance already, and whatever their misgivings about it, they were skittish about shifting to a new, untested system. Clinton and his advisers had hoped this problem, an obstacle to reform since the 1940s, would be less of an issue now that even people with "good" health insurance were finding it more expensive and less reliable. But faith in government had fallen even further since Clinton took office, and by the middle of 1994, as the health care debate was reaching a conclusion, it was below 20 percent.[18]

The print analogue to the Harry and Louise ads was a series of articles that ran in *The New Republic* and on *The Wall Street Journal* editorial page. Their author was Elizabeth McCaughey, whose qualification was a doctorate in American constitutional history, not health policy. Among her arguments was a false claim that the Clinton plan prohibited doctors from accepting private payments for services. *The New Republic* subsequently ran a pair of articles debunking McCaughey's pieces, but by that point, *Newsweek* columnist George Will and talk radio host Rush Limbaugh had conveyed her arguments to millions.[19]

That was generally the way it worked during the Clinton health care fight. Distortions and lies got scrutiny only after they had swayed public opinion, in the ultimate "triumph of misinformation," as *The Atlantic*'s James Fallows later put it.[20]

4.

Chip Kahn, a former Republican staffer who had gone to work for the insurance trade group, later said the goal of the Harry and Louise ads was just to get the administration's attention. Even many Clinton officials wondered afterward whether the ads would have made such a splash if the White House and its allies had simply ignored them.[21]

But the insurance industry's hostility was real. Smaller carriers, in particular, saw the Clinton plan as an existential threat, partly because the proposal prohibited the sorts of policies and selling practices that were their primary sources of revenue.

And it wasn't just insurers out to stop reform. The Clinton plan called for having the government negotiate prices directly with drug manufacturers, just as the governments of other countries do. The pharmaceutical industry didn't want to lose revenue, and it had the resources to make its voice heard—over the airwaves, through television advertising, and in person through direct lobbying on Capitol Hill.

The substance of the industry's argument was that regulations and reductions in payments would stymie innovation, depriving people of potentially lifesaving cures. A wide array of experts questioned whether profits and innovation were really so related or whether the kind of cuts the Clinton proposal contemplated were deep enough to have that sort of effect. But ultimately, it was the money behind the arguments, not their intellectual power, that made a difference. Between 1993 and 1994, special interests spent more than $100 million cumulatively to influence the health care debate, according to a report by the Center for Public Integrity.[22]

The Clinton administration and its allies had hoped to win over some traditional opponents—among them, doctors and hospitals who would see more paying customers, along with employers for whom the price of benefits was an ever-increasing burden. But doctors and hospitals were ambivalent, because the plan's controls on spending could limit their revenue too. Physicians had an added worry: Many were small employers and didn't want requirements that they pay for employee coverage.

Democrats accommodated this by limiting the employer requirement to firms with at least fifty workers, and in July 1994, the American Medical Association joined other groups, including AARP, in a broad endorsement of the Clinton plan's principles. It was a remarkable statement given the organization's historic hostility to reform, but it drew attacks from more conservative physician members and, one month later, from Republican officials. "We are dismayed by the actions of the leadership of the A.M.A.," Gingrich and his lieutenants wrote in a letter to the organization, warning that AMA leaders were "out of touch with rank-and-file physicians." At that point, AMA officials issued another statement, making clear they were not supporting Clinton's plan specifically.[23]

Employers proved to be an even fickler ally. Clinton and his supporters labored to gain the trust of the U.S. Chamber of Commerce, and for a while, it looked like they had succeeded. But the chamber isn't the only trade group that represents employers. The National Federation of Independent Businesses does too, only NFIB focuses on small companies that in the 1990s were less likely to offer their workers insurance. NFIB was opposing the Clinton plan strongly, running ads that, in all likelihood, had more impact on individual members of Congress than the Harry and Louise spots did.

The most dramatic illustration of the difficulty the Clinton administration faced with business groups may have come in February 1994, when a chamber official named Robert Patricelli testified before the House Ways and Means Committee. Patricelli had led a chamber task force that eventually endorsed the concept of universal coverage, including a requirement that employers contribute toward the cost of insurance. It was a real coup for the Clinton administration, one with potential to change the debate. And in prepared testimony that Patricelli submitted to the committee, he reiterated that position. But when Patricelli actually appeared in person several days later, he deviated from the prepared statement and said the chamber opposed the employer requirement.

Democrats were taken aback, and it wasn't until later that the full story came out via an article by the journalist John Judis. Ohio congressman John Boehner, then a rising Republican member of Ways and Means, had seen the prepared testimony and orchestrated a wave of phone calls from local business owners to the chamber, demanding that the organization come out against the Clinton plan.[24]

A different kind of blow came from a putative ally: the labor movement. In the middle of the health care fight, the administration was also promoting ratification of a new trade agreement with Canada and Mexico. Fearing that the agreement would hasten the exodus of high-paying manufacturing jobs across the southern border, unions spent dollars and time fighting it rather than promoting health reform. And as a show of protest, the AFL-CIO for six months halted regular contributions to the Democratic National Committee, which was supposed to be running the main grassroots campaign in support of Clinton's health care proposal.[25]

5.

For all these struggles, the Clinton administration might have succeeded if its partners in the Democratic Congress had been united. But while Democrats largely agreed on the need for reform, they did not agree on the form it should take.

On one end of the debate were those who favored single-payer proposals that would displace nearly all private insurance. On the other end were those who wanted to rely exclusively on private insurance and, in many cases, were content to stop well short of universal coverage. In between those extremes were Democrats holding a variety of positions consistent with their ideological and parochial preferences.

Every position entailed trade-offs that made agreement elusive. More conservative Democrats opposed the employer requirement, for example, echoing arguments from corporate groups that it would deter businesses from hiring new workers. But less money from employers meant less money to fund the program as a whole, which meant finding the dollars someplace else or helping fewer people to get insurance. Neither option sat well with liberal Democrats who thought the Clinton plan needed to be more generous, not less.

The Clinton administration's long internal deliberations did little to bring these factions together, and once the White House delivered its proposal, leaders on Capitol Hill made clear they intended to work through their differences on their own. "Your bill is dead on arrival," an adviser to John Dingell, chairman of the House Energy and Commerce Committee, told a delegation of administration officials when they arrived to brief him on the plan. "So let's talk about what we're going to do instead." Two House committees went on to approve versions of the Clinton plan, but Dingell's could not agree on legislation at all.[26]

Similar divisions existed in the Senate. Ted Kennedy's Labor and Human Resources Committee, as it was called back then, approved its own version of the Clinton proposal. But Moynihan, chairman of the Finance Committee, could barely hide his contempt for the Clintons, their proposal, and their refusal to take up welfare reform before health care. At one point, Moynihan pulled aside an adviser and said, "Do the Clintons not know I'm chairman of the Finance Committee or do they not care?" Finance ultimately approved a bill, but it was far less sweeping than its health committee counterpart.[27]

Leaders in each chamber did their best to stitch together proposals that could prevail in floor votes and provide the basis for compromise. But House leadership, already inclined to design a more generous, more expensive insurance program, pushed even further in that direction to establish a strong liberal bargaining position. Conservative Democrats and moderate Republicans pushed in the opposite direction, not just in the Senate but even within the House Democratic caucus, where Jim Cooper of Tennessee was touting a scaled-down reform bill of his own.

Working behind the scenes, the White House was providing technical assistance to both Cooper and Chafee. Administration officials had long assumed that they would have to accept a bill less comprehensive and aggressive than the initial proposal to secure passage; Paul Starr later likened the original proposal to an onion whose layers Democratic leaders could peel off as necessary. But the strategy would only work if all the parties were committed to reaching a deal, and by the summer of 1994, polls showed the public souring on not just the Clinton plan but also the idea of comprehensive reform.[28]

Conservative Democrats became especially anxious, because they typically came from states with voters who were most hostile to the plan, while moderate Republicans were under increasing pressure from leadership and their allies to dump the project for good. Politically, failure had become a lot less scary than success. When Dole announced his intention to filibuster, it was clear he had enough Republican votes to sustain it.

6.

In the late summer, as it became clear the Clinton effort was headed for failure, White House adviser Chris Jennings ran into an especially tough critic: his mother, who was also a health care activist. She had joined a bus tour that the DNC had orchestrated and, upon its arrival in Washington, asked her son a question: Why hadn't he and his colleagues tried single-payer?

In the coming months and years, many progressives would be asking the same thing. A single government health insurance program would have energized the grass roots and been a lot easier to explain to the public, the thinking went. That would have made legislation easier to defend against industry attacks—which, by the way, came even though Clinton's private-sector model for universal coverage was supposed to neutralize opposition. And the final product would have been better, progressives argued, since a single-payer plan would have eliminated the wasteful, frequently frustrating bureaucracy of private insurance.

But, as Jennings explained to his mother, nobody who understood Congress thought single-payer could get more than a handful of votes. There was no popular movement pushing it and no constituency among intellectuals or business leaders either. Had Clinton tried it, more industry groups would have fought it, and the conservative Democrats with sway over both chambers would have been even harder to corral.[29]

In the media and in professional political circles, the dominant critique was more or less the opposite one: that Clinton had tried to do too much. In this telling, Clinton ignored the political lessons about the Democratic Party's overreach. His proposal envisioned private insurers delivering coverage, yes, but the federal government would still be telling insurers how to act and then moving around hundreds of billions of dollars each year through taxes and spending. Voters were bound to be skeptical, especially in an era when so many Americans believed that the government was prone to waste and (in the view of white middle-class Americans) using their taxpayer dollars to help somebody else.

This was certainly Gingrich's view. And it is why, shortly after taking over as Speaker in 1995, he immediately launched an all-out assault on government programs, including dramatic changes to Medicare and Medicaid that would have reduced their funding over time and ended their basic guarantees of coverage. The resulting conflict with Clinton led to a full, extended government shutdown—one the public largely blamed on Republicans. They had to back down.[30]

A key element of Clinton's strategy was a vocal, explicit defense of Medicare and Medicaid. It was evidence that people were not so inextricably opposed to the idea of government-run health care, especially when they felt like they derived benefits from it. More proof still came from polling on Clinton's doomed health care proposal. People liked individual provisions, like the requirement that insurers couldn't discriminate against people with preexisting conditions. And they supported subsidies for people who couldn't afford coverage. The product wasn't popular, but the pieces were.[31]

Many disappointed reformers concluded their failure was more about the process than the substance. The biggest mistake, they said, was having the White House write legislation and hand it to Congress, which felt no sense of ownership. By the time committees had a chance to get their hands on it, in the fall of 1993, popular enthusiasm for the effort had waned, and political attention was shifting to the midterms.

The Clinton debate also reinforced perceptions that the health care industry is nearly impossible to beat. Clinton had taken on insurers and drug companies, while alienating hospitals. His efforts to win over employers failed. Future reformers would either have to rally more political power on their side or to find some way of neutralizing opponents.

The demise of the Clinton plan burned one other lesson into the minds of would-be reformers: Americans with private insurance from their employers were reluctant to give it up. Voters didn't believe Clinton's promises that they were getting something better, and propaganda from opponents reinforced their doubts. Next time around, reformers would need a plan that kept these people from freaking out.

Of course, supporters of universal coverage couldn't apply those lessons until another debate about health care was underway. And that wasn't going to happen for a while. Democrats needed time to recover from their political wound, and then they would need some evidence that a health care plan could actually become law.

It would take more than a decade, but they would get it. And it would come from a Republican.

Five

The Freedom Trail

1.

The Massachusetts State House is one of Boston's most iconic buildings, with its redbrick, Federal-style façade and golden dome that, for much of the city's history, was visible for miles. Tourists who take the time will learn that it was John Hancock who once owned land on which the statehouse sits and Paul Revere who applied the dome's copper covering, over which the twenty-three-karat gold gilding was eventually layered. Statues on the grounds honor Daniel Webster, Horace Mann, and John F. Kennedy, who not only served in the state legislature but also, for a time, lived in an apartment across the street. The memorials are reminders that the politics of Massachusetts have always shaped the politics of the United States, sometimes in ways that change the course of history.[1]

It's not clear whether Mitt Romney had such aspirations when he became governor in 2003. A straitlaced, teetotaling Mormon, Romney was an unusual figure in the famously parochial world of Massachusetts politics, where Irish and Italian American machines frequently conducted business at Catholic churches or local bars. He had grown up in Michigan and come to Boston when he was in his twenties, to get a joint business-and-law degree at Harvard. From there, it was off to a career in consulting and venture capital, where he accumulated a great deal of wealth.

Nobody was surprised at Romney's success in business, given his work ethic and brains. (He graduated from Brigham Young University with highest honors.) And nobody was surprised at his interest in politics, given his lineage. (His father had been governor of Michigan and then a cabinet secretary for Richard Nixon.) When state Republicans approached him about challenging Ted Kennedy for the Senate in 1994, he said yes and ran a strong, if unsuccessful, race. Soon after, Utah officials recruited him to rescue the troubled 2002 Salt Lake City Olympics. The turnaround that Romney engineered positioned him for another shot at public office. This time, it was for governor, and this time he won.[2]

Health care reform was not among ninety-three specific policy pledges Romney made during his campaign. But shortly before taking office, Romney had a conversation about his agenda with Tom Stemberg, founder and CEO of Staples, a longtime business associate and friend. Stemberg suggested Romney tackle health care costs by finding a way to cover the uninsured, whose reliance on emergency room care forced hospitals to raise prices, driving up costs for everybody else.[3]

Stemberg said later he didn't think Romney would take the suggestion seriously. And the prospects that Romney, in his first elected position, could get something as big and complex as health care reform through the state legislature seemed far-fetched. But Romney did take the idea seriously, and he did get a bill through the legislature, which is why, in April 2006, he was standing on the stage of Faneuil Hall, the colonial-era meeting place, to sign a law that would make sure nearly everybody in the state had health insurance.

Romney's staff had hired a colonial fife-and-drum corps, prompting him to joke that Cecil B. DeMille had organized the proceedings. On stage with Romney were the two most powerful members of the state legislature, both Democrats, which said a lot about what was in the bill and how it had gotten to Romney's desk. It sought to achieve a traditionally liberal goal through traditionally conservative means, by relying on private insurance to plug holes in the existing insurance system and imposing a requirement that everybody get some kind of coverage. "Today," Romney said, "Massachusetts is leading the way with health insurance for everyone, without a government takeover and without raising taxes."[4]

More than one observer thought the reforms would give Romney a signature achievement for an eventual presidential campaign. But the biggest national impact of the law was on the national debate over health care policy, because Massachusetts had succeeded precisely where Clinton-era reformers had failed—achieving universal coverage, or something awfully close to it, in a way that attracted bipartisan support and minimized disruption.

Nobody knew that better than Ted Kennedy. He had worked hand in hand with Romney, his erstwhile foe, to secure regulatory clearance from Washington and provide political cover for liberals uncomfortable with the plan's more conservative elements. Speaking at the signing ceremony, Kennedy joked about the incongruity of it all: "My son said something . . . when Kennedy and Romney support a piece of legislation, usually one of them hasn't read it." But then Kennedy turned serious. "This is a moment to savor, of hope and promise and achievement, for all the people of our Commonwealth—and perhaps for the rest of America, too."[5]

Kennedy's prophecy would prove correct; the Massachusetts reforms became a catalyst and template for what eventually became the Affordable Care Act. But the lessons from Massachusetts were not nearly as simple as outsiders and maybe even some insiders understood at the time.

Among other things, the state's success depended on Romney playing a political role that was falling out of fashion in national Republican politics. Among those who had played it before was Romney's father.

2.

George Romney was born in 1907, in Mexico, where his American parents had gone to join a Mormon colony. He grew up poor, got himself into college but never graduated, and eventually worked his way from a junior position at the American Motors Corporation, a rival of Detroit's big three, to become its CEO. His business success got the attention of local politicians, who asked him to lead efforts at rescuing the Detroit schools and then rewriting the state's constitution. That led to a successful run for governor. He was wary of regulations and taxes, in the way Republican businessmen typically are. But he worked well with unions, was an advocate for civil rights, and even supported a higher minimum wage.

Romney was by no means the only northern Republican to hold such positions. But by the early 1960s, he could see his archetype coming under assault from conservatives who were more hostile to both labor and civil rights and who were slowly growing more antagonistic to the welfare state. In 1964, those conservatives won a major intraparty battle when one of their own, Arizona senator Barry Goldwater, became the GOP nominee. At the convention that year, which took place in San Francisco's Cow Palace, Romney pressed for changes in the party platform to signal that more extremist conservatives had no place in the party.

His bid failed, and Romney, after giving an impassioned speech, made a show of walking out of the convention. It won him national acclaim and helped position him as a front-runner for the 1968 GOP nomination, only to have that bid fall apart after he blamed generals and diplomats for "brainwashing" him into supporting the Vietnam War. One of history's great hypotheticals is how American politics would have changed if Romney had been the 1968 GOP nominee. It is hard to imagine Romney adopting Nixon's Southern strategy, which stoked racial animus in angry white voters. It's impossible to see Romney, known for his high moral standards, engaging in the illicit activities that led to Watergate.[6]

Mitt was the youngest of four children. As a student at the tony Cranbrook School in suburban Detroit, he got good grades but was known less for his achievements than for his happy-go-lucky disposition and penchant for pranks—like the time he and friends stole the uniforms from his father's security detail and pulled over fellow students for speeding.

Still, growing up Romney came with obligations. George, determined not to let his children develop a sense of entitlement, made them get summer jobs while so many other Cranbrook kids were at the country club. Mitt also had a quiet determination about him. Once, when filling in for a runner on the track team, he nearly collapsed on the last lap of the race but refused help and staggered his way to the finish line. "He kept getting up, kept falling, but kept shouting at us—kept telling us not to touch him," one friend said. "He won a lot of people's respect that day. . . . In all my years, I never saw a guttier performance."[7]

Mitt started college at Stanford but after two semesters left for a two-year Mormon mission in France. It was during that period, away from home and out of his father's shadow, that he seemed to find himself, friends would later say. Upon his return, he transferred to BYU and married his high school sweetheart, Ann. From there, it was off to Boston and then to the world of business. He liked to say that his life goal at that point was to become president of Ford or GM, not the United States. But his father preached that the right time to run for office was after you made your fortune, so that nobody could own you, and that's precisely where Mitt found himself in 1994 when Republicans recruited him to challenge Kennedy.[8]

Kennedy was at his most politically vulnerable that year, partly because Democrats nationally were in such trouble and partly because Massachusetts voters seemed less willing to overlook his long history of personal misconduct. Notorious episodes included the 1969 Chappaquiddick incident, in which he fled the scene of a car accident in which his passenger drowned, as well as tales of boozing and womanizing that had long since made their way from the halls of Congress to the pages of well-respected magazines.[9]

Romney was in many ways the perfect "anti–Ted Kennedy," as *The New York Times* put it, in that he was sober and squeaky clean. And although Romney was central casting's idea of a politician, with a squared-off jaw and dark hair meticulously parted to the side, he could plausibly run as a political outsider because he had never held office. Throughout the campaign, Romney stressed his business acumen and distanced himself from Newt Gingrich's Contract with America. When he got a question about the Clinton health care plan, Romney said he identified with moderates seeking compromise: "I'm willing to vote for things that I am not wild with."[10]

In 2002, Romney adopted the same relatively moderate posture when he successfully ran for governor, emphasizing his status as an outsider who could "clean up" state government and keep the budget in check. That may help explain why Tom Stemberg's plea on health care got his attention. In Massachusetts, as in every state, health care programs were on their way to surpassing education as the single biggest expenditure. Figuring out a way to make those programs more efficient was precisely the sort of problem Romney had spent his career solving. Once in office, he started by looking at the numbers and consulting experts—one of whom, conveniently, worked in an office right across the Charles River.

3.

The economics profession didn't pay much attention to health care until the 1960s, when financial pressure on individuals, businesses, and government turned it into an urgent, intellectually novel subject, right at the time the profession as a whole was becoming more focused on mathematical analysis of real-world data to draw insights. Pathbreaking researchers of the era included Joseph Newhouse, whose experiments for the RAND Corporation in the early 1970s yielded evidence that people consume less health care, with mixed results, when their out-of-pocket costs go up; and Martin Feldstein, whose early work showed how a federal tax break for employer insurance led workers and businesses to spend more on benefits.[11]

Newhouse and Feldstein both taught at Harvard, and along with some contemporaries at other top universities, they trained a cadre of similarly minded health care economists whose advisory roles to organizations, candidates, and eventually elected officials would shape policy for decades. Among the most influential was a professor at the Massachusetts Institute of Technology named Jonathan Gruber.

Gruber had discovered economics as an MIT undergraduate. He was a math whiz who craved a way to apply it rather than study the subject for its own sake. College was also where Gruber discovered his political identity, because he saw more people trying to fix the human condition on the political left than on the political right. Graduate training at Harvard, under the tutelage of a Feldstein protégé named Larry Summers, reinforced Gruber's determination to be an empiricist—to follow the data wherever it took him. But more often than not, that journey ended in the place that Democrats were. Gruber was a big supporter of Medicaid, for example, in part because of a groundbreaking study he coauthored demonstrating that the program significantly improved newborn health.[12]

In the late 1990s, Gruber spent two years in the Clinton White House, supplying analysis to help shape administration initiatives on children's health insurance, smoking, and climate change. He liked how his work at Treasury had real-world impact and, before returning to his MIT faculty position, he sat down with Chris Jennings, who was still in the Clinton White House, to see how he could stay relevant. Jennings suggested Gruber focus on providing policy makers with projections on the impact of new health policy initiatives, because reformers were otherwise reliant on independent contractors (whose findings were less reliable) or the Congressional Budget Office (whose processes were slow and opaque).[13]

A few months after leaving the administration, Gruber got a call from Larry Levitt, who had also worked on the Clinton health care bill and was now at the Kaiser Family Foundation, a California-based nonprofit focusing on health care. It was 1998, and politicians, especially Republicans, were increasingly proposing new tax credits to offset the price of insurance. Levitt suggested he was the person to evaluate the impact. Gruber agreed and, drawing on available data about how people respond to different financial incentives, built a model that, among other things, showed a proposal from GOP presidential candidate George W. Bush would cover only one-third of the premiums for the typical uninsured family. Going forward, Gruber refined the model continuously, turning it into an all-purpose tool for guiding policy.[14]

Word got around, and one of the people who heard about it was Amy Lischko, a policy expert and top career official at a Massachusetts health care planning agency. She hired Gruber to make some preliminary estimates on the impact of coverage approaches, and the material came in handy when, shortly after Romney took office, his advisers summoned Lischko to brief the governor on who the uninsured were, how the state was paying for their care, and some options for redirecting the money more productively.

Lischko later remembered how nervous she was, and once at the meeting, she faced tough questions from two Romney advisers. The governor asked a lot of questions too, but he was unfailingly polite. Also, she quickly observed, he had a steel-trap memory for numbers. She had handed out a presentation on paper, and on more than one occasion, Romney interrupted her to ask about an apparent inconsistency with something she'd said ten or twenty minutes before. "You could tell he was excited about it," Lischko said, "that he loved that kind of thinking, about complex problems and just picking them apart piece by piece."

The policy proposals Lischko outlined included options to make employers contribute toward coverage as well as proposals to come up with new state funds, which would inevitably require major tax increases. Romney didn't like the sound of either and instructed his advisers to start thinking up alternatives. At that point, Lischko later remembered, she was still skeptical that anything would come of the effort.[15]

But other forces were propelling it forward.

4.

Massachusetts, whose role at the vanguard of American reform movements traced back to John Winthrop's "City upon a Hill" sermon in 1630, had spent decades debating major health care initiatives. And in 1988, Governor Michael Dukakis, then in the middle of his presidential campaign, signed a universal coverage bill that he promised would be a model for national legislation. That dream died when he lost to Bush, and the dream of universal coverage in Massachusetts died a few years later when the legislature repealed the law following a series of postponements. The program's big political weakness was an employer requirement that the business community had never fully embraced and later attacked as a job killer.[16]

"Psychically, you can't underestimate how deeply disappointed we were, having worked so hard, to see that Dukakis plan fail," Nancy Turnbull, a top Dukakis adviser, later said. But within a few years, the state's activists and stakeholders were back in conversation about the large numbers of uninsured and underinsured residents, along with the high health care costs straining public budgets and employers—only this time, the specter of recent failure focused attention on finding a consensus model that would endure politically.[17]

The Blue Cross Blue Shield of Massachusetts Foundation, which the state's top insurer had created in 2001 with a mission to help improve access to care, convened regular summits and underwrote two sets of key reports—one (by pollster and Harvard professor Robert Blendon) on public opinion and one (by the Washington-based Urban Institute) on the costs and benefits of expanding coverage. Health Care for All, an advocacy group that had been around since the 1980s, organized a coalition including faith-based and labor groups. The coalition wrote and gathered signatures for a ballot initiative on universal coverage, though the effort was as much about pressuring the legislature to act as attempting to bypass it. Many of the coalition members had their roots in providing one-on-one assistance to residents, on affordable housing, and other public services. Their focus was on concrete, achievable measures they hoped could help their target populations get health care quickly.[18]

Even with this political activity, reform might never have happened if not for one other critical factor: a threat by the federal government to cut off a big chunk of Medicaid funding.

Massachusetts operated its version of the program under a special waiver that allowed it to break some of the usual rules to improve health care access for the poor. Waivers are relatively common in Medicaid, and the ability of states to get approval inevitably depends on the inclinations of the administration in charge. Massachusetts got its original waiver during the Clinton administration, whose officials were eager to support coverage expansions and were so excited about the state's proposal that they effectively threw in extra money to subsidize care for the uninsured at some of Boston's safety-net hospitals.[19]

Waivers require renewal, and in late 2001, Kennedy used his clout from recent bipartisan education reforms to win approval from President George W. Bush. When that waiver was set to expire in 2005, Tim Murphy, Romney's top adviser on health care, got some bad news. The Bush administration was willing to renew it, but not that extra subsidy for the safety-net hospitals.

Word quickly spread through the Massachusetts political establishment that the state stood to lose as much as $385 million. The Romney administration's conversations about health policy suddenly had new urgency, although the waiver situation also created an opportunity. The Bush administration indicated it would let Massachusetts keep the extra money if it financed giving people insurance rather than subsidizing safety-net hospitals. This is actually what Romney and his advisers, as well as the advocacy and business communities, had been discussing. They had hesitated, in part, because the politically powerful safety-net hospitals would fight such a change. Now the hospitals were going to lose that money anyway. The question was whether Massachusetts could find a way to get the money and use it for a different purpose.

In late 2004, Bob Travaglini, Democratic president of the state senate, unveiled a proposal to use the waiver funding to finance a coverage expansion that would reach nearly all residents. Travaglini's announcement prompted Romney to write an op-ed promising he'd soon have a plan of his own. The op-ed wasn't overly specific, but he sent copies in advance to key figures like Kennedy, who saw the article as confirmation that Romney was serious. "If he's willing to work for this, let's work with him," he said, according to a retrospective by *The Boston Globe*'s Brian Mooney.[20]

On January 14, 2005, Kennedy and Romney met with Tommy Thompson, the Health and Human Services secretary. It was Thompson's last day in office, and after he signed the waiver, the three men went next door to a going-away party, where Kennedy and Romney got laughs by poking fun at their improbable partnership. Back in Boston, there was more celebration, though tempered by a realization that passing legislation was suddenly a lot more important.[21]

"Massachusetts put a financial gun to its head," John McDonough, Health Care for All's executive director, wrote later, "and the Bush administration provided the bullets."[22]

5.

Party leaders, stakeholders, and advocates had already come to a general consensus on what reform should look like, considering what they'd learned from the Dukakis effort and what they'd seen play out nationally when Clinton proposed his plan.

Instead of trying to upend the whole system through single-payer or some similarly transformative reform, legislation would focus mainly on those who didn't have insurance already. The state already had some regulations making insurance available to people with preexisting conditions, but the rules would have to be stronger, so that everybody could get comprehensive coverage at uniform, community rates. People who couldn't afford premiums would need some kind of financial assistance.

The question was exactly what combination of regulations and subsidies was required—and what other elements had to be part of the mix. This is where Christine Ferguson, who had been Senator John Chafee's health care counselor during the Clinton fight, became a part of the story. After leaving Capitol Hill, Ferguson had joined the Romney administration as commissioner of health. Early on, she raised the subject of an individual mandate—that is, a requirement that people who don't have insurance pay some kind of financial penalty, like her old boss Chafee had proposed.

An individual mandate, Ferguson told Romney, would give healthy people more reason to get insurance before they get sick. That would protect them against the possibility of crushing medical bills, plus it would make sure that insurance companies had plenty of healthy customers paying in premiums, offsetting the high medical bills of people with serious ailments and injuries. In other words, insurers would get that proverbial 80–20 mix, or something close to it, and be able to keep premiums lower across the board.[23]

Gruber ran projections on its impact. His estimate required more guesswork than usual, because no real-world data on a state-imposed mandate existed, but he was confident that he could simulate its effects. His calculations showed that adding a mandate to the mix of regulations and subsidies would allow the plan to cover three times as many people, nearly reaching universal coverage, for less than twice the cost. And the waiver funding could cover the difference.[24]

Romney's political advisers raised objections, noting the likely opposition from libertarian-leaning Republicans who would see it as the government dictating personal decisions. Romney had a different take. A big reason the uninsured problem had first attracted his attention was that free care for the uninsured wasn't actually free; doctors and hospitals just passed along the cost to everybody else. And while not everybody could afford insurance, some people could. By opting not to get insurance, Romney said, these people were shifting the financial responsibility for their future medical problems onto others. "It was literally him sitting there, arguing with his political advisers, saying it's the right thing to do, and we can do it, we can afford it," Gruber later remembered.[25]

Romney embraced the mandate with evangelical fervor, promoting it as "the ultimate conservative idea" in both public and private, at one point inviting Newt Gingrich to the statehouse for a PowerPoint presentation that spanned several hours. "It wasn't like a typical politician meeting, just skimming the surface and angling for political advantage," according to one aide who attended. "This was a deep policy discussion." Gingrich, who at the time was running his own small think tank on health care policy, was miffed Romney talked for nearly the entire time, barely asking for advice. But after the plan became law, Gingrich's newsletter lavished praise on it: "the health bill that Governor Romney signed into law this month has tremendous potential to effect major change in the American health system."[26]

Just as Romney's plan won praise from some conservatives, it drew criticism from some liberals—especially when it came to the benefits Romney seemed prepared to guarantee. Romney, always fond of car metaphors, liked to say that his plan would give people enough financial assistance so that everybody could get the insurance equivalent of a Saturn, not a Cadillac. Democrats and their supporters feared that too many residents would end up with a Yugo. (The Saturn was an inexpensive, no-frills car from General Motors; the Yugo was a cheap import from Yugoslavia with a reputation for low quality.)

Especially in the House, following the lead of Speaker Salvatore DiMasi, liberal Democrats pushed for more comprehensive insurance—by setting a higher standard for what policies had to cover and then by providing more financial assistance so that people could afford the more generous policies. Liberals also wanted to make sure employers had to contribute directly to the cost of insurance. If there was a mandate on individuals, which most unions opposed, there needed to be one on employers as well.

The differences were substantial. But the threat of losing that Medicaid funding had turned the usual political imperative on its head, because it was inaction, not action, that would cost the state money. A deal came together. There would be an individual mandate, but the penalties would have big exemptions for financial hardship. Employers would have to contribute, but the amounts would be modest. Low-income people would get fully subsidized insurance through a version of Medicaid.

The law kicked some key decisions, like the minimum standards for coverage, over to a quasi-independent commission that would oversee the entire program, including a new online marketplace through which people could shop and buy coverage. The idea of this "exchange" had come from the Heritage Foundation, a conservative think tank in Washington, where scholars believed such a marketplace could bring more competition into health care.[27]

The bill passed in April 2006. Romney used his line-item veto to knock out provisions he didn't like, including the employer requirement, but the Democratic legislature overrode it. That gave Romney some political deniability for what he assumed would be the feature most unpopular among conservatives, while giving Democrats something resembling the employer mandate they'd wanted all along.

6.

With less than a year to launch the new system, officials decided to keep the enrollment process simple by piggybacking on the existing Medicaid system, so that the state wouldn't have to build a complex IT system in a few months' time. To run the new insurance marketplace, called the Connector, officials hired Jon Kingsdale, who had worked at Blue Cross and then the Tufts Health Plan. Nobody knew more about the Massachusetts insurance market, and reform advocates didn't flinch at his six-figure salary, which, although less than Kingsdale had made in the private sector, was high for a state official. "Listen, this is not amateur hour," McDonough recalled telling a reporter. "We don't have room for failure here. We don't have room for people to learn on the job.... We are behind him a hundred percent."[28]

That spirit of cooperation among advocates and stakeholders carried over to other implementation tasks. A few days after the signing ceremony, representatives from virtually every major organization with an interest in health care sat around a conference table on the eleventh floor of the Prudential Tower, the 750-foot glass-and-steel skyscraper that looms over the redbrick row houses of Boston's nearby residential neighborhoods. Hospitals and insurers, employers and labor, faith leaders and activists—they were all in the room, mapping out a strategy for making sure people would enroll.[29]

A big focus was advertising, and the groups present agreed to contribute what they could, whether in the form of money, manpower, or both. Even Boston's beloved Red Sox got involved. The team (working through its community foundation) ran announcements about the new law during several games at Fenway Park and lent one of its most popular players, veteran pitcher Tim Wakefield, to appear in a public-service television ad from the Blue Cross Blue Shield of Massachusetts Foundation.[30]

The spot featured a twentysomething woman who, after getting health insurance, went to a doctor to check out a lump in her breast. It turned out to be cancer, but still treatable. "If I didn't have health insurance," she said, while sitting in the Fenway grandstands, "I might not be around today to tell my story, so it basically saved my life." Then Wakefield made his appearance on camera. "Jackie's story is just one example of how important it is for everyone to have health insurance, and in Massachusetts, we are leading the way," the famed knuckleballer said, before explaining where consumers could go to sign up for coverage. Kingsdale later likened the Red Sox partnership to Nelson Mandela partnering with South Africa's national rugby team to reach out to the country's white population.[31]

Even with the Red Sox vouching for the system, the program's architects worried about a backlash against the insurance requirement, which kicked in on January 1, 2007. "We were biting our fingernails," McDonough said. "It was New Year's Eve, people were out partying, and we were watching to see if they were marching in the streets." But there were no big protests. Although tens of thousands of residents would end up paying the penalty, people mostly responded to the law by signing up for coverage, just as advocates had hoped and as Gruber's model had predicted. Between 2006 and 2008, uninsurance among working-age adults fell by 70 percent, to 4 percent total—lowest in the United States. "The 2006 health reform initiative in Massachusetts has accomplished much of what it set out to do," an Urban Institute study concluded. "Nearly all adults in the state have health insurance."[32]

Not everybody who had insurance was happy with it or in good shape to pay medical bills. Single-payer advocates, including the organizations Public Citizen and Physicians for a National Health Program, released reports showing, among other things, that 13 percent of people in Massachusetts still did not have enough money to pay for their medication. One of PNHP's cofounders, a Cambridge-based doctor named Steffie Woolhandler, warned that the Massachusetts reforms had done nothing to reduce costs—and were, most likely, reinforcing existing incentives for people to seek costly (and sometimes clinically hazardous) high-tech medicine they didn't need. Journalist Trudy Lieberman reported that coverage was still too expensive for many because they were too wealthy to qualify for assistance but couldn't afford premiums on middle-class salaries. "Affordable health insurance is beyond their reach even under the health reform law," Lieberman wrote.[33]

But the law's biggest supporters understood that it would be a work in progress—and years later two governors, Democrat Deval Patrick and Republican Charlie Baker, each worked with the state legislature on follow-up legislation designed to get a handle on costs. By that time, researchers had the data they needed to assess the program's impact, and their findings were not ambiguous. The people of Massachusetts had better access to health care, and they were more financially secure as well.[34]

There was also evidence that people in Massachusetts were healthier and living longer. That may sound intuitive, but establishing links between insurance and better health has historically been difficult for researchers. A Harvard economist named Benjamin Sommers figured out a way to do it. He took statistics on various health outcomes in several Massachusetts communities and compared them to demographically similar communities in Connecticut, Rhode Island, and other bordering states. The Massachusetts residents were living longer after the state's health insurance program kicked in.[35]

7.

The political benefits of the program for Romney figured to be even clearer. Romneycare had won praise from a number of prominent Republicans. Experts at the conservative Heritage Foundation were excited about the insurance exchange and didn't express reservations about the mandate. The program "fundamentally shifts the state's health care system in the direction of greater patient and consumer empowerment and control," Edmund Haislmaier, a Heritage scholar, wrote. "Other governors and legislators would be well advised to consider this basic model as a framework for health care reform in their own states."[36]

But these supporters weren't speaking for everybody in the conservative movement. The Wall Street Journal editorial page congratulated Romney for addressing health care, then blasted him for passing a plan that Ted Kennedy could (and did) love. "The state is forcing people to buy insurance many will need subsidies to afford, which is a recipe for higher taxes and more government intervention down the road," The Journal warned. "By making a fetish of 'universal' coverage, Governor Romney has bought into a bidding war that Democrats and advocates of socialized medicine are bound to win in the end."[37]

Michael Tanner, a scholar at the libertarian Cato Institute, called the mandate "an unprecedented level of interference with individual choice and decision-making." And although "big-government" conservatives might like it, he said, "small-government conservatives" wouldn't. "There's no doubt that that split is going to be the key debate that takes place with the presidential contest and in the Republican Party over the next couple of years," Tanner predicted.[38]

Lurking behind these warnings was a fear that Romney's success would inspire copycats. The fear was well founded. Reform advocates all over the country seized on the Massachusetts success as evidence that such a plan could succeed as both politics and policy.

But if Massachusetts was proof of concept, it was proof that came with caveats. Officials didn't have to cut spending or raise revenue significantly to fund the new initiative. The task was a lot tougher when they did, as would-be reformers in California discovered. Despite similarly favorable political circumstances, including a moderate Republican governor eager to work with a Democratic legislature, talks broke down over financing.[39]

Massachusetts was also fortunate in that it already had some key legislation on the books. That included partial protections for preexisting conditions. Those rules meant insurers already had to account for insuring some very sick people. Making coverage fully available to people, regardless of medical status, wasn't such a big shift—which meant that insurers wouldn't have to hike premiums dramatically to cover the new expenses. This wasn't true in most other parts of the country and would turn out to be a huge issue years later when the Affordable Care Act took full effect. "It was a completely different dynamic," said Kingsdale.[40]

The officials who wrote the Massachusetts law and the officials who implemented it got lots of little things right. An example was a decision to set a fixed range for premiums, using actuarial studies as a guide, in what amounted to a loose version of price regulation. The worry was as much underpricing as overpricing; if insurers set premiums too low, to grab market share, they could take on massive losses that would force them to drop out later. This, too, would happen in many states under the Affordable Care Act.[41]

The other big advantage for Massachusetts was the commitment of so many individuals and groups to the program's success. And while that had a lot to do with the many years of collaboration by activists, stakeholders, and lawmakers, it also had a lot to do with Romney.

He had not set out to make sure every resident could afford health care. He simply wanted to use state resources more efficiently and, along the way, to stop people from passing the financial burden of their medical care on to others. But if Romney wasn't excited about creating new coverage guarantees, he wasn't opposed to them either. He understood that progress sometimes requires compromise, usually with people who hold different political views. Romney didn't love the welfare state. But he could live with it. And he could work with Ted Kennedy too.[42]

What would happen if reformers tried to run the Massachusetts playbook, but without all that money lying around, without administrators who knew how to get the details just right, and without a broad, bipartisan coalition of leaders committed to the program's success?

The rest of the country would find out soon.

Six

Audacity

1.

Barack Obama was at his rhetorical best on January 25, 2007, when he spoke at the annual conference for Families USA, a health care advocacy group based in Washington. "Plans that tinker and halfway measures" were not enough, he said, contrasting "the smallness of our politics" with the era of Truman and Johnson, when politicians pursued loftier, more ambitious goals. "Now is the time to push those boundaries once more," he proclaimed. Then he made a vow that got him national headlines:

"Universal health care for every single American must not be a question of whether, it must be a question of how. . . . I am absolutely determined that by the end of the first term of the next president we should have universal health care in this country."[1]

It was a bold promise, although not one to which anybody on the Obama team had given much thought. Obama, still only a first-term senator, had announced his presidential exploratory committee less than two weeks before. Although he had been pondering a run for more than a year, and although the media was already treating him as a top-tier candidate, he was just starting to build an organization. "We were in this position where we had to say something that was presidential candidate worthy," Dan Pfeiffer, an Obama adviser, told me, "and we had no policy yet."

Years later, none of his former aides were quite sure who first thought up the pledge. It was ambitious, which is what Obama always said he wanted to be, and it was consistent with his oft-stated desire to pursue universal coverage. At the same time, the pledge was vague enough that it wouldn't constrain him as a candidate or a president—although, aides later made clear, nobody was really thinking that far ahead. "In the third, fifth, or tenth day of the campaign, or whatever it was," said Pfeiffer, "actually having to pass health care in the first term seemed like a high-class problem to deal with." At some point, the speech went to Obama for review, and he signed off—although, again, nobody really remembered whether he gave it much thought. "It was funny," speechwriter Jon Favreau recalled, "the promise to pass health care was just a line to make news."[2]

A few weeks afterward, in March, Obama spoke again on health care—this time in Las Vegas. The Service Employees International Union, one of the most powerful labor organizations in the country, and the Center for American Progress Action Fund, a liberal advocacy group with close ties to the Democratic establishment, were holding a forum with each of the candidates appearing on stage, one at a time, and taking questions.

One of Obama's top rivals, Senator John Edwards of North Carolina, used the occasion to explain a newly released proposal that had already won praise from pundits. Senator Hillary Clinton, also at the forum, didn't have a plan—and didn't need one, because she was Hillary Clinton. Nobody running for president knew more about health care reform, and nobody running for president had invested more of her political life in the cause. She was Serena at Wimbledon, Springsteen playing the Meadowlands.

Obama's turn did not go as well. He didn't have a policy blueprint, and he didn't have the audience's trust. During the question-and-answer session, a young woman said she had checked his website for a proposal and couldn't find anything. "Right," Obama said. "Well, keep in mind that our campaign now is I think a little over eight weeks old." He promised that a detailed proposal was in the works and proceeded to explain some of its core principles, such as making sure medical care focused more on prevention. The moderator, journalist Karen Tumulty, pressed him on whether he could say something about the more important, politically difficult questions of reform—like, for example, whether he expected that most people would still be getting coverage through employers. Obama demurred, saying that his campaign was in the process of setting up roundtables with frontline workers and consumers to get their input before he would make final decisions.[3]

Andy Stern, SEIU's president and by then one of the nation's most influential advocates for universal coverage, had long thought of Obama as a potential star. But on this night, he was underwhelmed. "I just felt like the valedictorian had met the other valedictorians and suddenly realized that he maybe wasn't the smartest kid in the class anymore," Stern said. Sure enough, Obama had called a campaign aide right after the event and said, "I just whiffed up there." He needed to be better. And he needed a plan.[4]

2.

The Clinton health care fight hadn't merely exhausted Democrats. It had traumatized them too. The one major piece of legislation they managed to pass in its aftermath was the bipartisan State Children's Health Insurance Program. But that bill got through Congress in 1997 only because it targeted a politically sympathetic group, children of the working poor, and because it required what was, by budgetary standards, only a modest increase in spending. "The Democratic Party was so scared of health care reform after '93 and '94, even just talking about kids' coverage was hard," said Jeanne Lambrew, a Clinton administration health care adviser who continued working in Democratic politics afterward.[5]

Changes in health care reinforced Democratic reticence. Incomes were up in the late 1990s, and unemployment was down, easing feelings of insecurity at least among the middle class. Insurance remained expensive, but premiums weren't rising year after year as they had in previous years. A major reason for this was employers switching from traditional insurance over to HMOs and other forms of managed care, which saved money by subjecting treatments to review and limiting beneficiaries to specific networks of doctors willing to accept lower payments.[6]

These changes antagonized both providers and patients. Resentment of managed care was so widespread that it eventually bled over into popular culture, when audiences of a movie starring the actress Helen Hunt broke out into spontaneous applause when her character, the mother of a boy with asthma, blurted out, "fucking HMO bastard pieces of shit." And for a few years the idea of an "HMO bill of rights," to protect consumers from abusive insurance company practices, was a topic of debate in Congress. But for all the difficulties managed care created, some imagined and some very real, the new arrangements were also restraining health care inflation.[7]

The broader political environment was shifting too. Clinton had reacted to the 1994 rebuke by reestablishing his identity as a centrist Democrat, and in 1996, during the State of the Union address, he declared that "the era of big government is over." Late that summer, he signed one of the most controversial pieces of legislation of his presidency, a welfare reform bill that added work requirements and ended the guarantee of federal assistance for poor children.

It was bipartisan but really more of a Republican than a Democratic proposal and, arguably, the single biggest blow that Gingrich's Republicans would strike against a major government program. Nearly every member of the Clinton cabinet opposed the bill, and three officials at HHS resigned over it. One of them, Wendell Primus, had produced internal analyses predicting that it would push more than one million children into poverty. "To remain would be to disown all the analysis my office has produced regarding the impact of the bill," Primus said in a letter announcing his resignation.[8]

Health care's role in the 2000 campaign reflected these countercurrents. In the primaries, the plans from New Jersey senator Bill Bradley and Vice President Al Gore fell well short of what Clinton had proposed. In the general election, Gore tried to make health care an issue by focusing on George W. Bush's record in Texas, where he had opposed expanding coverage for kids. Gore also attacked Bush over his opposition to new managed-care regulations. Neither argument made much of an impression. And following Bush's victory, the political debate swung back to where it was in the Reagan era, with no serious consideration of universal coverage.[9]

But the United States was still the only country in the industrialized world that didn't treat health care as a right. The consequences for that peculiar form of American exceptionalism were becoming more apparent, thanks in part to a landmark 2002 report from the Institute of Medicine, an independent, government-chartered research organization. Following an exhaustive review of existing literature, the report's authors concluded that eighteen thousand people a year were dying prematurely because they didn't have insurance. The precise figure was debatable, but the report's gist was not. Seventy years after those Committee on the Costs of Medical Care reports, the same old problems existed, only they had gotten much worse.[10]

Out of public view, policy experts were busy thinking up new solutions or, at least, new ways to package the old ones. An early and influential project came via a small think tank called the Economic and Social Research Institute, which used funding from the Robert Wood Johnson Foundation to commission a series of new health care reform proposals, complete with detailed actuarial projections on how each would work. The project director, economist Jack Meyer, recruited liberals, moderates, and conservatives. The only requirement was that every proposal had to achieve universal coverage or something close to it. "The motivating factor was, how do we keep it going after the collapse in the Clinton plan," Meyer said. "How do we keep this idea alive?"[11]

Key interest groups were thinking along the same lines, and one in particular, from organized labor, would have a major impact.

3.

Unions had a long history of promoting universal health care, even after they had succeeded in securing coverage for their own members. Walter Reuther, who served as president of the United Auto Workers from 1946 until his death in 1970, had a pragmatic motive: He believed generous union benefits would generate resentment if the rest of the country didn't have equivalent insurance. But he also "thought of himself as an advocate for all working people, not just those in the UAW," as journalist Roger Lowenstein put it.[12]

When labor's influence declined in later years, some unions focused more on protecting the benefits they had won than on winning benefits for others. Especially in the building trades (carpenters, pipe fitters, and so on), many unions ran their own plans, with conspicuously high-paying jobs for the labor officials who ran them, giving them even less incentive to press for reform. But labor itself was changing, and the fastest-growing union was SEIU, whose membership base of janitors, security guards, and health aides included a lot of low-wage workers whose employers offered either skimpy insurance or none at all.[13]

During organizing campaigns, Andy Stern, the union president, kept hearing stories of hardship—including one in Iowa, from a woman who said her daughter had suffered from asthma and died four days after a doctor turned her away because of a past medical debt. The story stuck with him, because years before, he had lost a daughter to a medical error. "There was just a lot of anger," he told me. "And, you know, a lot of people saying, 'I cannot believe, in this country, this can possibly happen.'"[14]

Heading into the 2004 elections, Stern had observed the same thing about Democrats that party insiders like Jeanne Lambrew had. "You couldn't find a Democrat who was comfortable leading on anything but the most incremental health care plan," Stern said. SEIU committed to changing that mindset, setting up state-level campaigns with billboards that said,

"Running for president? Better do something about health care." Newly organized SEIU nurses went to candidate events, sometimes in scrubs and sometimes wearing purple, the union's signature color. "We basically stalked the candidates in 2004 in New Hampshire and Iowa," Stern said. "We had a squad of people . . . at every forum, and they would say, what's your plan for health care?"[15]

In the 2004 Democratic primaries, SEIU endorsed Vermont governor Howard Dean, a family physician who had successfully promoted an initiative that led to near-universal coverage for children in his state. As president, he promised to do the same thing—and help adults to get insurance as well. Despite near anonymity before the campaign, Dean's blunt attacks on Republicans resonated with primary voters eager to fight Bush, and for a while, it looked like he might actually win the nomination—only to have his candidacy collapse quickly after a poor showing in Iowa. Eventual nominee John Kerry endorsed a health plan promising a major expansion of insurance, though it was less ambitious than Dean's and well short of anything that might credibly be described as "universal."[16]

SEIU decided to push harder. For the 2008 cycle, it announced that candidates seeking its endorsement would have to do three things: follow in the footsteps of an SEIU health care worker for a day, propose a detailed plan that would actually get close to universal coverage for all ages, and take questions from SEIU members on health care in what amounted to a public interview. That last part is why the Democratic candidates were in Las Vegas in March 2007 and why the one who flubbed the audition knew he had so much work to do.

4.

Nobody had to tell Barack Obama about the struggles of people who can't pay their medical bills.

His mother, Stanley Ann Dunham, had died of cancer in 1995 at the age of fifty-two. She was by all accounts, including Obama's own, the dominant figure in shaping his character—whether by pushing him academically with extra homework in the mornings, cultivating his political conscience by having him listen to the speeches of Martin Luther King Jr., or steeling him for a complex, sometimes hostile world. "From a very early age, I always felt I was loved and that my mother thought I was special," Obama told journalist Janny Scott for the biography *A Singular Woman.*

He credited that attention and the emotional security it provided with his famously unflappable demeanor.[17]

Obama's mother was an energetic, fearless, and high-achieving anthropologist. Then the cancer hit, leaving her weak and emaciated—and struggling with medical bills. "I will never forget my own mother, as she fought cancer in her final months, having to worry about whether her insurance would refuse to pay for her treatment," Obama said in 2009. It was a disability insurer denying the claim, not a health insurer, as Scott later discovered. But the basic principle was the same.[18]

Dunham's death came at a critical moment in Obama's life, just as he was preparing to publish *Dreams from My Father,* a memoir of growing up in America as a mixed-race child. The book traced Obama's attempt to reconstruct the story of his father, who had been born in Kenya, left the United States shortly after his son's birth, and died when Obama was still an adolescent. The two barely knew each other, and the book's journey culminates with a scene in Kenya, alongside the graves of Obama's father and grandfather, with Obama crying as he finally comes to grips with his own African identity and the struggles the two men had faced in their very different lives. Friends and advisers would later speculate that Obama's uncertainty about his place in the world—part of so many communities and families, yet not quite a full-fledged member of any one—had a profound effect on his political identity by instilling in him a determination to create a world in which nobody would feel like an outsider.[19]

The book ends right when Obama is about to finish three years as a community organizer in Chicago and enter Harvard Law School, where he would eventually become editor of the *Harvard Law Review.* A key to his candidacy was his appeal to each of the factions on staff. Although he was a liberal, he got along well with the radicals and the conservatives, who appreciated that he took their views seriously. He was the *Review*'s first African American editor, making his election big news across the country and on campus as well. When a reporter from *The Harvard Crimson* asked what Obama hoped to do after law school, he said he intended to keep working in public service—and might even run for office someday.[20]

True to his word, Obama passed up more lucrative private-sector opportunities to join a Chicago firm that took on civil rights cases, represented tenants in disputes with landlords, and had a history of strong political connections. Obama also taught constitutional law at the University of Chicago, an experience he later said kept his intellect sharp by forcing him to explain and defend positions with which he did not agree. Then the state senate seat for his Chicago neighborhood opened up. Obama jumped into the race and won.[21]

Although health care had come up in his work as a community organizer, it came up more when he ran for office and began serving. He heard frequently from constituents about their medical bills, and noticed in particular the plight of the working poor whose incomes were too high to qualify for Medicaid. "A lot of people who are working full-time, maybe two or three jobs, still don't have health insurance," Obama explained in an interview that aired on a local cable station. It was a theme he circled back to almost two decades later, when he told me in an interview that he remembered specifically "those who didn't qualify for Medicaid were often much more vulnerable" than those who qualified.[22]

Helping the uninsured to get care became a top focus, as David Garrow chronicles in his exhaustive biography *Rising Star*. Obama made an annual tradition of introducing a constitutional amendment to establish health care as a "fundamental right." The amendment would be purely symbolic, but as a junior legislator in the minority, Obama figured that was as much as he could do. If nothing else, he hoped, it would push the conversation forward: "In discussing it with advocates, the thinking was that, if we could establish at least the principle that universal health care was an important goal for the state to pursue, then you plant a flag and build off of that—you build mechanisms to start providing care."[23]

Obama made more headway with legislation to expand eligibility for a children's insurance program, winning Republican support with a concession allowing families to choose a private option, as conservatives preferred. The bill passed, burnishing Obama's reputation as a Democrat who could work with the GOP. "He could not be accused of partisan aggression, but he got his way," recalled John Bouman, who as director of the Shriver Center on Poverty Law was a key player in the debate.[24]

5.

Obama's state senate seat became a lot more important in 2002, when Democrats got the majority and Obama became chairman of the health care committee. One of his first calls was to Jim Duffett, executive director of an advocacy group called the Campaign for Better Health Care. Together, the two hashed out what would become the Health Care Justice Act, a proposal authorizing a state commission to recommend a universal coverage plan and then instructing the legislature to vote on it, up or down, by a set date.[25]

Rallying public support was a big part of their strategy. Obama went all over the state to sell his plan, paying particular attention to downstate areas with more conservative voters. "You have to put political pressure on these politicians and you've got to keep on pushing and pushing," Obama told one audience, according to an account in Edward McClelland's biography, *Young Mr. Obama.* "If they say 'no,' don't give up. If they're a Republican, and they don't support this thing, keep on putting pressure on them, because they go back to the district and they say, 'Oh, my God, I'm really getting beat up on this issue. What's going on?' Same thing with Democrats."[26]

Insurance lobbyists fought the bill, Republicans were hostile, and conservative Democrats were mostly ambivalent. Obama kept at it, sometimes working at his desk late into the evening while Duffett, sitting on a couch nearby, would be dialing up skeptics to win them over. "I would say, you know, 'They're not budging, they're not budging,'" Duffett said to me later. "And he would just say, 'Try again, try again.'"[27]

At one point, Duffett and some of his allies met privately with Obama. They knew he was already thinking about running for the U.S. Senate in 2004. They also knew the health care push carried political peril, because it could alienate key power brokers and because it was making Obama the target of increasingly loud attacks by Republicans. If Obama wanted to let some other lawmakers take the lead, Duffett and his allies told him, they would understand.

Obama would have none of it, according to Duffett: "He said, 'Stop . . . this is going to happen and I'm committed to making it happen. And yeah, I'm getting beat up. Yes, I'm being called socialistic . . . but you've done a good job in pushing back and it's just a bunch of B.S. and we're going to figure it out.'"[28]

They did, although it required big concessions. Obama agreed to make the commission's recommendations nonbinding, in part because it wasn't clear whether forcing a vote was constitutional. Obama also altered the language to assuage insurance industry lobbyists (and the lawmakers they supported) who believed the original wording favored a recommendation of single-payer.

Even with those concessions, Republicans opposed the bill, in some cases stridently. State senator (and future U.S. representative) Peter Roskam, who had been the GOP's point person on health care, said it was a launching pad for "socialized medicine" and said Democrats were trying to ram a version of the old Clinton plan through the legislature.

The statement made Obama visibly angry, according to several accounts, although he delivered his response sternly and methodically, without raising his voice. "I would challenge you to find something in there that suggests anything remotely close to socialized medicine," Obama said. Then he told the story of an unemployed factory worker who couldn't afford the $4,500 in prescriptions his son needed for a transplant. "He's trying to figure out, once he loses his job and his health insurance, how in the heck he's going to be able to provide drugs to keep his son alive. . . . The notion that somehow that all is hunky-dory and we can characterize this with a bunch of ad hominem attacks and play politics with this situation is not going to satisfy that man and—and—and his wife," Obama said. "If you want to vote no on this bill, vote no on it, but don't lie about it."[29]

The bill passed without Republican support and became law. Years later, when Obama was in Washington, the commission concluded its deliberations by recommending a universal coverage scheme based on competing private insurance plans. When Governor Rod Blagojevich introduced a scaled-down version of the plan, the legislature refused to pass it. Many Illinois progressives, already unhappy with the compromises that went into the original law, said the outcome was proof that Obama had given away too much.[30]

Among those most disappointed was Quentin Young, a doctor who was on the commission and voted against its final recommendation. Young was a civil rights activist and past national coordinator of Physicians for a National Health Plan, the single-payer group. His partner in private practice happened to be Obama's personal physician, and for years Young had talked up Obama as a kindred spirit—in part because Obama frequently described himself that way, including at a 2003 AFL-CIO meeting, where he said, "I happen to be a proponent of a single-payer universal health care program."[31]

But in the final floor debate over the Health Care Justice Act, Obama said, "I want to say on record that I am not in favor of a single-payer plan. I don't think that we can set up that kind of plan, and if we were going to even attempt some sort of national health care, that would have to, obviously, be done at the federal level." Obama, Young said, had "sold out to the insurance companies."[32]

Duffett took a different view. After all those hours trying to win over hostile lawmakers, he became convinced the final legislation was as strong as it could be. Obama had always qualified his support for single-payer by saying it might not be possible right away, Duffett noted. And if the commission ultimately didn't lead to a big coverage expansion, Duffett said, Obama could legitimately take credit for the earlier Medicaid legislation, especially because he got that through while Democrats were still in the minority.

"Was he progressive on health care, on a scale from 1 to 10?" Duffett asked rhetorically. "You know, I'd probably give him an 8.75 or maybe 9 in that environment."[33]

6.

The Health Care Justice Act passed the legislature in the middle of Obama's 2004 campaign for the U.S. Senate and just weeks before he would make his national debut with a prime-time keynote speech at the Democratic National Convention in Boston. In an address that overshadowed every other speech that week, Obama laid out one of the big themes that would later guide his 2008 presidential campaign: his belief that political leaders were dividing Americans, who actually had a lot more in common than the familiar maps of red and blue states suggested. "There's not a liberal America and a conservative America," Obama said memorably, "there's the United States of America."[34]

Obama won and, upon taking his new Senate seat the following January, found himself once again in the minority party. Just as he had done in the Illinois legislature, he responded by reaching out to Republicans. He struck up a friendship with Tom Coburn, a staunchly conservative senator from Oklahoma, and forged a partnership on nuclear disarmament with Richard Lugar of Indiana.[35]

But as much as Obama liked to emphasize comity and common purpose, he also said it was important for leaders to stretch the boundaries of the possible and to take political risks for worthwhile causes. Although many politicians said those things, Obama could point to a specific, high-profile instance when he'd done it: back in October 2002, when he spoke out against the Iraq War, even though the 9/11 attacks were still a fresh memory and opposition was especially risky for a dark-skinned Democrat with the middle name of Hussein.

That stand made Obama a hero to a cadre of progressive activists who were pushing the Democratic Party to get out of its Clinton-era defensive crouch. A leading indicator of their power was the growth of MoveOn, the online-based grassroots organization that had started in the late 1990s as a way of fighting Clinton's impeachment and had turned into an all-purpose, highly effective vehicle for channeling anger over the 2000 Florida recount and the Iraq War. As of 1998, it had 500,000 members; as of 2004, it had 2.8 million.[36]

The visibility Obama had from his DNC speech and respect for his early opposition to the war put him into the conversation about potential 2008 presidential candidates. And eventually, Obama started thinking about it too, according to Richard Wolffe's *Renegade*, partly because Bush's plummeting popularity had made a Democratic victory in 2008 seem more likely. But first, Obama would have to get serious about policy in a way he hadn't before. And that very much applied to his thinking on health care.[37]

Obama already had a fully developed theory of America and how it should work. A key principle, which he laid out in a defining 2005 commencement speech at Knox College, was the idea that government has a vital role to play in providing economic security, including access to health care, because it draws "on our sense of mutual regard for each other, the idea that everybody has a stake in the country, that we're all in it together." But he hadn't done a deep dive on specific national health reform proposals, and the subject hadn't really come up in his 2004 campaign.[38]

The education process took place under the direction of adviser Karen Kornbluh, who convened a series of briefings in Obama's Senate office and, sometimes, at Washington restaurants. A policy expert and influential thinker in her own right, Kornbluh was unusually qualified for the position for policy director, which said something about the caliber of input Obama hoped to have around him. And during the discussions, Obama was an unusually engaging interlocutor, according to several accounts, although he rarely made pronouncements about his own thinking. David Cutler, a Harvard economist who would end up on Obama's presidential campaign, recalled later that Obama would stop him midthought and summarize what Cutler had said to make sure he wasn't missing the nuances, and then have him proceed without indicating whether he agreed.[39]

Cutler was a veteran of the Clinton health effort, as were several other health care experts who spoke with Obama. One session included Jeanne Lambrew, Ken Thorpe, and Chris Jennings. Jennings said later he could sense Obama's ambition to get beyond the incrementalism of recent years. "I remember being quite impressed, though also thinking he was perhaps overly confident that he could overcome the many barriers that had flum-moxed everyone else over the decades. I guess history proved me wrong."[40]

By 2006, a rough consensus about the ideal structure of reform was al-ready gelling within the Democratic establishment. The focus was on min-imizing disruption to existing insurance arrangements, since the threat of disruption had seemed to make the Clinton plan so toxic. Employer coverage would largely remain in place. Medicaid would too, but it would expand to cover all of the poor, not just those who fell into narrow catego-ries like pregnant women. And then there'd be some kind of new market of private insurance options—with subsidies and guarantees of coverage for preexisting conditions—for the remaining population. It was still a purely hypothetical notion when Jeanne Lambrew cowrote a paper describing it for the journal *Health Affairs.* Then Romney and his allies passed such a plan in Massachusetts.[41]

It was proof of concept, and it got everybody's attention—including Obama's. He still thought of himself as a single-payer fan, in principle, but he was also thinking a lot about the practical as well as the political chal-lenges to such a dramatic change. As longtime adviser and University of Chicago economist Austan Goolsbee frequently pointed out, single-payer only saved money if it dramatically reduced payments to doctors, hospi-tals, and other health care providers. That would be tough to do quickly—a point Obama made many years later in our interview. "We aren't starting from scratch. We have a legacy system that is one-sixth of the economy. And the idea that you could, in some way, dismantle that entire system—or even transition it entirely—to a single-payer system looked politically impractical and probably really disruptive."[42]

The Massachusetts model, Obama acknowledged, "wasn't elegant." But it had become law, and notably, it had done so with support of a prominent Republican governor. "It wasn't lost on any of us that, given filibuster rules in the U.S. Senate, even if we had a big majority we were likely to need and want some sort of bipartisan buy-in," Obama said. "And having a model that had been tested, had proven to work, and that had some conservative, free market bona fides—that looked like an attractive option."[43]

A similar thought process was playing out in the campaign of John Ed-wards, the Democratic senator from North Carolina who had been Kerry's vice presidential nominee. By 2006, Edwards was well into the process of sketching out an agenda that he hoped would establish him as both the most progressive and most policy-focused of the top-tier candidates. In part because of his wife, Elizabeth, whose battle with cancer had interested her in health policy, Edwards wanted his first big plan to be for universal coverage. His policy advisers, James Kvaal and Peter Harbage, prepared a memo describing three different approaches: a single-payer plan, a system where every American had vouchers to buy regulated private insurance, and a scheme like the one in Massachusetts.[44]

Edwards rejected single-payer right away. As ambitious as he wanted to be, Kvaal said, "he immediately felt like that was not something he could sell to the country." Edwards was more intrigued by the voucher idea, as was Elizabeth, because of its potential to wipe away all the inequities and screwy financial incentives baked into the employer system. At one point, advisers set up a conference call so that Ezekiel Emanuel, a physician and policy expert who had cowritten a book sketching out a voucher scheme, could debate Jon Gruber, who had become the best-known advocate for the Massachusetts approach. After listening, Edwards decided that the voucher plan, like single-payer, would be too disruptive, according to Kvaal.[45]

After working straight through Christmas to have the plan ready for the official campaign launch in January, Edwards and his political advisers decided to hold off until February so that the proposal would get more attention. And it did just that. "I won't trust presidential candidates on health care unless they provide enough specifics to show both that they understand the issues, and that they're willing to face up to hard choices when necessary," Paul Krugman, the influential economist and *New York Times* columnist, wrote. "And former Senator John Edwards has just set a fine example."[46]

The delay in the announcement was significant for one other reason. It gave Edwards time to give his plan one final, very important tweak—one that his rivals would also make and that, over the course of the next two years, would become a key part of the debate.

Seven

The Argument

1.

Political scientist Jacob Hacker wasn't a veteran of the Clinton health care effort. But he was perhaps its best student. Researching his dissertation about the plan's origins had involved poring over thousands of pages of internal administration memos, by hand, at the National Archives. By the time he was done, he likely knew as much about the Clinton plan as Hillary did.

Hacker was an unabashed liberal at a time when that label was still considered radioactive. He was convinced that public-sector health programs were both more efficient and more humane than private-sector alternatives. But his research into the Clinton plan led to the same conclusion that Obama and everybody else was reaching: single-payer wasn't politically feasible. Too many people would fear such a dramatic change, he thought, and the industries that profited from existing arrangements would fight successfully to block it.

But Hacker thought there might be a way to pave a new path that could lead to a single-payer system over time: by creating a government-run program that would be purely voluntary. If the intuition of liberals was correct, the program would attract more and more people with its lower prices and higher quality, relegating private insurance to an ever-shrinking part of the market and, maybe someday, nothing but a niche role. And if the intuition was wrong? Then the public option would still serve a purpose as an alternative for people who wanted it.[1]

The idea, like almost all ideas in health care policy, was not actually novel. One of Ted Kennedy's many universal health care proposals had envisioned offering a government-run program as a voluntary alternative to private insurance. The concept had come up in deliberations over the Clinton plan too. In the early 2000s, California officials crafted their own version as part of a possible reform plan. But Hacker was able to flesh out the idea at just the moment universal coverage proposals were in demand, first as part of that Jack Meyer "Covering America" series and then for the Economic Policy Institute, a liberal Washington-based think tank. Hacker called the idea "public plan choice." Somewhere along the way, people started calling it the "public option."[2]

One of the big selling points was that, in Hacker's conception, the public option would pay hospitals, doctors, and other providers of care at the same low rates Medicare used. This would allow the public option to offer lower premiums than private carriers, which would respond by lowering their prices or giving up their customers to the new government plan. Either way, the end result would be cheaper, more affordable insurance.[3]

The public option's ability to underprice private competition was precisely the feature that many health economists, including some advising Democrats, found objectionable; they thought it would distort normal competitive forces by setting prices either too low or too high. Politically, the public option promised to arouse opposition from industry groups, including not just insurers but also doctors and hospitals who saw a threat to their revenue streams. As it was, they said, they were losing money on their Medicare patients.

But the public option appealed to liberals who didn't like how the Massachusetts-style reforms shunted so many people into private insurance. The idea also had support from Health Care for America Now (HCAN), an advocacy group with $27 million in funding from the liberal Atlantic Philanthropies. Roger Hickey, the group's cofounder, and Diane Archer, its director, spent much of 2007 and 2008 promoting the idea, specifically targeting liberals who they knew preferred single-payer. "The good news is that people are ready for big change," Hickey told a New Jersey audience. "But the hard reality, from the point of view of all of us who understand the efficiency and simplicity of a single-payer system, is that our pollsters unanimously tell us that large numbers of Americans are not willing to give up the good private insurance they now have in order to be put into one big health plan run by the government."[4]

The survey Hickey referenced came from Celinda Lake, a prominent Democratic pollster. Her finding was consistent with other polling, as well as the intuition from the Clinton veterans that threatening employer coverage was a political death wish. It also resonated with congressional Democrats, whom Archer, a veteran advocate on Medicare issues, arranged for Hacker to brief. Among those most taken with the idea was George Miller, a California congressman and close ally of the new Speaker, Nancy Pelosi. Miller was also chairman of the Education and Labor Committee, one of three House committees with jurisdiction over health policy. That made him a valuable ally.

The public option appealed to one other group: the top Democratic candidates, all of whom were eager to secure the backing of prominent liberals. (Edwards had another reason to be enthusiastic: Peter Harbage, his health adviser, had worked on California's early version of the idea.) Edwards touted the public option frequently, telling interviewers and audiences that he didn't mind one bit if consumers marched en masse to the public option, eventually turning it into a single-payer system by default.[5]

Obama and his team were also taken with the idea, according to Jeffrey Liebman, a Harvard economist who had started advising the campaign in early 2007. "We spent quite a lot of energy in March and April considering different ways of inserting elements of the Hacker approach into our plan—ultimately landing on the public option within the exchanges," Liebman said. Still, Obama's rhetoric on the public option later in the campaign would prove less effusive than Edwards's, in an early sign that he supported the idea but perhaps didn't consider it as essential as some of his supporters did.[6]

Obama and his advisers made a series of key decisions during a two-part meeting that took place on May 2, with David Cutler leading the briefing. But they still had to litigate one big issue: the individual mandate. The advice Obama got from experts, including his own, was that a financial penalty was important. Without it, fewer healthy people would sign up. Insurers would be stuck with beneficiaries in relatively poor health, forcing them to raise prices, which would in turn scare more people away. The mainstream economic models showed this. It had been enough to persuade Edwards and had played a key role in winning over Romney.[7]

Obama remained unconvinced. He understood what the experts were saying, but according to Cutler, he also "wasn't comfortable requiring people to buy something" when it was still unclear exactly what it would cost. Obama also thought simply lowering premiums would bring in a lot more people, even healthy ones. "The reason people don't have health insurance isn't because they don't want it," Obama would say later, "it's because they can't afford it." Obama's political advisers had their own issues with the mandate: Voters might recoil at such a requirement, thinking that the decision to buy or not to buy health insurance was a personal one that the government had no business making. "I remember there being a view that it was a general election disaster," Dan Pfeiffer told me.[8]

Obama's policy team did have an alternative: automatically enrolling people in health coverage, the same way that private companies do with 401(k) retirement plans, and then giving people an option to decline. With the 401(k) plans, usually very few people turned down the contribution. The nudge worked. That was enough for Obama. A mandate for kids made sense, he thought, because they were cheap to insure, and he was comfortable requiring it. But for adults, he'd go with automatic enrollment and hold off on a mandate, at least until somebody could show it was absolutely necessary.

2.

The process and timing of putting together a campaign proposal was subject to all kinds of influences, some political and some personal. Cutler and Liebman, who lived near each other and had young children roughly the same age, sometimes conferred at a local playground; Gruber at one point told the campaign he couldn't turn around a calculation in time for a Monday briefing because of his child's bar mitzvah. But by the end of May the plan was ready to go and, on the Tuesday after Memorial Day, Obama formally introduced it during a speech at the University of Iowa.[9]

He had come a long way since the dispiriting Las Vegas forum. He'd beefed up his campaign staff, adding policy director Heather Higginbottom. As part of the rollout, his team put together a lengthy white paper on the proposal, and even by the standards of Democratic campaigns, it was thick with detail. It also included a special supplement on system-wide reforms that, Obama promised, would make health care less expensive for everybody using it.[10]

This was a big deal to Obama. Many of the constituents and voters sharing hardship stories with him over the years already had insurance. But they could barely keep up with premiums and out-of-pocket costs—and mostly, Obama knew, that was because so much money was flowing to doctors, hospitals, and drugmakers.

Once upon a time, reformers had proposed tackling that problem by dictating fees or setting budgets, the way European countries did. Nobody in U.S. politics was talking about that anymore. Instead, the focus was on "delivery reforms" designed to improve efficiency without direct government regulation of prices. The Obama campaign paper included some of the ideas most popular with experts—like streamlined billing to reduce waste and overhead; and encouraging doctors and hospitals to form integrated health systems, where providers could communicate more easily and coordinate care. All told, the paper predicted, these strategies could reduce health spending enough that, eventually, every American family would be saving $2,500 a year.

That number figured prominently in Obama's rhetoric and, although it sounded apocryphal to some, it had not come out of thin air. The experts on his team (Cutler, Liebman, and David Blumenthal, who was a professor at Harvard Medical School) had spent weeks reviewing literature on the impacts of various reform concepts, gradually increasing the savings estimate as they became more convinced the evidence justified it. But the figure also came with an asterisk. That $2,500 in savings represented a $2,500 reduction from the projected baseline—in other words, it was $2,500 less than projections suggested the average family would be spending if existing trends continued and nothing in public policy changed. Most likely, health care costs would still be rising for most families every year. The average person would have no idea that, if not for Obama's interventions, costs would likely be rising more quickly.

That misunderstanding would have political implications much later in the debate. But Obama had a more immediate problem on his hands. His decision to leave out an individual mandate had drawn scrutiny from experts and commentators who took it as a sign that he was not serious about universal coverage. "There is perhaps no more surprising fact about Obama's plan than that it is not universal," journalist Ezra Klein wrote in *The American Prospect*. "Its failing, somewhat ironically, is a lack of audacity."[11]

I had the same reaction, and while putting together an article for *The New Republic*, I asked Jon Gruber how much difference he thought the lack of mandate would make. Gruber said that he had not modeled Obama's final plan specifically and cautioned that it was difficult to predict the effects of automatic enrollment, as Obama was proposing. But a ballpark guess was that the number of people signing up for insurance would be lower by as many as fifteen million.[12]

Five days later, Edwards used the figure to attack Obama at a televised debate in New Hampshire. "We have a threshold question about whether we're going to have truly universal care," Edwards said. "The *New Republic* has estimated that his plan will leave about 15 million people uncovered. He says he will do something about that later. I believe that unless we have a law requiring that every man, woman and child in America be covered, we're going to have millions of people who aren't covered."[13]

Hillary Clinton didn't say anything about the individual mandate that night, in part because she had yet to unveil her own plan for expanding coverage. But she had already indicated she, too, was going to recommend a Massachusetts-like approach to coverage. Her advisers responded to Obama's announcement by making clear that her plan, just like the Edwards proposal, would have a penalty—which it did when they released it in September.[14]

The argument over the mandate became a fulcrum of conflict over the next few months as the nominating contest quickly narrowed to a two-person race. The arguments struck plenty of pundits as tedious, and at one point, *Saturday Night Live* poked fun at Clinton during a parody of one of the debates. "If you're just joining us, the first segment of tonight's debate, all three hours and forty minutes of it, was entirely given over to a discussion of health care—and sweet Georgia Brown, it was more boring than you could possibly imagine," the actor playing NBC moderator Brian Williams said. "A vitally important issue, to be sure, but when this one here [gesturing at the actress playing Clinton] gets to talking about it, it's all a person can do to keep the mind alive."

But the dispute had a nasty side, as well. Clinton was relentless in her attacks, suggesting that Obama's failure to include a mandate meant he was perfectly happy to leave an extra fifteen million people without access to health care, as if he hadn't been talking about universal coverage for his entire political career. Obama's campaign responded with mailers, one of which said, "Hillary's health care plan forces everyone to buy insurance, even if you can't afford it." In fact, Clinton (like all mandate advocates) had made clear there would be a hardship exemption, so that the penalty would only apply to people who, by the law's standards, could afford premiums.[15]

The mailer reminded many critics of the old Harry and Louise ads. When an aide handed one of them to Clinton at a campaign appearance in Cleveland, she summoned reporters for an impromptu press conference and let Obama have it: "Since when do Democrats attack one another on universal health care? I thought we were trying to realize Harry Truman's dream," Clinton said. "Shame on you, Barack Obama."[16]

Obama frequently expressed his exasperation at the back-and-forth, especially the debates, which he said were "not on the level" because they were more about one-liners than making cogent arguments. In practice runs, sometimes he would snap at advisers who were serving as stand-ins for his opponents or moderators. But he also understood that he had to play the game to win it, and even he later admitted that, by the time he had won the nomination, he had become a much sharper debater than he was at the outset.[17]

3.

One constant of Republican health care policy is that it's primarily been reactive; they put out proposals when it's necessary because a Democrat has done so first. Richard Nixon and John Chafee had each done this in their time. In 2008, it was presidential nominee John McCain's turn.

Although McCain had some more liberal instincts on a handful of issues, on health care he was a more conventional Republican—in other words, he didn't like the sound of more spending, more taxes, or more regulation. His proposal, put together by some veteran advisers, reflected these preferences. They came up with a plan to give people tax credits for buying coverage on their own; to pay for it, McCain would get rid of a tax break for employer-sponsored insurance. The underlying idea was to get more people out of employer coverage and shopping for plans on their own, in the hopes that competition for new customers would lead insurance companies to provide cheaper, better-quality plans for all.

A premise of McCain's plan, like Obama's, was that competition among insurance plans could lead to lower costs and better health care. But Obama's plan offered a lot more financial assistance to lower-income people, so that the net effect of Obama's plan would be tens of millions of people getting insurance, according to projections. McCain's plan was likely to have a much smaller impact, or perhaps no net impact at all.

At the same time, experts said, McCain's plan was likely to encourage a shift of people out of employer policies and into less generous individual coverage—that is, policies they would buy on their own, directly from insurers, with fewer benefits and higher out-of-pocket costs. That would be rough on people who were older or sicker and likely to run up bigger medical bills.

Obama's plan, by contrast, had multiple built-in protections to make sure everybody, including those with serious medical problems, got comprehensive benefits.[18]

McCain's willingness to change the tax treatment of health insurance in ways that could erode employer insurance created a political liability, one Obama and his strategists exploited with the same tenacious opportunism they had shown in their attacks on Clinton over the individual mandate. In a Newport News, Virginia, speech, Obama attacked McCain's plan as "radical," and warned that "under the McCain plan, at least 20 million Americans will lose the insurance they rely on from their workplace." Obama ads said that "McCain would make you pay income tax on your health insurance benefits. Taxing health benefits for the first time ever."

The attacks were more or less true, but they left out critical context—like forgetting to mention that most or all of those twenty million losing employer coverage would end up with alternative, albeit less generous, policies. The ads were also resonating with the public, so much so that Obama's political advisers urged him to say little else on health care. Polls showed he had a decided advantage on the issue, as Democrats generally did, and by the time of the general elections, other issues seemed more urgent.[19]

But Obama spurned the advice. Pfeiffer recalled one meeting at the Chicago campaign headquarters when he and other political advisers ticked off the reasons to avoid dwelling on health care. "He said he understood all of that," Pfeiffer remembered, "but said he was not going to drop it because he wanted to preserve the opportunity to do it." Neera Tanden, a top Clinton adviser whom Obama hired after winning the nomination, had similar recollections.[20]

And while Obama spent a lot of time zeroing in on the tax issue, he also emphasized what he believed was the fundamental difference between him and his Republican rival—a difference that wasn't an argument over specific policy choices so much as a clash of worldviews over what obligations society has to its most vulnerable members.

A particularly telling moment came on October 7, in Nashville, for the second of three presidential candidate debates. Moderator Tom Brokaw followed up an audience question by asking the candidates, "Is health care in America a privilege, a right, or a responsibility?" McCain said it was a responsibility, capturing the essence of GOP thinking. Although Republicans like McCain were willing to have government help people get health care—by, for example, offering tax credits that would make insurance cheaper—they rejected the idea that government should be in the business of guaranteeing it to everybody.

Democrats felt differently. Their proposals had evolved since Truman's day, but, Obama made clear, their motives had not. "I think it should be a right for every American," Obama said. "In a country as wealthy as ours, for us to have people who are going bankrupt because they can't pay their medical bills—for my mother to die of cancer at the age of 53 and have to spend the last months of her life in the hospital room arguing with insurance companies because they're saying that this may be a pre-existing condition and they don't have to pay her treatment, there's something fundamentally wrong about that."[21]

Health care mattered to Obama for practical reasons—because he had seen what big medical bills could mean to everyday Americans, whether it was his own mother or the people who approached him on the campaign trail. But it also mattered to him because, in his vision of America, nobody got left behind, and society's strongest banded together to protect the weak.

Pushing for universal coverage was bound to be difficult, he knew. But he wanted to be a transformational leader who took on such tasks. He was ready to go. The question, as he thought about a possible presidency, was whether the rest of the party would be too.

Eight

Workhorses

1.

The U.S. Capitol Building has more than a hundred "hideaways"—private offices that do not appear in public directories and frequently occupy corners in low-traffic, hidden hallways, giving them something of a Hogwarts vibe. Mostly, they are for senators, and the best ones are right near the floor, so that lawmakers can get work done between speeches and votes without going to their larger suites in the office buildings across the street.

The hideaway Ted Kennedy occupied for the bulk of his later years was among the most admired. It had a western-facing window offering an unobstructed view of the Mall, as well as a collection of personal mementos offering glimpses of his storied political and family history. On the wall, there was a portrait of Daniel Webster, and on the fireplace mantel was a large photo of Joseph Kennedy Jr., Ted's oldest brother, who died while flying a bomber over Europe in World War II. Kennedy treated the room like a museum and loved regaling visitors with the backstory of a fireplace where, supposedly, British troops in 1814 had lit the torches they later used to burn down the White House—an "Irish truth," as one aide who shared Kennedy's heritage called the too-good-to-check story.[1]

The aide was David Bowen, a Ph.D. neuroscientist who had joined Kennedy's committee staff in 1999, and he was with Kennedy one afternoon in May 2008, while they waited for a pharmaceutical executive who had an appointment. The executive was late, and typically, Kennedy would give such lapses only a few minutes before leaving. But Kennedy had something on his mind on this day. And so as they sat there, across a wooden table constructed from an old rudder on a Kennedy family sailing boat, the senator gave Bowen a new mission: writing a health care bill.

Introducing universal health care legislation was a biannual ritual for Kennedy, and usually, his bills called for either single-payer or some other reform scheme that relied on a large government program. But those proposals were thin on detail because they were purely aspirational, designed to affirm Kennedy's commitment to universal coverage, in its most progressive iteration, while he focused on narrower measures that could get through Congress.[2]

Now, Kennedy believed, universal coverage or something close to it was within reach—and, as much as anybody in Washington, he understood how rare and fleeting such moments were. He had long said that his greatest regret from public life was not pushing harder to finish negotiations with Nixon in the early 1970s. He had to wait twenty years for the next opportunity, only to see the Clinton effort fail. As the 2008 campaign unfolded, the political tailwinds seemed to be blowing again, in part because the cause had a new, capable champion in Barack Obama.[3]

Kennedy had endorsed Obama two days after the South Carolina primary but before Super Tuesday, when Hillary Clinton had what was probably her best chance to take a lead in delegates. Kennedy always said he liked and respected Clinton, but he was wowed by Obama, as were several of his nieces and nephews. Obama's ability to excite activists and younger voters, Kennedy thought, could give health care reform the boost it needed to get through Congress.[4]

Kennedy also understood the importance of timing, having seen the damage of delay in both the Carter and Clinton administrations. This time, Kennedy told Bowen, Congress needed to take the lead, and that meant preparing a bill now, even though the election was still months away, so that Democrats in Congress could begin hearings and markups in early 2009. "He was fired up," Bowen told me later. "And I was too."[5]

A few days later, Kennedy was at his family's compound in Hyannis Port, on the southern edge of Cape Cod. He was set to host a reception for a charity fundraiser that day: a bicycle race for Best Buddies International, a volunteer organization for people with mental disabilities, founded by one of Kennedy's nephews. It was the kind of event Kennedy had been doing a lot more frequently in his later years, in a second act of sorts—one in which he'd found the stability and sobriety so conspicuously absent earlier in life. Friends attributed the change to a combination of factors, including a willingness to give up his presidential ambitions to focus on Senate work, as well as finding love with Victoria Reggie, an attorney whom he had married in 1992.[6]

Kennedy had spent that morning as he frequently did, according to several published accounts, hitting tennis balls on the lawn to his Portuguese water dogs, Sunny and Splash. Later, while he was walking through his house, he suddenly felt weak and, unable to get outside for fresh air, slumped into a dining room chair. He was having a seizure. Soon he was on an ambulance to Cape Cod Hospital and then on a helicopter to Massachusetts General Hospital in Boston. Doctors ruled out a stroke, the initial hunch, and came back with a more devastating diagnosis. He had terminal brain cancer.[7]

Kennedy knew all about cancer. Two of his children were survivors, including Teddy Jr., who as a twelve-year-old lost a lower leg so that physicians could stop a tumor that had spread to and damaged the bone. Treatment included not just surgery but a then-experimental chemotherapy regimen; Kennedy would stay up with his son at night, holding him through the vomiting, and learned to inject drugs so that Teddy wouldn't have to go to the hospital so frequently. As grueling as it was, Kennedy realized, other families had it tougher. "He'd be there with all these other parents he'd come to know," David Nexon, longtime adviser and coauthor of a Kennedy biography, later told me. "They were wondering, how could they afford the drug . . . do they have to take a new mortgage on their house? Would their son or daughter maybe get half a dose? He always talked about that."[8]

Now, at age seventy-six, Kennedy was the one battling cancer, consulting medical experts, fighting for time. And the push for universal coverage was never far from his mind. In early July, while Kennedy was still in the middle of his treatments, a key funding bill on Medicare was one vote short of the sixty it needed to pass. Kennedy made a dramatic return to the Senate floor and put the measure over the top with his aye. He got a standing ovation, even from Republicans voting against him. Afterward, his staff lined up to welcome him, and he worked through the line, one by one, greeting each one with a hello until he got to Bowen, the health care staffer. Looking Bowen straight in the eye, he asked, "Where's my bill?"[9]

A month and a half later, Kennedy was in Denver for the 2008 Democratic National Convention. It was a return of sorts to the stage at which he'd given what many considered his most memorable performance: his address to the 1980 convention. That speech came after Kennedy's failed attempt to wrest the nomination from Carter, whose hesitancy to move aggressively on health care was among Kennedy's biggest grievances. "Let us resolve that the state of a family's health shall never depend on the size of a family's wealth," Kennedy had said at that speech, minutes before delivering his closing and most famous line: "The work goes on, the cause endures, the hope still lives, and the dream shall never die."[10]

In 2008, the dream was alive again, and Kennedy was eager to say so in person. But at the last minute, he had another medical crisis: a kidney stone. He got pain medication at a local hospital and went straight to the convention center, riding to the stage in a golf cart. "This is the cause of my life—new hope that we will break the old gridlock and guarantee that every American—north, south, east, west, young, old—will have decent, quality health care as a fundamental right and not a privilege," Kennedy said, to thunderous applause. He concluded the speech: "The work begins anew. The hope rises again. And the dream lives on."[11]

It was an update of his 1980 coda, although this speech was barely six minutes long. And he had required a great deal of assistance, from the Denver hospital staff treating the kidney stone to the family members carefully escorting him across the stage, never too far away in case he faltered.

That's how it was going to be, going forward. Kennedy was going to do everything possible to push major health care legislation forward. But he would need partners, including a senator who was in many ways Kennedy's opposite.

2.

The year was 2003, and Max Baucus was doing what Max Baucus did best: making deals with Republicans and making his fellow Democrats furious in the process.

George W. Bush was still president, and Congress was trying to write a bill that would help senior citizens pay for their prescription drugs. Baucus, the senior senator from Montana, was the ranking Democrat on the Finance Committee, which has jurisdiction over Medicare. He was working closely with his Republican counterpart, chairman Charles Grassley, to write a compromise bill that both parties could support.

Prospects for success seemed high, in part because the clamor for action was so loud. Medicare didn't cover prescriptions, because drug coverage wasn't a standard feature of health insurance when it became law in 1965, and Congress hadn't updated the benefits package. Some seniors had retiree drug coverage from their old employers, others were able to buy supplemental policies, and the poorest seniors were able to get prescriptions through Medicaid (which operated as a supplement to Medicare). But one-fourth of seniors had no drug coverage at all, and even some who did have insurance were stuck with co-pays and deductibles they couldn't afford. They coped by rationing their own treatment, which in practice meant taking half doses or none at all.[12]

Democrats in the late 1990s had proposed addressing this problem by creating a drug benefit for all seniors, regardless of health status or income. The program they had in mind would be part of traditional Medicare and operate in more or less the same way, with the government administering the benefit directly. Al Gore made such a proposal a focus of his 2000 presidential campaign, and even after he lost, Democrats in Congress, led by Kennedy and Senate majority leader Tom Daschle, made creating a prescription drug proposal one of their top priorities.[13]

As a general rule, Republicans were still more inclined to eliminate government programs than create them. But senior citizens were a universally sympathetic group and, increasingly, an essential part of the GOP's political coalition, so Bush, in his 2000 campaign, made a counterproposal—an initiative in which seniors could get drug coverage, as long as they enrolled in one of the insurance plans that private insurers offered as a substitute for traditional Medicare. Congressional Republicans took up the idea once Bush got into office, but it was a nonstarter with Democrats, who until 2002 controlled the Senate and who saw in the GOP alternative a scheme to lure seniors away from Medicare's original government-run program—in effect, privatizing it by attrition.[14]

In 2002, Republicans captured the Senate, and Bush pushed Congress to try again. That's when Baucus and Grassley got to work. They met over a meal every week and, as senators from rural states, saw one another as kindred political souls with interests that transcended partisanship. That proved critical in the Medicare drug discussions because, at the time, rural areas had few private Medicare options. If there was going to be a new drug benefit, Grassley wanted to make sure his constituents had an easy way to get it. Bush's notion of pushing everybody out of traditional Medicare to get prescription coverage just wouldn't do.

With that idea off the table, Baucus and Grassley were able to craft a compromise that still offered something for both parties. Private insurers, not the federal government, would be managing the new benefit. (That was the part for Republicans.) But the insurers would have to make coverage available even to seniors who stayed in traditional Medicare, and the program had to guarantee coverage for people in rural areas. (That was the part for Democrats, plus rural Republicans like Grassley.) The bill passed overwhelmingly on a bipartisan basis, with both Kennedy and Daschle endorsing it.[15]

That a Baucus proposal could generate such enthusiasm from those two liberal senators was no small thing, given the ill will he typically drew from that part of the caucus. Baucus, the son of a wealthy ranching family, was among the most conservative Democrats in the Senate. On health care, he'd first sparred with liberals in the late 1980s, when he served on the Pepper Commission and refused to endorse a universal coverage proposal—even after personal appeals from David Pryor, the Arkansas senator with whom he was close. More recently, in 2001, Baucus had broken with Democratic leaders and helped put together the 2001 Bush tax cut, which liberals despised.[16]

Liberals could understand and accept Baucus's record insofar as it was an expression of his home state's more conservative politics. They were less forgiving when it came to his close relationship with lobbyists and the industries they represented. *The Nation* magazine later dubbed him "K Street's Favorite Democrat," and his ties to the drug industry were especially tight. During the negotiations over a Medicare benefit, the industry's top strategist was a former top aide to Baucus. Along with the lobbying connections went fundraising ties; by the late 2000s, Baucus had raised nearly $4 million from health care industry interests, according to one accounting.[17]

Baucus apologized for none of this. He thought industry groups had expertise to offer, and he figured having his old staffers working for them made the legislative partnership more productive. As for campaign finance, he said he was all in favor of changing the laws about political fundraising, going so far as to cosponsor constitutional amendments to restrict donations. But as long as money was allowed to influence politics, he said, he was determined to have more of it than any would-be opponents. And if he voted with Republicans in ways that sometimes infuriated liberals, he also voted with liberals in ways that sometimes infuriated Republicans—like when he backed the 1994 assault weapons ban, despite the strong support for gun ownership rights in Montana. He was a Democrat, he would tell people, because he believed the government should help people struggling with basic needs. And the prescription drug bill he'd developed with Grassley was true to that spirit, he said.[18]

But drug legislation also required action from the House, and in that chamber, things went down a little differently. Led by Ways and Means chairman Bill Thomas, the Republican majority produced a bill that looked a lot more like Bush's original proposal. It had a strong push toward privatization, as well as less generous coverage for seniors. When it came time for the two chambers to merge their bills, Thomas allowed Baucus to be part of the negotiations but excluded all other Democrats except for John Breaux, a relatively conservative member from Louisiana who had previously supported privatization. Democratic leaders were incensed—at Thomas for his decision but, even more so, at Baucus for going along with it. Their fury only grew when they saw the final product, which, among other things, had extra subsidies for private Medicare insurers even as it skimped on coverage for seniors.[19]

In public, Democratic senators blasted the bill. In private, they blasted Baucus. Daschle, who nearly got into a shouting argument with Baucus when they met in a hallway one day, instructed his staff not to share his email distribution list for Senate health care aides. Baucus aides had to re-create the list on their own. At a weekly caucus meeting, Hillary Clinton, then a senator from New York, lit into Baucus, saying he was doing precisely what critics had accused her of doing with the 1993 health plan: brokering a terrible deal in secret. Baucus defended himself by saying the chance to spend $400 billion on health care for seniors was too good to pass up—and that, given Republican control of both the White House and Congress, some compromise was inevitable.[20]

After one of the final votes, Baucus and Breaux joined Grassley and Bill Frist, the Senate majority leader, for a press conference to celebrate the result. And if Baucus was upset at being ostracized by his fellow Democrats, he wasn't letting it show. At the time, he had two large bruises—one under his eye and one on his right temple—because he had fallen and hit his head on a rock eight miles into a fifty-mile ultramarathon a few days prior. Baucus finished the race anyway, and his running performance had already gained legendary status on Capitol Hill. "This guy is tough, look at his eye," Frist said at the press conference. "Fifty miles, six mile cut, blood coming down, he toughed it out, no stitches." Laughing, Baucus interrupted: "It wasn't there, it was in our caucus."[21]

The bill was unpopular and remained so even after Bush signed it, partly because of what it offered (or didn't offer) to do for seniors. Even with the new Medicare Part D fully in place, many seniors would owe thousands of dollars for prescriptions, thanks in part to a gap in coverage, known as a "donut hole." In one poll after passage, only 21 percent said they had a favorable view of it. But Baucus predicted it would grow more popular with time, as it eventually did, and said he was proud: "Nothing of major consequence passes in this body unless we work together."[22]

Baucus was so enthusiastic, in fact, that he told staff he already knew what he wanted to do next: universal coverage.[23]

3.

Kennedy was among those furious about the final Medicare drug deal, saying that it used seniors as "guinea pigs" for a conservative experiment with private insurance. He was particularly angry because his early work on the bill had given Baucus cover with liberal Democrats and interest groups.[24]

But Kennedy was too much of a dealmaker to keep a grudge. Over the years, he had worked with Senator Bob Dole on laws to protect people with disabilities and with Utah Republican Orrin Hatch on a law that helped millions of children get health insurance. The gregarious Kennedy treasured and nurtured these relationships, with personal touches whenever possible—like sending longtime aide Nick Littlefield, who happened to be a gifted vocalist, to sing tunes that Hatch, an amateur songwriter, had composed in his spare time. (Kennedy and Hatch were especially close, and after the cancer struck, Hatch wrote a song for him called "Headed Home.")[25]

Kennedy also did a lot of one-on-one lobbying, whether it was on his mobile phone (a BlackBerry that he always called a "blueberry" because it had a blue covering) or in person—even if that meant visiting much more junior members, in a reversal of protocol. "If you're a junior senator, then you're the one who had to schlep and hustle, and if you're senior . . . you don't go to people's offices, they come to you," Kavita Patel, a former policy adviser to Kennedy, said. "But Kennedy never felt like visiting a junior senator was beneath him. He would do what it took to make a deal happen."[26]

Kennedy was adept at pinpointing areas of shared interest to make allies out of adversaries—as he did in the early 1990s when he won over Strom Thurmond, the archconservative from South Carolina, for a fetal-tissue research bill that antiabortion groups opposed fiercely. Thurmond had a daughter with juvenile diabetes. Kennedy promoted the potential of fetal-tissue research to develop a cure. Thurmond gave his support.[27]

One reason that Kennedy could make these partnerships work was that he had a career's worth of goodwill from progressive groups. Abortion rights advocates would not punish him for working with Hatch, one of their staunchest adversaries, because Kennedy had fought hard to protect reproductive rights in health care legislation and judicial confirmations. Civil rights organizations wouldn't protest his partnership with Thurmond, who had risen to power as a champion of segregation, because Kennedy had been a vocal and effective ally since his inaugural Senate speech, in 1964, on behalf of the Civil Rights Act.[28]

But Kennedy's status as a liberal icon sometimes made him a less convincing salesman with the Democratic Party's more conservative wing, whose members hailed from rural and Southern states, where association with the face of American liberalism was politically treacherous. That was one reason the Massachusetts-style reforms excited Kennedy so much. They had the imprimatur of a Republican governor and a conservative think tank, making them easier to sell in those parts of the country. Even so, Kennedy would need an emissary—somebody his colleagues from Arkansas and Louisiana trusted to evaluate and promote legislation from a more conservative worldview. Baucus, who had become Finance Committee chairman when Democrats retook the majority in 2006, was the logical choice.

It was not the kind of partnership that seemed destined to succeed, given their ideological and temperamental differences. Baucus may have been a Stanford-educated lawyer, but he was among the Senate's less articulate members, stumbling over policy explanations and sometimes losing his place in speeches even when reading from a prepared script. Colleagues found him courteous but not outgoing, pleasant but not personable. Among those who dealt with him closely, he had a reputation for being prickly and thin-skinned—"always on the lookout for slights, either real or imagined," as one senior aide to another senator put it.[29]

Still, Kennedy and Baucus shared a reverence for the Senate as a deliberative institution—a place where lawmakers from different perspectives could convene, discuss matters of national importance, and eventually form coalitions strong enough to pass laws. Baucus also had a lot of experience crafting bipartisan deals on health care. In addition to the Medicare drug benefit, he had helped put together a bill reauthorizing the Children's Health Insurance Program that Kennedy and Hatch had crafted in the 1990s. Bush had wanted to limit funding, citing the need to restrain federal spending; Baucus helped recruit Republicans to support a bill that called for more money.[30]

Baucus's partner on that reauthorization was Grassley, just as it had been for the Medicare bill, and he believed that working with Grassley would prove the easiest, surest way to get a universal coverage bill as well. "That locking of arms with Grassley and Hatch . . . that collaborative effort, I think it gave us some confidence and some trust building around health care, something we could build on," Jon Selib, who was Baucus's chief of staff, later told me.[31]

Baucus also thought a bipartisan bill would be more politically durable. "He said many, many times to us in staff meetings [that] every major piece of social legislation in this country has passed with a large bipartisan majority," Liz Fowler, chief health care adviser to Baucus, recalled. "Social Security, Medicare, Medicaid, Americans with Disabilities Act, Civil Rights Act. He would name them, and he would know how many votes there were in the House and the Senate, and they were large majorities. He said, 'You can't have big social change without bipartisan support and you need it to be lasting—that's what makes it lasting.'"[32]

For this new push on health care reform, Baucus convened a daylong event at the Library of Congress called Prepare for Launch. It was one part media spectacle and one part seminar, designed to educate individual members about what needed to be done and why. An introductory video ended with a clip of the space shuttle *Discovery* blasting off, after which Baucus talked about the Apollo 11 mission, going to the moon, and how now all the "stars [were] aligned" for reform. He may have tortured the metaphor, but his message was clear: "We have to develop common understandings of our current system, the good and the bad . . . we will succeed only if we work together." For the keynote, Baucus recruited Federal Reserve chairman Ben Bernanke, who argued that health care reform would be good for the economy.[33]

The reaction from Republicans was exactly what he had hoped. "We agree . . . doing nothing is not an option," Kay Bailey Hutchison, a Republican senator from Texas, said. Right after the summit, Tom Price, a House Republican who attended as a guest, sent Baucus a handwritten note. "You know well the imperative of reform and the importance of patience," Price, an orthopedist and GOP leader on health care issues, wrote. "Thanks for your leadership! Let me know if I may assist." More effusive endorsement came from Robert Bennett, the conservative Republican senator from Utah: "I think, with a few diehard holdouts, just about every Republican is now willing to accept the idea that every American could be—should be insured."[34]

Bennett had reason to believe that. He was the lead Republican cosponsor of the Healthy Americans Act, a bipartisan bill designed to achieve universal coverage through what was basically a voucher system. All Americans, except those in the military or enrolled in Medicare, would get a credit they could use to buy a private insurance policy. The government would subsidize coverage for the poor and middle class. It would also regulate the insurance plans closely so that everybody could get a policy, regardless of preexisting conditions.

The bill's architect was Ron Wyden, Democratic senator from Oregon. The wonky, unabashedly earnest Wyden had introduced the plan back in December 2006, right after Democrats had won control of Congress in the midterms and weeks before John Edwards unveiled his health plan in the Democratic primaries—which means that, historically speaking, it was Wyden who first broke the informal taboo on universal coverage that Democrats had observed since the mid-1990s. "I think the country wants health care fixed," Wyden said. "There's been lots of rhetoric and position papers. It's time for action."[35]

On paper, the Healthy Americans Act was a thing of elegance, promising to cover nearly all Americans and to be self-financing within its first year, according to the Congressional Budget Office. But all the paeans in the world from policy journalists (including me) couldn't get Democratic leaders to consider it.[36]

Personalities had something to do with it; Wyden thought Baucus didn't take his ideas seriously, while Baucus thought Wyden was a pest. But mostly, the problem was political. The bill envisioned ending most existing insurance arrangements, including employer-sponsored plans. Wyden considered this feature a virtue, not a bug, given the unreliability of job-based policies. "Employer-based coverage is melting like a popsicle in the summer sun," he said. But if lawmakers had taken one lesson from the Clinton plan, it's the one they got from those Harry and Louise ads: Don't mess with employer insurance.[37]

Republicans had their own objections, because the bill required so much regulation and new spending. When pressed by reporters, most of the half dozen GOP cosponsors conceded that they didn't support the specifics. Only Bennett seemed sincerely committed.

Still, between the public endorsements of the Healthy Americans Act and hopeful rhetoric coming out of the Baucus summit, it was clear that a substantial number of Republicans now saw political value in publicly declaring support for universal coverage. That was a shift from the recent past. And it didn't happen by accident.

4.

Health care was an issue in 2008, first and foremost, because so many people were struggling. But veterans of past debates doubted that popular frustration would be enough to break through the usual political obstacles. One of them, Ron Pollack, was determined to do something about that.

A lawyer by training, Pollack had been leading health care advocacy efforts since 1983, when he helped to establish the Villers Foundation (named for philanthropists Phil and Kate Villers) with a mission of promoting better health care access for seniors and low-income Americans. In 1989, he and the group's board expanded the goal to include health care for all Americans and changed the name to Families USA.[38]

In the early 1990s, the group became the "de facto public relations manager" for the Clinton plan, as The New York Times put it. The campaign's highlight was a series of cross-country caravans with ambulances that would roll into cities, lights and sirens blaring, as a prelude to rallies for universal coverage. Clinton's subsequent failure convinced Pollack that success would require not just grassroots pressure but also a consensus among some traditionally hostile industry groups.[39]

Pollack began orchestrating meetings, including everybody from unions to the drug industry, eventually arranging a more formal series of discussions with eighteen of these "strange bedfellows." The conversations had agendas, professional facilitators, and analysts who, in between meetings, could crunch the numbers on proposals. The Robert Wood Johnson Foundation paid for the project. (Combined with some of its public-awareness campaigns and other efforts, Pollack estimated, the foundation plowed more than $100 million into developing support for universal coverage.)[40]

To organize the sessions, and to encourage participation from industry groups that might be wary, Pollack reached out to an erstwhile foe from the Clinton fight: Chip Kahn. Kahn had since moved from the health insurance lobby to run one of the big hospital trade groups. He also had credibility with Republicans, having managed Newt Gingrich's first two congressional campaigns and worked for then-senator Dan Quayle before joining the GOP Ways and Means staff in the 1980s.[41]

Even those industries that were profiting from the status quo could see that it was becoming unsustainable. Charity care, for people with either no insurance or punishing out-of-pocket costs, was putting a big strain on doctors and hospitals. Rising premiums were putting a bigger burden on the business community, while the savings managed care produced in the 1990s looked more and more like a onetime phenomenon. Although industry groups remained as suspicious of government intervention as ever, they were willing to talk, and bit by bit, the group was finding its way toward agreement on the goal of universal coverage—although, notably, consensus on how to finance it was more elusive.

Pollack's strange bedfellow meetings were just one of several dialogues taking place in and beyond Washington, with various subsets of the same groups and sometimes some very unlikely pairings—like when Andy Stern from SEIU joined Lee Scott, CEO of Walmart, to lead a labor-business coalition calling for reform.[42]

Among those following this progress was Kennedy's HELP Committee staff, which decided to convene its own set of discussions. They called it the "workhorse group," because the idea was to stay out of the headlines (i.e., not be a bunch of show horses) and instead develop a real, durable consensus for what legislation should look like. Frequently, the workhorse meetings would take place right after Pollack's, with participants sharing taxicabs to Capitol Hill.[43]

One October 2008 meeting would prove especially revealing. It included Pollack and Kahn, as well as Karen Ignagni, who was now president of America's Health Insurance Plans, the trade group that spoke for most of the country's insurers. Also present was John McDonough, the public health scholar and former director of Health Care for All in Massachusetts. Kennedy had recruited him to join the HELP staff.

At the meeting, McDonough laid out three scenarios for reform, each named for famous avenues in the nation's capital. Going down "Constitution Avenue" meant blowing up the existing insurance and financing arrangements, then replacing them with a single-payer program or a voucher scheme like Wyden's. Either would result in universal coverage and aggressive control of costs, and probably come closest to creating the sort of system that existed across Europe and East Asia. Either would involve the kind of wholesale changes to the welfare state never before attempted in American history.

An alternative route was "Independence Avenue." That meant pursuing a series of narrower, less ambitious reforms—some combination of subsidies for the poor, modest changes to insurance market rules, and maybe the creation of "high-risk pools" that would serve as last-chance insurance for people with preexisting conditions who were locked out of the individual market. This was the route of least political resistance, since it involved incremental expansions of existing programs. As policy, though, this would result in only slight progress on making health care more accessible and do little to manage the system's overall cost. It was easy to do, relatively speaking, because it proposed to accomplish so little.

The third possibility was to try "Massachusetts Avenue"—in other words, the Romney approach on a national scale. It was also the approach that Obama had endorsed and, at that point, was ahead in the polls.

Of the twenty participants, nobody wanted to try Constitution or Independence Avenues, but about fifteen said they liked the sound of Massachusetts Avenue. "Before the election," McDonough wrote later, "before the congressional process was actively engaged, a 2006 Massachusetts law had already become the essential template for national reform."[44]

5.

Another person who had taken notice of Massachusetts was Liz Fowler, the staff adviser to Baucus.

Fowler, who grew up in Kansas, was the daughter of a general practitioner, and she'd gone to college thinking she would go premed. Then she took a class on policy and decided it was America's sickly health care system, not individual patients, she wanted to cure. Fowler's trajectory from there included stops in the federal government (where she was a policy analyst on Medicare), Johns Hopkins (where she got a doctorate in public health), England (where she studied the National Health Service on a fellowship), and the University of Minnesota (where she got a law degree). After that she tried working at a Washington, D.C., law firm, hated it, and looked for a way back into the public sector—finding it on Capitol Hill, working for Baucus on the Finance Committee.[45]

The Medicare drug law had made her proud when it passed in 2003. It also left her mentally depleted. The prospect of more years in the minority didn't sound that appealing, especially given the disdain so many Democrats had developed for her boss, and there was a job opening at WellPoint, one of the nation's largest insurers. Fowler had decidedly mixed feelings, she told me later. But she also had tuition debts to pay off, and WellPoint didn't want her to lobby her old colleagues. She would simply be there to analyze and help formulate positions on public policy.

WellPoint was good to its word, she said. But WellPoint was positioning itself as the industry's most forceful reform opponent, just as support for it was on the rise. Fowler said she was especially unhappy to see WellPoint using its considerable clout to fight California's attempt at Massachusetts-style legislation. In February 2008, when her old job opened up, she jumped at the chance to take it.

Although hearings and the summit would occupy a lot of her energy for the first few months, her main focus that year would be writing the health plan Baucus had first vowed to craft back in 2003. Baucus originally wanted to write a full bill. Fowler persuaded him that it made more sense to produce a detailed white paper describing the basic structure of a new system while laying out options, without committing to specific choices, on the most politically sensitive issues. She kept in close contact with Kennedy's staff, especially Bowen, and in the fall she started speaking more frequently with Obama's advisers, who had tried unsuccessfully to stop Baucus from issuing the paper and settled instead for reviewing it beforehand.[46]

A week after the election, Baucus released the white paper. Nothing in the eighty-nine-page document was especially surprising, which is what made it so important. From a distance, the Baucus proposal looked like the Obama proposal, and both were national versions of the Massachusetts reforms that Kennedy backed. Although a clear purpose of the paper was to stake Baucus's claim to health care in the Senate, even those wary of him remembered the damage that Daniel Patrick Moynihan, an ambivalent, hostile Finance Committee chairman, had done to reform under Clinton. As Karen Tumulty observed, "This is a signal from the chairman of the Finance Committee—one of the biggest hurdles for any effort—that he is intent on moving forward."[47]

Ted Kennedy certainly took it that way. In a press release that circulated moments after the white paper's publication, Kennedy hailed it as "a major contribution" and said he was eager to work with Baucus—who promptly returned the favor, going out of his way to acknowledge Kennedy at a press conference: "I want to work with Senator Kennedy, the HELP Committee, and all my colleagues, especially those on both sides of the aisle . . . I've spoken three times with Senator Kennedy about this over the last few weeks, and we're very much on the same page."[48]

For advocates like Ron Pollack, who had labored to forge that kind of unity, it was a moment to savor: "The prospects for meaningful health care reform have never looked better."[49]

He was right—although, even with much-improved prospects, reform would prove more difficult than even the most jaded, battle-tested advocates ever imagined it could be.

Part II

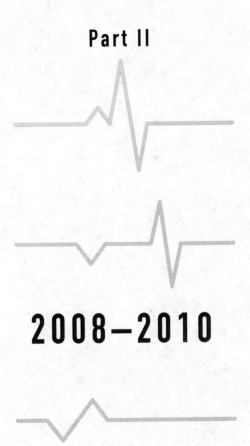

2008–2010

2008–2010

Nine

Hard Things Are Hard

Barack Obama, Nancy Pelosi, and Harry Reid were in the Oval Office on January 19, 2010. Nearly a year to the day after Obama had become president, their effort to pass health care reform was on the verge of collapse—all because, about 450 miles away in Boston, a Democrat was giving her concession in the special election for Ted Kennedy's old Senate seat.

Defeat in Massachusetts, one of the most liberal states in the country, had at one time seemed inconceivable. Martha Coakley, the state's accomplished attorney general, had been up thirty points in early polling. Her opponent, Republican state senator Scott Brown, had a résumé whose highlight was winning *Cosmopolitan*'s America's Sexiest Man contest when he was twenty-two.

But the voters in Massachusetts, like the voters around the country, were in a foul mood. And the health care effort was a big reason why, with Brown attacking it as a corrupt, secretive exercise by political insiders who didn't care about the average American. "Voters," Brown said, "do not want the trillion-dollar health care bill that is being forced on the American people."

It was a strange case to make, given that the prototype was Romney's Massachusetts reforms, which polls always found had majority support in the state. But Coakley proved especially inept at making connections with the voters, reinforcing Brown's argument. At one point near the end of the campaign, she had made just nineteen appearances to Brown's sixty-six, according to an accounting by *Politico*. When a radio host asked why she wasn't out on the trail more, she asked, "As opposed to standing outside

Fenway Park? In the cold? Shaking hands?"—referring, apparently, to an online video of Brown doing precisely that.[1]

The prospect of a Coakley loss had started to get attention at the White House about a week before the vote, when Patrick Gaspard, the director of political affairs, announced at a meeting that internal Democratic surveys showed her support collapsing. At the time, Obama and his advisers were in the middle of marathon negotiation sessions with Democratic leaders from the House and Senate, which had each passed bills, in the hopes of crafting a compromise version that could pass in both. But that would only happen if Democrats had sixty votes, and a Coakley loss would leave Democrats with just fifty-nine.[2]

Failing at health care reform because Democrats could not hold Kennedy's old seat was almost too painful a thought for its supporters to bear. But that was precisely what many Democrats started proposing once the polls closed and it was clear Coakley had lost. Conspicuous among them was Barney Frank, a stalwart Massachusetts liberal. "Our respect for democratic procedures must rule out any effort to pass a health care bill as if the Massachusetts election had not happened," he said.[3]

Obama, Pelosi, and Reid weren't ready to give up. They also didn't have a consensus on how to move forward. Days before, White House strategists contemplating contingency plans had determined the only viable path was to have the House pass the Senate's bill as written. But House leaders hated the Senate legislation, which they thought wasn't tough enough on the health care industry and didn't do enough to help low- or middle-income Americans pay for their coverage. Pelosi made clear the House wouldn't vote yes on the Senate bill, prompting Obama to ask whether she had an alternative. She didn't. The same went for Reid.[4]

After the meeting, Pelosi assured reporters that reform was not dead: "We will get the job done. I'm very confident."

There was no reason to take that claim seriously—and yet, two months later, in March 2010, there they were in the White House, watching Obama sign the bill virtually everybody in Washington was convinced would never pass. Reform had come back from the dead, and not for the first time.

The Democrats' success had a lot to do with the preparations for reform advocates had been making for more than a decade, as well as the skill and determination of party leaders, starting with those three who were in the Oval Office on January 19. No less important was the urgency of what they were trying to accomplish. If American health care hadn't been in such desperately bad shape, if so many people hadn't been suffering and in need of help, reform would not have had the support it needed to make it through the political process.

Not that the legislation Obama signed promised to solve all or even most of the problems Americans were facing. It was supposed to be a universal health care bill, but the official estimates suggested that it would, at best, reach only 92 percent of the non-elderly population. It was supposed to make health care less expensive, but few economists expected it to have a major impact on the overall trajectory of costs.[5]

One reason the law fell short of its original, loftier promises was due to the strategic decisions and substantive concessions its authors made along the way to neutralize or win over opponents. But if the choices of the law's champions were fair game for second-guessing, the reality is that Obama, Pelosi, and Reid were up against almost unimaginable political forces. They were trying to shake a legacy of failure that had bedeviled similar efforts for nearly a century, and even before the Massachusetts election they had no margin for error.

Looking back, it's remarkable they passed anything at all.

Ten

Yes We Can

1.

Obama's campaign for health care reform began the day his campaign for the presidency ended—on November 4, 2008, when a quarter of a million people gathered along Chicago's lakefront to celebrate his election victory. The crowd size was testament to the sheer historical weight of what had just transpired: the United States electing its first African American president. Even the anchors on Fox News said they could appreciate the significance of the moment, especially when one of their own, African American commentator Juan Williams, choked up describing how he felt.[1]

Obama had leaped from the Illinois state senate to the Democratic Party nomination so quickly that he was still a fresh face to most of the country, one who had produced little in the way of polarizing legislation or rhetoric that his opponents could use against him—although, to be clear, they tried. As his candidacy had become more serious, critics had tried to define him as a radical and somebody whom politically essential white voters should fear—seizing, among other things, on sermons by the Reverend Jeremiah Wright, Obama's former pastor, in which Wright had urged followers to sing "God Damn America" instead of "God Bless America" because of its history of racism.

Obama responded with what many considered the greatest speech of his career, condemning Wright's language but refusing to disavow his association with the pastor, because, Obama said, it was as much a part of his past and America's past as his white grandmother was. The real problem with Wright's sermons, Obama went on to say, was that he "spoke as if our society was static; as if no progress has been made; as if this country—a country that has made it possible for one of his own members to run for the highest office in the land and build a coalition of white and black, Latino and Asian, rich and poor, young and old—is still irrevocably bound to a tragic past."

Eight months later on the Chicago lakefront, speaking for the first time as president-elect, Obama emphasized the same point: "That's the true genius of America—that America can change," he said. "Our union can be perfected." He returned over and over again to the themes of forging unity and healing the nation's wounds, citing Lincoln and echoing his own words from the 2004 Democratic keynote. "We have never been a collection of Red States and Blue States: we are, and always will be, the United States of America."

The final part of the Election Night speech recalled somebody Obama had met on the campaign trail, a 106-year-old African American woman named Ann Nixon Cooper, and the expansions of opportunity and rights that she'd witnessed over the course of her lifetime: women's suffrage, the New Deal, the Great Society, and the civil rights revolution. Then he promised his supporters, as he had throughout the campaign, that they too could be a part of such transformations. "This is our moment . . . while we breathe, we hope, and where we are met with cynicism, and doubt, and those who tell us that we can't, we will respond with that timeless creed that sums up the spirit of a people: Yes We Can."

Obama, by all appearances, believed every word—that the United States could overcome its divisions of race, class, and politics; that America was a country of great flaws but great potential to remedy those flaws; that with enough hard work and determination, along with the right leadership, transformational reforms were still possible. And although he said not a word about policy in that speech, health care was reportedly not far from his mind. He later told aides, according to journalist Jonathan Alter's book *The Promise*, that during a quiet moment earlier in the day, he thought about what he hoped his presidency would achieve. As a candidate, he'd talked about so many ambitious initiatives on energy and education and a new vision for national security. But he kept coming back to health care, the cause that had animated and eluded so many of his predecessors.[2]

Obama had good reason for such ambition. Democrats had increased their numbers in both the House and Senate on Election Night, giving him bigger majorities than Clinton ever had. Better still, congressional leaders had already coalesced around the same basic vision for reform that he'd outlined in his campaign. A consensus existed, and it included key interest groups too.

But Obama's confidence was not widely shared—by outsiders or, as it turns out, by many of those close to him. Over the next two months, as Obama prepared to take office and then began to govern, many of his advisers would question whether to make health care a year-one priority and, if so, whether to pursue the kind of comprehensive reforms Obama had outlined in his campaign. Only a handful of advisers thought the answers to both questions should be yes.

2.

One of those advisers was Jeanne Lambrew, who was helping to direct the health care team in Obama's transition operation. As was customary in presidential campaigns, the transition effort had begun in the summer so that Obama could staff his administration, set an agenda, and be ready to govern if he won. At 9:00 a.m. on the morning after the election, while so many other people affiliated with the campaign were sleeping off a hangover, Lambrew convened a conference call with the members of the health care team.[3]

It was typical of Lambrew, whose singular devotion to work was as legendary as her singular focus on health care. It was something of a family tradition. Her grandfather was a general practitioner, her father a cardiologist, her mother a nurse. Her parents, who had met at a Manhattan hospital, both went out of their way to care for people who couldn't pay their medical bills. Sometimes her mother even brought patients into their home along the Maine coast, where Lambrew spent the second half of her childhood.

Lambrew admired her parents, but she had no interest in following their career paths because the sight of blood or needles gave her the heebie-jeebies. As an undergraduate at Amherst, she majored in English but was interested in public policy, and during one summer, she got an internship back home, researching Maine's nursing shortage for a state commission. She decided to get a graduate degree in health policy, studying at the University of North Carolina, where she met economist Kenneth Thorpe, who in 1993 left to join the Clinton health care team. When Lambrew finished her dissertation, in September, she went to work for him in Washington. He returned to UNC after the plan's demise. She stayed, working on incremental measures like the children's health insurance expansion. A notorious workaholic, she could frequently be spotted at her desk late at night, wisps of hair coming loose from her tightly pulled bun.[4]

Lambrew finally left the White House when Clinton did and, in the years that followed, she arguably did as much as any individual in Washington to lay the groundwork for the next big reform effort—all the while, with an eye on how to avoid the mistakes that had plagued the last one. She was partial to public programs like Medicare and Medicaid, and suspicious of private insurers. But she said the goal of universal coverage was more important than its form and urged allies to think the same way.

Lambrew did much of her work through her affiliation with the Center for American Progress, a think tank that Clinton confidant John Podesta had established for the purpose of incubating ideas and training people for a future Democratic presidential administration. Among Lambrew's projects was a series of ongoing discussions pairing up congressional staffers working on health care with experts in the field. The idea was to educate each group about the other, so that the staffers would learn more about health care policy and the experts would learn more about the political process, all while establishing working relationships for when legislating was once again possible.[5]

Lambrew's main connection to Obama came through her work with Tom Daschle, the former Senate majority leader whom she had helped recruit to work with the Center for American Progress after he lost his seat in 2004. Daschle, a former air force intelligence officer, had developed his own deep interest in health care, an issue he'd first discovered through service on veterans' affairs committees. Lambrew was his closest adviser on the issue, eventually coauthoring a book on the subject with him.[6]

In the interim, Daschle had also become one of Obama's most influential and visible supporters. The two first got to know each other in 2004, when Obama was coming into the U.S. Senate and Daschle, having narrowly lost reelection, was leaving. Obama, seeking veteran personnel for his Washington office, grabbed several of Daschle's suddenly unemployed staffers. He also started turning to Daschle for advice on policy and strategy, finding something of a kindred being in the soft-spoken South Dakotan with a reputation for steely political nerves.[7]

Daschle's early endorsement of Obama, at a time when most of the establishment was lining up behind Hillary Clinton, showed that Obama was a serious presidential contender and worthy of consideration by party leaders and financiers. That loyalty, plus Daschle's political experience, made him an obvious candidate for a high administration post in 2009, and Obama very nearly made him chief of staff. Instead, he offered Daschle a chance to run the administration's health care reform efforts by serving as both secretary of Health and Human Services and as a White House senior adviser on health care. The former would be necessary for managing implementation, the latter would be necessary for influencing legislation.[8]

Daschle only agreed to the post after Obama promised to pursue comprehensive health reform, rather than narrow, incremental measures. And he wasn't the only potential Obama adviser seeking such assurances.[9]

A few days after the election, Peter Orszag flew to Chicago to meet with the president-elect. A wunderkind whose first job in politics was as a twenty-something staff economist in the Clinton administration, Orszag had an outlook fairly typical of the Democratic Party establishment. He thought the government had an important role to play in fighting poverty, investing in public goods like education, and so on. At the same time, he was wary of leaning too heavily on public programs and thought deficit reduction should be a top priority. Bespectacled and known for carrying two Black-Berry devices on belt holsters, he liked to say that economists should have hard heads and soft hearts, adopting the motto of one of his mentors at Princeton University.[10]

But if Orszag occupied a familiar space on the philosophical spectrum, he had followed his intellectual curiosity to a relatively unusual place: a focus on the financing of health care. The main reason that deficits kept going up wasn't food stamps, foreign aid, or the Pentagon budget. It wasn't even Social Security. It was the two big government health insurance programs, Medicare and Medicaid. And while most economists who studied the budget knew this, most of them had little more to say about it, except that the main goal of policy makers should be to reduce the costs of those two programs— which, for many of them, simply meant reducing benefits.

Orszag, by contrast, believed that it was possible to save money by paying for care more intelligently. After a routine physical exam convinced him he needed to start taking better care of himself, he became a serious runner and a serious student of new research into patterns of medical care. The research, much of it produced by scholars at Dartmouth Atlas of Health-care project and popularized by medical writers like Shannon Brownlee, showed that tons of money was going into ineffective cardiac treatments and chemotherapies, or duplicate tests as patients shuttled between physicians who didn't consult with each other. And that was to say nothing of all the spending on treating the complications of diabetes because patients weren't getting regular checkups and insulin.[11]

In 2007, when the Democrats took control of Congress, they appointed Orszag to run the Congressional Budget Office (CBO), the nonpartisan accounting arm that produces estimates of how legislation will affect the federal budget. He made health care a bigger priority, hiring extra staff and commissioning studies on various delivery reforms—that is, policy changes with potential to alter the actual delivery of medical care in ways that would reduce its cost. His speeches and writings on the topic gained so much recognition that the Institute of Medicine, a prestigious division of the National Academy of Sciences, made him a member.[12]

One person who shared Orszag's passion for improving the quality of medical care was the president-elect. Partly, it was his interest in science. As a fledgling U.S. senator, he'd taken a special interest in disease management and public health measures. (That included global pandemics; Dora Hughes, a physician who worked on Obama's Senate staff, recalled him instructing her to research a then-obscure 2006 avian flu outbreak because he'd read about it in a medical journal.) Obama also understood that when medical care is too expensive, individuals feel it as higher premiums for private insurance, higher taxes for government programs, or higher out-of-pocket expenses.[13]

With Orszag on board, that was two top advisers pushing health care as a priority, or really three since Lambrew would be joining Daschle in the White House as his top deputy. But their perspectives were different in one very important way. Lambrew, and to some extent Daschle, put more emphasis on expanding access and getting to universal coverage. Orszag focused on managing the cost of care.

In theory, the imperatives to increase coverage and reduce costs were fully compatible. More access would lead to more efficient care, making it less costly to help people get access. That was what Obama had promised in the campaign, after all. In practice, the goals were sometimes in tension, in ways that would spark plenty of debate inside the administration over the coming months.

But that debate wasn't happening just yet.

3.

The focus, instead, was on whether Obama should try right away for comprehensive reform or settle on a much narrower, more easily achievable measure and circle back later to his big plan. Among those arguing for the latter was Rahm Emanuel, who had been representing the Chicago area in Congress and risen into the House Democratic leadership before Obama plucked him to be chief of staff.

Obama had chosen him over Daschle for that key post in part because of Rahm's hard-charging style. As a kid, he'd trained as a dancer and turned down a scholarship to the Joffrey Ballet in Chicago. As an adult, he was full of energy and not always the easiest person to be around. He was demanding and famous for his foul language—a habit Obama once mocked, during a charity fundraising speech, while describing a hand injury that Rahm had suffered while a teenager. "He was working at a deli, [had an] accident with a meat slicing machine, he lost part of his middle finger," Obama said. "This rendered him practically mute."[14]

Rahm was yet another veteran of the Clinton administration, where he had served as political director. Perhaps more than anybody else serving with Obama, Rahm carried around the scars of the 1993/94 reform effort. He remembered how every step of the process was more difficult than the president had anticipated. He remembered the infighting among Democrats, the hostility of Republicans, and the alienation of would-be allies, many of whom became adversaries. Most of all, Rahm remembered how, after investing so much time and political capital, there was nothing to show for the effort except plummeting poll numbers and, then, repudiation in the midterms. In a lengthy transition memo, Daschle and Lambrew addressed all these problems and sketched out a course for avoiding them, but Rahm was skeptical, and he wasn't afraid to say it.[15]

Neither were some of Obama's political advisers, especially David Axelrod, who'd been a mastermind of the campaign. Axelrod, who worked as a journalist before starting his own political strategy firm, understood better than most why health care reform was so important. His daughter had epilepsy, and years of sweating out premiums and fighting with insurance companies over treatments had shown him the U.S. insurance system at its worst. But Axelrod's job was to give the president political advice and, as he would frequently explain, the politics of health care were a lot more complex than a simple reading of the polls suggested. The majority of Americans with private insurance remained wary of alternatives, Axelrod said, echoing advice Democratic pollsters had given for decades. These Americans wanted help paying for their care, but they were apt to see reform as something designed to help the uninsured—in other words, somebody else.[16]

Axelrod had said this during the campaign, going all the way back to 2007. And he was not alone. But the arguments Obama advisers made against focusing on health care grew louder in 2008, especially toward the end of the year, because another issue was suddenly commanding everybody's attention. The economy was in free fall.

The tumbling had begun in the spring, when a collapse of the housing market triggered a collapse of the financial market, because banks had staked so much on high-risk mortgages (or, more specifically, high-risk mortgage-backed securities). The Federal Reserve quickly injected money into the economy, propping up struggling financial institutions. But the September bankruptcy of the investment house Lehman Brothers, similarly overexposed on housing-related holdings, sparked what was (to that point) the largest one-day drop in the Dow. By then, businesses across the country were shuttering, workers were losing their jobs, homeowners were getting foreclosure notices, and a full-fledged recession was underway.

The calamity may well have helped Obama win the election by reinforcing the public's desire for change (something Obama, as a relative newcomer to politics, offered) and support for government action (something Obama, as the Democrat and liberal alternative in the campaign, was already proposing). But it also promised to transform the complexion of his presidency, just as it had transformed the complexion of the campaign, because the economy became such an all-encompassing focus.[17]

The financial system remained on the brink of collapse; soaring unemployment and faltering state budgets demanded some kind of stimulus. The struggles of two iconic American carmakers, Chrysler and General Motors, would also require some kind of intervention, because so many other companies depended on them—from parts suppliers to restaurants feeding workers outside plants—that their imminent failure threatened to produce Great Depression–like conditions across the Midwest.

The original bank bailout, which passed before the election, had barely gotten through Congress and depended on a push from Speaker Pelosi because so many Republicans opposed it. A new one would be even tougher to pass, given the growing fury at Wall Street. (Rahm for that reason had urged Obama to mete out some "Old Testament justice" to Wall Street; Obama didn't take the advice.) The Detroit automakers were also short on friends, having alienated many Democrats with their opposition to emissions rules, while the kind of stimulus that the economy needed was going to be well into the hundreds of billions and maybe even more than $1 trillion, in an era when nearly all Republicans and many centrist Democrats believed federal spending was already too high.

Each of these initiatives was going to require work on policy and politics. But a president's time and staff, like a president's political capital, are limited resources. A day Obama spent promoting his health care initiative would be a day not spent defending the terms of the financial rescue package. Even promoters of a big health care push understood that. "Everybody was presenting exactly the right arguments to the president," Lambrew later told me.[18]

4.

These arguments kept coming up, informally over coffee and formally over spreadsheets, first in Chicago and then in Washington when the Obama operation moved there. The debate became more intense following the inauguration, during a series of meetings in the Roosevelt Room, the windowless conference room on the middle floor of the West Wing and across the hall from the Oval Office. One of the most passionate arguments against prioritizing reform came from Vice President Joe Biden, who said he didn't want to see health care undermine Obama's presidency the way it had previous presidents. "It was very, very strongly phrased and very long, and I have heard very few things like it over the years," one meeting participant said, likening Biden's soliloquy to a "tirade. . . . It was just, 'We shouldn't do this. This will be terrible for us. I know politics, I know people, I've been doing this for thirty-six years.'"[19]

The health team was underrepresented in these sessions, because Daschle, the member with the most seniority and closest relationship with Obama, was in North Carolina, at the hospital bedside of his brother, who was undergoing cancer treatments. That left Lambrew as the health team's senior member. She had thought hard about what she could be doing to act as an effective adviser to the president and promoter of good policy. Back on New Year's Day, she went to lunch with Chris Jennings to get his advice. At the restaurant, they spotted Obama legal adviser Elena Kagan sitting by herself, and Jennings proposed inviting her over to their table. Lambrew said no, because she wanted to talk shop about health care. (Lambrew, who at five-foot-ten was hard to miss, said she felt terrible about it afterward but never got a chance to apologize. The next time she saw Kagan was in 2012, inside the Supreme Court hearing room, when Justice Kagan was on the bench and hearing the first constitutional challenge to the Affordable Care Act.)[20]

At one particular meeting, Lambrew found herself on the spot, having to make the case for prioritizing reform in what felt to some in the room like a make-or-break moment. It did not go well. Exactly what she said and why it was unpopular is a bit unclear; accounts differ. But a redo of the meeting followed, this time with Mark Childress, another Daschle adviser, giving the health team's perspective. At yet another meeting, neither Lambrew nor Childress was present, and Obama, according to one participant, stopped the conversation because there was nobody to push back on the economists and political advisers skeptical of undertaking a full health care effort in year one.[21]

One issue in deliberations was whether the president's first budget should set aside a fixed sum in a "reserve fund" for health care and, if so, how big it should be. The president's budget isn't a binding document, since the real budgets—the annual templates for federal spending that Congress uses as a guideline when it appropriates funds—are passed by joint congressional resolution without presidential signature. But the president's budget is important as a signal of presidential priorities, especially when a president's party controls Congress and he or she is embarking on the first year of his or her term. The proposed health care allotment wouldn't specify what reform would entail; the point was simply to show Congress that Obama was serious about reform in his first year.

Childress, whose experience included tenures on the Senate staffs for Daschle and Ted Kennedy, had been arguing that Congress needed that kind of signal—in part because, in the absence of a budget commitment, Congress would take the budget as a sign that Obama was open to postponing the reform effort. At one point, Obama asked for a show of hands over whether to create a large reserve fund. Childress was the only one who raised his, some officials later remembered.[22]

Obama avoided definitive statements about his plans at these meetings, just like he had in his 2006 Senate office briefings. And Daschle, hearing about the proceedings, was nervous enough that he requested a one-on-one with Obama when he returned from North Carolina shortly after the inauguration. He came to the White House on a Sunday night, first meeting with Rahm, who reiterated his concerns that health care would do to the Obama presidency what it had done to Clinton's. Then Obama walked in. He put his arm around Daschle and, after asking about his brother, assured him that health care remained a year-one priority.[23]

At the time and years later, some administration officials would say the enthusiasm for prioritizing health care was greater than it seemed—that the debate about the reserve fund, for example, was less about whether to pursue health care and more about exactly what kind of political marker to place in the budget. As for Obama, some of the people closest to him said they never doubted he would pursue comprehensive health reform right away. They said it was simply his style to hear out all arguments, to ask people to challenge him. They noted that he especially liked seeking out younger advisers who had done enough research to form an opinion but might shy away from expressing it, because they were more junior; he thought that was a good way to encourage diversity of opinion.[24]

They also pointed out that Obama had put together a staff geared up to do health care, with not just Daschle, Lambrew, and Orszag but also key advisers like legislative counselor Phil Schiliro (former chief of staff to Henry Waxman, a House committee chair who would lead any health effort), deputy chief of staff Jim Messina (former chief of staff to Baucus), and domestic policy chief Melody Barnes (who, like several other West Wing aides, had come from Kennedy's office). Further, planning for a major White House summit on health care, set for early March, had begun in January.[25]

Still, the pressure to postpone a big push was intense, from both outside and inside. The main reason it didn't make a difference seems to be that Obama wouldn't let it. He said repeatedly that he wasn't about to drop his biggest campaign promises, even though the economic crisis required his attention—especially in the case of health care reform, which he believed essential for the country's long-term economic health. As for political risks, Axelrod and Pfeiffer remembered Obama saying, "What are we supposed to do, put our approval rating on the shelf for eight years and admire it?"[26]

"Not surprisingly, there were those outside the administration who suggested we shouldn't do anything other than the economy," Obama told me many years later, looking back on the early period. "And we had a serious debate about, as Rahm put it, how many planes we could land on the runway during a two-year legislative session before the midterms."

But, Obama said, he was committed to an early agenda that would also include legislation on climate and financial regulation, and the only question in his mind was the precise sequence to push them through Congress.

"There was no point at which I believed that it made sense for us to abandon those three major legislative initiatives," Obama said. "I've looked at enough history of the presidency to know that you don't get those first two years back, especially when you have large majorities in both chambers. And so I wouldn't say that there was a serious argument about not doing health care. The question was, how do we time these various initiatives to maximize the possibility that we can get them all done?"[27]

Eleven

Party Lines

1.

Nobody questioned whether Senators Max Baucus and Ted Kennedy were committed to health care. Right after the 2008 election, while Obama was still filling out his administration, Baucus and Kennedy had moved on to the first-order question about process: How, exactly, should legislation go through their chamber?

Arguably, no other strategic decision would have a greater effect on what reform ended up looking like. And the most important factor in that decision was the makeup of the Senate.

The Democratic caucus had fifty-eight members to start the year, their biggest majority since LBJ. And there was a good chance they would soon have fifty-nine, depending on the outcome of the Senate race in Minnesota, where the razor-close margin between GOP incumbent Norm Coleman and Democratic challenger Al Franken had led to a recount and then litigation. But unrestrained use of the filibuster had created a de facto sixty-vote requirement for most legislation, which meant Democrats would need at least one or two Republican votes to pass almost anything of consequence.[1]

And it wasn't as if leaders could take Democratic votes for granted. Blanche Lincoln of Arkansas, Mary Landrieu of Louisiana, and Ben Nelson of Nebraska were among the more conservative Democrats sure to resist legislation with so much liberal-sounding spending and regulation. Even more ideologically sympathetic senators were likely to raise objections because of regional interests, donor preferences, or any of a number of other reasons.

One alternative was to move health care legislation through budget reconciliation, the process protected from filibusters so that bills could pass with a simple majority. But the notion got even less serious consideration than it had in 1993. Several administration officials shared Baucus's belief that bipartisan reform would be easier to sustain politically in the years after enactment, plus there were practical considerations. Moving quickly to reconciliation could alienate more conservative Democrats, who desperately craved the political cover a bipartisan bill would provide. "There were a whole bunch of senators who were hoping that this would be bipartisan both substantively and politically for their own electoral outcomes," Peter Orszag said to me later. "Reconciliation was just seen as too big of a partisan stick."[2]

Among the senators wary of reconciliation was Kent Conrad of North Dakota. That was no small thing because Conrad was chairman of the budget committee, which normally would be the one to determine what goes through reconciliation. In theory, Harry Reid could bypass Conrad or badger him into submission. But when Reid first campaigned for leader, in 2004, he promised to defer to his chairmen. Insisting on reconciliation over the objection of Conrad could backfire, and worse, poison relationships that Reid would need for other legislation.[3]

The same argument applied to changing Senate rules to eliminate the filibuster altogether, an option that never came up in serious conversation at the leadership level—quite probably because it stood virtually no chance of winning majority support even among Democratic senators. A not-so-secret secret about senators was that the sixty-vote requirement made every member's decision even more valuable. Individual senators were reluctant to give up that leverage.[4]

The rules were a whole other complication. The whole point of using reconciliation was to stop small factions from blocking legislation essential to running the government or to controlling deficits. Only bills with clear, practical effects on revenue or spending could move through reconciliation. And they had to reduce the deficit, both in the first ten years and in the decade that followed.

Nobody could dispute that health legislation affected the budget. And for some Senate Democrats, as well as key administration officials like Orszag, the potential to reduce deficits was the single most important reason to take up reform in the first place. But fixing the insurance market was bound to include new insurance rules like preexisting condition guarantees, and the relationship of those provisions to the budget was more tenuous.

Decisions about what qualified and didn't qualify for reconciliation would fall to the Senate parliamentarian, a relatively obscure official appointed at the beginning of every session, and there was no way to be sure in advance what the final rulings would be. Although a majority of senators could overrule the parliamentarian, politically, that seemed as difficult as eliminating the filibuster altogether. "We could have spent either a month or an hour discussing reconciliation," Phil Schiliro, who was in charge of legislative strategy at the White House, told me, "and the conclusion would have been the same."[5]

Of course, it helped that both administration officials and congressional leaders thought bipartisanship was achievable. And nobody on the Democratic side believed that more fervently than Baucus.

He got to work right after the election, organizing a mid-November 2008 meeting with the Senate Democrats and Republicans whose committee jurisdictions gave them the most direct sway over health care. For the Democrats, besides Baucus and Kennedy, that meant Jay Rockefeller, of West Virginia, who was chairman of the Finance subcommittee on health care and a tenacious defender of Medicaid and the Children's Health Insurance Program; and Chris Dodd, of Connecticut, who served on the HELP committee and was increasingly taking on some of Kennedy's responsibilities. Charles Grassley and Orrin Hatch were there for the Republicans, as was Mike Enzi, from Wyoming, who was the ranking Republican on HELP.

A staff memo preparing Baucus for the session laid out three goals, the second of which was to "secure a commitment to work together on a bipartisan approach." Grassley had his history with Baucus. Hatch, just a few months before, had quietly dispatched staffers to approach Kennedy aide David Bowen with an offer: If Kennedy were willing to go it alone and work with Hatch directly, they could hammer out a health care reform bill together. (Kennedy declined, but his staff passed word of the interest on to their counterparts working with Baucus.) Enzi's history of bipartisan cooperation on health care consisted mostly of a narrow, business-oriented bill that he crafted with Nebraska's Ben Nelson, one of the most conservative members of the Democratic caucus. Still, the memo stated, "Enzi is enthusiastic about health reform and believes Republicans can play a productive role in the debate."[6]

The meeting took place right after lunch on November 19 in Kennedy's new hideaway, which made up for its lack of ambience with a prime location, literally steps from the Senate floor. (Reid gave it to the ailing Kennedy, whose presence was becoming more sporadic, so that he wouldn't have to walk as much.) According to the notes of one attendee, Baucus kicked off the meeting by repeating his Ready to Launch mantra, that the "stars were aligned" for reform. Kennedy, acting as cohost, recited the history of health care reform failures, going back to the early twentieth century, and said that "this time is the time to get it done."

The meeting's focus was mostly on process, not substance, with Baucus and Kennedy saying the committees should coordinate, including both majority and minority staff, to figure out areas of agreement and disagreement. Baucus asked everybody present to refrain from discouraging or demanding public statements. "Let's not negotiate through the press."

Enzi said, "I'm encouraged by all your comments," and suggested somebody make a list of negative words they should try to avoid in their public statements. Hatch was even more upbeat. "We have great staffs," he said. "They can get to work at it. I'm grateful for this meeting." Grassley was probably the most encouraging: "I like what I hear about the process. I haven't heard anything here I don't like. I can't think of an issue that isn't compromise-able—except abortion. But there are always places to compromise."[7]

2.

No sooner had Obama reaffirmed his commitment to health care in late January than the effort ran into a serious problem. Tom Daschle, the man Obama had entrusted to lead the effort, was gone.

Daschle's appointment as HHS secretary required Senate confirmation, and just prior to his formal nomination, Daschle had paid more than $100,000 in back taxes (including interest and penalties) for the personal use of a limousine offered by a friend. Daschle had said it was an accounting oversight. But the friend who had provided the car service was a well-connected Democratic financier who owned an equity company, for which Daschle was providing consulting services and had received more than $2 million in compensation over two years.[8]

As a candidate, Obama had pledged to stop the influence of wealthy special interests over the lawmaking process, in part by not having lobbyists in his administration. Although Daschle's job description included only the provision of strategic advice, not contacting old colleagues on behalf of a special interest, his insider's knowledge was helping a private firm with rich, powerful clients get what it wanted out of Washington. Worse still, the news came out right after a controversy over tax problems for another Obama nominee, Treasury secretary Tim Geithner. And Daschle's nomination would have to go through the Finance Committee, where Baucus was in charge and seemed in no particular hurry to make the controversy about his old antagonist go away. On February 3, Daschle withdrew his HHS nomination and announced he wouldn't be serving in his post as head of the White House health reform office either.[9]

Obama gave an NBC interview that day and took responsibility for the mess: "I'm frustrated with myself, with our team," he said. One day later, on a short flight back to a speech in Williamsburg, Virginia, he and his aides discussed possible replacements, with a focus on the White House post. They quickly zeroed in on another Clinton administration veteran, Nancy-Ann DeParle.[10]

DeParle's résumé featured a familiar academic pedigree, including Harvard Law and Oxford via a Rhodes Scholarship. But the path she took to acquiring it was atypical. Her parents split up when she was about four and she never really knew her father, a Chinese immigrant engineer. Afterward, her mother, a Tennessee native and former U.S. Army nurse named June Cooley Min, took DeParle and her two brothers back home to Rockwood, an Appalachian town small enough that it didn't have its own exit on the interstate.

Min provided for her family by working as a secretary at an elementary school, then as a clerk for the state department of conservation, and DeParle always remembered her mother crying because she couldn't afford braces even though DeParle needed them. (DeParle got them years later.) But the salary covered rent and then mortgage payments on a small house, plus it put food on the table. It also provided health insurance, which became especially important during DeParle's junior year, when Min was diagnosed with lung cancer.

The treatment, a combination of chemotherapy and radiation, was almost an hour away in Knoxville; DeParle would get out of school early to drive her mom back and forth. Min lived long enough to see DeParle's high school graduation, defying the doctors' prognosis, and insisted DeParle proceed with her planned enrollment at the University of Tennessee in the fall. During that first semester, Min kept working, in part because she wanted to log more days at the office. That way, if the illness forced her to leave work for good, she could hold on to her health insurance for as long as possible. Just before the winter holidays, right when DeParle was heading home for break, Min got a respiratory infection and was admitted to the hospital. She died two days after Christmas, DeParle at her bedside.

DeParle, a perfectionist with a stoic streak, didn't miss class and didn't tell people at UT about her mother. "I was so determined to succeed and move forward—I think I was afraid that if I started feeling sorry for myself, I would stall out and fall apart," she told me. Her favorite time to hit the library, she later recalled, was on football Saturdays because that was when it was quietest. She was eventually elected student body president, the first woman ever to hold that title, and graduated as valedictorian. *Glamour* magazine included her on its annual list of top-ten college women.

After law school and Oxford, DeParle joined a private law firm in Nashville. But she had gotten a taste of politics in college, because, as student body president, she would lobby the state government on behalf of student causes, which included everything from lower tuition to changes in rules for on-campus drinking. One of the elected officials she got to know was Democrat Ned McWherter, who brought her onto his gubernatorial campaign and, after winning, tapped her to run the state human services agency. She was just thirty upon taking office, making her the cabinet's youngest member, and the job put her in charge of human services. When Bill Clinton became president, she went to the Office of Management and Budget to work on health care reform. She remained after the reform effort ended, eventually taking over the agency in charge of Medicare and Medicaid until the end of his term.[11]

DeParle said she had decidedly mixed feelings about the prospect of working with Rahm again. Her last interaction with him was during the Clinton years and, characteristically, it included several expletives (from him). Returning to government work would also mean less time with her two children, both in grade school, plus leaving a private equity firm right when she had a share that was about to vest.

At a weekend White House meeting to discuss the possibility, Rahm was more congenial and mature than DeParle had remembered. They talked about their memories of the Clinton effort and the strategic error they both believed Clinton had made by not negotiating more seriously with Republicans like John Chafee early in the process, when a deal might have been more likely. Rahm suggested they "pinkie promise" not to make the same mistake if they worked together. But DeParle still wasn't sold on the job. Eventually, Rahm came around the table, until he was standing inches away from her. "You know you have to do this," he kept saying, pointing a finger in her face. Ah, the old Rahm, DeParle thought—and continued to say no.

Rahm then said he had to excuse himself for a few minutes and asked DeParle to wait. She knew what was coming. She'd spotted the dress-uniform Marine outside the Oval Office, which meant the president was there; Obama was about to walk through the hallway connecting it to his chief of staff's and make a pitch directly. She didn't think she'd be able to say no to his face, so she told a crestfallen Rahm that she, too, had to go.[12]

Back home, however, DeParle found herself thinking about the job—especially when her husband, author and *New York Times* reporter Jason DeParle, told her that she'd regret saying no if this was finally the time when comprehensive health reform actually became law. (Also, he was already planning on reducing his hours to spend more time with the kids.) On Sunday night, she called Rahm to accept the position. Good, he said, because the administration was planning on announcing her appointment the very next day, along with the naming of Kansas governor Kathleen Sebelius as the new HHS secretary. With Daschle gone, administration officials decided it was easier to keep the cabinet and White House posts separate. It meant, among other things, that DeParle could start immediately, without going through a weeks-long confirmation process.[13]

It all happened so fast that DeParle never had a chance to speak with Obama until just before the announcement, when they had a few minutes in the Oval Office. He asked about her background, she later remembered, as if he were probing for things they had in common—which he found when she mentioned being raised by a single mother who died relatively young from cancer. Many years later, Obama in his memoir described DeParle as the health care adviser he relied on most heavily, noting that shared experience and admiring what he called her "crisp professionalism." In an administration full of expressive alpha-wonks, DeParle was thought by many to have the administration's best poker face, taking in dissenting views without a tell.[14]

Following the announcement of her appointment, DeParle didn't have much time to get up to speed on internal discussions, because the big White House summit on health care took place just two days later—on March 4, 2009. Everybody was there: congressional leaders from both parties, officials from industry and advocacy groups, plus the president and his team. It started with an Obama speech in the East Room, followed by breakout sessions and then a town hall in which Obama called on some of the attendees for comments. Among them was Karen Ignagni, head of the insurers' trade group.

"On behalf of our entire membership, they would want to be able to say to you this afternoon, and everyone here, that we understand we have to earn a seat at the table," Ignagni said. "You have our commitment. We hear the American people about what's not working. We've taken that very seriously. You have our commitment to play, to contribute, and to help pass health care reform this year."

The statement was a notable gesture, given the role insurers had played in killing past reforms. Obama responded in kind, making clear his interest in accommodations. "If there is a way of getting this done where we're driving down costs and people are getting health insurance at an affordable rate and have choice of doctor, have flexibility in terms of their plans, and we could do that entirely through the market, I'd be happy to do it that way," Obama said. "If there was a way of doing it that involved more government regulation and involvement, I'm happy to do it that way, as well. I just want to figure out what works."

The emotional highlight of the day was another appearance by Kennedy, whose entrance again prompted long applause. He walked slowly, but he didn't look especially weak or gaunt, and his face lit up as he spoke. "If you look over this gathering here today, you see the representatives of all the different groups that we have met with over the period of years," he said. "You have the insurance companies, you have the medical professions, all represented in one form or another. That has not been the case over the history of the past, going all the way back to Harry Truman's time. . . . I'm looking forward to being a foot soldier in this undertaking, and this time, we will not fail."[15]

The day after the summit, Kennedy invited Baucus to his Georgetown home for lunch. Their top aides, Bowen and Fowler, came along. Kennedy loved to offer tours of the house, which like his Senate office was full of family artifacts, although his favorite feature was a bar hidden behind a swiveling bookcase in the library. It was a holdover from Prohibition, Kennedy explained, and it was great for playing hide-and-seek with his nieces and nephews. He'd send them out of the room and make them count to a hundred. When they got back, they couldn't find Uncle Teddy, until he magically reappeared from behind the bookcase.[16]

After lunch, Kennedy and Baucus met privately. They discussed the progress that each of their committees was making, as well as what they had been hearing from colleagues. But, Baucus said later, he had the impression that this meeting was less about legislative details and more about passing the baton on reform. "He essentially said, 'Max, this is up to you.'"[17]

3.

The bipartisan bonhomie of the summit captured the spirit Obama had hoped he would bring to Washington. But by that point, he and his aides had already seen how Republican leadership planned to treat Democratic initiatives and the extent to which Republican members of Congress would fall in line. One episode in particular had been instructive: the battle over legislation to address the economic crisis.

The best way to restart growth, experts from across the ideological spectrum agreed, was to have the government inject money into the economy, so that individuals and businesses would start spending again. The debate was over how much money to inject and how to inject it. Obama's opening bid was for a package of about $800 billion, which was actually less than advisers like Christina Romer thought necessary but the maximum of what they thought Congress would approve. More than $300 billion of the proposal was in the form of tax cuts that Republicans had championed. Most of the rest of the money was in the form of infrastructure projects, unemployment assistance, and aid to state and local governments that, if not the type of spending that typically made Republicans excited, was also not the type that typically made them apoplectic.[18]

It was a preemptive act of compromise, and it had little perceptible effect on Republicans. Back in December 2008, as the journalist Michael Grunwald later reported for *Time*, Virginia congressman and minority whip Eric Cantor had convened a meeting of his lieutenants. "We're not here to cut deals and get crumbs and stay in the minority for another 40 years," Cantor said. A month later, at a retreat for Senate Republicans, Mitch McConnell offered a similar message—that Republicans should stand together in opposition. "If Obama was for it, we had to be against it," former senator George Voinovich, an Ohio Republican, told Grunwald. "All he cared about was making sure Obama could never have a clean victory."[19]

House Republicans attacked the proposal as full of waste and too big, even though their own alternative was nearly the same size, and voted against it in lockstep. As for the Senate, Obama and the Democrats ultimately pried away three Republicans. But it was clear McConnell had most of his caucus behind him. "We worked very hard to keep our fingerprints off of these proposals," he told *The Atlantic*'s Joshua Green two years later. "Because we thought—correctly, I think—that the only way the American people would know that a great debate was going on was if the measures were not bipartisan. When you hang the 'bipartisan' tag on something, the perception is that differences have been worked out, and there's a broad agreement that that's the way forward."[20]

The stimulus experience loomed large when it came time for the House and Senate to write their respective budget resolutions—and decide, once and for all, whether to include reconciliation as an option for health care. Republicans had drawn a hard line at its use, saying it would scuttle any chance for cooperation. Baucus had made clear, in public and private, that he did not intend to try reconciliation preemptively— a pledge Obama, Kennedy, and Reid all reaffirmed. But they wanted to preserve negotiating leverage, plus they wanted a fallback in case bipartisanship failed. The solution, they agreed, was to include reconciliation instructions in the final budget but make clear to the Republicans that it was there only as a last resort.[21]

That still meant persuading Kent Conrad, the Budget Committee chairman. A full-court press from the administration followed. Orszag, whom Conrad trusted from his days when Orszag was CBO director, emphasized the administration's commitment to reforms that would pay for themselves. Obama conveyed the same message directly. He also sent a gift package, including a doggie collar for Dakota, the white bichon frise that Conrad frequently brought to the office. "Rahm idea, Obama execution," as one senior administration official put it. Conrad relented, and the final budget resolution, which ultimately passed in April, included reconciliation instructions.[22]

The Republicans were not pleased. But a bigger affront, to Hatch and especially to Grassley, was how Obama and the Democrats had managed the session's first health care debate, over reauthorization of the Children's Health Insurance Program. Grassley and Hatch had hoped to pass something like the 2008 bill that they'd negotiated with Baucus and Kennedy and gotten through Congress, before Bush vetoed it. But the previous Congress considered two versions. Under the second, immigrant children legally in the country were eligible right away; Grassley and Hatch opposed that, as did most conservatives. Upon taking office, Obama pushed for that version and, relying on Democratic votes plus a handful of Republican votes, got it through Congress. Grassley and Hatch said they were furious at Democratic leaders.

Grassley told Baucus he remained committed to working on broader health reforms and said so publicly in a floor speech that both excoriated Democrats and pledged to work on comprehensive reform. But according to Baucus, Grassley was already getting a lot of grief from Republican leaders, especially after he appeared alongside Baucus at a press conference to discuss progress on legislation. Later that day, Baucus later told me, Grassley said that he couldn't appear alongside Baucus in such settings anymore, because McConnell had threatened to "saw him off" and support a primary challenge.[23]

Grassley, through a spokesman, said that he recalled no such conversation and that McConnell never made such a threat. But nobody disputes that Grassley was under pressure from his own party—and that the pressure got worse with time.[24]

Twelve

House Rules

1.

With all the attention on the Senate, it was easy to forget that getting health legislation through the House had historically been difficult, as well, and that infighting among chairmen had helped snuff out the Clinton plan in 1994. By 2007, when Democrats took back control of the chamber, many of those same chairmen were still around, and they sensed another opportunity coming. Like all the other reformers who lived through the Clinton failure, they were determined to get it right this time—not least because, at their ages, they understood it might be their last chance. "They were in legacy mode," as one aide later put it.[1]

The list included John Dingell Jr., the Michigan congressman who was in his eighties and, up through the end of the Bush presidency, still presiding over the Energy and Commerce Committee. National health insurance was a cause he inherited from his father, former congressman John Dingell Sr., who in 1945 had cosponsored what historians consider the first serious universal coverage bill. Dingell Jr. picked up the cause when he took over the seat, and in 1965, for the vote on Medicare, Dingell was the presiding officer. Every year thereafter, he would introduce his own national health insurance bill as a reminder to his colleagues and his constituents that it was still his most important priority.

Another longtime health care warrior was septuagenarian Pete Stark, who represented a district in the East Bay Area near San Francisco and led the health subcommittee inside the powerful Ways and Means Committee. (Ways and Means controls revenue and spending, giving it roughly the same portfolio that the Finance Committee has in the Senate.) An MIT-trained engineer and air force veteran, Stark founded a community bank whose sole purpose, he said, was "to fulfill the financial needs of working people"—a mandate he carried out by offering free checking accounts, child care, and buses so that African American workers in the Oakland branch could get to the bank's headquarters fifteen miles inland. Originally a Republican, he became a Democrat because he opposed the Vietnam War, and he came to Congress in 1973. One way he put his social justice instincts to work was by making universal health care his primary crusade.[2]

One thing Dingell and Stark had in common was that they were more feared than loved on Capitol Hill—Dingell for the ferocious control over legislation he wielded, Stark for the ferocious rhetoric he unleashed on opponents. In 2007, after attacking Bush for sending American soldiers "to get their heads blown off for the president's amusement," Stark's sorry-not-sorry apology expressed his love for the troops while still attacking Bush and his allies. "I respect neither the commander in chief who keeps them in harm's way nor the chicken-hawks in Congress who vote to deny children health care," Stark said.[3]

Both Dingell and Stark were partial to single-payer. Dingell's annual proposals usually included some variation on that same original concept. In the 1993/94 debate, Stark was the primary author of a plan to create a new Medicare Part C that would be open to everybody without employer-based insurance—which, although not a full-blown single-payer plan, was basically an early and ambitious version of the proposal Jacob Hacker helped develop into the public option a decade later.[4]

Ways and Means passed a version of the Stark bill, but Clinton and Democratic leaders dismissed it quickly as too liberal to gain approval by the chamber as a whole (not to mention the Senate). As if to prove the point, Dingell's committee wouldn't even approve a more market-oriented proposal modeled on Clinton's, because that bill still had too much regulation and spending (read: it was too liberal) to suit the preferences of its more conservative members. "I tried, damn, I tried," Dingell told *The New York Times* afterward. "It was simply not possible to do."[5]

Twelve years later, Dingell, Stark, and their fellow House leaders decided to lay the foundation for another reform effort, so that they would be ready if a Democrat became president in 2008. It was the same thing Baucus and Kennedy were doing in the Senate, but with less focus on outside stakeholders and Republicans, and more on their caucus. The feedback was encouraging, with lots of interest in the Massachusetts model. It had that Goldilocks quality—not too much government-led change but also not too little. Dingell and Stark could live with that, despite their preference for single-payer. "Everybody understood that just wasn't practical," Cybele Bjorklund, a health care staff member on Ways and Means, said later. "In terms of public opinion, in terms of the finances of it, in terms of the special interests . . . it would have been legislative malpractice. We would have ended up with nothing."[6]

Neither Stark nor Dingell would end up playing the role in reform that they had hoped—Stark because illness kept him from participating in the debate fully, Dingell because he lost his chairmanship when another California congressman, Henry Waxman, challenged him and won after the 2008 election.

Waxman cast a long shadow over the federal code that belied his five-foot-five stature. As a determined environmentalist, he had been the driving force behind the 1990 Clean Air Act amendments, the 1986 and 1996 Safe Drinking Water Act amendments, the Food Quality Act of 1996, plus myriad other laws regulating the release of toxic substances. On health care, his other passion, he was among the officials most responsible for the Orphan Drug Act and, as the title suggested, the Waxman-Hatch Amendments. The former helped accelerate development of drugs for people with rare diseases; the latter brought down drug prices by allowing more competition for established, name-brand drugs.[7]

Waxman was in many ways the House analogue to Ted Kennedy, with whom he frequently partnered on legislation, although the two came from different backgrounds and operated in different fashions. Waxman grew up in the Great Depression, in an apartment over his father's grocery store. He attended UCLA for college and law school, got interested in politics, and worked his way up through the state assembly into a congressional seat. He wasn't especially religious but took seriously the Jewish commandment of *tikkun olam*—to repair the world—and he relished the role of underdog. "Nearly every worthwhile fight in my career began with my being badly outmatched," he said.[8]

Waxman was telling the truth. Much of what he accomplished happened while he was taking on powerful interests thought to be unbeatable or when his party was in the minority. And he didn't do it with charm.

George Miller, fellow Democrat from California, once said that he thought Waxman's first name was "sonuvabitch, because everyone . . . kept asking, 'Do you know what that sonuvabitch Waxman wants now?'" Years later, when Waxman announced his retirement and word reached a retreat of House Republicans, spontaneous applause broke out, as Karen Tumulty reported for *The Washington Post*.[9]

Waxman was the master of using congressional investigative powers to highlight industry practices that would generate outrage. And in the course of legislative negotiations, he would use his mastery of policy to outwit whoever was sitting across from him at the table. "He and his staff were always the smartest and most prepared, but his most effective tool was to wear people down with negotiations over countless provisions and never-ending questions about policy flaws of his opponents," one former staffer said. "Beside besting Republicans, I saw him repeatedly outlast Democrats—whether it be the [rival] House Ways and Means Committee or the Democrats in Finance Committee at the end of virtually every budget agreement conference."[10]

Waxman had a special interest in Medicaid, which he'd come to see as an all-purpose weapon against poverty. He waged a decades-long campaign to add benefits and make more people eligible, frequently by introducing formulas that automatically broadened the program over time—a strategy that came to be known as the "Waxman wedge." Tom Scully, who ran Medicaid for the Bush administration in the early 2000s, once quipped that "fifty percent of the social safety net was created by Henry Waxman when no one was looking."[11]

Waxman in late 2008 wanted to shape legislation on energy and health care, and the best way to do that was to take the helm of Energy and Commerce, where Dingell wanted to remain chairman. The contest that emerged was partly about style, with Waxman emphasizing that Obama's election had signaled a desire for change and it was time for Dingell to step aside after three decades at the helm. To the extent it was about substance, the focus was environmental policy and their ongoing clashes over automobile emission rules.[12]

On health care, Waxman and Dingell were largely in agreement, so much so that advocates for universal coverage found the contest painful to watch. But it also meant that the committee's orientation toward big action on health care wouldn't change, substantively or strategically, with Waxman in charge. He, too, preferred a single-payer system or at least a system where the government was the primary insurer for everybody without employer insurance. But like Dingell and Stark, Waxman was convinced the support for such a proposal wasn't there. And Waxman knew better than anybody what a difference less-than-perfect legislation could make.[13]

2.

Members of Congress send letters to the White House all the time—to express approval or criticism of a particular proposal, or simply to thank the president for visiting a district. A letter from three congressmen to Obama on March 11, 2009, was a lot more significant than that.

It was from Waxman and the other two committee chairmen with jurisdiction over health: George Miller from Education and Labor and Charles Rangel from Ways and Means. And it was a pledge to cooperate on health reform. "As chairs of these committees and veterans of past health reform debates, we have agreed to coordinate our efforts," the chairman wrote. "Our intention is to bring similar legislation before our committees and to work from a harmonized approach to ensure success."[14]

The idea for the letter had come from the White House, administration officials said. Rahm thought it would be another way to demonstrate to the media and key Washington power brokers that reform had forward momentum. But the foundation for that cooperation among the three committees was those three chairmen and their aides. At a March 3 Capitol Hill meeting, which Rangel convened, they had agreed to work together with "no daylight conceptually and on the common goal," according to one summary memo. All those years in the minority, between 1995 and 2007, had forced Democrats to put aside jurisdictional disputes, because they could exert more power standing together. The staff got accustomed to sharing notes, collaborating on proposals, and referring potential hires to one another. It helped that most of these aides had been with the leaders for many years, giving them an implied proxy for their members during negotiations. Karen Nelson, Waxman's chief adviser on health care, had been working for him so long she was basically an extension of his brain.[15]

Something similar was happening in the Senate, where Kennedy aide David Bowen and Baucus aide Liz Fowler had been staying in contact since her return to Capitol Hill in the spring of 2008. Their relationship had more potential for tension, given the inevitable ideological and strategic conflicts between HELP and Finance. Over Thanksgiving, the two had a long telephone conversation in which they agreed they would avoid jurisdictional pissing matches and make sure each committee knew what the other was doing. (Bowen later described it as the "Tucson Zoo conversation," because he was there with his family during the call, watching polar bears lick their way to pieces of meat encased in ice.)[16]

Once DeParle took over the White House operation, she invited the staff from both houses to the White House for lunch. It was supposed to be a casual, get-to-know-your-colleague sort of gathering, although many already knew each other well, whether it was through their many prior collaborations, attendance at stakeholder conferences, or their teamwork on the Recovery Act, which included extra Medicaid funding and a big investment in electronic medical records. Soon the aides were having daily and eventually twice daily standing phone calls with staff from the White House.[17]

That level of coordination, which continued until the day the Affordable Care Act became law, was highly unusual. Looking back, more than one staffer noticed a distinct gender pattern among the dozen or so top Capitol aides working most intensely on health care and, in particular, the coverage issues. In addition to Bjorklund and Nelson, the House delegation included Chiquita Brooks-LaSure (who worked on Ways and Means), Debbie Curtis (who worked for Stark), Purvee Kempf (who worked on Energy and Commerce), Liz Murray (who worked for majority whip Steny Hoyer), Megan O'Reilly and Michele Varnhagen (who worked on Education and Labor). Key Senate staff besides Liz Fowler included Kate Leone (Reid's adviser on health care) and Yvette Fontenot (Fowler's colleague on Finance). There were some men too, as there were in the administration—although, as work on legislation got serious, DeParle and Lambrew increasingly became their primary points of contact. "This is studied in business schools all the time, how men and women lead differently," Bjorklund said later. "I just think there was a strong collaborative spirit there."[18]

White House officials played two key roles in these deliberations. One was as a coordinator and messenger, making sure that every committee knew what every other committee was discussing. This was not always fun. Lambrew frequently drew the duty of talking with Senate Finance staff as they were putting together their bill, then walking across the Capitol Building to brief House staffers bewildered at the choices Baucus was making. The other was to set basic parameters for the program, so the different committee bills would be close enough to merge into one measure that Obama could sign.

Administration officials didn't want to write the bill, for reasons Daschle's transition memo from December laid out: "If we offer to do more than offer guidance in the early phase, members of Congress will have less incentive to work through the policies and politics and wait for the plan to arrive. They will also feel less ownership of the process and product." That was why, for example, the health reserve fund in Obama's budget didn't include specifics on the sources of savings. As Gene Sperling, a Treasury official, later explained to me, putting out too many details "would expose it to attacks much earlier, before Congress could work through it, making it harder to pass a bigger bill."[19]

Still, the president had clear goals for both coverage and cost that he wanted the committees to meet. On coverage, the Massachusetts-style model would never have the reach of a European-style system. Too many people wouldn't realize they were eligible for public programs or would decline insurance. But Obama wanted to get close. He also wanted a public option, although it was obvious to advisers and lawmakers he considered it a secondary priority.

As for what the insurance would look like to a policyholder, Obama wanted to minimize financial exposure to medical bills, especially for low-income Americans, although he expected most other people would bear some out-of-pocket costs. When meeting with advisers, he would go over spreadsheets from Jon Gruber, who was serving as a paid consultant, showing what different proposals would mean for people in different hypothetical situations. DeParle later remembered discussions about one imaginary household, a young family of three that owned a small business in Northern Virginia. "He asked questions like, 'Will they value having insurance? Will they be more annoyed with having to pay premiums—assuming they have low medical costs—or would they rather have a low deductible so when they use the insurance they will get help right away?'"[20]

Obama understood the program would be an expensive undertaking for the federal government. Early on, advisers presented a number of options to him, showing how different levels of outlays would result in different levels of coverage. Obama said he would be fine with a price tag that went above one trillion over ten years, which was the most expensive of the options, although that would be a massive commitment of federal spending relative to the price of other recent federal initiatives.

But he was insistent that the program pay for itself and then start to reduce the deficit through some combination of new revenue and cuts to existing government health programs. He was especially interested in the "game changers" and "delivery reforms" from Peter Orszag and two top aides, Zeke Emanuel (Rahm's brother and an oncologist) and Bob Kocher (an internal medicine doctor serving on the National Economic Council). Many of these proposals were designed to shift the financing of medical care away from separate payments for each visit, test, and procedure—and toward lump-sum payments for each patient or at least every condition—on the well-established theory that paying a fee for every service creates incentives to do more. The hope was that, over time, health care costs would grow more slowly, thus "bending the curve" of what the federal government and society as a whole would be spending.[21]

In May, Obama seized on a *New Yorker* article by Atul Gawande, who had helped Bill Clinton craft his health care policy back in 1992 and had since turned into one of the nation's most respected physician-writers. The article focused on a particular community, McAllen, Texas, where Medicare spending was unusually high compared to nearby communities where the health problems were similar. Gawande, relying in part on the Dartmouth research about regional disparities, argued that the explanation was different treatment patterns. Basically, doctors and hospitals in McAllen had gotten in the habit of providing more intensive care, like operating preemptively on gallstones rather than giving medication and diet changes a chance to work.[22]

Orszag posted an item on his official blog, highlighting the article and noting that the McAllen patients weren't actually doing better, despite all the medical interventions. Obama circulated it to aides and brought it up in a meeting of senators, as Ron Wyden later told *The New York Times:* "He, in effect, took that article and put it in front of a big group of senators and said, 'This is what we've got to fix.'"[23]

3.

How to meet those different goals in a way that could get enough support in committees and then in floor votes was the central question that Democrats spent the spring and summer of 2009 trying to answer.

Trade-offs were everywhere. Covering more people or raising insurance standards would raise the price of the program, requiring higher taxes, more dramatic changes to the financing of public insurance programs, or some combination of the two. Every upside had a downside, every benefit a cost. The administration had its share of internal turf fights, particularly early on when Orszag and DeParle vied for influence. But the most consequential clashes were over substance—like whether to limit the profits and overhead of insurers aggressively, a favorite idea of Lambrew's that was unpopular with the economic team. When meeting with his advisers at the White House, Obama would frequently raise his two hands like he was manipulating a Rubik's Cube, twisting it this way and that, as if health care legislation were a puzzle to solve.[24]

Which it was. But it was a puzzle with more than one solution and, in June, the three House committees offered theirs.

Everybody with income of up to 133 percent of the poverty line would be eligible for Medicaid. People with incomes higher than that, and without access to employer coverage, could buy private policies through an online exchange. It was an analogue to the Massachusetts Connector, where insurers would have to sell at uniform prices, regardless of preexisting conditions, with only modest variations based on age. Financial assistance would be available to exchange buyers with income of up to four times the poverty line—or about $43,000 a year for an individual and $88,000 for a family of four, in 2009 dollars.

That threshold, well into the middle class, was just one of the ways the House committees had pushed in a more liberal direction. Their plan also had a public option of the kind Jacob Hacker had recommended and advocacy groups like HCAN and MoveOn were promoting. To finance the expansion, House leaders were proposing to cut Medicare payments for various industry sectors and to raise taxes on the wealthy.[25]

The proposal included an individual mandate, the idea that Obama had rejected (except for kids) and then attacked during the 2008 primaries. Obama had formally signaled his acceptance of the idea in early June 2009 by writing a formal letter to Baucus and Kennedy with a statement that "I am open to your ideas on shared responsibility." *Shared responsibility* was the euphemism supporters used for the mandate.[26]

But by the time of Obama's letter, the decision was something of a fait accompli. House leaders had agreed in principle to a mandate back in early March, as Ezra Klein first reported in *The American Prospect*, while Baucus and Kennedy had embraced the idea long before then. As for Obama, he had started musing about the mandate's upsides privately as soon as the 2008 primary campaign was over—persuaded, he said, both by Clinton's strong arguments and the advice of economists who said it would make the program more effective. It came up frequently in conversations after that, and in January, Daschle told Baucus privately that Obama was open to a mandate. At a late April 2009 meeting with advisers, Obama signed off on the idea in principle, as journalist Steven Brill later reported in his book *America's Bitter Pill*. The letter had come at Baucus's request, to provide the Finance bill (and Baucus) with some political cover.[27]

With the mandate in place, 94 percent of the non-elderly population would end up with insurance, according to an estimate from the Congressional Budget Office. (A big chunk of the remaining uninsured would be undocumented immigrants; covering them was assumed to be so politically toxic that the idea had minimal support even in the Democratic caucus.) That wasn't quite up to Massachusetts standards, but it wasn't far off. At higher incomes, even relatively thin insurance would be pricey, though still less than 12 percent of income. At lower incomes, coverage would be significantly more comprehensive and dramatically less expensive, especially for people below and just above the poverty line. They'd be eligible for Medicaid, which covered pretty much everything for free. Altogether, the insurance provisions would require about $1 trillion in new outlays from the federal government, and aside from pushing back the implementation date by two years, to 2013, the proposal was mostly free of the budget gimmicks legislators typically used to disguise the true costs of their proposals.

The proposal was still just a starting point; each of the three committees had to take it up individually, debating and then adding amendments before voting on the final package. Miller got the bill through the Education and Labor Committee with relative ease; Rangel did the same at Ways and Means. Henry Waxman had a harder time. He may have taken over the committee in 2009, but the membership included a significant delegation of more conservative "Blue Dog" Democrats Dingell had picked to resist what he considered overly aggressive environmental legislation. And by July, they were in an ornery mood.[28]

The reason was legislation for a "cap and trade" emission control system that had just gone through their committee. Waxman wrote it, Pelosi supported it, and Obama pushed for it, because he was as determined not to give up on climate change legislation in his first year as he was determined not to give up on health care. It won approval from the full House on June 26, following personal appeals from Obama at the annual congressional picnic and lobbying by Pelosi, who somehow pulled eight Republicans to her side. But its chances of surviving the Senate seemed increasingly meager, with coal country Democrats already coming out against it, while environmental groups were backing off the bill because of compromises sponsors made to get it through the House.[29]

"All of the members who had voted for that bill from marginal districts were getting the shit kicked out of them and getting no backup from environmental groups," a Democratic aide said shortly afterward. "There was a guy at a caucus who stood up and said, 'Nancy, there's an ad in my district, and it's with you and me, which would be nice, but we're both being struck by lightning.'"[30]

Now Waxman was coming to some of those same members with a health care bill that was likely to end up on a similar path, with a skeptical Senate and disillusioned supporters unwilling to fight for lawmakers who voted yes. It had a lot of regulation and spending—not as much as liberal Democrats wanted, but more than conservative Democrats did. And the thing was paid for with taxes and reimbursement cuts to well-connected industries whose donations and advertisements could swing a close race one way or the other.

Waxman could afford to lose six votes in committee, assuming no Republican support, and right off the bat, he thought he had four no votes and two more likely noes—in other words, his margin was down to zero. On the first day of hearings, a group of Democrats including several Blue Dogs declared their opposition, enough to sink the bill. Even worse, according to a memoir that aides Bryan Marshall and Bruce Wolpe published later, Waxman feared that the committee's ranking Republican, Joe Barton of Texas, would try to get the committee Blue Dogs to join him on some kind of alternative measure that, by peeling off moderates, would undermine the entire enterprise when it got to the full House. This was always the real problem. The Blue Dogs Waxman was struggling to corral were just like the ones Pelosi would need on the floor. And there were more than fifty of them, which meant they had enough votes to stop legislation if they stuck together.[31]

Waxman was exasperated, as much by the substance of the Blue Dog complaints as their impact. They criticized the bill for its high level of government spending, but they also opposed what Waxman thought were the most effective ways to bring the cost down. That was especially true for the public option. As the Congressional Budget Office had attested, it could save money by paying for inpatient and outpatient services at rates close to Medicare, which were much lower than what private insurers would pay. The Blue Dogs said it would introduce unfair competition into the market, making it impossible for private carriers to keep up. Waxman thought the low payment rates were proof the public option would work—and that the real problem, for many Blue Dogs, was lobbying by insurers plus provider groups unhappy with the prospect of getting lower reimbursements. Many Blue Dogs, he knew, relied heavily on these industries to finance their campaigns.[32]

Still, Waxman needed their votes, and so he made a major concession. The bill would have a public option, but it would have to negotiate reimbursements just like a private insurance plan, thereby giving up one of its main advantages. He then brought in the White House, including Peter Orszag, to assure the Blue Dogs of the White House commitment to a bill that would hold the line on spending and reduce the deficit, even if that meant less money for coverage.

It turned out the Blue Dogs were excited about one of Orszag's favorite ideas: an independent board of experts that would recommend changes to Medicare payments based on whether treatments worked. Waxman was decidedly not a fan, because he didn't want Congress giving up so much discretion. But he accepted it and was actually surprised that Blue Dogs liked the idea, given that the board's recommendations could reduce payments to providers he presumed Blue Dogs were trying to protect. At one meeting, Waxman told me, a Blue Dog congressman realized that possibility and commented, a note of concern in his voice, that the board could mean less revenue for providers. Waxman said he just grinned, acknowledging the possibility.[33]

One final hurdle was an issue related to biologics, which are drugs harvested from living things and then transformed into blood products, gene therapies, and other treatments for chronic or severe conditions, including some cancers. The industry group representing these firms wanted an exclusivity period (that is, a period during which they would face no competition from generic manufacturers) of twelve years, arguing that it would reward investment in research and ultimately lead to more innovation. They had a champion in Anna Eshoo, a Democratic Energy and Commerce member whose Silicon Valley district included a number of firms that manufactured biologics and whose fundraising rolls included quite a few industry leaders.

Waxman thought the idea was outrageous, and the experts he consulted thought the innovation argument was wildly overblown, if true at all. But Eshoo had support from some more conservative Democrats as well as committee Republicans (including Barton), and they attached their amendment to the bill. It was a major blow. That was twelve years that biologic manufacturers could pretty much dictate the price of their wares, raising costs for individuals and insurance programs and, eventually, the new health care program. It was another example of how a group complaining about the cost of health care reform was, simultaneously, demanding changes that made it more expensive.[34]

Waxman wasn't alone in his frustration. Obama was just as worked up—so much so that, when he got a chance to meet with representatives of the drug industry, he brought up the twelve-year exclusivity period as something he thought excessive and hoped to change before legislation got to his desk.[35]

But on another key issue related to the drug industry, Obama wouldn't fight the deal. He would endorse it.

Thirteen

On the Bus

1.

Billy Tauzin was famous in political circles for what he did in Congress. But he was more famous for what he did when he left.

A lawyer who represented a district from the New Orleans suburbs, Tauzin had helped establish the Blue Dog Coalition and served as a Democrat for more than a decade until 1995, when Republicans took control of the chamber and he switched parties. He served on Energy and Commerce and became its chairman, playing a key role in writing Medicare drug legislation. Then he abruptly retired to become president of the Pharmaceutical Research and Manufacturers of America (PhRMA). His reported salary: at least $2 million a year.[1]

The quick jump from Congress to leading an industry he'd overseen was brazen, even by Washington standards, and Obama, as a presidential candidate, frequently used Tauzin's story to illustrate the kind of special interest power he was determined to fight. "I don't want to learn how to play the game better," Obama had said. "I want to put an end to the game-playing."[2]

But while Obama was making those statements, Tauzin was participating in Ron Pollack's strange bedfellows group, along with representatives from all the other industry associations. He was part of the conversations with Kennedy and Baucus.

For Kennedy, dealing with industry groups was a necessity. They had shown their ability to kill reform in the Truman and Clinton fights. If Democrats wanted to succeed this time, they would have to neutralize those industries, or at least most of them, as LBJ and his allies had done to pass

Medicare. Baucus was less inclined to see them as adversaries. The providers, producers, and payers of medical care would have to live with the new system. He treated them more like partners, especially since some of his former aides were now their lobbyists.

The idea behind the negotiations was that more people with insurance meant more paying customers, so that industry could live with lower payments—in effect, making up in volume what they'd be giving up on price. To guide the discussions, Baucus brought on an accounting expert, Tony Clapsis, who made projections of just how much extra the drugmakers, for example, would make because the newly insured could afford to pay for their prescriptions. "He was our secret weapon," according to Jon Selib, chief of staff to Baucus. When industry lobbyists challenged those figures, Baucus and his staff appealed to the groups' self-interest: The alternative might be even bigger cuts, because the Democrats needed to find money for their plan somewhere. Their mantra was, "At the table or on the menu"—or, sometimes, "On the bus or under the bus."[3]

Obama embraced the strategy, praising industry participation at the March summit and bringing in representatives for discussions of how, together, they could find savings through more efficient care. (Visitor logs, which the Obama White House had made public, showed that Tauzin was among those with frequent meetings inside the West Wing.) "There was never going to be a scenario in which we could get this done without at least some of them," Jim Messina told me later. "We'd hoped to get all of them. . . . But we knew we had to at least get a bunch of them."[4]

The drug industry was first to cut a deal. Armed with a Clapsis estimate, Baucus thought the industry could live with policy changes that would generate between $100 and $130 billion in savings. The drug companies were thinking more like $20 to $40 billion, with a stipulation that legislation not include two popular reform proposals: allowing the importation of cheaper drugs from Canada and allowing the federal government to negotiate directly with manufacturers over price. Drug industry representatives also demanded that the deal get endorsements from both the White House and Senate leadership, so that the terms wouldn't change once the bill had left the Finance Committee.

In April, the two sides settled on $80 billion. House leaders were livid—at Baucus, for not extracting more savings, and at the White House, for endorsing the deal. "Stabbed in the back" is how one aide put it to me.

When Waxman announced that he didn't feel bound by the agreement, drug lobbyists demanded reassurances at a Roosevelt Room meeting. "We are in," Rahm told them, according to a report by the *Washington Post*'s Ceci Connolly.[5]

But the arrangement remained controversial within the drug industry, and in 2010, Tauzin left his position—officially for personal reasons, though amid reports that several major executives were angry he hadn't gotten a deal more favorable to industry. It was an example of a hidden dynamic behind legislation; interest groups also have their own internal politics, with members who disagree over priorities. And it nearly unraveled yet another deal—the one with the hospitals.[6]

Hospitals didn't have the same reputation for greed as drugmakers, even though their practice of suing the uninsured and underinsured over exorbitant bills had generated embarrassing media coverage. They also didn't have the same reputation for exerting influence, even though they were the largest employer in many congressional districts and typically had politically well-connected board members.[7]

The deal hospitals cut was for even more savings: $155 billion over ten years. The theory behind having the hospitals give up more money than the drugmakers was that they accounted for a much larger share of national health care spending. But many individual hospitals didn't see it that way. They didn't have the huge profit margins of pharmaceutical companies, and in any event, some officials felt like they hadn't given their proxy for this kind of dealmaking. Richard Umbdenstock, president of the American Hospital Association, came under intense criticism.[8]

Aides like Jon Selib said the deals were necessary because "everybody knew what the hospitals and the pharmaceutical companies could do—and the proof point is what the insurers did do." He was referring to revelations, from Bloomberg's Drew Armstrong more than a year later, that insurers had spent $86.2 million financing an advertising campaign against reform that the Chamber of Commerce ran in 2009. Insurers never reached an agreement with the White House and Senate Finance, despite extensive negotiations, and had the other industry groups spent similarly to fight reform, they might have prevailed. Ron Pollack later remembered a PhRMA official saying, back in the pre-2009 meetings, that the group had a $200 million war chest ready to spend on health care reform. When Pollack asked if it would be for or against, the official told him he wasn't sure yet. Pollack thought back to how interest groups had fought the Clinton plan and knew the implied threat was not idle.[9]

Amid all of this, Messina and Selib secured a promise from PhRMA to spend $150 million on a pro-reform ad campaign. It was not technically part of the legislative arrangement, although everybody could see that they were related. Whether or not the ads actually swayed anybody, it represented $150 million drugmakers were not spending to stop legislation. That felt like a big win to the White House and Baucus. But the deals generated lots of negative, politically damaging publicity—in the *Los Angeles Times,* where reporter Tom Hamburger first reported the details; in *HuffPost,* where correspondent Ryan Grim got his hands on a lobbyist memo; and in editorial pages and opinion publications, where supporters of reform were as furious as Waxman had been. "President Obama's handshake with Tauzin is easily the dumbest mistake he's made in shepherding health reform through Congress," Timothy Noah wrote in *Slate.*[10]

The deals also put hard limits on legislation's potential to extract savings directly from providers and producers of medical care. That had far-reaching effects on reform's budget math and, ultimately, what the program would mean for everyday Americans.

2.

The commitment that reform would pay for itself and then reduce the deficit was one of the most important decisions Democrats made, because it established boundaries on what their plan could do—and what it couldn't.

The promise reflected strategic calculation. Between the Blue Dogs in the House and self-described deficit hawks like Kent Conrad in the Senate, no bill was getting through Congress if its spending significantly exceeded revenue. Polls also suggested that voters associated deficits with Democratic spending programs and held it against the party, in part because they saw it as a proxy for irresponsible governing, even though it was Republicans who had been running up deficits.[11]

For Obama, though, reducing the deficit was never just about politics. The federal government faced a real financing problem in the long run, he thought, with the gap between spending and revenue growing over time. As debt piled up, interest payments would siphon money needed for other purposes. The economy would be weaker, too, as Washington's demand for dollars made it harder (that is, more expensive) for businesses to borrow what they needed to finance their own operations and expansions.[12]

Years later, more economists would question whether deficits were so dangerous—or at least whether reducing them needed to be such a focus of policy making. But in 2009, Obama's outlook was widely shared in the nation's political and economic establishments and got plenty of reinforcement from its members inside the White House. At a July meeting, according to one participant, Axelrod presented poll numbers showing that deficits had become the voters' number-two concern, while Tim Geithner said deficit neutrality was essential. Peter Orszag, meanwhile, made it clear that reducing the deficit was not merely a precondition for health care reform; it was, to his mind, a primary goal.[13]

Questions about the expense to the government had been a recurring theme in arguments over major health care bills, going back to the original debate over Medicare. But Obama had to make the case for his reforms in a world where health care spending and debt levels were higher than they had been in LBJ's day. And while Johnson could dismiss deficit worries as the product of rough, loosely informed guesses by a small handful of government actuaries, Obama had to contend with estimates from what had become one of Washington's most powerful and respected institutions: the Congressional Budget Office.[14]

The CBO was an outgrowth of fights between Nixon and Congress in the early 1970s, following his efforts to impound spending on housing, environmental programs, and other initiatives Congress had authorized. Although the courts put a stop to that, Congress rewrote the rules for budget making and decided it needed its own, independent organization to study and make predictions about federal finances. In the course of three decades, CBO's staff and mission had expanded dramatically, as had its credibility— thanks in part to the appointment of directors who, whatever their ideological or partisan backgrounds, resisted efforts to tailor estimates in ways that particular lawmakers wanted. In an era when independent institutions like the media, think tanks, and universities were losing public trust because of perceptions they were becoming more partisan, CBO stood out as a rare exception.[15]

Orszag had primed the institution to play an active role in health reform, using an estimate of the 2007 Wyden-Bennett bill as a trial run of sorts and producing a separate volume on options for reducing health care costs that he imagined handing to Congress and a new president in 2009—that is, before he signed up to work for him. Orszag's successor was Doug Elmendorf, who also recognized what a big deal health care would be. He told lawmakers from both parties that his office would proactively share information on CBO's scoring methods and try its best to produce estimates quickly. Frequently, Elmendorf said, that meant staff ran calculations until 2:00 a.m., with Elmendorf, an early riser, picking up the work at 4:00 a.m.[16]

But predicting the impact of health legislation was inherently difficult because of the many variables that went into it. A projection about legislation's effect on the budget had to consider how the new financial incentives it provided would affect both people's propensity to buy insurance and then to consume care—which in turn affected the price of insurance, which then altered the cost of federal subsidies. And the underlying data was never perfect, forcing CBO to make judgment calls on how to weigh it.

Such guesswork was necessary on a critical issue: the individual mandate's impact. "I remember this discussion about how . . . in Massachusetts the mandate seems to really matter," Elmendorf told me. But some of his economists wondered whether it'd be as effective in other states, since in liberal Massachusetts residents had a reputation for accepting and following government instructions. After studying the issue, CBO decided to assume significant effects, partly on the theory that if Congress passed legislation with a mandate in it, "then maybe the country is more like Massachusetts in this one way."[17]

Staff from both sides appreciated CBO's spirit of collaboration, as well as its commitment to impartiality. But Democrats got frustrated with the assumptions that went into CBO calculations, including deep skepticism of many cost-cutting initiatives. CBO's position was that, absent hard evidence that such reforms would actually save money, it couldn't credit big savings, no matter how promising the ideas seemed.

Democratic exasperation erupted into public view in July, after Elmendorf was on Capitol Hill to give regularly scheduled testimony before the House Ways and Means and Senate Budget Committees. "I'm going to really put you on the spot," Conrad, the Senate Budget chairman, said. "From what you have seen from the products of the committees that have reported, do you see a successful effort being mounted to bend the long-term cost curve?" Elmendorf's answer was no. Legislation might be able to pay for itself, Elmendorf explained, but CBO did "not see the sort of fundamental changes that would be necessary to reduce the trajectory of federal health spending by a significant amount."

Within hours, news websites were carrying headlines like "Health Reform Bills Won't Reduce Costs," and Republicans were on the attack. Mike Pence, then a GOP congressman from Indiana, said, "Today's announcement by the independent CBO confirms what Republicans have been saying all along: The health care proposal by Congressional Democrats amounts to a government takeover of our health care economy." David Wessel, an economics columnist for the *Wall Street Journal* news section, called it an "emperor has no clothes moment."[18]

3.

Inside the White House, the president's team was in a "tizzy," one aide said at the time. Even Orszag found CBO's extreme skepticism of some cost-control proposals vexing. But along with other members of the economic team, Orszag agreed with CBO that legislation was missing an essential element on cost control. That element was some kind of change to tax treatment of employer health benefits.[19]

Back in the 1940s, the federal government had made a critical decision: If an employer provided an employee with insurance, the premiums wouldn't be subject to income taxes. The effect was to make a dollar of health insurance more valuable than a dollar in wages, and over the long run, it helped entrench job-based insurance as the primary source of coverage for working-age Americans. But the exemption (or *exclusion*, as it was officially called) gave both workers and employers incentive to devote more money to health care—incentive that, most economists argued, discouraged cost consciousness in health care, leading to more spending, eventually leading to higher costs for everybody.

This belief, which traced back to Martin Feldstein's old research, was the sort of thing economists at universities all over the country would teach as a bedrock principle of health financing. And the most straightforward solution, they would say, was simply to take away that special treatment, so that a dollar of insurance would look like a dollar of regular income to everybody. Over time, workers and employers would make better decisions about how to make trade-offs between insurance and wages, gravitate toward insurance policies that didn't cost so much, and spending would come down—since cheaper plans, by definition, would be finding ways to spend less.[20]

Not every economist agreed on the exclusion's impact. And adjusting or eliminating the exclusion was by no means the only way to hold down costs. Overseas, countries with national health systems brought down costs by simply regulating prices—that is, establishing fixed fees for everything from physician visits to MRI scans, usually after some kind of negotiation with whoever was providing the care or producing the equipment. But that kind of price regulation had long since fallen out of favor in the United States, as part of the decades-old intellectual and political backlash to big government. And while a reform plan like the House bill promised to hold down the cost of Medicare and Medicaid by cutting what those programs paid for services, it had no way to apply similar pressure on private insurance without changes to the exclusion—a point Orszag, Emanuel, and other members of the White House economic team kept making.[21]

To seal the deal, Obama's advisers invited Elmendorf and several other economists to meet with the president in the Oval Office. Obama had also grown weary of the CBO; at one point, as *The New Yorker*'s Ryan Lizza later reported, he told advisers to start referring to the agency as "a banana" because he was tired of hearing about it. But he approached the meeting like he had the Senate briefings in 2006, asking Elmendorf to explain CBO modeling and the prevailing assumptions on health care spending. Republicans would later blast Obama for trying to intimidate Elmendorf. The tone of the conversation, according to several people present, was the opposite—deferential to Elmendorf and the agency, with the air of an academic seminar that got deep into the weeds of economics and why America's health care system was so screwed up.[22]

The idea of changing the tax treatment of insurance was almost unthinkable to some of Obama's strategic advisers, who remembered attacking John McCain over a similar proposal in 2008. David Axelrod made the health care team watch ten minutes of old campaign ads, just to hammer home the point, as Noam Scheiber later recounted in his book, *The Escape Artists*. But Obama prided himself on being the kind of leader who took unpopular positions when necessary, and he'd come to believe, as his economic advisers did, that the tax change was necessary to get health care costs under control. In a public letter to Baucus, he signaled his willingness to go along with some sort of modification, although he didn't specify what form it should take.

The Montana senator was pleased, because he had long eyed changes to the exclusion as both a way to finance the coverage expansion, since more taxable income would mean more tax revenue, and to bend the curve. He also liked it better than the House alternative for financing, which relied heavily on taxing the rich. Conrad was just as happy.[23]

Satisfying those two was important politically, given their committee perches and influence over more conservative Democrats. But if tampering with the exclusion solved some political problems on Capitol Hill, it created others, especially among liberal Democrats and those with ties to organized labor.

Unions over the years had negotiated generous health insurance benefits for their members, frequently forgoing wage increases to do so. A change in their tax treatment would make these plans more expensive. Economic theory held that the workers would end up getting that money back as higher wages. But as unions argued, and as many economists quietly conceded, that was unlikely to happen evenly or right away. It would depend on bargaining dynamics.[24]

And what was true for unions might be true for other workers, as well. In the optimistic scenario, businesses would react to the tax change by demanding insurers provide a better product, prompting insurers to demand lower prices or more efficient care from providers. In other words, market forces would push the entire health care system to better quality for less money. But it was possible (and likely, in some tellings) that employers would just start slashing benefits by saddling individuals with bigger deductibles and co-pays. People in good health might be fine. But those with chronic illnesses, especially those with lower incomes, would decide not to fill prescriptions or get checkups they needed to avoid more serious complications.[25]

An extra source of frustration for liberal Democrats was that the push for this tax change was coming from senators like Conrad, whose insistence on fiscal responsibility somehow seemed less insistent when their own interests were at stake. Conrad had been publicly critical of both the House and Senate HELP bills because, he said, they weren't serious about deficit reduction. But as the Finance Committee (where he also sat) was writing its bill, Conrad lobbied for a key provision: an increase in what Medicare paid rural hospitals in the Great Plains and western states. That increase, which Baucus wanted for his constituents as much as Conrad did for his, would make the bill more expensive.[26]

This boost, which eventually came to be known as the Frontier package, had a defensible rationale. Rural hospitals tended to run on smaller margins and sometimes lost money, because they didn't have the economies of scale that large urban hospitals did. The start-up costs of an intensive care unit are enormous, for example, making them much harder to afford in a small hospital with just fifty beds as opposed to five hundred. But most of the priorities that liberal Democrats wanted had policy rationales too. Somehow their priorities were subject to strict budget constraints, but Conrad's weren't.[27]

All of this might have been easier for more liberal Democrats to accept if their adherence to CBO guidelines were helping them in the public relations battle. But Democrats were still the party that had the reputation for running up deficits to pay for new programs when, in fact, it was the Republicans who time and again had enacted programs without paying for them, as writers like Jonathan Chait and Paul Krugman repeatedly pointed out. The most recent example was the Medicare drug benefit, which had literally no offsetting revenue or spending cuts. Even Orrin Hatch later conceded that, during the Bush years, "a lot of things weren't paid for and that wasn't right."[28]

Of course, the reality was that most voters simply weren't paying that much attention to the details of health reform. All they could see was that the process was ugly. And it was about to get uglier.

Fourteen

Death Panels

1.

Few figures in American politics were more associated with the rise of the modern Republican Party than pollster and strategist Frank Luntz.

The child of a Connecticut dentist, Luntz had degrees from the University of Pennsylvania and Oxford and made his first big impression on American politics in 1994 when he helped Newt Gingrich choreograph the Republican takeover of Congress. Luntz had a boyish face and natural, inquisitive charisma that translated well on television, where he had steady work running on-camera focus groups after debates and speeches. Between those gigs, his political and corporate work, and his speaking, Luntz did well for himself. The $6 million Los Angeles mansion he called home for many years had its own bowling alley.[1]

Luntz's genius was really as a political wordsmith, somebody who could repackage political losers as winners. Instead of trying to repeal the "estate tax," he recommended, Republicans should talk about a "death tax." And stay away from the phrase "drilling in the Arctic," he said. Call it "energy exploration." "I'm not a policy person," he told Deborah Solomon of *The New York Times*. "I'm a language person."[2]

Still, he had his opinions. He preached about the importance of hard work and the dangers of too much government, which he said created dependency. "You should not expect a handout," he told the journalist Molly Ball. "You should not even expect a safety net. When my house burns down, I should not go to the government to rebuild it. I should have the savings, and if I don't, my neighbors should pitch in for me, because I would do that for them."[3]

That worldview made him suspicious of Democratic health reform plans. In April 2009, as committees were getting to work, he circulated a memo laying out "the ten rules for stopping the 'Washington takeover' of healthcare" with a focus on the rationing of care. "Nothing will anger Americans more than the chance that they will be denied the healthcare they need for whatever reason," Luntz wrote. "So say it. 'The plan put forward by the Democrats will deny people treatments they need and make them wait to get the treatments they are allowed to receive.'"

To make horror stories from countries like Canada resonate, Luntz advised, Republicans should personalize them. "In countries with government run healthcare, politicians make YOUR healthcare decisions," Luntz suggested Republicans say. "THEY decide if you'll get the procedure you need, or if you are disqualified because the treatment is too expensive or because you are too old. We can't have that in America."[4]

Soon Republican leaders like Eric Cantor and Mitch McConnell were making arguments about a "government takeover" and rationing of care—accusations that, whether inspired by Luntz's memo, had little resemblance to what Democrats were actually proposing. The plans coming out of the House and Senate committees, like the one that Obama had sketched out as a candidate, lacked the kind of central control that characterized the Canadian and European systems (which, by the way, didn't actually ration care in the way conservatives frequently suggested). The decision to go with a Massachusetts-style plan had, for better or worse, meant the federal government simply wouldn't have that kind of power.[5]

Democrats pointed this out. Media fact-checkers backed them up. It didn't stop the arguments from circulating and getting more egregious with time. In June, conservative analyst Elizabeth McCaughey appeared on a talk radio show with what she claimed was an explosive revelation: Democratic legislation "would make it mandatory—absolutely require—that every five years people in Medicare have a required counseling session that will tell them how to end their life sooner."

McCaughey's reemergence gave some veterans of the Clinton fight flashbacks to her deceptive arguments from 1993. Now she was making incendiary claims about the Obama effort that, sure enough, were wildly inaccurate. All the Democrats were proposing was to have Medicare reimburse doctors for time they spent advising patients who wanted to write advance directives. The hope was that, with the reimbursement, doctors would give patients their undivided attention for more than just a few minutes, to make the process of writing those instructions easier.

Once again, fact-checkers said McCaughey was wrong. Once again, it didn't stop the stories from spreading—especially on Fox, on which more conservative voters were increasingly relying as their source of news. A few weeks after that, Sarah Palin, the former Alaska governor and GOP vice presidential nominee, offered her own version of the argument. "Government health care will not reduce the cost; it will simply refuse to pay the cost," she posted on her Facebook page. "And who will suffer the most when they ration care? The sick, the elderly, and the disabled, of course." Palin, who had a child with Down syndrome, went on to say, "The America I know and love is not one in which my parents or my baby with Down Syndrome will have to stand in front of Obama's 'death panel' so his bureaucrats can decide, based on a subjective judgment of their 'level of productivity in society,' whether they are worthy of health care. Such a system is downright evil."[6]

Palin, by that point, was a celebrity in conservative circles and a beloved figure to many parents with special needs children. But her statements made little sense. The only thing in the legislation remotely resembling the panel Palin had described was a whole other provision: Orszag's proposed Medicare spending panel, the one Henry Waxman had reluctantly agreed to accept. The idea, like so many in the emerging legislation, was the subject of real debate even among serious students of health care. But the idea that it would be denying treatment to children with Down syndrome was as far-fetched as McCaughey's claim about end-of-life counseling.

Among those outraged by the distortions was Johnny Isakson, a conservative Republican senator from Georgia who wrote the provision on end-of-life counseling that had ended up in the Senate HELP bill. "It's to protect children or a spouse from being put into a situation where they have to make a terrible decision as well as physicians from being put into a position where they have to practice defensive medicine because of the trial lawyers," Isakson told journalist Ezra Klein. As for how that proposal got a reputation for encouraging euthanasia, Isakson said, "I have no idea. . . . How someone could take an end of life directive or a living will as that is nuts."[7]

But inside the GOP, Isakson's voice was a lonely one. Most Republicans said nothing, and quite a few repeated versions of the argument. John Boehner, the Ohio congressman who was now leader of the House Republicans, sent out an official statement warning that the end-of-life counseling provision "may start us down a treacherous path toward government-encouraged euthanasia if enacted into law."[8]

Chain emails from GOP supporters were even more alarmist. One of them, which the organization Factcheck.org said it got from a reader, warned that Democrats were trying "to push SUICIDE to cut medicare spending!!!"[9]

2.

For the White House and its allies, the death panel myth was a politically damaging distraction. For one administration official, it was also a personal attack. That official was Zeke Emanuel.

Zeke was the oldest of the three high-achieving Emanuel brothers, whom more than one person had likened to a modern-day version of the Kennedys, only Jewish and less focused on politics. In addition to Rahm, who was serving as Obama's chief of staff, there was Ari, the Hollywood talent representative who had built one of the entertainment industry's biggest and most powerful agencies. Growing up, the three boys were energetic, outspoken, and highly competitive with one another. As grown-ups, they were pretty much the same, except that Zeke's conversational style had not taken the colorful turn that his brothers' had. (Ari Emanuel was supposedly the model for the fictional character Ari Gold, the expletive-spewing agent on the HBO series *Entourage*.) Of the three, Zeke was the most academically inclined and accomplished. He had a medical degree and a doctorate from Harvard, where he also won the annual Toppan Prize for the government department's best dissertation.

Benjamin Emanuel, their father, was a pediatrician, though Zeke always said medicine was not the preordained path for him many had assumed. He had other interests and considered pursuing them. But he readily conceded that he inherited something else from his family: a drive to get involved in public life and work on fixing the world's problems. His grandfather was a union organizer, his mother a dedicated civil rights activist, and his father crusaded to eliminate lead paint from housing in order to protect children, especially in low-income areas.

As a medical student and future oncologist, Zeke watched families struggle with difficult choices about treatment for dying patients no longer able to make their own decisions. Drawing on his background in philosophy, he and his then wife, Linda, created a basic form they called "The Medical Directive" designed to let patients think through and specify, in some detail, their preferences for four medical scenarios in which they could not consciously make decisions for themselves. The Emanuels published it in *The Journal of the American Medical Association* and made copies available, for a dollar plus a self-addressed stamped envelope, by request. It became a widely used template for living wills. Later, he joined the National Institutes of Health, where he launched its bioethics division, and churned out a few books, including the universal coverage blueprint that had gotten the attention of John Edwards's advisers back in 2008. Wiry and bursting with energy, Zeke somehow found time along the way to become a well-known foodie, eventually developing and producing his own line of exotic chocolate.[10]

As a member of Orszag's staff, Zeke's primary focus was on the game changers for medical care, because he had seen up close the waste in the health care system. He worked closely with Bob Kocher, a fellow physician, and met with various groups from the health care industry, trying to persuade them that reforms like "bundled payments"—a way to move away from fee-for-service—were less threatening than they might seem. Zeke had a reputation around Washington for expressing his views bluntly, loudly, and, sometimes, without anybody asking. Among those close to him, he also had a reputation for quiet acts of kindness, like reviewing medical files for relative strangers seeking advice on cancer treatments.[11]

Zeke didn't watch television or follow social media, so it took him a few days to realize that the controversy about death panels had become a controversy about him. McCaughey had gone through Zeke's past work and, writing in the *New York Post,* said that he believed "medical care should be reserved for the non-disabled. . . . Translation: Don't give much care to a grandmother with Parkinson's or a child with cerebral palsy."[12]

On the House floor, Michele Bachmann, a junior Republican who was fast getting her own following in conservative circles, read excerpts of the McCaughey article and then recounted the care her late father-in-law had received in his final weeks. "Apparently, under the Democrats' health care plan, my father-in-law would not have received the high quality of care that he received in his last two months of life. Or if you're a grandmother with Parkinson's or a child with cerebral palsy, watch out."[13]

Emanuel seemed to his friends genuinely shocked, not least because he had spent so much of his career trying to improve end-of-life care. The quotes McCaughey pulled out came from academic papers about truly scarce resources, like organs for transplant, and the ethical questions that different criteria for allocating them would raise. In other publications, Zeke had written whole articles against doctor-assisted suicide, and in a book on end-of-life care, he criticized a high-profile court case in which a judge allowed doctors to discontinue treatments of an incapacitated patient because of the parents' wishes.

"I'm an oncologist who has cared for scores, if not hundreds, of dying patients," Zeke told *The Wall Street Journal* after the McCaughey article, headlined DEADLY DOCTORS, started to get attention. "It's a perversion of everything I've done to take one or two quotes completely out of context, without any of the qualifiers I've added, and distort them."[14]

The White House mounted a full defense. So did Zeke's network of contacts and supporters, including high-profile conservatives like Stuart Butler, a scholar at the Heritage Foundation who had been involved in GOP politics since Reagan's day. "These personal attacks on good people like Zeke are outrageous," Butler said. "There are real policy issues that should be debated vigorously, but slandering a good person's name is beyond the pale." Gail Wilensky, another longtime Republican adviser who was by then a senior fellow at the global health organization Project Hope, said she was "shocked by the comments about Zeke."[15]

Wilensky's voice was the kind that, at one point, would have carried a great deal of weight in Republican circles. She was among the most formidable health policy experts in the country, a University of Michigan–trained economist who had run Medicare and Medicaid under President George H. W. Bush. When she said government programs were prone to waste and inefficiency, she spoke as somebody who had seen that waste and inefficiency up close. She was an early critic of the legislation that eventually became the Affordable Care Act, because she thought it was trying to do too much too quickly—and relied too heavily on the wisdom of government agencies that, in her experience, were not really that wise.

But Wilensky's critiques of Democratic legislation were conspicuous for what they did not include. She did not attack the individual mandate on philosophical grounds, because, as a health economist, she believed it took that kind of incentive to make private insurance markets work properly. "I'm not against requiring insurance, in principle," Wilensky explained to me in an interview two years later. "We've already made the commitment to not having people die in the streets." And although she was no fan of government spending, she conceded that "if we're going to fix the problems of the uninsured . . . we have to put money on the table initially."[16]

That kind of nuance was not consistent with GOP rhetoric, and it didn't excite conservatives, which perhaps was why figures like McCaughey were getting all the attention. "It's not like I don't know how I could look more attractive to the loudest voices in the Republican Party right now, in terms of making more extreme statements," Wilensky said. "I just don't think that's ultimately how to be most helpful in trying to solve issues."

3.

On July 17, 2009, Jim DeMint spoke on a conference call to conservative activists from across the country. DeMint, a first-term South Carolina senator, had emerged as a leader in the movement to stop health care reform from passing. The August recess was approaching, and the call's host, a group called Conservatives for Patients' Rights, was helping to organize protests to greet members back home.

"If we're able to stop Obama on this it will be his Waterloo," DeMint told the activists, "it will break him."[17]

DeMint hadn't always seemed so hostile to universal coverage. In 2007, he had praised Romney's Massachusetts reforms and signed on to a letter written by his Democratic colleague Ron Wyden, vowing to work on bipartisan legislation to "ensure that all Americans would have affordable, quality, private health coverage, while protecting current government programs."[18]

But in 2009, DeMint was attacking Democratic reforms as a "government takeover." He had also introduced a plan of his own, the Health Care Freedom Act, with a very different, mostly familiar set of conservative ideas—like reform of medical malpractice laws and allowing the purchase of insurance across state lines, plus a tax credit too small to help most of the uninsured afford premiums. If enacted, it would require far less spending and regulation than what Democrats were proposing. It would also come nowhere close to ensuring that all Americans had affordable coverage.[19]

DeMint came from the world of marketing. He got interested in politics through a client who served in the U.S. House, representing one of the state's most conservative districts. DeMint ran for the seat when it became open, at one point saying that gays shouldn't be allowed to teach in public schools and that unmarried pregnant women shouldn't either. He later apologized for the comments, without disavowing the underlying sentiments. He won easily.[20]

DeMint was an early proponent of the theory that Democrats had solidified the support of poor people and African Americans by offering them benefits that made them dependent on the government—and, as a result, protective of the party that supported those benefits. (He eventually fleshed out the theory in a book called *Saving Freedom: We Can Stop America's Slide into Socialism.*)

"The more dependent on government Americans become, the more insecure and fearful they become," DeMint wrote. "Democrats use this fear to manipulate their votes at election time." But if Democrats were guilty of creating this incipient socialist state, DeMint wrote, Republicans were guilty of doing too little to stop it. Too many GOP lawmakers had accommodated themselves to expansion of the welfare state, just as long as they could get projects for their districts—a strategy he called "Democrat lite."[21]

As a congressman and then a senator, DeMint compiled one of the most conservative voting records in Congress—breaking with party leadership, along with President Bush, to oppose the Medicare drug benefit and Bush's failed-effort bipartisan immigration reform. McConnell's strategy of total opposition following the 2008 election meant DeMint was back in sync with leadership, although there was a critical difference between the two men. McConnell was primarily focused on gaining and keeping power for his party. DeMint was trying to change the party itself.[22]

DeMint had lots of company. Advocacy organizations like Americans for Prosperity, funded by conservative financiers Charles and David Koch, had spent years pushing the GOP to take a harder line against government spending and regulation. In 2009, they were as determined to stop Democratic health care reforms as DeMint was. Operating through an umbrella group called the Health Care Freedom Coalition, they financed bus transportation to events and anti-reform advertisements—and let Republican officials know that supporting a Democratic bill would incur their wrath in 2010. As an example, they would point to their support of Pat Toomey, a conservative congressman in Pennsylvania, who announced he was challenging incumbent GOP senator Arlen Specter following Specter's vote in favor of the Obama economic stimulus package.[23]

That challenge from Toomey had a major effect on health reform, because it convinced Specter to switch parties in April, giving Democrats fifty-nine votes in the Senate. Two months later, the Minnesota Supreme Court rejected final challenges to recounts of that state's contested Senate election, effectively awarding the seat to Al Franken—and bringing the Democratic majority to sixty, which meant they had enough to overcome a filibuster. If conservatives wanted to stop reform, they would have to persuade at least one Democratic senator or a bunch of House Democrats to vote no.

Town hall meetings felt like the place to make that happen. Conservative activists started descending upon them in late July, right around the time of DeMint's Waterloo press conference, and many seemed to be following a script, later obtained by Lee Fang of ThinkProgress, that a volunteer had posted online at a widely read conservative bulletin board.

"Spread out in the hall and try to be in the front half," the volunteer wrote. "The Rep should be made to feel that a majority, and if not, a significant portion of at least the audience, opposes the socialist agenda of Washington." The posting included policy talking points from groups like FreedomWorks, another organization in the anti-reform coalition, and it encouraged activists to disrupt the normal flow of conversation. "You need to rock-the-boat early in the Rep's presentation. Watch for an opportunity to yell out and challenge the Rep's statements early. . . . The goal is to rattle him, get him off his prepared script and agenda. If he says something outrageous, stand up and shout out and sit right back down."[24]

4.

A scene just like that unfolded in a western Detroit suburb one evening in early August. The overflow crowd that arrived to meet John Dingell was so big that staff agreed to have a second meeting right after the first. One activist had brought a poster of Obama with a Hitler mustache drawn on it. Another had a sign that said, "Abortion is not health care." As Dingell prepared to speak, and the initial applause died down, a man named Mike Sola started shouting, "Mr. Dingell, I have a question!" Then he came forward, pushing his adult son in a wheelchair, until he was just a few feet away from the congressman.

"I have a question for this young man," Sola said several times, vigorously jabbing his finger toward the floor each time. "I'm his father, and I want to talk to you, face-to-face, not put a question on paper that you're going to avoid. Under the Obama health care plan, which you support, this man would be given no care whatsoever, because he is a cerebral palsy handicapped person." Dingell started shaking his head, to say no. Sola kept going. "Dr. Ezekiel Emanuel stated, people with cerebral palsy are no good." Dingell, whose glare had for decades petrified so many committee witnesses in Washington, was taken aback and started to talk about an amendment in the proposal. Sola was having none of it: "You voted a death sentence for this young man. . . . You're a fraud, and you're sentencing this person to death under the Obama plan." Clips of the scene played on the evening network news and went viral on right-wing message boards.[25]

A day later, Dingell invited Sola to meet with his staff one-on-one. When he got no response, he posted an open letter to Sola making the case for Democratic reforms, with particular attention to how he thought it would help people with disabilities. As it happens, this had been one of the messages Dingell had hoped to convey at the meeting. The introductory speaker was Marcia Boehm, a local social worker and small business owner with a disability. Boehm talked about the difficulty she had encountered trying to find insurance because of her preexisting condition, and said the debate was about "who deserves health care and who doesn't."[26]

She, too, got interrupted. "She's a plant," one audience member said of Boehm, who stood less than four feet tall. "Go home, lady," said another.[27]

Reform supporters had turned out in large numbers, as well, and this was no accident. As soon as news of the coming protests spread in late July, liberal organizations like MoveOn and HCAN began alerting their members and mobilizing a response. By the end of the month, they were frequently showing up in greater numbers than the anti-reform activists, though they got less media attention.[28]

Among the talking points they emphasized was how the big conservative organizations, supposedly out to protect the disabled and elderly, had long pushed to cut or privatize Medicare and Medicaid, on which disabled and elderly Americans depended. The liberals also noted that Conservatives for Patients' Rights, the group that had convened DeMint's Waterloo call, was funded and led by Rick Scott. Scott had become famous—and very rich—as the head of Columbia/HCA, a hospital company that, after his departure, had to pay more than $1.7 billion in criminal fines and civil damages for fraudulent Medicare billing.[29]

That history led some reformers to write off the health care protests as "astroturfing," the practice in which advocacy organizations promoting unpopular positions finance grassroots demonstrations to give their agendas the veneer of popular support. But Chris Savage, a liberal Michigan activist who was at the Dingell event, warned against making assumptions. "I know it's popular these last few days to talk about astroturfing and corporate sponsorship of protesters," Savage wrote in a blog post. "However, I don't think much of that was going on tonight. These people are angry and afraid. . . . These people were there tonight because they wanted to be."[30]

They were also part of a broader conservative uprising, the Tea Party movement, which traced its lineage back to a rant about Obama's economic plans that CNBC commentator Rick Santelli made back in April 2009. Santelli's big complaint was that, under Obama's plan, relief money would be going to people who defaulted on home loans, and many of them should never have taken out the loans in the first place. As Santelli put it, Obama and the Democrats wanted to "subsidize the losers' mortgages."[31]

This distinction between the deserving and the undeserving—and the associated argument that liberals were always using taxpayer dollars from the former to support the latter—had been a politically potent pillar of conservative rhetoric going back to the days of Reagan's attack on welfare queens. It was also an animating sentiment behind the Tea Party movement, as a trio of Harvard political scientists, including Theda Skocpol, later concluded after an exhaustive review of public opinion data and in-depth interviews with activists. "Tea Partiers are not monolithically hostile toward government," the scholars wrote. "They distinguish between programs perceived as going to hard-working contributors to U.S. society like themselves and 'handouts' perceived as going to unworthy or freeloading people."[32]

Democrats were hyperaware of political danger that the welfare stigma posed to health care reform. Especially at the White House, officials did their best to inoculate themselves and legislation by emphasizing how reform was supposed to reduce costs for middle-class people who already had insurance—and by deemphasizing how much money would be going to a dramatically expanded Medicaid program.[33]

But the promises on lower costs provoked as much disbelief as hope, while the emerging legislation really did envision a massive increase in spending on low-income Americans. And many of them had dark skin.[34]

5.

The racial subtext to the conservative backlash was impossible to miss, in part because sometimes it was the text. Rush Limbaugh said the emerging legislation was actually "a civil rights bill, this is reparations, whatever you want to call it." Posters depicting Obama as an African witch doctor appeared regularly at Tea Party protests.[35]

Conservative leaders dismissed such displays as the product of a fringe element. But those signs and slogans were consistent with survey information showing that Tea Party voters were substantially more likely than other Americans, and even other conservatives, to agree with statements like "if blacks would only try harder they could be just as well off as whites."[36]

These sentiments were rooted, Theda Skocpol and her colleagues found, in a deeper anxiety that the election of an African American president had triggered. "Rather than conscious, deliberate, and publicly expressed racism, these racial resentments form part of a nebulous fear about generational societal change. As we have seen, many Tea Partiers are deeply concerned that the country they live in is not the country of their youth—and that they themselves are no longer represented by the US government."[37]

It is impossible to know how much these sentiments affected perceptions of the emerging legislation. Certainly, there were plenty of conservatives who opposed Democratic reforms for substantive or political reasons that had nothing to do with race. But the black-white divide on Obama's health care effort was bigger, by twenty points, than it had been for Bill Clinton's, according to one study. Another found evidence that Obama's sponsorship of health reform was a "source cue" that activated white racial animus.[38]

Administration officials, aware of these dynamics and how Obama's ability to win over skeptical white voters had fueled his political rise, were eager to steer the conversation away from race. "If we appeared to be dismissing opposition to Obama's policies as racism, it would enrage all those who had honest concerns about his legislative priorities, including millions who had voted for him," David Axelrod wrote in his memoir. But stopping the conversation about health care from becoming a conversation about race was a constant struggle for Obama and his team—never more so, perhaps, than in a late July news conference in the East Room.[39]

It was a week after DeMint's Waterloo comments, which Obama had been using in his own remarks to decry GOP tactics. Now Obama had a chance to answer some of the policy attacks coming from the right—going on for several minutes, at one point, to explain why getting data on the effectiveness of treatments wasn't the same thing as establishing a death panel. But coverage the next day focused almost entirely on the evening's last question, which wasn't on health care. It was about an African American professor at Harvard whom police had arrested at his own home, after a bystander called to report a possible burglary.[40]

The professor, Henry Louis Gates Jr., couldn't get his front door open and eventually walked around the back, letting himself in with a key. The arresting officer, who was white, said that Gates had responded belligerently to requests for information when police arrived. Obama chastised the police, noting that "there's a long history in this country of African Americans and Latinos being stopped by law enforcement disproportionately." Days of controversy followed, with police unions demanding an apology and critics accusing Obama of unnecessarily turning the arrest into a racial incident.[41]

Obama, who had staked so much of his political life on bridging racial divides, said afterward he wished he had spoken more carefully, so as not to malign the arresting officer or the Cambridge police. He also invited the officer and Gates to the White House to chat over afternoon drinks on the patio. The Beer Summit, as it came to be known, put the controversy to rest, more or less, although the reaction to the episode was another reminder of race's potency in politics. Twenty-six percent of blacks thought Obama acted stupidly, according to a CNN poll. Among whites, the percentage was 63.[42]

6.

Whatever role race was playing in public perceptions, support for the health care effort was falling. In April, 51 percent had approved of Obama's handling of health care, while only 26 percent disapproved, according to the Pew Research Center. In July, only 42 percent approved while 43 percent disapproved.[43]

The original plan had been to move the legislation out of committee and maybe even get through floor votes in both houses before the August recess, so that the two chambers could spend the early fall negotiating over a final version and Obama could sign it before Thanksgiving. The House and Senate HELP were on that timeline. Finance wasn't, because Baucus was still on his quixotic bid to win Republican support.[44]

At one point in the late spring, Baucus had his staff draw up a list of every Republican senator who could conceivably vote in favor of reform, based on the reaction he'd gotten in one-on-one meetings over the past months. It included sixteen Republicans. But the list quickly winnowed to four negotiating partners, and in June, one of them, Orrin Hatch, signaled he, too, was out.[45]

As much as any Republican senator, Hatch made overtures to Democrats, going back to late 2008 when he had his staff approach Kennedy's about a one-on-one collaboration. Nancy DeParle, who met with dozens of Republican lawmakers over the course of the year, later recalled that it was a meeting with Hatch at the Capitol that may have gone on for the longest time—because they'd gotten deep in the weeds of policy, and Hatch wanted to keep the conversation going but was constantly stepping out for floor votes. She ended up staying there for several hours.[46]

But however serious Hatch was or wasn't about legislating, his substantive views did not overlap with Democrats' enough to make a deal possible. He opposed the new regulations and the proposed expansion of Medicaid, which he said would put too great a strain on state finances. He was likewise against any bill with spending that approached $1 trillion, as Democratic bills did. In short, he was still a conservative representing a conservative state—and he believed that what Democrats were trying to do would be bad for the country. "I really commend them for the effort," Hatch said, announcing his departure. "What I don't want to do is mislead people by continuing to be in the meetings when I disagree with much of the direction I feel they have to go."[47]

Of the three remaining Republicans, Wyoming's Mike Enzi seemed the least likely to say yes, and even some Republican staffers wondered why he was there. During the Gang of Six meetings, Enzi would say little; then, when giving updates at Republican caucus meetings, he would report that he was hard at work, pushing the negotiations in a Republican direction. "We all watched that and went, 'What?'" one GOP aide said later. "I don't want to call a sitting senator disingenuous but that's not what was happening."[48]

Olympia Snowe, from Maine, was a different story. She represented a New England state that, despite some more conservative, rural pockets was generally liberal and supportive of Democrats. She also liked to bury herself in policy detail. Obama met with her several times, as did Peter Orszag, who visited Snowe while on vacation in Maine. During these discussions, Snowe would provide lists of requests that aligned frequently with Democratic priorities. She talked a lot, for example, about making sure subsidies were sufficiently generous to make coverage truly affordable. But whenever Baucus and the White House would say okay, she would say she needed more time to think.[49]

If Snowe seemed to many Democrats painfully indecisive, Charles Grassley seemed just as conflicted. Throughout the spring and summer, he would use his Twitter account to launch disjointed, inscrutable missives. When Obama, during a trip to France, said he wished the Senate would move along more quickly, Grassley responded quickly. "Pres Obama while u sightseeing in Paris u said 'time to deliver on healthcare' When you are a 'hammer' u think everything is NAIL I'm no NAIL." But sometimes Grassley spoke fondly of the president, at one point telling a delegation of Iowa business leaders that Obama "wants to get it done yesterday, and that's about the only thing that's inflexible about President Obama. On the issues that are key, he is willing to look at compromises."[50]

Still, Grassley was under pressure from fellow Republicans, including his Senate colleagues. At one caucus meeting, Judd Gregg of New Hampshire ripped into him, literally yelling (according to one staffer's account) that Grassley was defying conservative principles and helping Obama simply by being part of negotiations. Back home, Grassley was facing threats of a primary challenge from the right. "There's so much talk of primarying Chuck Grassley now," Bill Salier, an Iowa conservative, said during a radio broadcast. He went on to say that Grassley's experience would mean "bupkis if what you do with that power is work with Max Baucus to try to advance socialized medicine."[51]

Those sentiments helped explain why Grassley had wanted Enzi to stay at the table. He'd said frequently he didn't want to be the only Republican supporting reform. And Snowe, an apostate from New England, didn't count.[52]

Grassley kept telling Baucus he wanted to keep the discussions going. Baucus, in turn, reported as much to the White House, promising repeatedly that a deal was nearly at hand. Back in late June, Baucus had said he would have a "chairman's mark" (the format that Senate Finance uses to write legislation) by July 1, according to one aide's notes. The date came and went, and no mark appeared. The negotiations continued, and sometimes Obama would call Baucus directly, pulling him out of Gang of Six conversations as they were happening; Baucus would tell the president that they were making progress, then return to the table. On Capitol Hill, frustrated Democratic staff schemed for ways to win over Grassley. Among the ideas that came up in discussion were promising Grassley that SEIU would canvass on his behalf if he supported the legislation, one Democratic aide told me. (It's not clear how serious the discussion got or whether SEIU would have agreed.)[53]

One evening in July, DeParle arrived at Grassley's office for a late meeting. As she waited, a Grassley aide pulled her aside to say that the senator still wanted to find a way to yes, but that his decision might hinge on whether he had decided on seeking reelection. Inside the office, Grassley—who had grown up on a farm and still owned one—stared out the window while the sun set, musing about how much he liked driving a tractor. DeParle took it as a sign he was leaning against running, which meant his vote was still in play. Later that month, with the August recess approaching, Grassley fueled those hopes with an interview on National Public Radio. "We're on the edge, and almost there," he said.[54]

But for every hopeful sign on Grassley, there was a discouraging one. Whatever his intentions going into negotiations, whatever his true feelings about reform, it became increasingly clear he wasn't going to break with his leadership. At a White House meeting with the Gang of Six, Grassley and Obama got into a one-on-one conversation. Exactly who said what and in what sequence remained the subject of dispute long afterward, but multiple sources recalled Obama asking Grassley whether he'd promise to vote yes if every one of his demands were met—and Grassley saying no.[55]

The real tell about Grassley's intentions, for many officials, was something he said publicly, in the middle of August at a constituent event in Iowa. "There is some fear because in the House bill, there is counseling for end of life," Grassley said. "And from that standpoint, you have every right to fear. . . . I don't have any problem with things like living wills. But they ought to be done within the family. We should not have a government program that determines if you're going to pull the plug on grandma." DeParle, who later said she was among the White House aides who had held out the most hope for bipartisanship, saw the clip and realized it was time to move on.[56]

Baucus's staff did too. But their boss hadn't. He kept talking about how he'd crossed party lines to support Grassley on the Medicare drug bill—and all the Grassley ideas, like a requirement that drug and device companies disclose payments to doctors, that Baucus had incorporated into the bill. He was "clinging with his fingernails," as one senior Senate aide put it.[57]

7.

The controversy over the special interest deals, the protests at the town halls, the futility of the Grassley courtship—it was precisely the kind of political quagmire skeptics had always predicted and, for the president and his advisers, a potential inflection point.

At an Oval Office meeting in August, Axelrod gave an update on dismal private polling, which matched dismal public polling by news organizations. Rahm, more convinced than ever he was reliving the Clinton nightmare, proposed the president look for a deal on a much smaller package, maybe something focusing primarily on kids.

Phil Schiliro was less pessimistic. Lanky, with permanently arched eyebrows and a broad, easy smile, Schiliro was so unflappable it sometimes unnerved colleagues. At a meeting with DeParle and Sebelius a few months earlier, he had sketched out his vision for how legislation would get through Congress—not in a memo, but on the back of a scrap of paper. He drew a straight line for about an inch, then a bunch of up-and-down squiggles, and then an inch of straight line again. ("He had lots of turbulent lines in the middle," Sebelius mused later.) That drawing, he said, was what it would look like from the outside: an organized start followed by a bunch of chaos until, almost miraculously, Congress would come together and pass something.[58]

By summer, the debate had clearly entered the chaos-squiggle phase. Schiliro asked Obama if he felt lucky, and Obama, reprising a mantra about his improbable rise to the White House, said, "My name is Barack Obama. I'm president of the United States. I wake up every day, and I feel lucky."[59]

One aide, less confident than Obama or Schiliro, remembered leaving the meeting and thinking, "Holy shit, we're doing this because the president feels lucky." Axelrod, also skeptical, later told me that he wasn't surprised—and thought back to a conversation a few weeks earlier, when he'd been in the Oval Office shortly after the president had returned from a trip to Wisconsin.[60]

"I reported to him that we were losing altitude, and health care was a big reason for it," Axelrod recalled. "And he said, 'Yeah, but I just got back from Green Bay and I met a woman, she's thirty-six years old, two kids, married, has health coverage, she's got stage three breast cancer and she's hitting her lifetime cap. And you know, she's scared she's gonna die and leave her family bankrupt. . . . That's not the country we believe in, so let's just keep fighting.'

"There's plenty of folks who were encouraging him to stand down," Axelrod said. "He just refused."[61]

Fifteen

Madam Speaker

1.

For Democrats, the low point of August was the death of Ted Kennedy, who finally succumbed to brain cancer.

It was not a surprise to anybody, and although Kennedy had kept in close touch with his staff until nearly the very end, he had for several months been handing over his responsibilities on health legislation—metaphorically to Baucus, who was leading his negotiations at the Finance Committee, and literally to his friend Chris Dodd, who was effectively running Kennedy's HELP committee for him. The Connecticut Democrat was another senior statesman with a talent for dealmaking, and Kennedy had been proud on July 15 when, with Dodd presiding, HELP became the first of the five committees working on reform to pass a bill. "As you vote today, know that I am with you in heart and mind and soul," Kennedy said in a statement that Dodd read aloud.[1]

Not a single Republican voted for it, even though it included literally dozens of GOP amendments, and Enzi, who served on HELP as well as Finance, slammed it as the foundation for a "government takeover." Hatch, who also served on both committees, would later say chances for bipartisanship on the committee had ended when Kennedy could no longer lead discussions—although the same reservations that led Hatch to step away from Baucus's bill might have led him to part ways with Kennedy, as well.[2]

The memorial and funeral mass at a 130-year-old church in Boston offered a respite from the partisanship of the health debate—and featured, among its many tributes, a poem Hatch said he wrote by hand on his way to Massachusetts for the services: "He leaves the earth a better place. In the end, the good things won. He cared for all the human race. . . . I will miss my Irish friend. God be with you till we meet again." Obama's eulogy took the full measure of Kennedy's life, touching delicately on Kennedy's "personal failings and setbacks" while praising his personal and political magnanimity—and recognizing his deep impact on American society. "He was given the gift of time that his brothers were not," Obama said, "and he used that gift to touch as many lives and right as many wrongs as the years would allow."

Obama was back in Washington a week later, where he and several officials ended up in yet another conversation about whether to scale back their ambitions. It ended the same way every other such conversation had: with Obama saying he was determined to keep pursuing a comprehensive bill, not a narrowly focused one. "Download on POTUS. I don't want to do targeted and leave out group," one aide wrote down at the time.[3]

But Obama and his advisers also thought it was time to assert more control over the process.

They decided, first, to write their own legislation and let Baucus know they were preparing to give it to Reid. Best-case scenario, they figured, the prospect of ceding control to the White House would prod Baucus into presenting a bill to his full committee for markup. Worst case, Baucus would do nothing. In that case, they'd go ahead and give the bill to Reid, who could then combine it with the HELP bill and present it to the full Senate for consideration. The legislation was to be a secret project, with a single paper copy that aides could see only by entering a locked room. "No fucking leaks," one aide remembers Rahm warning. Another recalled Rahm making a threat involving the removal of key anatomical parts.[4]

Obama would also give a speech. He had great confidence in his ability as a persuader—and he wanted a chance to make his case, the way he wanted it, in front of a prime-time national audience.

The speech was scheduled for the Wednesday after Labor Day. Speechwriter Jon Favreau worked furiously to finish a first draft before the weekend, because his friend and fellow White House staffer Ben Rhodes was getting married in Los Angeles. Favreau had offered to stay in Washington; Obama, who also knew Rhodes, said Favreau should go. But at 6:00 a.m. California time, on the morning after the wedding, Favreau woke to a phone call from Reggie Love, Obama's personal assistant; the boss needed him back right away because he had extensive revisions to discuss.

Favreau found the first flight he could, and when he landed in Washington, his BlackBerry was full of new, increasingly urgent messages from colleagues about his whereabouts. Favreau went straight to the White House, wearing a beer T-shirt and ripped jeans, talking his way through the northwest gate because his security badge was at home. (Secret Service eventually found an agent who recognized him.) "What happened to you?" Obama chuckled when Favreau finally arrived in the West Wing. "You don't look too good."

Obama had written out his revisions in neat longhand, as he customarily did, filling the margins and spaces between paragraphs and carefully drawing arrows to the passages that needed changes. Mostly, Obama wanted to hit harder on responding to the attacks critics had made on the bill. This was very much the opposite of what communications strategists typically recommend. To answer a criticism, the thinking goes, is to repeat and amplify it. Obama said this situation was different. The arguments about death panels, blowing up the deficit, and destroying employer coverage were out there already. This was his best chance to refute them.[5]

On the night of the speech, Obama did just that and provoked what for many people was its most memorable moment. One of the arguments circulating among conservatives was that reform would provide insurance to undocumented immigrants. It was an especially powerful charge because it fed right into Tea Party tropes about the deserving and undeserving. In reality, Democratic leaders had gone out of their way to avoid spending government money on undocumented workers, though many thought it was the right thing to do, precisely because they knew it was politically toxic.[6]

When Obama said as much, explaining that "the reforms I'm proposing would not apply to those who are here illegally," Joe Wilson, a Republican congressman from South Carolina, shouted, "You lie!" Behind the podium, Pelosi whipped her head around, mouth open and eyes wide in disbelief. Biden looked over and then down, shaking his head in disgust. Obama stopped himself from starting his next line, paused, and said, "It's not true."[7]

The last part of the speech was also its most emotional—and for one final time in the health care debate, Ted Kennedy supplied the inspiration. The day before the speech, his widow, Vicki, had faxed over a letter that Ted wrote in the spring, to be delivered upon his death. The main subject of the letter was health care reform, which Kennedy described as "that great unfinished business of our society," and Obama decided to quote from it. "'It concerns more than material things. What we face,' he wrote, 'is above all a moral issue; at stake are not just the details of policy, but fundamental principles of social justice and the character of our country.'"

That last part, Obama told the assembled lawmakers, made him think about Kennedy's life—and how the bedrock idea of Kennedy's liberalism was not that the government had all the answers but that the government was the way Americans came together to help one another in times of need. "Ted Kennedy's passion was born not of some rigid ideology, but of his own experience," Obama said. "It was the experience of having two children stricken with cancer. He never forgot the sheer terror and helplessness that any parent feels when a child is badly sick. And he was able to imagine what it must be like for those without insurance, what it would be like to have to say to a wife or a child or an aging parent, there is something that could make you better, but I just can't afford it.

"That large-heartedness—that concern and regard for the plight of others—is not a partisan feeling," Obama went on to say, echoing some of the arguments he'd made back in Springfield years before. "It, too, is part of the American character—our ability to stand in other people's shoes; a recognition that we are all in this together, and when fortune turns against one of us, others are there to lend a helping hand; a belief that in this country, hard work and responsibility should be rewarded by some measure of security and fair play; and an acknowledgment that sometimes government has to step in to help deliver on that promise."

There were no signs that Obama's closing paean to bipartisanship moved any Republicans. But the invocation of Kennedy, along with Wilson's outburst, had succeeded in rallying the Democrats—in the country and, especially, in the House chamber.

"He didn't have to move the public as a whole," one adviser said later. "He needed to move one hundred nervous people sitting in the room there with him."[8]

2.

Hours before the speech, Baucus had announced that he wasn't waiting on the Gang of Six anymore. He formally released a summary of his proposal, which reflected negotiations up to that date, and said the Finance Committee would formally take up the measure in two weeks, regardless of whether any of the GOP members had signed on to it by then.

Whether Obama's speech and threat to submit his own bill prodded Baucus to act is unclear; administration and Finance aides tell the story differently. Either way, the process was moving forward again—not just in the Senate but also in the House, where Pelosi had held off taking legislation to the floor. She wasn't going to subject her members to another tough vote, like she had on cap and trade, until she was sure the Senate was moving ahead too.

But after Obama's speech, Pelosi was angry. And the reason wasn't Joe Wilson's breach of protocol. It was a single passage in the address, the part where Obama explained that reform "will cost around $900 billion over ten years."

Over the past few months, while death panels, drug industry deals, and town hall protests had been soaking up all the media attention, the magnitude of reform legislation—that is, the number of new dollars the government would be spending under the plan—was a constant preoccupation for Democratic officials and lawmakers. The vast majority of new spending would be paying for people's health insurance, either through Medicaid or federally subsidized private coverage. As a result, the dollar size of the bill was the single best way to measure how much help it would provide the American people, which in turn was the single best way to measure just how "affordable" health insurance would become.

All year long, the debate had hovered around $1 trillion in outlays. It wasn't enough to finance insurance for everybody or to guarantee the kind of generous coverage that European, Canadian, and East Asian systems provided. But it represented the maximum that many political strategists felt lawmakers could (or would be willing to) defend before their voters. And now Obama was knocking it down by another $100 million.

The figure hadn't come out of thin air. Conservative Democrats, especially in the Senate, had been pushing to keep spending below $900 billion. But House leaders felt like they had already stretched the dollars as far as they would go—by, for example, relying more heavily on Medicaid, which was cheaper per person than private insurance—while largely avoiding superfluous congressional giveaways that would add to the bill's total price tag. Reducing expenditures further was going to mean less help for people who needed it.[9]

Worst of all, House leaders later said, the White House hadn't even given them a heads-up that the $900 billion figure was coming. Pelosi and her lieutenants learned about the number when they read it in the advance copy or heard it during the speech. One former aide later remembered it as a "total gut punch and surprise to all of us."[10]

Afterward, several administration officials went to Pelosi's office. The Speaker didn't curse, except by implication. She was known to say things like, "What is this cow pie?" But she let the officials have it; they reassured her the figure had some built-in flexibility. Pelosi accepted that and, with her leadership team and staff, began finalizing a bill that she believed could get the 218 votes it needed to pass.[11]

3.

Pelosi was good at this, even her critics conceded, and maybe as good as anybody who had held the job in modern times.

She had learned the art of transactional politics from her father, Thomas D'Alesandro Jr., a congressman and later mayor of Baltimore. She understood that the key was developing a detailed sense of each member's preferences and needs—on papers and index cards, but preferably by memory as well. She made sure she understood each lawmaker's political vulnerabilities, and no less important, she made sure each member knew she understood their political vulnerabilities—so that, when she needed to ask for a tough vote, they believed she was still looking out for their well-being and would find some way to help them later. She also believed acts of personal kindness made a difference. When she learned a member's parent or close relative had died, she would make sure to call or send a note at the holidays, just to say she knew how difficult that time of year could be after the loss of a loved one.[12]

Pelosi had been a supporter of government health programs since the late 1980s, when she was a new House member from San Francisco rallying support to fight the AIDS epidemic. She did not mind the label "liberal," at least for herself, and would have been pleased with legislation that created a European-style system. She was in that sense an old-school Democrat who believed the government's job was to provide for the welfare of its citizens, and she didn't see any need to rely on private insurance companies to do it.

But Pelosi was hyperaware of the competing demands within her caucus, as well as the party's reliance on financiers who looked askance at too much government spending and regulation. She was a prolific fundraiser and had been since even before she got to Congress, back in the 1970s and early 1980s, when she hosted events for Democrats at her home. She did not consider "compromise" a dirty word, and neither did the people around her. Her health care adviser was Wendell Primus, who had publicly resigned from the Clinton administration rather than support a welfare reform bill he believed would punish the poor. But he drew a distinction between a bill he thought would hurt vulnerable people and one that, however short of his ideals, would help many millions of them.[13]

The legislation Pelosi introduced to the full House in late October lived up to that standard and had just a few notable modifications from the three committee bills upon which it was based. The new proposal envisioned more people going into Medicaid, by setting the eligibility threshold at 150 percent of the poverty line rather than 133. The minimum coverage standard for middle-class people buying insurance on the new exchanges was not as strong; in other words, the new bill had a lower "floor" on benefits.

The new House bill had a public option, but it would not get to take advantage of Medicare's low payment rates, which pleased more conservative Democrats and their backers in the health care industry. Future generations would have to improve on that, as they would for other provisions. But the bill's reach was still substantial; thirty-five to thirty-six million people would get insurance, according to the CBO, leaving just 4 percent of non-elderly legal residents without.[14]

With the legislation public, Pelosi began lining up the votes, working at her typically frenetic pace. Day after day, the diminutive sixty-nine-year-old lawmaker would outhustle younger counterparts—and exhaust her staff—by pigeonholing colleagues on the floor, scampering from meeting to meeting, and making calls anytime she had a few minutes to spare. During one day in health care negotiations, the *Los Angeles Times* reported, she got on the phone with fifty different members of her caucus. She still found time for fundraisers, speeches, and ceremonial duties, typically by working late into the evening and frequently past midnight. "Apparently she doesn't sleep or eat," Louise Slaughter, a Democratic congresswoman from New York, told the *Times*.[15]

But as of early November, the bill remained about 18 to 20 votes short of the 218 needed to pass. Even with the public option concession and even with a lot of help from Steny Hoyer, the majority whip who had better relationships with conservative Democrats, Blue Dogs were coming out against the bill, saying it was too much government and too much spending. Pelosi and her allies tried tinkering with regional funding formulas, specific employer requirements—really, anything that could get a vote or two. Obama lobbied wavering members personally. Nothing was working.[16]

Pelosi had one big play left, a play she had wanted very badly not to run.

4.

Abortion came up every time Congress considered starting or reauthorizing a program that provided health care to women. Four years after the Supreme Court legalized abortion in 1972, Henry Hyde, a Republican congressman from Illinois, won approval for a new requirement, valid for one year, prohibiting federal Medicaid funds from financing abortion. Each year after, abortion rights opponents in the House would introduce the Hyde Amendment to the annual HHS appropriation bill, eventually applying it to all federal health programs. It passed every time, thanks in part to support from Democratic lawmakers who said they supported keeping abortion legal but not asking taxpayers to fund it. (Among those Democrats was Joe Biden. He switched his position and renounced the Hyde Amendment in 2019, right as he was preparing to run for president.)[17]

Leading Democratic advocates for abortion rights had long wanted to eliminate the Hyde requirement, although they weren't looking to do so with the health care reform bill. They didn't want to jeopardize the legislation and thought the bills out of the three House committees were actually consistent with Hyde anyway. Under the language in those proposals, private insurance plans available through the new regulated marketplaces had to have a separate pool of money for abortion services. And that pool could not include any money from government insurance subsidies. Several states used similar arrangements in their Medicaid programs.[18]

A group of antiabortion Democrats, led by Michigan's Bart Stupak, said they considered the proposed segregation of funds meaningless. Stupak represented Michigan's upper peninsula, a rural area that had more in common politically with Appalachia than Detroit. He told Pelosi that he was following the guidance of the Conference of Catholic Bishops, a group that had been making this case for weeks. The subject had even come up at Ted Kennedy's funeral, when, as *The Washington Post* subsequently reported, the archbishop of Boston pulled Obama aside to say that the bishops were enthusiastic about reform but had big concerns about the abortion arrangements.[19]

This was too much for abortion rights advocates. Under every projection, the majority of people buying private insurance through the new markets would be getting some kind of federal assistance. If insurance companies covering abortion had to turn away those customers, then they would simply decide not to cover abortion rather than lose the business—

effectively making insurance coverage for abortion unavailable to millions of people buying private insurance on their own. This wasn't respecting the Hyde Amendment, these Democrats said. This was expanding it.

Pelosi felt the same way. She had grown up in a devout Catholic family and treasured a photo from an eighth-grade family trip to Rome when she accompanied her father to meet the pope. She talked about her faith frequently as a source of her morality and would say that she was personally opposed to abortion. But in Congress, she was a fierce defender of abortion rights, because, she said, a woman's ability to control reproductive decisions was a fundamental human liberty. "The church has their position, and we have ours, which is that a woman has free will given to her by God," she explained in a *New York Times* interview years later.[20]

But Pelosi needed Stupak and the members whose votes he carried with him. When she couldn't find a compromise, she invited leaders of the pro-choice caucus to her suite of offices and told them she had no choice: She'd have to give Stupak what he wanted.[21]

Some tears followed, and some tempers flared—with Rosa DeLauro, a liberal Connecticut Democrat, yelling at Pelosi's closest confidant, George Miller, according to one account. (DeLauro said later she didn't actually yell; she merely expressed her anger.) But when they saw Pelosi's whip count, and no way to get 218 without Stupak's bloc, they said they would live with her decision. "I stood my ground," DeLauro later told *Politico*. "The speaker does that, Mr. Miller does that, Hoyer does that. We all stand our ground. We also know, we all know, that you must focus on the endgame, and that's to pass health care."[22]

Even with the Stupak deal in place, it was touch and go. A group of House Democrats, led by Wisconsin's Ron Kind, were balking because they didn't think the bill did enough to align Medicare payments with quality—and because they thought the formula in place would punish states where providers had already found ways to be more efficient. These controversies over regional disparities got almost no attention in the national press, but they were a constant source of tension, and at a late-night meeting before the floor vote, they threatened to blow up the whole process when a frustrated Kind got up to leave. Pelosi promptly blocked his path to the door, clasped his hands, and said he needed to hear her out. He sat down after about a minute and listened, while Pelosi appealed to his sense of practicality (his district would still see enormous benefits, she said) and history (this would be a once-in-a-generation achievement, she reminded him), while promising to revisit the issue at some later date. Kind would end up voting yes.[23]

With the wavering factions on board, it was time to vote. First up was a Republican reform alternative, which John Boehner, the minority leader from Ohio, had introduced days before. Like most of the other Republican health plans that had been circulating in Congress and in conservative think tanks, it relied primarily on tax breaks to make insurance more affordable. The total financial assistance amounted to less than one-tenth of what House Democrats were proposing to offer, according to the CBO, and as a result, the GOP bill would cover less than one-tenth as many people. And by allowing the purchase of insurance across state lines, a favorite conservative reform, it would undermine existing regulations on what insurance had to cover. (Insurers, like credit card companies, would likely gravitate to the states with the fewest rules.) One side effect was that, even as insurance became less expensive for some healthy people, it would become more expensive for some with serious medical problems. That bill failed.

Then it was time for the Democratic bill, which passed with 220 votes—including a lone Republican, Anh "Joseph" Cao of Louisiana, who had switched from no to yes when Stupak got his way. But otherwise, it was a party-line vote, with many Republicans denouncing it harshly. Paul Ryan, a Wisconsin Republican, called it "perhaps the worst bill I have seen come to the floor in my 11 years in Congress."

Even some Democrats signaled their votes were reluctant. "This bill will get better in the Senate," said Jim Cooper, a conservative Tennessee Democrat who'd said the legislation was too expensive and had too many regulations. "If we kill it here, it won't have a chance to get better." Diana DeGette, a Colorado representative and cochair of the Pro-Choice Caucus, made clear she was still angry about the Stupak compromise.

Pelosi, mindful of reform's history, expressed no such qualms. "What a night," she said at a press conference following the vote. "For nearly a century, leaders of every party and political philosophy—as far back as Teddy Roosevelt—have called for health care for the American people. For generations, the American people have called for affordable, quality health care for their families. Today, the call will be answered."

But the call was not answered yet, because the path to reform also went through the Senate.

Sixteen

March or Die

1.

Baucus gaveled the Senate Finance Committee into session on the morning of September 22: "My colleagues, this is our opportunity to make history." He had been building to this moment for more than a year, going back to the summer of 2008 when he presided over the Ready to Launch summit. The goal then had been to assemble a broad, bipartisan coalition for reform. That is why he spent so much time in the Gang of Six negotiations with Grassley, Enzi, and Snowe. But Grassley was out, and Enzi, from the looks of things, was never really in. Snowe was the only Republican left.[1]

The proposal Baucus presented to his full committee was mostly the same as the version that, in late July, Grassley had described as "almost there." It was by far the smallest of the bills any of the five congressional committees had produced, with total projected outlays of less than $900 billion over the next ten years. Partly as a result, it proposed to reach the fewest people, cutting off financial assistance at 300 percent of the poverty line rather than 400 percent. In practice, that meant leaving a much bigger chunk of the middle class to buy insurance without the help of federal subsidies.

The Baucus bill had an individual mandate but not a public option, just like Baucus had always said. For financing, it relied heavily on that controversial change to the tax treatment of employer health insurance. For that reason, the CBO said it was the bill with the most potential to "bend the curve" over time.[2]

But the tax change had a twist to it. Working with the White House, Baucus had agreed on a way to scale back the employer tax break while, in theory, staying true to Obama's pledge not to raise taxes on middle-income Americans. The idea, which came from John Kerry, was to tax the insurers directly whenever premiums exceeded a certain dollar threshold. It was a roundabout way of curbing the incentive for generous insurance. That was why the CBO believed it would lower health spending. Employers would push insurers to avoid the tax; insurers would respond by finding new efficiencies or simply offering less generous coverage.[3]

Proponents called it a "Cadillac tax," because the tax would affect only the most expensive insurance plans (i.e., the Cadillac plans). But plenty of people with these plans were the kind of people who, in actual life, drove Chevys. They just happened to work for companies that provided generous benefits, which frequently meant the kind that unions had won in collective bargaining. To the economists, it was a politically clever way to reduce an underlying cause of out-of-control health spending; to the unions, it was a deliberately deceitful way to stick their members and some other middle-class workers with less generous insurance.[4]

The Finance Committee had eight days of hearings, during which it took up 135 amendments. Several of the amendments came from Snowe, including one cosponsored by Chuck Schumer, the New York Democrat, on an amendment reducing the individual mandate penalty for people who did not have insurance. That amendment set off alarms in the insurance industry, which, despite extensive negotiations, had never reached a deal with Baucus.[5]

Like every other group at the bargaining table, insurers had self-interested reasons to be there. The status quo seemed unsustainable, and their reputation as an industry that made profits by excluding sick people was getting worse. At some point, the pressure for action would become impossible to resist. And depending on the details of legislation, reform could end up helping insurer finances by giving them more customers. One person making this case was Karen Ignagni, head of America's Health Insurance Plans (AHIP), who was a former Democratic staffer in Congress and had also worked for the AFL-CIO.

But insurers were still wary of too much change—and worried, especially, that rules requiring them to cover preexisting conditions would saddle them with too many beneficiaries who would run up huge medical bills. The best protection against that, they felt, was a strong individual mandate to keep plenty of healthy people enrolling. With the Schumer-Snowe amendment, they worried that a weak mandate had just become weaker.

In September and October, groups of insurers circulated a pair of reports they had commissioned from private actuaries. Each predicted dramatic premium increases if the bill were to become law. The goal of the reports, industry insiders later said, was merely to show the dangers of an insufficient mandate. But Democrats and their allies interpreted the reports as an effort at sabotaging legislation and a deceptive one at that, because the reports selectively focused on the parts of reform most likely to drive up premiums.[6]

The perception that insurers were being heavy-handed riled up senators like Jay Rockefeller, who had previously accused them of "banditry" because of their treatment of people with preexisting conditions. Rockefeller's vote had been in doubt, partly because Baucus refused to add a public option. But he voted yes, as did all the panel Democrats.[7]

Snowe did too, giving Baucus and the White House their prized Republican vote—a reward for all those hours spent going through her lists and all those amendments added to the final bill. But, Snowe warned, she might still oppose legislation on the floor.

"My vote today is my vote today," she said. "It doesn't forecast what my vote will be tomorrow."[8]

2.

Searchlight, Nevada, is an old mine town about an hour's drive south of Las Vegas. In the late nineteenth and early twentieth centuries, when gold rush activity peaked, some state leaders thought it should become the capital. But the town's bounty proved difficult to extract, and the Great Depression hit hard, interrupted only by a boom from the Hoover Dam project that went bust when construction finished. By the late 1930s, when Harry Reid was born there, the mines had mostly closed, and Searchlight's population, which had peaked decades before at 1,500, had dropped to around 500.[9]

Reid's house, built partly from old railroad ties, didn't have hot water or an indoor toilet. As a teenager, he worked in the mines. He grew up with an abusive father who eventually committed suicide. Reid developed a pugilistic streak that a high school teacher channeled into boxing. "The black eyes and soreness to me were badges of honor to wear the next day," Reid wrote in his memoir, "and I'd fight every chance I got."[10]

Searchlight had no high school; Reid said he would hitch rides to one in a nearby town. He also said it had no doctors. Decades later, he still remembered the time that the state-operated tuberculosis wagon came through and his mother's X-ray was positive. She was petrified but couldn't afford or find care, so did nothing, hoping for the best, and got lucky because the test turned out to be wrong. They handled other medical situations the same way. "My brother broke his leg on a bicycle," Reid told me in an interview. "He laid in bed, his leg is bent even today. So did health care mean a lot to me? It sure did. You bet it did."[11]

Even so, Reid had never made health care reform a priority. He had started in politics as a city attorney and worked his way up from there: state assemblyman, lieutenant governor, chairman of the Nevada gaming commission, U.S. congressman, and finally, in 1987, senator. He wasn't a Baucus or a Kennedy—or a Rockefeller or a Wyden—who sat around thinking up ways to fix the U.S. health care system.

But in January 2009, Reid was the Democratic majority leader for a newly elected Democratic president who wanted to pass health care reform, and he had two powerful committee chairmen equally committed to the cause. "We're going to start getting educated," Kate Leone, his health care adviser, remembered Reid telling her at a staff meeting. "You're going to pick a topic every week, and we'll spend an hour, two hours working on it. You're going to get me up to speed on this."[12]

If Reid didn't have strong feelings on what health care legislation should look like, he did have strong feelings about how it should move through Congress. Reid had a reputation for using bare-knuckle tactics—as he did years later, in 2012, when he would accuse Romney, then running for president, of having never paid taxes. (Romney had, although at a low rate; Reid refused to apologize.)

But Reid was among the Democratic leaders resisting reconciliation, and throughout the spring and summer, he would tell colleagues and the White House to show patience with Baucus—much to the chagrin of some fellow senators and administration officials who thought Reid could be pushing harder. "Max rubbed a lot of people the wrong way," Reid told me, "but I understood Max Baucus." Reid wanted to save his political capital with Baucus for substantive issues, according to one adviser, plus he thought letting the committees work through the bills would improve the chances of passage by giving wavering lawmakers time to get comfortable with the idea and develop some sense of ownership. "It was never-ending," Reid said, "but nobody felt like they were being pushed."[13]

Once the Finance Committee had voted, Reid set out to merge its bill with HELP's, just as Pelosi had done with her committees' work. But compared to the three House bills, which one aide likened to siblings, the Senate bills were more like cousins—the kind who nursed grudges for years. HELP, whose Democratic membership was more liberal than Finance's, had produced legislation that would result in more generous coverage for more people, at a significantly higher cost to the government. Reid had to come up with a fusion that would stay true to White House guidelines and the Baucus industry deals while getting sixty votes from a caucus whose ideologies covered a broad spectrum.

Just to make things more complicated, Reid had to consider the specific policy concessions that individual senators had won and were determined to protect—as well as the concessions they had not gotten but said they still needed. Some senators had more than a dozen asks, and a handful had more than twenty, according to a fourteen-page internal memo detailing them.

The list included major policy priorities, like Wyden's push for waivers, so that states could experiment with different reform models, and Rocke-feller's insistence that CHIP remain a separate program, because he worried that private insurers would not meet children's needs as consistently. But the compendium also included narrower, more parochial requests, like Schum-er's for extra funding of academic medical centers. (New York has a lot of teaching hospitals.) Mary Landrieu, of Louisiana, wanted more Medicaid funding for her state. Evan Bayh wanted to reduce a proposed tax on the device industry, which had a major presence in Indiana and a history of bankrolling his campaigns. Joining him were the senators from Massachu-setts and Minnesota, home to some of the nation's largest medical device makers, plus a few others.[14]

Some of these appeals had more defensible rationales than others. Louisiana's health system, in particular, was still reeling from Hurricane Katrina in 2005. But their impact on the total legislation and Reid's task were the same. Every dollar he agreed to spend on some senator's project or priority was a dollar not available for other purposes, including more generous subsidies.[15]

And then there was the matter of the public option, which was a top priority for more liberal Democrats.

They had blanched at the industry deals, which they believed to be out-rageous giveaways designed (at best) to buy off would-be adversaries or (at worst) exchange favors for future campaign support. They had seethed while Baucus held up the entire process to court a small handful of Republicans who, except maybe for Snowe, had no shared interest in universal coverage.

"We knew that if Baucus could come up with an agreement that Mike Enzi was for, Chuck Grassley was for, it wouldn't be worthwhile," Sherrod Brown, a progressive Democrat from Ohio, said to me later. He was particularly upset because the Gang of Six members represented such a small portion of the population: "The combined number of congressional districts they had in those states were fewer than Ohio." Brown's math was correct. At the time, the combined total of congressional seats from the Gang of Six states was thirteen. Ohio alone had eighteen.[16]

The public option wasn't the only thing liberals wanted to see in the merged Senate bill. But it was the simplest to explain, it was popular with the public as a whole, and it fired up progressive activists. They were making their stand there, and Reid couldn't ignore them.

At the same time, Reid knew, at least a half dozen Democrats had come out against the idea, with more communicating their reservations in private. And one in particular was likely to be a tough sell.[17]

3.

Joe Lieberman of Connecticut was a political anachronism. His home state, like most of the Northeast, was among the most reliably liberal in the country. But on key issues, including the economy and foreign policy, Lieberman was one of the most conservative members of the caucus. During the fight over the Clinton health care plan, Lieberman was, as activist Richard Kirsch later noted in his book, *Fighting for Our Health*, "the only Democratic Senator north of the Mason-Dixon Line who did not endorse a universal health reform bill."[18]

That record didn't stop Al Gore from picking him as a running mate in 2000, and the prospect of Lieberman becoming the first Jewish vice president was enough to make even skeptical progressives excited about his nomination. But the rift between Lieberman and the party's liberal base grew when Lieberman, a vocal proponent of the Iraq War, continued to defend the enterprise long after most Democrats had turned against it. In 2006, a more traditionally liberal Democrat in Connecticut, future governor Ned Lamont, challenged Lieberman in the Senate primary and won.

Lieberman held on to his seat by running as an independent. Afterward, he decided to keep caucusing with Democrats, who agreed to let him keep his chairmanship of the Homeland Security and Government Affairs Committee. Neither side felt great about the arrangement, but it was mutually beneficial. Democrats would still have their 51–49 majority, which they needed as long as a Republican vice president could break tie votes, while Lieberman would still have his committee.

Then came the 2008 presidential campaign, when Lieberman endorsed John McCain. The two were longtime friends and had worked closely on national security issues. But even Democrats inclined to cut Lieberman slack were aghast when he spoke at the Republican convention and used the opportunity to criticize Obama as a neophyte unwilling to stand up to his party or to special interests. After the election, many Democrats wanted to strip Lieberman of his committee chairmanship. It didn't happen, because Reid and Obama were against it. They hoped a show of forgiveness would turn Lieberman into a more reliable ally.[19]

On health care, Lieberman said that he supported the party's basic approach. But he expressed qualms about the public option, which he predicted would run deficits and require extra taxpayer subsidies. Liberals suspected Lieberman's position had less to do with the size of the national debt and more to do with the influence of some large insurance companies, including Aetna and Cigna, that had headquarters in the Hartford area. Still others thought Lieberman was simply acting out a grudge against party leaders who, back in 2006, had backed Lamont after the primary.[20]

Reid's first attempt to bridge the divide was to include a public option in the Senate bill, with a stipulation that states could reject it. Lieberman said no, and, importantly, he threatened to support a filibuster. (Snowe did the same.) Reid then asked a group of ten senators to craft a compromise. Sherrod Brown of Ohio, plus Rockefeller and Schumer, were among the liberals, and Lieberman was supposed to be among the moderates. When he declined to show up, sending a staffer instead, Delaware's Tom Carper took his place.[21]

The group settled on an idea that Howard Dean, who had just finished a term as chairman of the Democratic National Committee, had injected into the conversation: allowing people fifty-five and older to buy into a version of Medicare. For liberals, it was more than a consolation prize. Many had long eyed gradual expansion of Medicare eligibility as a way to move toward single-payer, plus they knew it was older Americans near retirement who frequently struggled the most to find insurance. Lieberman had supported the idea during his 2006 Senate bid and had spoken favorably about it as recently as 2009, in an interview with a Connecticut newspaper. A similar proposal had been part of the official Gore-Lieberman platform in 2000.[22]

Reid announced the deal on the evening of Tuesday, December 8. What happened next was another one of those instances where accounts diverge. Lieberman said that he was wary of the idea from the get-go, felt like Reid was using the announcement to box him in, and sent the majority leader a letter listing his objections. Reid said that Lieberman signed off on the Medicare buy-in and that, as late as Saturday night, he believed Lieberman was a yes. "He agreed to do it," Reid told me. "And then the night went by, and he called me in the morning, and said, 'I'm not going to go with it now.'"[23]

Whatever transpired between the two, on Sunday morning, Lieberman formally announced his opposition to the idea during an appearance on CBS's *Face the Nation*. "We've got to start subtracting some controversial things," Lieberman said. "You've got to take out the Medicare buy-in."[24]

Reid called an emergency meeting in his office. One by one, the key leaders came in: Baucus, Brown, Dodd, and Schumer from the Senate; DeParle and Rahm from the White House. "Everybody was just devastated," Brown said. "I remember Dodd turned to me and said, 'We couldn't even pass a fucking civil rights bill with this crowd.'" Lieberman, summoned by Reid, showed up eventually, and the two talked one-on-one. A day later, Reid decided he was out of alternatives; he was going ahead without the public option.[25]

On Tuesday, when Reid made his decision public, progressives reacted with fury. "This is essentially the collapse of health care reform in the United States Senate," Dean said in a radio interview. "Honestly, the best thing to do right now is kill the Senate bill, go back to the House, start the reconciliation process, where you only need 51 votes and it would be a much simpler bill."[26]

Democratic leadership didn't agree, and neither did Obama, which wasn't surprising given that he and his advisers had never promoted the public option with the enthusiasm liberals had hoped. "The public option, whether we have it or we don't have it is not the entirety of health reform," Obama had said back in the summer in a town hall. "This is just one sliver of it, one aspect of it." His frustration with the bill's detractors on the left lingered even a decade later. In an excerpt from his 2020 memoir, Obama said that he found the "brouhaha exasperating" and recalled grousing to staff, "What is it about sixty votes these folks don't understand?"[27]

The exasperation was entirely mutual. Progressive activists by the fall had compiled a long list of grievances with Obama, who they believed was too quick to give up on their priorities, too timid about pressuring recalcitrant senators, and too in the thrall of centrist advisers who were either out of touch with average Americans (an example was Orszag, who kept pushing the Cadillac tax) or had ties to the health care industry (an example was DeParle, who had served on the boards of health care companies before joining the administration). "They were very good at making it look like they wanted a public option in the final bill without actually doing anything to make it happen," blogger Jane Hamsher told *Politico*, referring to Obama and Reid. "It's hard to believe that the two most powerful people in the country—arguably the world—could not do more to achieve their desired objective than to hand the keys over to Joe Lieberman."[28]

MoveOn called for a vigil at the White House—and put together a sock puppet video, which quickly went viral, of a grouchy Lieberman turning down every effort by his Democratic colleagues to find a compromise he could support. "I would rather see all health care reform die," the puppet Lieberman said in the video, "then cave to the demands of my constituents. And by the way, I've got some demands of my own, people. I'd like to be senator for life. I'd like my name inserted into the Pledge of Allegiance where it said flag before. And I want a pony."[29]

MoveOn, which reported raising more than $1 million from the video over two days, called on its members to contact lawmakers and urge them to block the Senate bill from passing. But none of the lawmakers did, not even the high-profile progressive champions. Although they vowed to fight for a public option in conference committee negotiations, when the House and Senate would have to work out their differences, they said the legislation was too important—and the political process too delicate—to threaten more aggressive action.

"I saw no reason to walk," Sherrod Brown told me later. "I don't think that way. I think you grab what you get. And then you move forward."[30]

4.

Bernie Sanders also wasn't ready to stop reform. But he wasn't ready to pledge his vote yet either.

Sanders, a senator from Vermont, cared about health care as much as anybody on Capitol Hill. His devotion grew out of personal experience—

although, unlike most politicians, he almost never talked about it. According to an account Sydney Ember put together for *The New York Times*, Sanders's mother, whose childhood bout with rheumatic fever had left her with heart damage, died in her forties after a lengthy hospitalization while Sanders was still just a teenager. Her final years were spent dealing with both pain and medical bills the family couldn't pay. Years later, when Sanders became the mayor of Burlington, Vermont, he started to take notice of the people who had gotten health care across the border, in Canada's single-payer system, and became convinced it was what the United States should have as well.[31]

When Sanders first came to Washington as a congressman in 1991, he joined the single-payer crusade that Democratic lawmakers like Paul Wellstone (a Minnesota senator) and Jim McDermott (a Washington congressman) and outside groups like Physicians for a National Health Program had taken up. But their influence did not grow in the ensuing years. If anything, it waned, as the Democratic establishment rallied behind less disruptive reform schemes and eventually the Massachusetts-style reforms, which emphasized the use of private insurance, not public. Single-payer didn't get much attention from the most credentialed and influential economists, who saw more downside than upside in so much government control.[32]

Sanders, who described himself as a democratic socialist and wouldn't formally affiliate with the Democratic Party, did not mind the role of ideological gadfly. In 2009, he freely acknowledged that single-payer had nowhere near the votes it needed to pass. Like other progressives, he had pinned his hopes for reform on a robust public option, partly in the hopes it would be the first step toward single-payer that outside advocates hoped it would be. Like other progressives, he was livid that moderates had forced it out.

Sanders had a reputation as something of a loner—a member who enjoyed making fiery speeches and introducing politically fanciful legislation more than working with his colleagues on policy negotiation. "I'm not good at backslapping," he conceded in an interview with the *New York Times* editorial board years later. "I'm not good at pleasantries." That also made him more inscrutable, and throughout the fall, DeParle worried that he would hold up reform legislation for a ransom the White House and its allies couldn't pay. When she met with him as part of her regular rounds on Capitol Hill, Sanders rarely brought up specific issues the way most lawmakers did. As she later recalled, he would just sit there on his drab, government-issued couch—a conspicuously spartan piece of furniture compared to the ornate furnishings of most Senate offices—and listen to her pitch. Then he would cross his arms, furrow his brow, and say in his thick Brooklyn accent, "Tell Barack Obama to call me."[33]

White House officials more familiar with Sanders weren't so worried, and neither was Reid, who had developed a fondness for Sanders and his gruff manner. Nor was Reid surprised to hear, in December, that Sanders's big ask was for $10 billion in new funding for community health clinics, which cared for people who couldn't afford to pay on their own. Even if legislation passed, Sanders reminded Reid, millions would still not have insurance. And even those who had insurance might have trouble finding care if they lived in low-income neighborhoods, where, typically, doctors were less likely to practice.[34]

The $10 billion for clinics was still $10 billion Reid would not have for other uses, like subsidies. But it was $10 billion going directly to providers of care for people who needed it and not, for example, the medical device firms that Evan Bayh was so determined to protect. Reid signed off, and Sanders pledged his vote, with just one other condition—that he get a chance to introduce a single-payer amendment on the floor. Later, when Republicans threatened to use the amendment to delay proceedings by forcing an out-loud reading of the amendment, Sanders withdrew the demand—proof, Reid would later say, that Sanders was more of a team player than his reputation suggested.[35]

Sanders's vow of support meant Reid needed just one more vote, and in theory, Snowe was an option. But Reid was running into the same problem that the White House and Baucus had. She wouldn't commit to yes. Instead, she was pushing to postpone a vote until after the Christmas break, because, she said, neither she nor the other lawmakers had enough time to work through the details in legislation.

Democratic leaders were stupefied. They had been debating reform since the spring, with hundreds of hours of hearings and hundreds more spent in private negotiations, a big portion of them with Snowe at the table. She had spent more time with administration officials, including the president, than any other Republican and many Democrats, as well. (Obama once joked that he'd move into an apartment, and give Snowe the White House, if it would help.) But her position was clear. If a bill came up in December, she was voting no.

That left Ben Nelson, the senator from Nebraska and the last holdout in the Democratic caucus. A lawyer by training, he had worked in the insurance industry before getting into politics as the Nebraska insurance commissioner. He later returned to the industry before getting back into politics, this time as Nebraska's governor—where, over the course of two terms, he cut taxes, cut spending, and introduced welfare reform years before Bill Clinton did at the national level. Since coming to the Senate, he had compiled the most conservative voting record of any Democrat.

Still, he wasn't a Republican, and his record included support of government programs to help low-income people, especially children, in Nebraska. During the economic stimulus fight, early in the year, he had served as Reid's ambassador to the three Republicans—Snowe and Specter, plus Susan Collins of Maine—who eventually voted yes. Nelson had said he wanted to support legislation but could not if it contained certain key features. One was the public option, which Lieberman had killed. Another was language allowing funding of abortion, an issue Reid had addressed through language similar to, though less restrictive than, the House version. After some negotiation with two more liberal senators, California's Barbara Boxer and Washington's Patty Murray, Nelson said okay.[36]

The final item on Nelson's list was Medicaid expansion, which Nelson said he opposed because it would force states to spend more money on the program. This was another argument that drove liberals nuts. Under the emerging legislation, the federal government would be picking up nearly the entire cost of any new enrollees. And while it was true that expansion would require additional state spending, especially in later years, it was also true that projections suggested states would generally be better off financially, given that extra Medicaid spending would generate more economic activity (and thus more tax revenue) while reducing the need to subsidize charity care at public clinics and hospitals.[37]

Nelson's preference was to make the Medicaid expansion optional; in states that chose not to do it, low-income residents could get private insurance through the new marketplaces, with the help of subsidies fully funded by the federal government. The problem with that, Reid knew, was that it would ruin reform's delicate budget math. Subsidizing private insurance was a lot more expensive for the government than expanding Medicaid. A bill that covered substantially more people through private insurance would either cost a lot more or cover far fewer people. Neither was acceptable to the majority of the caucus or to the White House.

An alternative—which Reid later said he suggested to Nelson, rather than the other way around—was to let Nebraska, and only Nebraska, off the hook for any new Medicaid expenses by having the federal government pick up the entire cost. Doing that for the entire country would have added tens of billions of dollars to the bill. But doing it for Nebraska, one of the least populated states in the country, would mean only tens of millions. Nelson accepted that.[38]

Reid's staff went to adjust the language in the bill and pondered ways of disguising the provision, so that it wasn't such an obvious giveaway to a lone senator and state. That was standard practice in situations like these, and they had done something similar with the Louisiana Medicaid supplement by specifying that it would apply only to states in which every single county had been declared a federal disaster area in recent years. (Louisiana, because of Katrina, was the only state that met that criterion.) But any attempt to cloak the feature was bound to backfire, they figured, and so they just put the name of the state, Nebraska, into the legislation.[39]

In the days and weeks to come, the deal would come to be known as the "Cornhusker kickback," and it would become a source of major controversy—proof, to critics on the left and right, that the legislation was full of corrupt bargains. It wasn't even popular in Nebraska, where Nelson was left to defend the deal by saying he intended it as a placeholder, in the hopes that all states would eventually get the same deal.[40]

Reid never understood the fuss. The "rifle shots" (the term for legislative provisions like the Nebraska deal) in the final bill were all pretty minor by the standards of major legislation and not even in the same universe as the giveaways in the 2003 Bush Medicare drug bill, which the GOP practically gift wrapped for the pharmaceutical industry. Legislating was all about balancing the needs of senators from states with different interests, and Nelson was just sticking up for the preferences of his conservative constituents. "I think Ben handled that wrong," Reid said. "I think he should have gone back and boasted about that."[41]

Still, Reid said he felt nothing but admiration for Nelson, who had told Reid the health care vote could end his career in politics. That prediction proved correct. In late 2011, amid repeated GOP attacks on the Cornhusker kickback and discouraging poll numbers, Nelson announced that he wouldn't seek reelection.[42]

The following November, his seat went to a Republican.

5.

Nothing with health care reform was ever simple, and before Reid could bring a bill to the floor, he faced one last procedural hurdle.

The Senate had a series of must-pass bills to get through before the year's end. Reid had scheduled votes on them in rapid succession, so that the Senate could finish its work in time for Christmas. And he made sure that each piece of legislation had the sixty votes necessary to break filibusters Republicans were sure to try to delay proceedings and consideration of health care.

The annual appropriation for the Defense Department posed a particular challenge because Russ Feingold, the progressive Democrat from Wisconsin, had consistently voted against that measure to demonstrate his opposition to the Iraq War. Reid started canvassing Republicans and thought he had a commitment from Mississippi's Thad Cochran so that a motion to end debate would still have sixty votes. But after the bill was on the floor, Cochran warned Reid that he was leaning toward supporting the filibuster after all.[43]

No other Republican was willing to break ranks. White House officials, who by this point were basically an extension of Reid's whip operation, thought trying to win over Feingold was hopeless and were thinking up other ways to get the defense bill off the floor. Obama said he wanted to talk to Feingold directly and called him from Air Force One. After that conversation, Feingold addressed the Democratic caucus and announced that he was voting yes on the defense bill—prompting a rousing, lengthy cheer from his colleagues.[44]

The caucus meetings had been getting testy in the fall, especially when Reid was negotiating with Lieberman. But while liberals hadn't gotten the public option, they had gotten some other big concessions, including some of the HELP bill's insurance regulations and a boost in the subsidies so that they would reach people making up to four times the poverty line instead of three. Whether it was determination or fatigue or both, the caucus was ready to move ahead—especially after Rhode Island's Jack Reed, a West Point graduate and former U.S. Army Ranger, rallied them with his mantra: "March or Die."[45]

It was time to vote, and at 7:00 a.m. on the morning of Christmas Eve, Reid opened the session with an homage to Kennedy: "The work goes on. The cause endures . . . and yet here we are, minutes away from doing what others have tried but none have achieved." When it was his turn in the roll call, Reid was so exhausted that he accidentally said no before realizing his mistake, waving his hands in the air, and changing his vote to yes. Sanders arrived a few minutes later, briskly walking across the chamber to his seat, and provided the final "yes" that the legislation needed to pass.[46]

The final tally was 60–39, with one Republican senator absent. Snowe had voted no, as promised, calling both the bill and final debate over it "extremely disappointing." Grassley was equally dismissive, while McConnell, describing the bill as a "monstrosity," vowed that "this fight is far from over."[47]

Sentiments across the aisle were as mixed as they had been after legislation passed in the House, with more liberal Democrats like Brown and Rockefeller vowing to push for a public option and other concessions during conference committee negotiations—and more conservative members like Lieberman and Nelson warning they would vote against final legislation if it changed too much.

But the historical import of the moment was palpable, especially at the White House, where Obama said, "This will be the most important piece of social policy since the Social Security Act in the 1930s, and the most important reform of our health care system since Medicare passed in the 1960s."[48]

Obama cautioned that more work awaited: "We now have to take up the last and most important step and reach an agreement on a final reform bill that I can sign into law." But that step would wait. Congressional leadership thought members needed a break—a chance to spend time with their families over the holidays. Surely an extra ten days wouldn't make a difference.

Seventeen

A Big F***ing Deal

1.

Formal negotiations over a final bill started on Wednesday, January 6, 2010, at the White House and neighboring Eisenhower Executive Office Building. House and Senate leaders had to hash out a compromise that they could then take back to their chambers for a final vote of approval so that it was ready for Obama's signature.

Nobody thought the talks would be easy. Few thought they would be so hard.

From a distance, the bills from the two chambers looked alike, and similar to their antecedents in Obama's campaign plan and the 2008 Baucus white paper. But the House bill did significantly more to help people get insurance, because its expansion of Medicaid and spending on private insurance subsidies were larger. The Senate bill promised to do more to reduce costs, at least by the CBO's reckoning, mostly because of the Cadillac tax.[1]

The delegation from each chamber came to the January negotiations determined to pull a final compromise in its direction. But each team had divided internal constituencies to satisfy. The more liberal House had to account for Blue Dogs who thought their chamber's bill had too much spending and regulation. The more conservative Senate had to address liberals still hoping to get a public option. The White House had its own, familiar tensions, with some advisers focused more on coverage and others focused more on cost. And all of them were listening to political advisers anxious about how long the whole thing was taking.

The congressional math seemed likely to push the final agreement a lot closer to the Senate bill. The reality was that Pelosi had votes to spare in her caucus. Reid didn't. And because of the Senate's small-state bias, more conservative members had disproportionate power there. Some of these senators didn't simply prefer a bill that did less and cost less. Their commitment to the whole reform project seemed weaker, giving them extra leverage—as Sherrod Brown had warned liberal activists back in the fall, while Reid was first making his concessions on the public option: "The problem is that they are willing to kill reform, to walk away. We are not. We're doing our best and I'm as frustrated as you are. The problem is, the negotiating table isn't even."[2]

Pelosi wanted to change those dynamics. As far as she and her lieutenants were concerned, the House bill wasn't simply more progressive. It was more carefully crafted too, because her side wasn't frantically rewriting language until the last minute to put together the votes. The public option might not be possible, she knew, but she thought even more conservative Democrats could grasp the logic of more financial assistance for people with private insurance, which would show up as savings for middle-class consumers, and the simplicity of a single national insurance marketplace rather than fifty-one versions for the states and District of Columbia.

As the main discussions began around the long table in the Cabinet Room, Pelosi's strategy sounded to many participants like Michael Corleone's in *The Godfather, Part II*: Her offer was nothing.

Instead, she would talk about what she said were the Senate bill's many deficiencies—that it depended too much on state goodwill to function well, that it let the drug companies off too easily. Reid and his chairman reacted with a mix of defensiveness, sheepishness, and understanding, all while reminding Pelosi they had to make sure whatever came out of their discussions still had support from more conservative caucus members. Pelosi knew all about those constraints but kept pushing, even if it meant breaking with her own delegation. At one point, after the Senate delegation offered a concession, Waxman said he thought it was an encouraging gesture. Pelosi said that Waxman "does not speak for the House."[3]

Plenty of people in the room agreed with Pelosi on the merits. Baucus's own advisers thought many of her demands made sense. In a January phone call, White House officials told Reid they were fine adding $160–$185 billion in new outlays, so that the total spending was around $1 trillion. But, as always, there were those trade-offs. New spending would require new offsets, and they were hard to find. "We were in this box,"

Karen Nelson, Waxman's health care adviser, told me. "We had only so much we could spend, and there were things that needed to be done in that bill, cost-sharing help and subsidies. But that took money and it was a constant struggle on how we were going to balance it out."[4]

2.

Presiding over all of this was the president. Traditionally, the two houses would work out differences in legislation on Capitol Hill through a formal conference committee in which leaders in each house picked a delegation. It was rare to have those kinds of discussions in the West Wing, rarer still with the president right there at the table.

And he was very much in charge. He was already familiar with the bills at a detailed level, but he had DeParle brief him again. Like Waxman, Obama knew that information was an advantage in these situations. He wanted as much of it as possible.[5]

At the outset, Obama believed, as he always believed, that reason would prevail. But as the discussions went on for hours and then days, he found that belief increasingly difficult to sustain. During a break one evening, as a handful of advisers huddled in the Oval Office, Rahm encouraged Obama to show his frustration and walk out of the negotiations, according to one official who was present. When the group returned and the two sides got to fighting again, Obama announced that he didn't need to be there anymore, because they were stuck on so many small issues and neither side was giving ground. In some retellings of Obama's scolding, which many people in the room remembered, Obama said the members were acting like children; in others, Obama said he was going to spend time with his children.[6]

Years later, when I asked about the episode, Obama said he didn't recall the specifics but doubted he needed Rahm's prodding to show his displeasure. "I don't think you needed to engineer my being frustrated," he said with a wry grin. He remembered the refusals to compromise on various member priorities ("We were in the weeds on a whole bunch of pet programs") and the ill will between the two sides ("The degree of suspicion and bad blood between the House and the Senate negotiators was trying").

Obama said he could sympathize, given the political environment and difficulty of getting Republican votes in either house. "I think one thing that's important to remember in defense of the Democrats in this entire process is that we're telescoping a really big, complicated bill, trying to do it really quickly, in an environment in which the entire other party has made a determination that we are going to try to defeat and obstruct at all costs," Obama said. "There's no play in the joints."

Still, Obama said, he thought few of the negotiators seemed to grasp the real-world political constraints and the urgency of moving forward. "I completely understood the House's frustration, because this is a frustration they've been going through all year," Obama continued. "By that time, the House has passed a year's worth of progressive legislation, only to see it get watered down or wither and die, or they've had to swallow compromises they don't like. I actually agreed with the House on many of their positions. . . . But by that point, it's clear that we are working with a very narrow window to get historical legislation done. And there was no sense of give on either side. There was this attitude that we had all the time in the world, as if the political world wasn't deteriorating around us.

"There was a little bit of an air of unreality about this," Obama continued. "And so at that point, I do recall standing up and saying, 'You know what? This is it, we've got to move on. We have to make decisions. I'm going to step away and I expect that, when I get back, there are going to be some decisions you guys will have made. Otherwise, I'm going to make them and I will make the public aware of the fact that, at this point, what's holding us back is the inability of Democrats to cooperate.'"[7]

The conversation continued when Obama left the room, with Rahm orchestrating some deals that, together, brought the two sides closer by tens of billions of dollars. And there was progress on some other fronts too. Economic adviser Jason Furman, working with the unions, brokered a deal on the Cadillac tax, so that it affected fewer plans at first but phased in more quickly. Jeanne Lambrew, whose record of promoting coverage expansions gave her extra credibility with liberals, persuaded House Democratic staff that the distinction between a national exchange and a state-based system was overblown, since in either case the national exchange would be available in states that opted against building their own.[8]

The original goal was to have legislation ready for final votes in the House by the twenty-first or twenty-second of January, followed by the Senate a few days later, and then signing around the end of the month. The president could give the State of the Union address right afterward, still basking in the glow of success, and launch his second-year agenda, which would focus on jobs and the economy and positioning Democrats for the midterms.[9]

Three weeks later, that timetable was no longer realistic. But the negotiators were getting close, and they probably needed only a few extra days—which they had, until Scott Brown won in Massachusetts.

3.

On the morning after the Massachusetts election, while the news of Scott Brown's victory was still sinking in, a handful of negotiators showed up at the White House. The rest stayed on Capitol Hill and made an early exit for the bars. "We had a very sinking feeling," Debbie Curtis said later. "A number of us had been through this ten years before. We had drowned before. You really try to be positive, but at that point in time, you were really like, 'Wow, how does this happen?'"[10]

About the only reason for hope was the fact that Democrats had invested so much time into the effort—and that, having voted for legislation in both houses, those Democrats had already taken on reform's political liabilities. One person making that case was Chris Jennings. He had not joined the administration, because his past lobbying work disqualified him under the new Obama rules, but he knew virtually everybody working on health care in the White House and in Congress. They would turn to him for guidance and, sometimes, emotional support.

Jennings had predicted the panic on Capitol Hill. He had also predicted that Democrats would get over their panic and finish the job, with the House passing the Senate bill and then both chambers passing what modifications they could through reconciliation, where the threshold was just fifty votes. The key was making sure nobody in leadership declared that the effort was over. He said as much in private conversations, and three days after the Massachusetts election, he published those thoughts in *The New Republic*. "The truth is that there is no political option other than to pass health reform," Jennings wrote.[11]

Ron Pollack agreed, and as a precaution days before the election, he had sent a memo recommending the same reconciliation strategy to his contacts in Congress and the administration. But while White House officials were also contemplating that option, they weren't sure whether Obama would settle on that approach or whether it was feasible. Pollack said he soon got a call from Jim Messina, who was furious, because the memo was forcing the administration into a response when nobody had decided what that response would be. (Messina later told me he had no memory of such a call.)[12]

Indecision was a real issue. Obama, Pelosi, Reid, and the committee chairmen were pushing, with varying levels of energy, to pass legislation. But there was confusion and disagreement over how to do it, because the only way forward depended on the House approving the Senate bill, and Pelosi was telling everybody the votes were not there. At one point, Henry Waxman let Pelosi know he thought the strategy made sense; "Yeah, go sell that to the caucus," he recalled her saying. At a Democratic Senate retreat in early February, when an angry Al Franken asked David Axelrod why the White House wasn't just telling Pelosi to pass the Senate bill, Axelrod shot back, "If you have a piece of paper with 218 votes on it, give it to me, and I'll walk it over to the Speaker right now. I don't think she has such a list."[13]

She didn't. She was short by at least thirty votes, and maybe many more, depending on who was doing the counting. Making matters worse, Obama had sent ambiguous signals when he gave an interview to George Stephanopoulos on ABC News. He shot down the idea of trying to pass legislation in the remaining days before Scott Brown's swearing in and said, "There are many different things that we can do to move forward on health care, but we're not making any of those decisions now." Obama noted that the House and Senate bills mostly overlapped—suggesting, perhaps, that he still wanted to pass a version. But then he talked about coming together on "core elements" that Democrats and Republicans both supported, which sounded a lot like seeking a dramatically scaled-down compromise in a bid for some GOP support.[14]

That option had always been on Rahm's mind, and with no clear path to passing comprehensive legislation, he had some officials resume work on a much smaller plan that would insure children only. But Obama wasn't leaning in that direction. If anything, he seemed more and more determined to give the full bill one more try, starting with a full-throated defense during the State of the Union address. A few days later, at the end of January, he spoke at a House Republican retreat in Baltimore and proceeded to take detailed policy questions for ninety minutes. Although the questions touched a variety of topics, Obama's performance sent a signal to his allies that he wasn't about to retreat on his agenda.[15]

Inside the White House, Obama told advisers that they were at the two-yard line and he didn't want to settle for a field goal. They had made it through the town hall protests and the near collapse of talks in the Senate. They could make it through this too.

The night before that meeting, Zeke Emanuel texted me with a status report. "Dead Dead DEAD." The next morning, Zeke sent a one-word update: "Alive."[16]

4.

Obama and his advisers thought they needed to change the dynamics one more time by sketching out what the Senate bill could look like with some modifications through reconciliation and convening a bipartisan summit. As a candidate, he'd promised to conduct negotiations over major bills on C-SPAN—a wildly unrealistic boast that critics had, predictably, used to show that Democrats had been scheming behind closed doors. The summit wouldn't be a substitute, but it was a nod in that direction. He'd also get a chance to engage the Republicans on policy substance one last time.[17]

An administration official later admitted to thinking the idea was "goofy." Around Washington, many said it seemed like a waste of time. But a handful, like longtime Democratic Party power broker John Podesta, thought time had significant value. "It just froze the game," Podesta said. "Everybody just decided, 'OK, let's see what happens a month from now [at the summit].' It stopped people from jumping ship."[18]

And that gave Pelosi an opportunity.

For the past year, Reid's job had been more difficult. He was the one with no votes to spare. He was the one with all those ambivalent centrists, always threatening to abandon reform. He was the one with the two distinct committees, one run by a chairman, Max Baucus, whom a large chunk of the caucus couldn't stand.

Now Pelosi was the one facing the bigger challenge. In public, her strategy was to keep stating that reform was moving forward. "We will go through the gate," she said at a January 28 press conference. "If the gate is closed, we will go over the fence. If the fence is too high, we will pole vault in. If that doesn't work, we will parachute in. But we are going to get health care reform passed." She also made clear to the White House, through the press and in private meetings, that she wanted no part of what she described as Rahm's "eensy weensy spider, teeny-tiny" bill that would help children only.[19]

With her caucus, Pelosi made a point of listening but not wavering. At a meeting after the Massachusetts election, junior and vulnerable members lined up at the microphones, decrying reform as a "suicide mission." Pelosi, with Hoyer at her side, heard out every one—and then made a speech of her own, declaring her determination to go forward because they had come so far.

Chris Murphy, who in 2010 was finishing his second term representing a suburban House district outside Hartford, Connecticut, said later, "I just felt like the momentum was heading in the direction of surrender. Pelosi just did not allow it to happen. By sheer will, she turned that room around. People like me, I still wanted to do it but I don't know that I had the confidence to stand up to this tidal wave. She breathed confidence into everybody in that room who wanted to stay the course."[20]

Pelosi also started bringing her members along to the reconciliation strategy by promising that there were ways to address the Senate bill's weaknesses. Many aides later wondered whether that had been her intention all along, that her insistence the House wouldn't pass the Senate bill—and maybe her stubborn posture in the pre–Scott Brown negotiations as well—were actually acts of performance art designed to keep her leverage with the Senate while convincing skeptical House members she was standing up for them.

At one point, Pelosi brought in DeParle to brief House members on the Senate bill and, for an introduction, said that DeParle had already admitted the House bill was the "best bill that's ever been passed in history." But, Pelosi sighed, that wasn't an option anymore, so DeParle was here to talk about how they'd fix up the Senate legislation instead.[21]

Pelosi and the reform effort got some unexpected (and, surely, unintended) help from the insurance industry in early February, when Anthem–Blue Cross, California's largest for-profit insurer, announced rate hikes of up to 39 percent. It was the second consecutive year of significant double-digit increases for people buying coverage on their own and provided the Democrats with fresh evidence that the status quo needed reform. "You handed the politicians red meat at a time when health care is being discussed," an alarmed Fox Business host told an executive at WellPoint, Anthem's parent company, during an interview. "You gave it to them."[22]

House members were slowly coming around to the idea of the reconciliation strategy but worried the Senate would renege on its part of the deal. One option, which House staff presented to the White House and Senate, was to have both houses pass the reconciliation bill first and then have the House pass the Senate bill. Karen Nelson and Wendell Primus even worked up language for the measure. But the technicalities of passing a bill to modify a bill that wasn't yet law proved too difficult to pull off.[23]

Distrust was still an issue when the summit took place on February 25. The president was there, along with nearly forty administration officials and congressional leaders, all sitting around long tables forming a square. The conversation didn't lead to any new understandings, although it spanned almost seven hours. It was more each side restating its basic arguments. But the seating plan put Pelosi right next to Reid, and one senior administration aide noticed a great deal of conversation. "They were leaning in, whispering, talking to each other. Not that they weren't friendly before, but this had been a tense time . . . and now you could almost see they're realizing, 'My best friend in the whole world is sitting right here, and we're going to get this done.'"[24]

By this point, administration officials and Capitol Hill staff were working feverishly to figure out how much they could do in reconciliation, which was a question both of what would keep at least fifty senators on board and what could get approval from the Senate parliamentarian. Fear of the parliamentarian disqualifying key legislative provisions and turning a bill into "Swiss cheese" was one reason Democrats had not tried reconciliation in the first place. But now they were talking about a much narrower set of fixes, and the most important ones, like changes to the subsidies and modifications to the Cadillac tax, easily qualified because they had clear budget impacts—though reconciliation's requirement that legislation reduce the deficit in its second decade limited how much Democrats could do.

Two key steps remained. Holdouts in the House wanted some kind of guarantee that reconciliation would get through the Senate. Reid gave Pelosi a letter, signed by fifty-five of the fifty-nine Democratic senators, vowing to vote for it. Waiting after that was one final controversy over abortion rights, because the restrictions in the final Senate bill weren't as tight as the ones in the House bill. (It was one of the few places where the Senate bill was, arguably, more progressive than its House counterpart.) Four months after negotiating with the Pro-Choice Caucus to get their agreement on Bart Stupak's amendment to block subsidies from going to insurers that covered abortion, Pelosi found herself negotiating with Stupak all over again to get his agreement on the Senate bill.

Pelosi scheduled a vote for the weekend of March 20, although Stupak was still holding out, which meant she was still anywhere from five to fifteen votes short of a majority. More negotiation followed, with Steny Hoyer making an appeal and then John Dingell, a fellow Michigander, whom Stupak considered a mentor. The White House proposed an executive order that would have nearly the same effect as the original House bill language. The Conference of Catholic Bishops said that wasn't satisfactory, but Sister Carol Keehan, head of the Catholic Health Association, said it was. Stupak said yes.[25]

5.

For the first few weeks after the Massachusetts election, Obama said relatively little publicly about the situation in the House to avoid the impression that the White House was bullying members. But as momentum developed and the crusade so many pundits had declared hopeless suddenly showed hope, he started giving rally-style speeches. One was in the suburban Cleveland district of Dennis Kucinich, a progressive Democrat who supported single-payer and had voted against the House bill in November as a show of protest. After Obama praised Kucinich for being "tireless on behalf of working people," an audience member shouted, "Vote yes!" Obama, stopping himself midsentence, said, "Did you hear that, Dennis? Say it again!" Two days later, Kucinich announced that this time, he would be a yes.[26]

Obama's final pitch came in the Capitol Building complex on the day before the vote, when he addressed the full House Democratic caucus. He acknowledged the imperfections of the Senate bill. Even with reconciliation fixes, the legislation would leave people buying insurance exposed to higher costs than House negotiators (or Obama) had wanted. Still, Obama said, the program would help millions. "Some of you know I get 10 letters a day that I read out of the 40,000 that we receive," Obama said. "Started reading some of the ones that I got this morning. 'Dear President Obama, my daughter, a wonderful person, lost her job. She has no health insurance. She had a blood clot in her brain. She's now disabled, can't get care.' 'Dear President Obama, I don't yet qualify for Medicare. COBRA is about to run out. I am desperate, don't know what to do.'"

Obama said he knew this was a risky vote for many members and even mentioned a few by name. Then he reminded them why, he imagined, they had all come to Congress in the first place: "Every once in a while, every once in a while a moment comes where you have a chance to vindicate all those best hopes that you had about yourself, about this country, where you have a chance to make good on those promises that you made in all those town meetings and all those constituency breakfasts and all that traveling through the district, all those people who you looked in the eye and you said, you know what, you're right, the system is not working for you and I'm going to make it a little bit better. And this is one of those moments."

The weekend was its own self-contained drama, with Tea Party activists rallying outside Capitol Hill and some of them wandering the halls of congressional office buildings. Hecklers hurled homophobic slurs at Barney Frank. Three African American congressmen, including civil rights icon John Lewis, said they heard protesters using the N-word. Inside the House chamber, while deliberations were taking place, a few anti-reform activists started shouting from the visitors' gallery. Several Republican congressmen cheered and then walked out to the balcony to salute the protesters on the lawn. As a show of determination and solidarity, Pelosi, Hoyer, Lewis, and several other members locked arms and walked across the street from the House office buildings to the Capitol itself. Pelosi was holding the gavel that Dingell had used for the 1965 vote on Medicare and that she planned to use again that evening.[27]

A little past dinnertime, the visitors' gallery filled up with staff and administration officials who had worked on the legislation. Nancy-Ann DeParle brought her son, who sat on her lap; Jeanne Lambrew, who had never been inside the House chamber, sat by Kathleen Sebelius. Zeke Emanuel got a hug from AFL-CIO president Rich Trumka, even though Zeke had fought for the Cadillac tax the unions hated so much; Jason Furman sat with Pelosi's family. The line to get into the gallery grew quickly, eventually snaking down two of the large flights of marble stairs in the corridor. By the time Liz Fowler got through, all the seats were gone. She grabbed a few square feet of open space in the stairway aisle, which was soon packed as well.[28]

On the floor, members from each side made their closing arguments while Pelosi and her whips made their final vote checks. The final Republican orator was John Boehner, who accused the Democrats of defying the public's wishes and putting together a bill in secret. "Shame on us," he said, nearly shouting at points. "Shame on this body. Shame on each and every one of you who substitute your will, and your desires above those of your fellow countrymen."

The Republican side of the chamber roared with an intensity that raised eyebrows in the gallery and hinted at a political future that few could yet imagine.

Then it was Pelosi's turn. Her entrance, to a standing ovation, was more dramatic than her speech, which was characteristically stilted and sounded more like a laundry list of poll-tested buzzwords than a call to history. But Pelosi's job had never been to make the public case for reform. It was to build a coalition that could pass a bill. And she had. Members watched as the tally reached 215, perched tantalizingly on the edge of a majority for a few moments. "One more vote . . . one more vote," they chanted, until the board switched to 216 and applause broke out.[29]

A few minutes later, the presiding officer banged the gavel and read the final tally: 219–210. In the end, Pelosi had three votes to spare.

6.

Obama watched the proceedings on television, inside the Roosevelt Room, sitting at the long table next to Biden and with a few dozen advisers and staff standing around them. After the count hit 216, he stood and clapped, then worked his way around the room—stopping for a high five with Rahm and a particularly long embrace with Schiliro.

Obama left to give prepared remarks on television but told the crowd to join him afterward for a reception in the residence. It was an uncharacteristically warm night for March, and the event was on the Truman Balcony, overlooking the sprawling back garden and with the Washington Monument visible in the distance.

Guests got champagne. Obama had a martini. He made a point of mingling, thanking almost every person individually for their work over the past year, and addressed them as a group—reminding them that, thanks to their hard work, millions of Americans would now get health care, but warning that important work lay ahead. He led cheers for DeParle and Schiliro. When he noticed that Lambrew wasn't there (she had stayed behind at the Capitol), he borrowed a staffer's phone so he could thank her. They spoke for several minutes. Then he said good night to the crowd, though he invited everybody to stay for a while. "You all are younger than me," he said. "So you can work on three hours of sleep. But I cannot."[30]

The signing ceremony took place two days later in the East Room, where Obama had launched the health care campaign a little more than a year before. This time, no Republicans were in attendance. It was just the Democrats, some two-hundred-something of them, who had carried the bill to passage on their own. Special guests included Vicki Kennedy and Sister Carol Keehan, who helped break the abortion logjam; each would get one of the twenty-two ceremonial signing pens. When the audience took their seats and the official proceedings began, Biden spoke first. As he stepped away from the podium and gave Obama a bro hug, the microphone captured his "BFD" comment to the president.

Obama talked about some of the benefits Americans would see right away, like a provision allowing young adults to stay on a parent's insurance until age twenty-six—and about the historical significance of what the Democrats had just done, recalling a crusade that had started with Theodore Roosevelt and been carried on most recently by Obama's own secretary of state, Hillary Clinton. As he finished, he predicted the debate would shift, now that H.R. 3590, the Patient Protection and Affordable Care Act, was about to become law of the land. "It is fitting that Congress passed this historic legislation this week," Obama said, "for as we mark the turning of spring, we also mark a new season in America. In a few moments, when I sign this bill, all of the overheated rhetoric over reform will finally confront the reality of reform."

He was right about that coming confrontation—although, as he later admitted, he didn't realize how it would play out.

To be fair, nobody else did either.

Part III

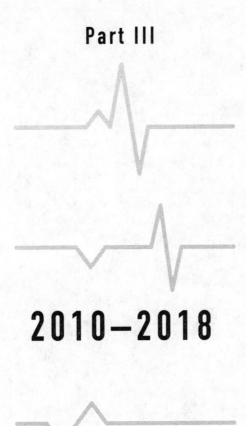

2010—2018

Eighteen

The Last Stand

The news was less than forty-eight hours old: Donald Trump was going to be president. His victory in the 2016 election felt like a total repudiation, of both Obama and Obama's presidency. But the outgoing incumbent wasn't ready to give up just yet. Trump was on his way to Washington, with a formal visit to the White House early on the agenda. Obama thought he could still influence him—and, perhaps, save the Affordable Care Act.

Their meeting was supposed to last fifteen minutes. It lasted ninety. Obama, determined to show Trump the same courtesy that George W. Bush once showed him, walked through the steps of presidential transition and talked about some of the weightier, ongoing issues that Trump would confront, especially on national security. Then he put in a plug for the health care law, which even he had come to call Obamacare. Trump had promised its repeal, yes, and the Republican Congress was primed to make that happen. But perhaps Trump should think about keeping its popular features. Trump said he would and repeated as much in a pair of interviews, with *The Wall Street Journal* and *60 Minutes,* where he said that protecting people with preexisting conditions "adds cost, but it's very much something we're going to try and keep."[1]

One month later, Trump was back in New York in his office at Trump Tower, in another lengthy meeting about his presidency. Strategist Steve Bannon and outgoing Republican National Committee chairman Reince Priebus were there, along with Jared Kushner, Trump's son-in-law. Together they were listening to Paul Ryan, Republican Speaker of the House, who had brought a set of Gantt charts laying out a first-year agenda.[2]

Obamacare repeal was first on the list. Ryan recommended repealing the law through budget reconciliation, since Republicans had just fifty-two seats in the Senate, and then delaying the effective date by a year or two or three. That would allow time to craft and pass a replacement plan—ideally, through regular order, on the theory that the GOP could get support from some conservative Democrats once repeal was a done deal.

As the conversation moved forward, Trump went "sideways" a few times, as one person familiar with the conversation later put it. He talked about his plans for updating Air Force One and his frustration that Amazon wasn't paying more taxes, and took a call from MSNBC host Joe Scarborough. But the president-elect was focused enough to wonder aloud whether voters would get skittish about repeal if they didn't know what Republicans intended to put in its place. Ryan acknowledged the possibility but said it would not get in the way of passing a bill. Incumbent GOP lawmakers had already voted for a repeal legislation, he noted, when they approved a 2015 bill Obama vetoed. That meant they could move quickly now, just as Trump wanted.[3]

Trump gave Ryan the green light to proceed, and a few days later, GOP leaders in the House sketched out their plan: Within the first one hundred days of the Trump administration, they would pass a law repealing the Affordable Care Act. They would do so using the reconciliation process, so that the bill could get through the Senate with just fifty votes. But the repeal law would not take effect for two years, so that there would be time to come up with a replacement. "Republicans will provide an adequate transition period to give people peace of mind that they will have those options available to them as we work through this solution," Kevin Brady, Ways and Means chairman, said in December.

Brady seemed confident, as did Ryan, and it was easy to see why. The Affordable Care Act had never been as stable or popular as programs like Medicare; lots of people were unhappy with it. But the law had achieved a lot more than Trump and his allies conceded—and, perhaps, a lot more than they realized. Tens of millions were getting coverage they never could before, or were saving money, or had peace of mind despite their ongoing, chronic medical problems. Those stories didn't get a lot of media coverage, but they were real, and they would make the Affordable Care Act more difficult to take away.

Obama knew this as well as anybody. He also remembered how difficult passing the health care law had been, how every single tweak Democrats wanted to make ran into objections from a new political constituency—and how change, any change, scared the bejesus out of voters. In 2009 and 2010, that sentiment had worked against him and his allies; in 2017, it would just as surely work against Trump and his.

Republicans had no idea what they were about to face, Obama kept saying. And they might just fail.

Nineteen

This Honorable Court

1.

The Republican assault on the Affordable Care Act began officially on March 23, 2010, the same day Obama signed the law and possibly while the ink on his signature was still drying.

It took place on several fronts. One of them was the federal courts, where Virginia attorney general Ken Cuccinelli filed a lawsuit. The subject was the individual mandate, the provision Obama had opposed during his 2008 campaign but accepted after experts (and Hillary Clinton) convinced him that it would prod healthy people into getting coverage. If that didn't happen, insurers would have to raise premiums higher and higher—and, quite likely, many fewer people would end up with insurance.

But the question in court wasn't about the mandate's wisdom. It was about its legality. To justify the mandate, supporters had to show it was consistent with at least one of the enumerated powers, like raising an army, that the Constitution gave explicitly to Congress. Or, at the very least, they had to show it was one of the implied powers that could plausibly be read into the document.

The Affordable Care Act's advocates believed they could do so easily. The consequence for failing to get insurance was a financial penalty, to be paid as part of annual income taxes. Congress has the power to levy taxes, the law's architects noted. Nobody disputed that. In addition, the law's supporters said, the mandate was a way to make health insurance markets function better. That meant it fell within the power Congress had to "regulate commerce . . . among the several states." Nobody disputed the existence of that authority, either, although its meaning had changed over time.[1]

Up through the 1930s, the Supreme Court interpreted the Commerce Clause power narrowly, striking down key New Deal programs because they didn't have sufficiently direct effects on trade across state borders. A pivotal 1941 ruling about an Ohio farmer named Roscoe Filburn signaled a shift. Filburn raised poultry and cattle, plus he grew wheat that he used mostly to feed the livestock and his family. He was subject to restrictions on how much he could grow, because the federal government was trying to stabilize the price of wheat following the collapse of the farming economy in the Great Depression. In 1941, officials fined Filburn $117 because he grew 23 acres of wheat, more than twice the 11.1 acres the rules allowed. Filburn sued, claiming the federal government had no right to limit his crop output if he wasn't even selling it.

The Supreme Court rejected his argument. It didn't matter whether Filburn was selling the crop, the court ruled. He was changing the demand for wheat on the open market, thus affecting its price. And while the extra 12 acres he was growing might have a minuscule impact nationally, the accumulated effect of more farmers doing the same would be significant.[2]

Some seventy years later, supporters of the Affordable Care Act thought the ruling in *Wickard v. Filburn* provided authority for a mandate designed to stabilize the price of insurance. They also thought the health care law was in the spirit of the New Deal programs that *Wickard* and related cases had upheld. Like FDR and his allies, Obama and the Democrats were using regulation and spending to make a broken market work again.

The Affordable Care Act's critics, which included libertarian scholars Georgetown professor Randy Barnett, veteran conservative litigator David Rivkin, and George Mason professor Ilya Somin, disagreed. They said the mandate was a novel, distinct use of federal power, because it was compelling people to engage in commerce rather than making rules for commerce already taking place. Congress had wide-ranging authority to regulate activity, they agreed, but nothing in the Constitution said it could regulate inactivity, and nothing in the *Wickard* opinion did either.[3]

The National Federation of Independent Businesses (NFIB), eager to get the law off the books, hired an attorney to file a suit making that claim. It was one of several that landed in federal district court. And after judges in Michigan and Virginia rejected the lawsuits, ruling in favor of the Affordable Care Act, Roger Vinson in Florida sided with the plaintiffs and declared the law unconstitutional. He also invoked an analogy that would become something of a mantra for conservatives challenging the law: If the federal government could make you buy insurance, Vinson said, there would be nothing to stop it from making you buy broccoli.

Vinson's ruling was especially alarming to the law's supporters because he said that the entire statute had to come off the books. Typically, laws include severability clauses, indicating that, should the courts find a portion unconstitutional, the rest can stand. The Affordable Care Act contained no such clause—quite possibly because nobody thought to add one during the intense writing and rewriting of the original Senate bill. And nobody caught the mistake during the conference committee process, as would normally happen, because the Scott Brown election meant that process never took place.

In principle, the lack of a severability clause shouldn't have mattered. Long-standing doctrine held that, when invalidating a provision of a law, courts should leave the rest of the law standing if at all possible. Vinson decided that wisdom didn't apply, because the law's components were too interconnected.

2.

Vinson had been appointed to the federal bench in 1983 by a Republican, Ronald Reagan. Every judge who subsequently ruled against the Affordable Care Act was also a Republican appointee. There were quite a lot of them—thanks, in part, to a patient, effective crusade by conservative activists.

The crusade's leader was the Federalist Society. It started in the 1970s as a law students' organization; it soon grew into an association for conservative, politically active lawyers and scholars in all stages of their careers. Its founding purpose was to challenge what conservatives perceived as liberal hegemony over both academia and the courts. Its agenda included everything from reversing decisions on abortion (which conservatives said rested on a nonexistent right to privacy) to limiting government's power to enforce the Voting Rights Act (on the theory that the Justice Department was encroaching on state power). The initial faculty sponsors were Antonin Scalia, the future Supreme Court justice who at the time was a professor at the University of Chicago, and Robert Bork, who was a professor at Yale.

Bork was also supposed to be a Supreme Court justice. But when Reagan appointed him, Democrats set out to defeat him. Ted Kennedy led the charge, warning that in Bork's America, women would be getting back-alley abortions and African Americans would still be sitting at segregated lunch counters. He was referring to Bork's writings questioning the logic of court decisions legalizing abortion and enforcing civil rights; Republicans objected that he was distorting Bork's views, making him sound sexist and racist. Democrats prevailed, and the outcome left a deep scar on the conservative psyche. Decades later, Republicans would cite that episode as proof that it was Democrats, not Republicans, who broke conventions of fair play and made politics bitterer and more dishonest and partisan.[4]

The Bork episode also convinced Republicans to redouble their efforts at populating the judiciary, and those efforts had made an impact—including at the Supreme Court, which in the fall of 2011 agreed to hear the mandate case. Five of the nine justices were Republican appointees, making for a working conservative majority, although sometimes one or more of them broke ranks.

Anthony Kennedy was the most likely of the five conservatives to join the liberals, as he had done in abortion cases and some other high-profile decisions. But Kennedy also had an appetite for big, sweeping rulings. If he didn't buy the government's arguments on the mandate, he might decide it required sweeping away large swaths or the law or maybe even, as Judge Vinson thought, the whole thing.

Scalia was also a candidate to side with the Democrats, in spite of his reputation as the court's most outspoken conservative. In a 2005 decision about marijuana prohibitions, he had affirmed the federal government's authority to do whatever was "necessary and proper" for carrying out its constitutional powers. The Affordable Care Act's defenders used the same argument. They said the mandate was a "necessary and proper" method of regulating insurance prices, which in turn fell within congressional power to set rules for interstate commerce.[5]

And then there was the chief, John Roberts. A veteran of the Reagan and Bush administrations, Roberts had the judicial record of a committed conservative and loyal Republican. Since joining the Supreme Court in 2005, he had written or supported decisions limiting the federal government's power to enforce the Voting Rights Act and limit political contributions by independent groups. One study found him among the most likely justices in the modern era to overturn precedents. Still, Roberts had the court's institutional reputation to protect; chief justices in particular frequently saw that as part of their duty. And a ruling against the mandate was sure to be controversial.[6]

As the case had moved up through the courts, the plaintiffs had recruited a talented group of lawyers who specialized in appeals. NFIB had picked Michael Carvin, a veteran conservative advocate who had served in the Reagan administration and whose past appellate work included representing the tobacco industry and the winning side in *Bush v. Gore*, the 2000 Florida recount case. He was optimistic because he thought government lawyers couldn't identify a "limiting principle"—that is, a clear line indicating when the government could compel somebody to buy a product and when it couldn't. Or, to put it as Judge Vinson did, the government didn't have a clear answer for why it could make you buy insurance but it couldn't make you buy broccoli.[7]

The Obama administration lawyer handling the case was Don Verrilli, who had become solicitor general less than a year before but had been involved with the case from the very beginning, when he was in the White House Counsel's office. He, too, thought the Commerce Clause arguments might run into trouble, given that the Supreme Court in 1995 and then again in 2000 had established new limits on the Commerce power. That hadn't happened since the 1930s, and it suggested the justices might be in the mood to circumscribe the power again. "In the world of twenty years ago, I think I would have said this is clearly constitutional under the Commerce power—I could have easily won that case," Verrilli said to me later. "But I was really worried about it."[8]

Verrilli's all-consuming preparations included briefings on health care economics and the workings of the Affordable Care Act. He did multiple moot court exercises—two for each of the different parts he would be arguing but with an extra (for three total) on the mandate arguments. In those sessions, he sensed again that the defense of the Commerce Clause power wasn't holding up as well as he had hoped.

The argument that the mandate was constitutional under the power to tax held up better in the practice runs, although the argument was tricky for the administration politically. Obama as a presidential candidate had pledged not to raise taxes on the middle class, and during a 2009 television interview, he had said specifically he did not think of the mandate as a tax increase. Making the tax argument in court would enable Republicans to argue that Obama had lied.

Back in 2010, when the administration was first preparing briefs to defend the mandate in the lower courts, Verrilli had helped prepare a decision memo, the kind that filled Obama's briefcase every night. It explained the situation (including Obama's statement on TV) and recommended use of the tax argument, notwithstanding the political risk. At the end of the memo were three boxes: agree, disagree, discuss. Verrilli got the memo back with a mark in the "agree" box. Obama was a politician, but he had been a constitutional law professor first.

The tax issue had not gotten much attention in the lower courts. But for the Supreme Court hearing, the justices had set aside three days for arguments, with each day covering different aspects of the case. That would give Verrilli a chance to flesh out the argument, finally. Among other things, Verrilli wanted to emphasize the principle of constitutional avoidance, which holds that if a court can find a constitutionally plausible rationale for a law, it should not strike it down. In other words, the tax argument alone would be enough.[9]

Outside of the solicitor general's office, the potential of the tax argument got a lot less attention. Years later, Carvin admitted that he was sure of very few things going into the case. But one of them, he told me, was that the mandate wasn't going to survive simply because of the taxing power.[10]

3.

Oyez, oyez, oyez. . . . God save the United States and this honorable court.

At 10:00 a.m. on Monday, March 26, 2012, the clerk called the Supreme Court into session to hear *NFIB v. Sebelius* and the related cases. The named defendant, Kathleen Sebelius, was there in the courtroom. So were some other officials and lawmakers who had roles in the law's creation, including Liz Fowler and Jeanne Lambrew. Ron Pollack, who happened to be a member of the Supreme Court bar, was present too. The range of outcomes included upholding the law in its entirety, striking the whole thing down, or a mixed decision allowing only some of the program to go forward.[11]

Day one was the one most people thought they could ignore. The focus was a relatively obscure law called the Anti-Injunction Act, which effectively prohibits lawsuits challenging taxes that the government hasn't yet collected. The government's position was that, for purposes of the Anti-Injunction Act, the mandate was not a tax, and thus it was fine for the court to rule on the case now, rather than waiting until after 2014 when the law and the mandate were set to take full effect.

In making this case, the government was careful to say that its argument applied only for purposes of the Anti-Injunction hearing. When it came to questions of constitutional authority, which the court would take up on Tuesday, the mandate was still a tax—a point Samuel Alito, the conservative justice skilled at needling liberal advocates, noted dryly: "Today you are arguing that the penalty is not a tax. Tomorrow you are going to be back and you will be arguing that the penalty is a tax."

Roberts also asked a question, one that would prove significant. He noted that the mandate didn't seem like a "command" to get insurance when the only punishment for violating it was a higher tax bill. "What happens if you don't file the mandate? And the answer is nothing"—referring to the lack of criminal sanctions. The full comment was a bit difficult to parse and got little attention at the time, although Verrilli picked up on it: "At that moment I said, 'Oh, he gets our point.' The chief gets it, that the only consequence is that you pay a tax, and therefore it can be construed as not being a command and just being an exercise in tax power."[12]

Tuesday, with its focus on the mandate, was the day of drama. And it did not start off well for Verrilli. He was tired and a bit out of sorts that morning, because the alarm system in his house had gone off twice during the night. Adrenaline took care of the fatigue, but before he started speaking, a sip of water went down the wrong pipe. A few seconds into his opening remarks, he had to pause to take another drink. "Excuse me," he said, as the sound of a clinking glass echoed through the vast, silent courtroom.

Verrilli resumed talking and quickly found his rhythm. But almost immediately, he came under attack from the conservatives—especially Scalia, Roberts, and Kennedy, whose seats together in the middle of the elevated bench made them physically as well as rhetorically intimidating. "Can you create commerce in order to regulate it?" Kennedy wanted to know, channeling an argument from the challengers' brief. Roberts indicated he was wondering the same. Alito, who as a more junior justice was sitting off to one side, posed a hypothetical about burial services in which he and Verrilli were walking around downtown Washington at lunchtime, approaching random young people, and making them pay in advance for the funerals. Scalia asked about broccoli.

Just like that, four conservative justices had expressed extreme skepticism of the Commerce Clause argument. (The fifth, Clarence Thomas, never asked questions in oral arguments but would presumably vote to strike down the mandate.) When the plaintiffs' attorneys, Carvin and Paul Clement, gave their presentations, they got some rough queries from the liberals, especially Obama appointees Elena Kagan and Sonia Sotomayor, who as the two most junior justices were sitting at the two far ends of the bench. But their pincer action was nothing like the interrogation Verrilli had encountered.

Day three didn't go much better for the Affordable Care Act's defense. The morning focused on whether finding one part of the law unconstitutional would require invalidating the entire statute. The question suddenly loomed large, given the justices' skepticism of the mandate on Tuesday. Kennedy's questions, emphasizing the difficulty justices would face trying to figure out which parts of the law were interconnected and which ones were distinct, made it sound like he was ready to throw out the whole thing.

The afternoon session was on the Medicaid expansion, the case's sleeper issue. The lawsuit claimed that the financing arrangements were coercive to states, because states that declined to expand their programs would lose all federal Medicaid funding, including money to run their existing Medicaid programs. It was, in other words, an offer that states couldn't refuse. The counterargument was that the courts had never questioned the government's authority to make funding conditional on states following federal guidelines. Even many conservatives thought the plaintiff's argument was far-fetched— although, curiously, the justices seemed to be taking it seriously.

The consensus after the hearings was that the Affordable Care Act was in big trouble and that Verrilli's performance hadn't helped. The Republican National Committee turned audio of his opening stammers into an attack ad, editing selectively to make the pauses sound longer than they actually were. At the end, it said, "Obamacare: It's a tough sell."[13]

Verrilli's colleagues thought the reaction was unfair. He'd made all his points, even though the questioning was unusually tough. Several members of the administration, including the president, reached out with support. Verrilli said he was fine, made a point of checking on the spirits of his own deputies, and maintained that they still had a good shot of winning.

Few people believed him.[14]

4.

The justices discuss cases on the Fridays immediately following oral arguments. They meet alone, with no clerks or other staff present, and normally details of those conversations only become public many years after the fact—if they become public at all.

The discussion that took place two days after oral arguments in the Affordable Care Act case was an exception, thanks to reporting by three well-sourced journalists: Joan Biskupic, Jan Crawford, and Jeffrey Toobin. Based on their writings, a few things about that meeting later became clear. All five conservative justices indicated they were not persuaded by the Obama administration's arguments on the Commerce Clause, which, as Verrilli had suspected, they were prepared to limit again. Roberts assigned himself the majority opinion. The four other conservative justices left that meeting believing Roberts would vote with them to strike down the mandate, leaving only the question of whether to leave remaining parts of the law in place.[15]

Only Roberts will ever be sure what he was actually thinking at the time. But he knew that the difference between upholding the act and rejecting it was the difference between twentysomething million Americans having health insurance or having none. Many millions more would gain or lose protections from insurance company practices that made it difficult for people with preexisting conditions to get decent coverage and pay their bills. The decision would also affect a sector that, roughly speaking, was responsible for one-sixth of the nation's economic output each year.

Arguably, only a handful of decisions in the court's recent history promised to have such a direct, dramatic impact on the everyday lives of so many Americans—*Brown v. Board of Education,* maybe *Roe v. Wade,* and one or two others. But *Brown* was a 7–2 decision, and *Roe* was 6–3. Once, in an interview with the journalist Jeffrey Rosen, Roberts mused about the fact that chief justices were more memorable for their failures than their successes—and that a court overturning laws and precedents on closely divided, party-line votes would look, to future historians, like a failure. Yet since becoming chief, he'd presided over plenty of 5–4 rulings. A decision to strike down the Affordable Care Act was going to break down the same way.[16]

Those past cases had something else in common. They raised fundamental questions about the government's right to achieve a particular policy outcome. Could the government outlaw abortion? Could it prohibit segregation? In those cases, the court was grappling with real debates over whether the federal government had any business even trying to reach those objectives. The advocates challenging the Affordable Care Act certainly believed their case was about a similarly weighty issue; they were trying to prevent the government from forcing people to buy a commercial product. But not even they questioned whether the government had a right to make health insurance widely available. They understood that a program like Medicare was perfectly constitutional.[17]

Whatever Roberts was thinking, he decided at some point he wasn't ready to throw out the entire law, according to those subsequent journalistic accounts. That put him in conflict with the conservatives, including Kennedy, who, as he had intimated in oral argument, was ready to toss the entire program. And while Roberts wasn't about to change his mind about the limits of the Commerce Clause, he had already been thinking about the taxing power, as his question in oral arguments indicated. He started writing a decision to uphold the mandate as a tax.

As word reached the other GOP appointees, either some of them or some of their clerks started venting outside the chambers, because news of Roberts's possible treachery quickly circulated through conservative political circles. It led to a series of cryptic columns by conservative writers in *Newsweek, The Wall Street Journal,* and *The Washington Post,* each fretting that Roberts might let the law stand.[18]

Then, on June 2, *National Review* editor Ramesh Ponnuru told a Princeton University alumni reunion panel that "my own sort of educated guess, based on people I talk to at the Supreme Court, is that—well, as I'm sure people know, there's an initial vote the same week, on the Friday of the oral arguments. And my understanding is that there was a 5–4 vote to strike down the mandate and maybe some related provisions but not the entire act. Since then, interestingly, there seem to have been some second thoughts. Not on the part of Justice Kennedy but on the part of Chief Justice Roberts, who seems to be going a little bit wobbly."[19]

Verrilli had heard the stories too. He didn't believe them, because rumors about impending decisions were rarely accurate. He also didn't know when a decision was coming, since the court doesn't say in advance. It just indicates what days it intends to issue rulings. With the term drawing to a close, Verrilli went every day, sitting at the government lawyer's table and listening to the rulings—until there was just one left.[20]

5.

On June 28, the room was just as packed as it had been for the oral arguments, the mood just as tense, although this time, it was tinged with a greater sense of trepidation from the law's supporters. A whistle sounded, and the justices each stepped forward from the curtained area behind the bench, taking their seats. Roberts spoke, dispensing first with some routine orders. Then he said, matter-of-factly, "I have the announcement in case number 11–393, *National Federation of Independent Business versus Sebelius,* and the related cases."

Justices reading from the bench read excerpts or summaries of their decisions because it would take too long to read them in their entirety. Even so, Roberts spent about six minutes talking about the government's Commerce Clause arguments on behalf of the mandate—and why, in the opinion of five justices, those arguments were wrong. It was the challengers' logic almost verbatim. The government could regulate activity but not inactivity; the administration's lawyers had not come up with an acceptable, definable limit that would stop the government from making other commands. The broccoli argument had prevailed.

Then Roberts got to the taxing power.

Roberts did not change his inflection at this point or at any point in the oration. For all the emotion in his voice, he could have been reading the terms and conditions on a software purchase. But Verrilli didn't need tonal cues to recognize a turning point when Roberts said, "Under our precedent, if there are two possible interpretations of a statute and one of those interpretations violates the Constitutions—the Constitution, courts should adopt the interpretation that allows the statute to be upheld."

This was a reference to the theory of constitutional avoidance. As Roberts went on to explain, if the taxing power argument was even somewhat reasonable, the Supreme Court had a duty to uphold the mandate as constitutional. And that is what the court had decided, in an opinion where Roberts joined the four liberals.

Outside the courtroom, where activists on both sides had gathered, it was confusion and then bedlam. CNN, seeing that the justices had rejected the Commerce Clause argument, announced that the court had struck down the mandate. Fox News did the same, prompting the law's challengers to celebrate. Then the Associated Press and SCOTUSblog, a website that had become the go-to for politicos following the case, pushed out the correct report—that the mandate and most of the law would stand, thanks to the taxing power. Soon CNN and Fox were issuing corrections. Now it was the law's supporters cheering.[21]

Their euphoria was so overwhelming that few noticed the second part of Roberts's ruling, in which he sided with the plaintiffs on Medicaid, supporting an argument even some of the law's legal critics considered a stretch. The federal government was holding a gun to the heads of the states, Roberts said. The court wasn't going to throw out the entire Affordable Care Act because of that problem, Roberts said, but it declared invalid the threat to existing state Medicaid funds. Two of the liberals, Stephen Breyer and Elena Kagan, joined this part of the decision in what many assumed was part of an implicit deal to solidify Roberts's upholding the mandate.[22]

The Medicaid ruling would have vast, long-term consequences because it effectively made the expansion optional, giving conservative states the ability to reject it. But for the law's defenders, that was a discussion and a fight for another day. In the car on the way back to the Justice Department, Verrilli got a phone call. It was Obama, offering congratulations and his thanks. "It was my honor," Verrilli said. Later, at the office, the team celebrated with grocery-store sheet cake. Joe Palmore, an attorney who'd worked on the case from the beginning and had been sitting at the table next to Verrilli, walked into his office, closed the door, and broke down crying—able, finally, to let loose some of the anxiety and trepidation his psyche had accumulated over the last seventeen months.[23]

The mood on the other side of the fight was one part astonishment, one part fury at Roberts for betraying them with an argument they deemed unserious. Defeatism set in too. They had worked so hard to fill the judiciary with conservatives, but they had lost on their signature cause, and they wouldn't get another chance.

Except they would.

Twenty

The Anti-Universal Club

1.

Michael Cannon says that he wasn't always a libertarian. He grew up in the Virginia suburbs of Washington, hearing and accepting the social justice teaching of his Catholic faith. Then he got to college at the University of Virginia and started reading Friedrich Hayek, the Austrian economist who preached the virtues of the free market. Cannon was shedding the "economic and social authoritarianism" of his youth, as he later explained it to me. He became convinced that government transfers of wealth were wasteful and that ingenuity, unfettered by prescriptive regulation, delivered more progress and prosperity than social welfare programs. "I was the guy asking the upper-level undergraduate course instructors, 'Why don't we have any [free-market champion Milton] Friedman or Hayek on the syllabus?'"

After graduating college in 1994, Cannon found work at the right-wing group Citizens for a Sound Economy and then the Senate Republican Policy Committee, focusing on health care because, he said, there was a lot of work to be done and few staff to do it. It was the first time that he perceived a "wonk gap" between the parties. The greater Democratic Party universe was teeming with activists and experts who had made health care their life's work. The Republican Party had only a handful, and many of them, like Cannon, had found their way to it by accident. "There's a joke I like to tell," Cannon said, "which is, what do Christian Scientists and Republicans have in common? They just don't do health care."

Cannon theorized that the lack of Republican interest was a by-product, in part, of the political environment. Liberal Democrats got to work on creating and then maintaining programs that gave people clear, tangible benefits. Nobody ever lost votes by promising seniors new Medicare benefits. Republicans would try to downsize or eliminate those programs. That was usually unpopular, and so Republicans gravitated to other issues like taxes and national security, where they could portray themselves as delivering relief or providing protection.

Cannon didn't think it had to be this way. He believed that stripping away government regulations and subsidies would result in cheaper, better health care, and that the voters would reward that. Those policies required an investment of time and political capital that few Republicans had been willing to make. But he was. After about four years on Capitol Hill, Cannon joined the Cato Institute, a libertarian think tank that used to go by the name Charles Koch Foundation in recognition of the man whose donations underwrote it initially. Its main preoccupation was economic policy, with a focus on tearing down regulation and taxes.[1]

Cannon took notice in 2006 when Mitt Romney signed the Massachusetts reforms—"Panic would not be too strong a word," he said—and was not surprised to see top Heritage scholars involved in it. The Massachusetts system, with its regulation of plans and individual mandate, made perfect sense if the goal was to make sure everybody had insurance. But Cannon kept arguing that universal health care ultimately led to worse access and worse care and that requiring people to have insurance, whether public or private, was fundamentally immoral. In 2007, he declared himself the president of the "anti–universal coverage club."[2]

Cannon said he didn't vote for either major party candidate in the 2008 election, although he added that he had preferred Obama because of his opposition to the Iraq War, and because the United States finally having an African American president would be such an important milestone. But Cannon strongly opposed Obama's health care proposal and admitted surprise that the Democrats managed to pass it even after Scott Brown's election. He respected what Democrats had accomplished, admired it, even. Clearly, universal coverage mattered enough that the president and his allies were willing to risk their political careers on it. At the same time, he wasn't about to concede defeat.

Although repealing a major piece of social welfare legislation was virtually unheard of, Cannon knew, the one exception in U.S. history was the Medicare Catastrophic Coverage Act, the Reagan-era initiative to fill gaps in the program's benefit structure. It passed with strong bipartisan support, but opponents kept attacking it, focusing on the higher costs some seniors would face. It became so unpopular that a nearly equivalent bipartisan coalition voted to get rid of the law a year later. Cannon thought something similar might be possible with the Affordable Care Act, which he believed was grotesquely mistitled and which had aroused a large, intense backlash even before it became law.

That backlash had helped Republican gubernatorial and state legislative candidates across the country to win in the 2010 elections. Cannon thought he could best serve the cause by educating these newly elected Republicans, many of whom had touted their opposition to the health care law but didn't really grasp how it worked or how much power they had to undermine it. "One of the first things I realized," Cannon explained later, "is that you want to keep the negatives high and that a good way to do that would be to convince states not to implement the law."

At that point, after the election and before the Supreme Court decision in *NFIB*, Cannon believed the main choice states faced was whether to create and maintain the new insurance exchanges. The alternative was to let the Department of Health and Human Services in Washington do it. Cannon understood why state management might appeal to governors and state lawmakers, especially conservatives eager to avoid federal control. But this was a misconception, he told state officials, because the law didn't leave them as much leeway as they thought. It dictated how insurers could price their products; states had some flexibility to set benefits but, crucially, they'd maintain that flexibility even if HHS ran the exchanges. As Cannon later recalled, his message was, "Don't just do something—stand there. I was asking them to sit on their hands and politicians are actually surprisingly good at that."[3]

Cannon began a tour of sorts, with Virginia among his first stops. In a June 2011 appearance before the state's joint commission on health care, Cannon emphasized that building an exchange would divert resources: "Every dollar that Virginia spends on an Exchange is a dollar it cannot spend on roads, education, or police." By refusing to take part in the enterprise, Cannon added, Virginia lawmakers would send a message about the strength of popular opposition to the law, thus lending credibility to the lawsuit against the mandate that their own attorney general had helped launch.[4]

After that testimony, Cannon later said, he got an email from Jonathan Adler, who taught constitutional law at Case Western Reserve University and shared Cannon's libertarian sensibility. It was about a wrinkle in the Affordable Care Act, the peculiar wording of a specific passage, that seemed to create a significant legal vulnerability—although even Adler did not seem to appreciate how significant it was.[5]

2.

"This bastard has to be killed as a matter of political hygiene. I do not care how this is done—whether it's dismembered, whether we drive a stake through its heart, whether we tar and feather it and drive it out of town. . . . I don't care who does it—whether it's some court someplace or the United States Congress. Any which way, any dollar spent on that goal is worth spending. Any brief filed towards that end is worth filing. Any speech or panel contribution toward that end is a service to the United States."[6]

The speaker was Michael Grieve, a George Mason University law professor affiliated with the conservative American Enterprise Institute. The venue was an otherwise sleepy AEI forum on opportunities for lawsuits against the Affordable Care Act. It was December 2010 and the mandate lawsuits were already underway. The purpose of this forum was to find new methods of attack, and one of the other panelists, a South Carolina attorney named Thomas Christina, thought he had found one.

Christina, an employment benefits expert who had served in Reagan's Justice Department, had started studying the Affordable Care Act because his firm advised clients who would need to comply with its rules. It was in the course of that work he came across a clause about calculating tax credits, the federal subsidies to make private coverage on the exchanges more affordable. The clause referred to "an exchange established by the state" and said nothing about those established by the federal government when a state declined to take action. "This could be an unintended consequence," he told the AEI forum, "but the lesson appears to be, there will be no tax credits for taxpayers who live in non-capitulating states."[7]

Adler passed this information along to Cannon, who knew instantly what a big deal that was. Without the subsidies, the exchanges would fall apart. Too many people wouldn't be able to afford insurance.

Cannon incorporated the tax credit ambiguity into his counsel for Republican state officials. "I explicitly made the pitch that, if you want to stop the ACA, then, as a state official, this is the most important thing that you can do. Because if they stick to the statutory language and [a large number of] states don't establish exchanges, Congress will have to reopen the law. And the President will have to make some sort of deal." Cannon and Adler also started taking up the possibility of court challenges on the lecture circuit and at conferences, boosting conservative spirits following the disappointment of *NFIB*. Eventually, two lawsuits were funded and coordinated by the Competitive Enterprise Institute, a libertarian think tank where counsel Sam Kazman saw the same potential to thwart the Affordable Care Act that Cannon did.

The institute did most of the heavy lifting on the legal side by finding plaintiffs with standing to sue (one of whom Cannon helped recruit) and paying for their lawyers. Cannon and Adler focused on researching the case. Like Thomas Christina, they initially assumed the wording of the key clause was an accident—not a drafting error per se but rather a failure to recognize what the law's language would imply. That was not a great way to win a case, because judges would be reluctant to block the law's implementation because of sloppy wording. But after digging into the legislative history they developed a new argument—that the lawmakers who wrote that section "100 percent intended to restrict subsidies to state-established exchanges," in order to make sure states did their part.[8]

That argument picked up credibility when a Philadelphia financial adviser named Rich Weinstein dug up some old academic lectures by Jonathan Gruber, forever memorialized on YouTube, in which he said, "What's important to remember politically about this is if you're a state and you don't set up an exchange, that means your citizens don't get their tax credits." Gruber's high profile, as both an adviser to reformers and advocate for the Affordable Care Act, made the video especially damning.[9]

When those videos came out, Gruber said he couldn't remember why he would have said that. The whole point of the program, he said, was to make sure financial assistance was available everywhere, not make it dependent on state officials. Among those vouching for that view was Liz Fowler, who was as closely involved in the law's drafting as any other person in Washington. Although generally press shy, she spoke up to say the Cannon-Adler theory was not representative of her thinking—or that of her boss, Max Baucus, or any other legislators she heard. John McDonough, who had helped craft the law and then written a definitive tome on it, said the same thing. Timothy Jost, a Washington and Lee law professor who advised Democrats throughout the process and who knew the statute's nooks and crannies as well as anybody, was unequivocal. "These claims are simply false. The legislative history of the ACA establishes that Congress understood that premium tax credits would be available through both federal and state exchanges."[10]

Reporters on the beat were just as bewildered. "As someone who has covered Obamacare and the people who wrote it for five years, the argument that Congress actually didn't know how it intended for subsidies to work rings hollow," wrote Sarah Kliff, who had covered the law's crafting for *Politico* before moving to *The Washington Post* (and later *Vox* and *The New York Times*). "Legislators knew exactly how the subsidies were meant to work, and they intended for them to work in every state, no matter who built the exchange." Julie Rovner, a National Public Radio correspondent who had been covering health care since the 1980s, posted on her Facebook page that "I also had 100s of conversations with people writing the bill in 2009 and 2010, and I never had anyone mention the idea that subsidies would only be available in state exchanges."[11]

As for why the key legislative clause had the language it did, one theory came from Greg Sargent, a *Washington Post* columnist, and Larry Levitt, who from his position at the Kaiser Foundation provided regular policy feedback to staff working on health legislation. The original Senate Finance bill had state exchanges only; the HELP bill envisioned a state option with a federal fallback. When Harry Reid's staff merged the two, they pulled pieces of language from each—and the meaning of the clause in question, which came from the original HELP bill, suddenly became more ambiguous. The intention, to allow tax credits everywhere, never wavered.[12]

These sorts of recollections and theories on the legislative process would have no weight in court. But logic could, and Nicholas Bagley, a law professor at the University of Michigan, pointed out the absurdity of using the loss of tax credits as a threat to states and then making the threat so difficult to detect. "When Vito Corleone in *The Godfather* made a man an offer 'he couldn't refuse,' he wasn't subtle about it: 'Either his brains or his signature would be on the contract.' That's how you threaten somebody. The phrase 'through an exchange established by the state' doesn't cut it."[13]

And while *Godfather* references might not be enough to persuade the justices, experts like Bagley knew of a powerful legal argument that might. Under accepted doctrine, the government's interpretation of the ambiguous wording didn't have to be the best one. It merely had to be plausible.

3.

The Supreme Court agreed in November 2014 to take the case, following conflicting circuit court rulings in which, once again, the only judges to rule against the Affordable Care Act were Republican appointees. The hearing for *King v. Burwell* was in early March, a little less than three years after *NFIB* appeared before the justices.

This time, it was just one session of oral argument, not four. And although it was Don Verrilli facing off against Michael Carvin one more time, the dynamics were conspicuously different. Now Carvin was getting tougher questions, including several on why the law's architects would have tucked such an important provision into a relatively obscure part of the statute. "I mean," Kagan said, "this took a year and a half for anybody to even notice this language."

Sotomayor mentioned the potential to create a "death spiral," because the subsidies (more so than the mandate) were essential to keeping healthy people enrolling. She was getting at another key argument by the law's defenders—that the Affordable Care Act's architects would never have deliberately created a program that contained the ingredients for its own destruction, so that it was at "war with itself."[14]

This possibility also got Kennedy's attention. He seemed especially concerned that, by forcing states to choose between managing their own exchanges or risking a death spiral in their insurance markets, the federal government was effectively coercing them. As he'd made clear in his vote to strike down the Medicaid provision in *NFIB*, he did not think the federal government should have that power. "There's a serious constitutional problem if we adopt your argument," Kennedy said to Carvin.

The decision came in June: Another ruling to uphold the law, this time by a vote of 6–3. Tax credits would continue to go to all states. Roberts had written the decision, with Kennedy providing the sixth vote, just as his questions had hinted he would do.

Roberts's opinion was, by the standards of the court, straightforward to the point of terse. He conceded that the phrase "established by a state" made that particular clause ambiguous. But, he went on to say, it was "implausible" that Congress intended to jeopardize insurance for so many millions and risk severe damage to state insurance markets. "Congress passed the Affordable Care Act to improve health insurance markets, not to destroy them. If at all possible, we must interpret the Act in a way that is consistent with the former, and avoids the latter."

The chief was careful not to pass judgment on the law itself: "In a democracy, the power to make the law rests with those chosen by the people. . . . In every case we must respect the role of the Legislature, and take care not to undo what it has done."

It was in some respects a banal statement of the judiciary's role in the American system of government. But it also felt like a message from Roberts to the Republican lawmakers who worked across the street: Get rid of Obamacare if you'd like, just don't ask me to do your work for you.

On that, they were happy to oblige.

Twenty-one

Purification

1.

The first bill proposing to get rid of the Affordable Care Act got to the clerk of the U.S. Senate on March 23, 2010, right around the same time the first constitutional challenge landed in federal court. The bill's sponsor was Jim DeMint, the South Carolina senator who had hoped 2009 Tea Party protests would bring about Obama's Waterloo. The bill had twenty-two cosponsors, which was actually more than the total number of words in the legislation's one-sentence text: "The Patient Protection and Affordable Care Act, and the amendments made by that Act, are repealed."[1]

Republicans in the House and Senate would file several more repeal bills in 2010, each one with roughly the same substantive content as DeMint's. "Repeal and replace" was the party's official motto, but the bills were all repeal, no replace. The legislation was primarily a way to show voters, financial supporters, and sympathetic interest groups that Republicans remained inextricably opposed to Obama's health care reform effort. They would have to win back Congress to repeal it for real.

Republicans were calling it Obamacare by this time, and they used it to bludgeon vulnerable Democrats like Wisconsin's Russ Feingold with television ads warning that the health care law would mean higher taxes and insurance premiums along with lower quality—and that it would cut more than $500 billion from Medicare. The basis for that last claim was the law's reduction in Medicare payments, including cuts that Democrats had negotiated with the hospitals and other groups, to offset the cost of the coverage expansion.[2]

In reality, Democrats had gone out of their way to protect benefits for individual seniors. The one change retirees were likely to see and feel was extra help with prescription costs, because the Affordable Care Act would fill in the "donut hole" gap in Medicare's drug coverage. But that would happen gradually, starting in 2011. Especially for voters exposed only to right-wing media, the argument about Medicare cuts validated suspicions that Obama and the Democrats were reducing benefits for hardworking Americans to finance a giveaway to other, less deserving parts of the population. Ron Johnson, the Tea Party Republican challenging Feingold, predicted that Obamacare "will destroy our health care system."[3]

On Election Day, Democrats took a "shellacking," as Obama called it afterward, with net losses of six seats in the Senate and sixty-three in the House, more than enough to swing control of the chamber back to the Republicans. Pelosi's reign as Speaker was over after just four years, and Obama's opportunity to pass major legislation was gone with it. He would spend the rest of his presidency on defense, not offense.

But something else had changed in the election. The Republican caucuses became more ideologically and temperamentally extreme.

In the House, the GOP's leader was John Boehner, whose impassioned floor speech against the Affordable Care Act on the night of its passage remained an emotional lodestar for many of his colleagues. Later in 2010, rallying conservative voters, he vowed, "We're going to do everything—and I mean everything we can do—to kill it, stop it, slow it down, whatever we can." Still, Boehner was an old-school legislator, well practiced in the art of screaming at his opponents one minute and making a deal with them the next. He was a doctrinaire Republican, but he wasn't on a mission to rewrite the federal code. He didn't even hate Obama in the way some members of his caucus did. He got along with the president just fine.[4]

Incoming Budget Committee chairman Paul Ryan, on the other hand, was a crusader whose beliefs were more indicative of the emerging Republican approach on policy. Ryan, frequently seen around Wisconsin in his hunting gear and on Capitol Hill with his poster-sized fiscal charts, had developed a following among conservative intellectuals by sketching out blueprints for lower taxes and a thinner, more privatized welfare state. He believed that large entitlement programs were bankrupting the government and that programs for the poor created dependency. For Medicare and Medicaid, he proposed to end the guarantee of benefits they provided and reduce their spending dramatically over time.[5]

This was of course precisely what Republicans were accusing Democrats of doing with the Affordable Care Act, only Ryan's plans really were likely to cut benefits and leave seniors facing much bigger medical bills. But Ryan got little grief about his proposals from within the party. On the contrary, he had support from across the GOP caucus, because his agenda lumped opposition to older, more cherished government programs (to the delight of establishment conservatives and their financial backers) with opposition to the Affordable Care Act (to the delight of the Tea Party and its allies). Ryan was also popular with white, blue-collar workers back home, despite his designs on Medicare, presumably because his anti-Obama—and anti-Obamacare—posture appealed to them too.

If Ryan was the GOP's ego, Michele Bachmann was its id. Bachmann was a lawyer in the northern Minneapolis suburbs who decided to stay home when she had her fourth child. After helping to establish a charter school for her kids, she clashed with state education officials who said its Christian orientation violated the law. She became a conservative activist, won a seat in the state legislature, and then, six years later, in the U.S. House.[6]

In 2011, she was just beginning her third term and had no major legislative efforts in her record. Under the old, unwritten rules of how Congress worked, she would have been a classic backbencher, toiling away in obscurity until she finally had enough seniority to shape laws and secure projects for back home. But Bachmann was already a Tea Party hero. She'd first gotten national attention during the 2008 campaign, when, as a freshman member, she'd called Obama and his allies "anti-American." During a 2009 speech in Colorado, she likened taxes to "slavery" and rallied her supporters to fight the Democratic health care bill: "This cannot pass," Bachmann said. "What we have to do today is make a covenant, to slit our wrists, be blood brothers on this thing." It was around the same time she was reading her version of Betsy McCaughey's death panel screed into the *Congressional Record*.[7]

Bachmann's celebrity status on the right gave her power. After the midterms, Bachmann threatened to attack Boehner publicly when he balked at her demand for a better committee assignment, according to a subsequent account by *Politico*'s Tim Alberta. "I'm going to go to Rush, and Hannity, and Mark Levin, and Fox News," she said, "and I'm going to tell them that John Boehner is suppressing the Tea Partiers who helped Republicans take back the House." Boehner felt that he couldn't say no. "She had me by the balls," he told Alberta. "She had all the leverage in the world, and she knew it."[8]

A similar transformation was underway in the Senate. Ron Johnson had taken Feingold's Wisconsin seat, and Pat Toomey had taken Arlen Specter's from Pennsylvania. Their strong conservative credentials hadn't prevented them from winning two swing states, demonstrating just how willing even moderate voters were to oust Democrats in 2010. Utah's new senator was Republican Mike Lee, another Tea Party darling. At the state party's nominating convention, he had beaten incumbent Robert Bennett, the well-regarded Republican whom nobody ever confused for a liberal but whose transgressions included partnering with Democrat Ron Wyden on his bipartisan health care bill.[9]

Hostility to Obamacare intensified with these new arrivals, and in January 2011, right at the beginning of the session, DeMint decided to introduce a new repeal bill. Most of the caucus signed on right away and the few stragglers joined in short order, even though it still left unfulfilled the GOP promise to include a replacement that so many Republicans had promised would come. Some veteran advisers took notice.[10]

"There are Republicans who were Republicans before 2009 and those who came after, and the ones who came after were a very different brand of human," Rodney Whitlock, who was a Grassley aide until 2015, told me later. "Those of us who were here before, we began to realize that the rules have changed, and the rules are no longer—I hate to use this word, but it's right—rational. . . . Post-2010 election, the transformation begins almost immediately, that there is no peace to be had here."[11]

This lack of peace would be a defining feature of national politics going forward. It would make life miserable for Democrats and also for some Republicans, especially one who had his eyes on the presidency.

2.

Mitt Romney was in his natural habitat: standing in an auditorium, wearing a crisp white button-down shirt, and giving a PowerPoint presentation.

The date was May 12, 2011. The venue was at the University of Michigan Medical School in Ann Arbor. Romney's campaign for the presidency was still in its soft-launch phase, in advance of a formal announcement. He had been planning to run ever since losing to John McCain in 2008. This time, Romney was the front-runner, with high name recognition, loads of campaign cash, and endorsements from across the Republican establishment. But he also had a major political liability, and cruelly, it was the accomplishment he considered his leg-acy from Massachusetts.

Romney was proud of the health care law he had signed. A printed copy of it was one of two objects he requested be part of his official portrait that would hang forever in the Massachusetts State House. (The other was a desk-frame picture of his wife, Ann.) But conservative support for the program, especially the individual mandate, vanished when Obama used it as a prototype for national reform. Among those repudiating the mandate were Grassley and Hatch, who had spoken favorably about the concept as recently as 2009. Now, two years later, Romney was coming under attack for it. An editorial in *The Wall Street Journal* under the headline OBAMA'S RUNNING MATE called Romney "compromised and not credible."[12]

Rather than disown the law, as many conservatives might have preferred, Romney defended it. "I had half a million people whom I was elected to serve and who were frightened because they didn't have health insurance," Rom-ney said at the Michigan event. "As a result of the plan I put in place, 400,000 were insured and I'm pleased we were able to accomplish that." Then, using the PowerPoint slides, Romney walked his audience through the logic of the mandate and repeated the argument he'd perfected in the statehouse meeting with Amy Lischko, Tim Murphy, and Jon Gruber: "We told people either pay for your insurance or we're going to charge you for the fact that the state will have to pay for your care."[13]

Romney made clear that while he thought the mandate made sense for Massachusetts, it was not something to impose on the rest of the country, as Obama had. And that was only one of the problems with the Affordable Care Act, Romney said. The federal law raised some income taxes, Romney said, and the Massachusetts plan hadn't. Near the end, Romney sketched out some ideas he hoped to pursue as president. It was a vague list of the usual conservative reforms, including tax credits and allowing the purchase of insurance across state lines.

Romney's effort to distinguish Romneycare from Obamacare left out some pretty important context. No, the Massachusetts scheme didn't raise taxes on individuals. But mostly that was because Massachusetts was get-ting extra money from the federal government to finance the expansion. And while Romney in 2011 said the mandate was something for states to try on their own, years before, he had proudly touted it as a national model in a book he wrote. (The paperback version scrubbed those lines.)[14]

Still, his basic position, that a mandate might be fine in Massachusetts but not in other parts of the country, had a logical consistency to it. It was also right in line with the case that conservative lawyers were in the process of bringing before the Supreme Court. The central claim in *NFIB* was about federal power—specifically, that nothing in the Constitution gave Congress the authority to impose such a requirement. The lawsuit said nothing about whether states could impose one at their discretion.

The problem for Romney was that the conservative uprising against Obamacare wasn't a nuanced argument about federalism or the finer points of constitutional law. It was an objection to the whole idea of requiring people to be part of a universal coverage scheme—and, more generally, an objection to the Obama presidency. As Ryan Lizza observed in *The New Yorker,* "Romney could give his PowerPoint presentation in every living room in Iowa and New Hampshire until every Republican understood the technical differences between the two plans, and it would not change the core of his dilemma."[15]

Romney's most formidable rival in the primaries was former Pennsylvania senator Rick Santorum, who attacked Romney's health care record relentlessly. "We have a candidate . . . who is the worst possible person in the field to put up on this most fundamental issue in this campaign, and that is Gov. Romney," Santorum said at one event. "The plan he put together in Massachusetts is in fact 'ObamaCare' on the state level."[16]

Romney survived the challenge, in part because Santorum, whose popularity with evangelicals carried him in early contests, alienated even many Republican voters with more extreme positions. He didn't just oppose gay marriage. He had opposed allowing gays to serve openly in the military. Santorum also didn't have the money to keep up with Romney, who was able to finance advertisements highlighting Santorum's own inconsistencies. It turned out that Santorum, like so many other Republicans, had once made favorable comments about the idea of an insurance mandate.[17]

Once Romney secured the nomination, he picked Paul Ryan as a running mate, giving the ticket a little extra vigor (Ryan was just forty-two years old) and reassuring conservatives upset about Romney's role as the Obamacare instigator. But the addition of Ryan to the ticket saddled Romney with a much broader policy agenda that, however popular with opinion editors at *The Wall Street Journal,* turned out to be deeply unpopular once it got wider public exposure. Medicare and Medicaid, the programs most squarely in Ryan's sights, were beloved by most Americans—even those who were part of the Tea Party.[18]

This tension between the Republican ruling class (which wanted to scale back or privatize all entitlement programs) and less upscale parts of the Republican base (which wanted to preserve and strengthen entitlement programs from which they benefited directly) was a perennial issue that Democrats had successfully exploited before—most memorably back in the 1990s, when Bill Clinton used Newt Gingrich's attacks on Medicare and Medicaid to revive his presidency and reputation among middle-class voters. Obama pursued the same line of attack, highlighting the impact of Ryan's Medicare cuts and what they would mean for average Americans.[19]

Obama also started talking about the Affordable Care Act a lot more, embracing the Obamacare moniker and linking it to more cherished parts of the welfare state. "You know what?" he said at a Texas rally. "They're right. I do care." In 2010, Obama and party leaders had been wary of elevating the issue, fearful that it would hurt vulnerable candidates in swing districts. But in 2012, a debate on health care highlighted the contrasts with Romney, whose record in venture capital left him open to attacks as a soulless corporate raider—just as it had in 1994, when he lost that Massachusetts Senate race to Ted Kennedy.[20]

Obama's victory in November felt to many in Washington like a turning point. Months after the Supreme Court had upheld the Affordable Care Act, the electorate had given its approval—it not to the program itself, then to the president who'd created it. "Obamacare is the law of the land," Boehner conceded in a postelection interview.

But almost immediately afterward, Boehner's office issued a statement reaffirming Boehner's commitment to repeal, along with a tweet: "Our goal remains #fullrepeal." Boehner and his aides could sense that the GOP base remained committed to the program's destruction, political circumstances notwithstanding.[21]

"We messaged from 2010 to 2012, and we convinced everybody that we were going to repeal and replace Obamacare," one former GOP aide said later. "Somehow, everyone in the core conservative part of the Republican Party missed the memo on the fact that to repeal and replace Obamacare, we actually needed a Republican president."[22]

3.

In December 2012, Jim DeMint announced that he was leaving the Senate to take over the Heritage Foundation. The decision was not as surprising as it seemed at first blush. Although he didn't have a doctorate or the typically mild-mannered sensibility of a think tank leader, he was going to Heritage at a time when the institution was in the final stages of a transformation that mirrored changes in the Republican Party and conservative movement.

Heritage, a pillar of the policy infrastructure conservatives erected in the 1970s, had supplied the Reagan administration with a governing agenda and had a standing reservation at a weekly meeting of Republicans in Congress. Among its most influential scholars was Stuart Butler, who applied a Thatcher-era, pro-privatization sensibility from his native England to American debates—by, for example, seeking to turn Social Security into a system of investment accounts.[23]

On health care, Butler found the U.S. system inscrutable and unreliable. It was the same reaction many progressives had, except that Butler thought the best solution was to have everybody get private insurance. A plan he introduced in the late 1980s and fine-tuned afterward envisioned minimal, "catastrophic" policies, but his plan also included an individual mandate. That put him on the right side of the mainstream debate during the Clinton health care fight, when he was helping Republicans devise their alternatives. A decade later, it was Butler's colleagues at Heritage who advised Romney and spoke up for the Massachusetts reforms, including a mandate, when they became law.[24]

The grief Heritage got from some conservatives when Romney embraced the mandate got more intense in 2009, when Obama and the Democrats put one in their plan as well. Heritage did everything it could to distance itself from the idea, and Butler did too, pointing out that he had plenty of other objections to the Affordable Care Act. But Heritage's standing within conservative circles took a hit. (Butler, whose work increasingly focused on helping low-income children, would eventually leave Heritage.)[25]

In 2010, the year the Affordable Care Act became law, Heritage made a critical decision about its structure. It followed the lead of other ideologically aligned think tanks (including the liberal Center for American Progress) and spun off a separate, technically independent organization. Heritage Action fell under section 501c(4) in the tax code, which meant that it could not accept tax-deductible contributions. In exchange for giving up that source of support, it could engage in direct political advocacy—by, for example, endorsing congressional candidates or financing advertisements to influence lawmakers.

Heritage Action got right to work on fighting the Affordable Care Act. One of the first congressmen to file a repeal bill in 2010 was Steve King, the Iowa Republican who was becoming infamous for his nativist views. About the only thing that seemed to rile King as much as immigration was Obamacare, and to get his repeal bill onto the agenda, he was trying to use a discharge petition that would force a floor vote that Democrats could not block. The key was getting a majority to sign it. Heritage Action took up the cause as its own, sending out alerts to the foundation's email list, which numbered more than six hundred thousand, advising recipients to contact their members of Congress and lobby them to sign. "What's the point in having a conservative party if we're not going to fight a massive federal intervention in health care?" Michael Needham, Heritage Action's cofounder, told Robert Draper of *The New York Times*.[26]

Tom Price and Mike Pence, then congressmen representing Georgia and Indiana, respectively, were among the Republican congressmen who signed the petition. And although the effort came up about forty signatures short, the 2010 GOP takeover in the House emboldened Heritage Action to keep pushing total opposition—an effort that sometimes put it in conflict with Republicans who were, or at least thought themselves to be, every bit as committed to the law's repeal. In 2012, when Eric Cantor, the Virginia congressman and majority whip, was promoting a bill to eliminate the Affordable Care Act's Medicare payment commission, Heritage Action came out against the proposal because it might "muddy the water" and distract from full repeal.[27]

A few months later, DeMint arrived at Heritage, where he had authority over both the think tank and advocacy wings—and where his first big crusade would be an effort to kill Obamacare by defunding it.

4.

The timing was almost too perfect. Obamacare had survived the Supreme Court, and Obama had survived reelection. The first provisions, including one allowing young adults to stay on their parents' policies, were already in place. But the big expansions of Medicaid and opening of exchanges with subsidized insurance would not start until 2014—or, from a more practical perspective, on October 1, 2013, when people could begin enrolling. October 1 was also the end of the fiscal year, which meant basic government operations could not continue until Congress authorized new spending.

DeMint and his allies wanted House Republicans to pass an appropriations bill with zero funding for the Affordable Care Act and present it to the Senate as a take-it-or-leave-it proposition. Harry Reid would presumably say no, but DeMint said that public anger would force Reid to relent. Then a bill would go to Obama, who would similarly buckle under pressure and agree, finally, to reopen negotiations over the health care law, resulting in repeal.

Or something like that. The plan seemed positively nutty to most of Washington, including House Republicans like Charlie Dent, who was co-chairman of a moderate GOP caucus called the Tuesday Group. Shutdown tactics had backfired since Gingrich's day, because voters always blamed Republicans. The only thing more far-fetched than Reid conceding was Obama agreeing to go along with the gutting of his legacy domestic policy achievement. "There was no chance of success," Dent said later. "There never was. And everybody knew it."[28]

It wasn't just members of the GOP's shrinking moderate wing who felt this way. "To create the impression that we can actually defund Obamacare, when the only thing we control, and barely, is the House of Representatives, is not intellectually honest," Tom Coburn, the conservative Oklahoma senator, said. A former GOP aide heard a Heritage Action official say Obama would look ridiculous for shutting down the government. "Or maybe we'll be the ones who look ridiculous," the aide thought.[29]

But the Defund Obamacare movement had one powerful ally: Ted Cruz, the newly elected senator from Texas.

An accomplished lawyer with longtime political aspirations, Cruz had challenged the sitting lieutenant governor, David Dewhurst, in a Republican primary that turned into a pitched battle between the GOP's establishment and Tea Party wings. Dewhurst had the backing of the governor, Rick Perry, and a number of high-profile state officials. Cruz had endorsements from Sarah Palin and Rick Santorum. Cruz prevailed in the final GOP runoff with 57 percent of the vote, then dispatched his Democratic opponent in the general election with relative ease.

Cruz, the son of a Cuban immigrant who first came to the United States with one hundred dollars sewn into his pants, prevailed on the strength of an innovative campaign that relied heavily on social media and attacked Obama for trying to bring "European-style" socialism to America. "His substantive ideology is profoundly dangerous," Cruz said in one flourish. "I think Obama is a creature of the elite academic institutions of this country, and he reflects their far-left radical ideology."[30]

Cruz was also a creature of those institutions or at least a product of them, with degrees from Princeton and Harvard Law School plus an impressive record as a top college debater. Later, he had a Supreme Court clerkship with Chief Justice William Rehnquist. Cruz didn't try to hide these credentials from the voters—or from anybody else, for that matter. His reputation for intellectual arrogance went back to his days in law school, when, as Jason Zengerle later reported in *GQ*, Cruz preferred his study group draw exclusively from graduates of Harvard, Yale, and Princeton, rather than "minor Ivies" like Brown and Penn.[31]

That same attitude didn't make him especially popular in the Senate, where Lindsey Graham, another South Carolina Republican, later quipped that "if you killed Ted Cruz on the floor of the Senate, and the trial was in the Senate, nobody would convict you." But it wasn't just Cruz's personality that rubbed so many senators wrong. It was his willingness—eagerness, even—to attack Republican colleagues who didn't share his ideological purity. Which was nearly all of them.[32]

Inside the caucus, Cruz had stepped into the role DeMint once occupied, only DeMint was still involved from the outside, and the two partnered up on the Defund Obamacare movement. Cruz dispatched his father to join DeMint on a nine-city bus tour that Heritage Action was sponsoring. And when the tour got to Dallas, Cruz made a special appearance. "We've all seen this movie before," Cruz said. "President Obama and Harry Reid are gonna scream and yell 'those mean, nasty Republicans are threatening to shut down the government.'" Not to worry, Cruz assured the spectators; he and the Republicans could overcome that. "One side or the other has to blink. How do we win this fight? Don't blink!"[33]

Back in Washington, Cruz made the same case—and did so in person to a group of conservative House members, urging them to confront the "surrender caucus" within their leadership ranks. The conservatives didn't need convincing, though several thought a smarter, more realistic strategy was to demand merely a one-year delay in Obamacare funding. As for more moderate House members, they didn't like either position. But they feared the wrath of Heritage Action, the Tea Party groups, and right-wing media. The shutdown became, as one former Republican aide put it, a "purification test."[34]

Boehner, facing the same pressures as his members, put the Defund

Obamacare appropriation on the floor and backed it despite his own misgivings. It passed, prompting a confrontation that unfolded in precisely the
way all the skeptics figured it would.

Reid refused even to consider the House legislation, demanding instead
a "clean" spending bill with no special provisions defunding the Affordable Care Act. At the White House, Obama blasted House Republicans for
using brinkmanship to achieve goals out of step with public sentiments.
Cruz cheered on the House from the Senate, and DeMint did the same
from Heritage, although neither was having much luck persuading more
senators to join the cause. Republican standing in the polls plummeted,
and eventually, McConnell worked out a clean spending agreement with
Reid. Boehner folded, and the shutdown ended after a little more than two
weeks.

It was yet another moment of political vindication for the Affordable
Care Act—or at least it would have been if the program itself had been
working.

Twenty-two

Shock

1.

Click . . . click . . . click.

Denis McDonough, the White House chief of staff, was in his West Wing office and trying to log on to HealthCare.gov, the new website for the federal insurance exchange. He'd press the button on his mouse, watch the display refresh, and every time, it ended up with the same error screen.[1]

McDonough had expected glitches. So had the president. So had everybody else. But this went way beyond glitches.

Almost nobody who tried to sign up for insurance could get past the online registration screen. Those who did ran into other problems. On October 1, administration officials were initially thrilled because their data showed a surge in traffic. But the site didn't have instrumentation to show how far people were getting. It was only through social media, anecdotes, and soon press accounts that officials learned how completely the system had broken down. Only six people managed to sign up for coverage that first day.[2]

Some of the states running their own exchanges fared better. Connecticut and Kentucky had mostly functional websites. But Maryland and other states were having the same problems that the feds were, to the great frustration of newly trained enrollment counselors. "The IT system is so messed up at the moment," said the outreach director at a clinic in Prince George's County, a Maryland suburb of Washington. Staff were turning away hopeful applicants and telling them to try again in two weeks.[3]

Without Ted Cruz and the shutdown to divert attention, HealthCare

.gov would become an all-consuming political controversy and a genuine policy crisis—"Nothing short of a disaster," as Michigan GOP congressman Fred Upton put it. The setback was especially devastating to Obama, who had said people would be able to find insurance the way they shopped for electronics on Amazon or bought airline tickets on Kayak.[4]

One of his theories of change, going back to his days as a community organizer, was that success begets success. Show the people that a government program can make a meaningful difference in their lives, and they will support programs in the future, restoring for the public sector the kind of trust it had until the 1960s.

That would only happen if programs functioned, a message Obama conveyed when staff gave briefings on Affordable Care Act implementation. "All of that is well and good," he would say, "but if the Web site doesn't work, nothing else matters."[5]

2.

The Obama administration figured to be in a good position to do that. Both the 2008 and 2012 campaigns won acclaim for their use of technology as an organizing tool. And the president recruited Todd Park, a highly regarded tech entrepreneur, to serve as chief technology officer—first for HHS, then for the entire federal government. Both were new positions.

But Park's mandate was to find ways to improve the delivery of care. He wasn't directly responsible for HealthCare.gov. The administration had instead handed management over to a division within HHS called the Centers for Medicare & Medicaid Services, known as CMS.

The behemoth agency had experience running large government insurance programs and working with the private sector. But a big reason CMS got the job was political circumstances. In the final stages of writing the Affordable Care Act, Democratic leaders had agreed to reduce funding for administering the law's programs, from $15 billion down to $1 billion, to free up extra money for subsidies. They figured they could always get funding to administer the program from Congress, through routine appropriations, not realizing that Republicans would win the House in a few months and use that leverage to block new spending on the law.[6]

Putting administration of the Affordable Care Act inside the same agency that ran Medicare and Medicaid gave it an infrastructure relatively safe from Republican meddling—although, even with that arrangement, the program's administrators felt they didn't have nearly enough money to do the job right. "The staff was heroic and dedicated, but we did not have enough money, and we all knew that," said Don Berwick, who served as chief CMS administrator in 2010 and 2011.[7]

That wasn't the only way fear of political attacks shaped launch preparations. The law put critical decisions about insurance design and other factors affecting the exchange websites in the hands of the HHS secretary, in part to preserve flexibility. But with an election looming, the administration waited on issuing some key guidance and rules, since every announcement was bound to raise objections somewhere. "They just held up these regulations way too long because they were concerned about the 2012 election—and doing anything that could upset the applecart," one former senior administration official said later. "They totally went into this defensive crouch," said another. "And they just stayed there. If they could avoid a fight or push it off until later, they did it."[8]

These delays had consequences, because enrolling people in insurance promised to be a lot more complicated than hawking books or airline tickets. The system had to verify identity status, cross-check income with available payroll data, figure out eligibility for Medicaid or tax credits, show insurance buyers their options in a user-friendly way—and then, for people getting private plans, send a packet of data with all the relevant information over to the insurers, who could then add them to the rolls and get payment.

Every step of that process entailed its own unique challenges. Verifying residency and immigration status in real time, something essential given the determination not to cover undocumented residents, required building an interface with computers at the Department of Homeland Security— which, in turn, required special legal and technical arrangements. Even something as simple as establishing household size, necessary for determining eligibility for Medicaid and federal insurance subsidies, was complex because the criteria for each program were different.[9]

CMS hired contractors, as it generally did for such big projects. But government procurement rules, designed primarily to thwart fraud and favoritism, limited bidding to firms that already had approval to do such work—even if, as many later argued, other tech companies were better suited to the task. As work got underway, contractors complained of confusing instructions and an inability to get quick answers to queries, because every decision required sign-off from multiple officials. Government managers, in turn, said the contractors were missing deadlines, not coordinating, and constantly blaming one another for lapses.[10]

In September 2011, an internal government report warned that implementation, including website development, was already behind schedule. In June 2013, the Government Accountability Office found a long list of unfinished business, including "the core exchange functional areas of eligibility and enrollment, plan management, and consumer assistance." The report stated that "much remains to be accomplished within a relatively short amount of time." In all, according to a subsequent Inspector General's investigation, CMS got eighteen "documented warnings" about problems with the website build between July 2011 and July 2013. Some were "scathing," the report said, and all had "substantial detail about the project's shortcomings."[11]

In the late summer and early fall of 2013, officials hastily downsized their ambitions by delaying introduction of such key features as a Spanish-language version. But in late September, as *The Washington Post* later reported, a test run with just five hundred hypothetical customers brought the system to a halt. Kate Steadman, a young HHS staffer who was working on the registration pages, remembered thinking in the final weeks that surely somebody was going to postpone the launch. No such order came. One reason was a fear that postponement—or, really, any admission that everything wasn't hunky-dory—would fuel GOP criticism. "They made very clear they didn't want us talking publicly about problems before the launch," said one state-level official who raised warnings.[12]

Insurers had been working with CMS and testing the system; they may not have supported the Affordable Care Act, but it was in their interest for the website to work. At a meeting days before the launch, they proposed a delay, only to have CMS officials rebuff the suggestion.[13] A *Wall Street Journal* article cowritten by Louise Radnofsky relaying insurer concerns elicited a similar response, with officials disputing predictions of impending disaster.[14]

One person who had predicted trouble was David Cutler, the economist who had helped shape Obama's campaign plan. Back in May of 2010, he sent a memo to his old academic adviser, Larry Summers, warning that CMS leadership was not up to the task of implementing the law and questioning the agency's ability to manage large enterprises.

Cutler's memo, which he said he was writing at the urging of administration officials who shared his concerns, was a volley in broader conflict over management of the new program. And that conflict had some familiar contours, with the economic and health policy teams at odds once again. The economic team wanted to manage implementation itself or appoint somebody who would—in part, to make sure the delivery reforms got enough attention. Obama had instead turned implementation over to Nancy-Ann DeParle, in whom he'd developed so much trust during the effort to pass legislation. DeParle in turn relied on the health team, especially after January 2011, when she became deputy White House chief of staff and inherited new responsibilities.

DeParle left the administration altogether in January 2013, which put Jeanne Lambrew, who had become a special assistant to the president, in charge. But her broad portfolio included nearly every aspect of health care reform implementation, not just the website, and inside CMS, no one person had direct responsibility for the whole enterprise. (DeParle had tried to recruit Jon Kingsdale, who had run the Massachusetts Health Connector under Romney; he said no.) Lines of authority were opaque, not only to frontline workers but also to top officials, according to the Inspector General's report. Sometimes people were afraid to share bad news. Other times, they weren't sure who should get it.[15]

Exactly who in the chain of command was most responsible for the failures was the subject of much angry conversation afterward. Some blamed DeParle and Lambrew; others pointed fingers at Sebelius, who after all ran HHS, or Marilyn Tavenner, a nurse and longtime public servant who took over CMS in late 2011. Of course, it was Obama who had put HealthCare.gov in their hands, even though none of them had experience managing this kind of project. "We hadn't ever built anything like this," Tavenner told Steven Brill for his book *America's Bitter Pill*. "We didn't know what we didn't know."[16]

In the end, Obama administration officials weren't asleep at the switch so much as they didn't understand how to operate it. Because of that, the president's signature domestic policy program was literally not functioning.

And that wasn't even the biggest problem they faced.

3.

The most notorious promise that Obama made about health care may have actually started with his 2008 campaign rival, Hillary Clinton. "If you have private insurance you like, nothing changes—you can keep that insurance," Clinton said in a speech describing her health care reform plan, as the *Washington Examiner*'s Rebecca Berg reported years later. At some point, Obama started making the same claim about his proposal, which mostly had the same structure.[17]

The likely provenance of the promise in Clinton's rhetoric was a clue about its original intended meaning. Democrats wanted to distinguish the new plan from the 1993/94 effort by showing it would leave employer-sponsored coverage largely in place. "You can draw a straight line from the nervousness about losing your current insurance during the Clinton health debate to President Obama's promise that you could keep your plans," Larry Levitt noted later.[18]

But reform was always going to have more profound effects on insurance for the small minority of people buying on their own, or what policy professionals call the "non-group" market. In fact, changing that insurance was one of reform's major goals.[19]

It was here that insurers were charging higher premiums or denying coverage to people with preexisting conditions. And it was here that insurers sold policies with massive gaps that were difficult for consumers to spot until they were sick or injured, went to get care, and discovered their policies came up short.

Sometimes when a beneficiary would file a big claim, the insurer would go back through old medical records to find evidence that it was a preexisting condition—and, then, either refuse to pay the bill or cancel the policy altogether. In Florida, an insurer would not pay for a beneficiary's ovarian cancer testing because the patient had previously reported instances of irregular menstrual periods. In Iowa, a carrier canceled the policy for a woman with a heart problem because they said her application misstated her height by an inch and her weight by five pounds. In California, one insurer paid bonuses based on how many individual policies analysts canceled; another sent physicians copies of patient insurance applications, asking the doctors to report immediately any preexisting conditions they thought the patients hadn't disclosed.[20]

But as with every other part of health care legislation, there was a trade-off to changing the industry's behavior. Insurers would be laying out a lot more money to cover all those medical bills they'd dodged before. They weren't going to eat those costs. They were going to pass them along to customers in the form of higher premiums or bigger out-of-pocket expenses.

The Affordable Care Act's tax credits were designed to mitigate the effect, and for millions of consumers, they did. But for some middle-class consumers who got only a little financial assistance or none at all, the money would not be enough to make up the difference.

During the law's drafting, liberal Democrats had worried about this. It's why they kept pushing to make the tax credits more generous. It's why they were so dismayed that outlays had to stay under $1 trillion—and borderline apoplectic when Obama, in his September address to Congress, took it down to $900 billion. It's also part of why they wanted a public option, which they believed would reliably provide a cheaper insurance alternative. In the media, progressive bloggers Jon Walker and Marcy Wheeler had crunched the numbers and warned, presciently, that the emerging reform legislation would still leave some people facing punishing costs. "For the middle class," Wheeler wrote, ". . . this remains unaffordable."[21]

The law had one other provision to protect people who already had insurance from paying more under the new system. Under a grandfather clause, insurers could keep policies that were already in place in March 2010, when the Affordable Care Act became law. They couldn't sell the plans to new customers, but they could maintain them for existing customers who wanted to stick with them.

But the non-group market was notoriously volatile. Lots of people buying insurance on their own did so for only a year or two, or just a few months. Then they would get a new job or get married or go through some other major change in life circumstances—and, once they did, sign up for an employer policy, Medicaid, or some other type of insurance. Insurers, for their part, were constantly dropping and adding policies and making changes to the ones they had. "Turnover is so significant in the ordinary course of business," law professor Timothy Jost noted in 2010, "that relatively few policies will remain grandfathered for any significant period of time."[22]

A big concern for Lambrew and some other officials was how to prevent insurers from exploiting the grandfather clause to prop up precisely the sort of shoddy insurance that the law sought to eliminate. Under the final rules that the administration issued, insurers could add benefits or make small increases in premiums and out-of-pocket costs. But they couldn't make significant pricing changes, and they couldn't take away benefits, either—which, given how frequently insurers modified those policies, meant that as many as two-thirds of plans would lose grandfather protection every year, according to the government's own estimate.[23]

Insurers warned that the rules would lead to major disruptions, Steven Brill later reported. And in the fall of 2013, letters from carriers about canceled plans started showing up in mailboxes around the country. It was never clear how much insurers had shut down old policies because the rules required it and how much they did so simply because they felt like it was a good business decision. But beneficiaries didn't care, and most didn't realize that their new plans plugged gaps in the old ones. All they knew was that Obama had promised that they could keep their insurance—a vow they had taken at face value, and not some sort of generalization.[24]

This conflict between expectations and reality wasn't unforeseeable, although quite a lot of people in politics and the media (including me) hadn't foreseen it. The issue started attracting serious attention in late 2012 and the early months of 2013—when Robert Laszewski, an industry consultant, began warning readers of the Health Care Blog to "get ready for some startling rate increases" and Avik Roy, then a scholar at the Manhattan Institute, started writing about "rate shock" in conservative publications.[25]

Articles on rate shock frequently downplayed the impact of the law's subsidies, which meant that even policies with high sticker prices would be inexpensive (and sometimes dirt cheap) for people at lower incomes. And they rarely mentioned why premiums were higher: because the insurance was more comprehensive and available, finally, to people with pre-existing conditions. But the only way for people to learn these things firsthand was to check at HealthCare.gov or a state website, most of which weren't working in October and November 2013. Absent that information, policyholders assumed they would have to pay the full sticker price—or that they couldn't get coverage at all.

The blistering news coverage that followed included an NBC News story noting that the 2010 regulatory guidance, published in the *Federal Register,* had predicted a wave of premium hikes and cancellations: "White House knew millions could not keep plans under Obamacare," was the headline on the web version. Clips of Obama promising people that they could keep their plans ran over and over again on the news. PolitiFact declared it "lie of the year," the distinction it had given to death panels back in 2009.[26]

In Congress, Democrats were nearly as merciless as Republicans. "I don't know how he f***ed this up so badly," one told *Politico,* speaking about the president. As for the public, opposition to the Affordable Care Act hit 57 percent in an ABC–*Washington Post* poll, while Obama's disapproval rating hit 55 percent. Both were record highs for his presidency.[27]

4.

Andy Slavitt learned about the problems of American health care the way most people do: through a story of personal tragedy.

Slavitt was in his early thirties, living in California, and in the relatively early stages of a career in finance and management that was already making him wealthy. He was married, with a new baby, when he got a call from Jeff Yurkofsky, his college roommate. Yurkofsky had terminal brain cancer. And although he was a physician, he was just out of residency with little in the way of savings and no life insurance. He wanted Slavitt to look after his wife and newborn twins.

When Yurkofsky died five months later, his widow and the twins moved across the country to live with Slavitt and his family. The out-of-pocket medical bills for Yurkofsky's treatment followed, totaling about $60,000, and Slavitt realized they were so high in part because Yurkofsky's widow wasn't getting the discounts that large insurers negotiate with providers.

Slavitt was able to bargain the amounts down and perceived a business opportunity. He created a company, called HealthAllies, that negotiated lower fees for patients who didn't have insurance. UnitedHealth later acquired HealthAllies, and Slavitt, who stayed on, eventually became an executive vice president for the Minneapolis-based insurer.

Despite a résumé that also included stints at Goldman Sachs and McKinsey, Slavitt had interests that extended beyond finance and business. He'd grown up in Evanston, Illinois, the northern Chicago suburb, with parents who preached the importance of social justice. After seeing *The Year of Living Dangerously* and Mel Gibson's portrayal of a journalist, Slavitt dreamed of being a foreign correspondent. He was editor of his high school newspaper, and although he got a degree from the Wharton School of the University of Pennsylvania, he also got one in English literature—and, at McKinsey, gravitated to projects that dealt with crafting public policy. HealthAllies was a profit-making venture, but, Slavitt said, part of the appeal to him was the potential to help people struggling with medical bills.[28]

In 2013, Slavitt was an executive at UnitedHealth with a portfolio that included oversight of QSSI, one of the HealthCare.gov contractors. QSSI's job was to create the data hub for exchanging information and appeared to be one of the few parts of the site that, for the most part, was working like it was supposed to work. When HealthCare.gov crashed, Slavitt called about helping with the repair effort, offering up his own expertise. Soon he was on the phone with Jeff Zients, who had been preparing to join the Obama administration's economic policy team but had instead taken on the HealthCare.gov crisis.

Zients was assembling a team of outsiders, including some Google and Twitter veterans, to work with Todd Park on rescuing the project. He wanted Slavitt to be part of it and wanted QSSI to handle the contract work. A few days later, Slavitt was on his way to Washington, where, along with the rest of the team, he would spend the next few weeks working. The group had already made a key decision by the time Slavitt arrived: Fixing the website made more sense than wiping away everything and starting over. They set a deadline of late November for making the system operational.

Nobody was entirely confident that timetable was realistic; the system lacked basic documentation on its architecture and coding that made it difficult to pinpoint breakdowns. But some of the engineers who had been part of the project were eager to see it through, as were the CMS staff. Although overworked and demoralized, they were more capable than the HealthCare.gov debacle suggested.

The newcomers brought in a Silicon Valley mentality and recognized, right away, one of the biggest errors: trying to roll out the entire system at once, instead of through a series of smaller soft launches. "You can't name a major technology project in the history of this country that hasn't been behind budget, behind time—or delivered with all the right features and functions right away," Slavitt said later. "And so the first issue is that there was no tolerance for that. The kind of normal thing that happens in technology, which is that you do small releases and you test and improve and so forth, just didn't happen."[29]

Some of the fixes were pretty straightforward, starting with a repair to make a browsing tool available to site visitors who just wanted to check out their options, rather than set up an account. That helped to clear the initial bottleneck. And although the list of problems was long, with a punch list that peaked at more than four hundred items, the analysts, engineers, and coders made their way through it. By late November, HealthCare.gov was functioning; by the middle of December, it was ready to handle a million visitors per day.[30]

One of the biggest remaining problems at that point was the enrollment information the website sent to insurers. It was full of errors, and administration officials worried that, come January 1, people who needed prescriptions wouldn't be able to get them, because insurers hadn't straightened out the records yet.

Something similar had happened in 2006, when the Medicare drug benefit took effect. To avoid a repeat, CMS officials worked with trade associations to make sure pharmacists would fill those prescriptions anyway, and then had staff ready to field emails and hotline calls as the calendar turned to 2014. Phil Schiliro, who had returned to the White House in December to help with implementation, said, "We had a whole team of people, most of whom volunteered to work, on New Year's Eve day, New Year's Eve night, New Year's Day, the days after, so that if anybody showed up into an emergency room anywhere, and there was confusion over their insurance status, we could resolve it."[31]

The preparations turned out to be unnecessary. Despite intense media attention, reports of people having insurance trouble were sporadic and quickly resolved. For the first time since the launch, the news about Health-Care.gov was about a calamity that its operators had managed to avoid.

Techies and volunteers couldn't do anything about the grandfathering issue, rate shock, and Obama's "keep your plan" promise. That was for the president and his top policy advisers to address—and he started by apologizing, although he did so with some roundabout Washingtonspeak that sounded a lot like he still wasn't taking full responsibility. "I am sorry that they are finding themselves in this situation based on assurances they got from me," he told NBC. He was more direct at a White House briefing, when he acknowledged that he "fumbled" the HealthCare.gov rollout and said that it was on him to restore the voters' trust. "I think it's legitimate for them to expect me to have to win back some credibility on this healthcare law in particular and on a whole range of these issues in general."[32]

In November, with Obama's approval, the administration issued regulatory guidance stating that state officials could allow insurers to keep offering any plans still in place as of 2013, regardless of whether those plans qualified under the old grandfathering standard. Now more people could keep their plans, as long as states said okay and insurers could make it happen.[33]

The authority to create this "grandmothering" rule was extremely dubious; even sympathetic legal scholars thought it went beyond what the statute allowed. Health care experts worried aloud about what the change would mean for the stability of the new markets. The more that insurers maintained the old, noncompliant plans—and the more that healthy people kept up their enrollment—the more that the beneficiaries in the new plans would skew toward the unhealthy, forcing up prices. For that reason, officials in states like California didn't back off the tighter standards.[34]

"People could have kept their cheaper, bad coverage, and those people wouldn't have been part of the common risk pool," said Covered California director Peter Lee, who noted that he was getting complaints from his own sister-in-law, whose rates were going up 50 percent. "We are better off all being in this together. We are transforming the individual market and making it better."[35]

But while plenty of administration officials shared the concerns, they thought they had no choice politically—especially with a Democratic senator, Louisiana's Mary Landrieu, threatening legislation that would have made the same change. They said they had to make good on the president's keep-your-plan vow, however misguided and misunderstood it had been.

5.

By January 1, more than two million people had gotten insurance through the exchanges. But overall, the pace was still well behind projections. Going into the open enrollment season, CBO had predicted more than seven million people would get coverage. After the website problems, it lowered the prediction to six million—a figure that still seemed highly optimistic to most of the political universe.[36]

But getting people to sign up was one part of implementation that the Obama administration had really thought through. It also had some outside help. After the Affordable Care Act became law, Ron Pollack and Families USA spun off a new nonprofit, Enroll America, whose sole mission was educating people about the new insurance options and signing them up. Its founding director was Anne Filipic, whom Pollack recruited from the White House Office of Public Engagement, very much with the White House's blessing.[37]

Enroll America had a multimillion-dollar budget and used it to deploy resources (ads, counselors, events) in states like Florida and Ohio, where demographics and the particulars of the insurance market meant there was likely to be heavy interest. Some of the organization's money came from insurers, a few of whom complained that they felt compelled to donate because of the close White House ties—especially when HHS secretary Kathleen Sebelius asked them to contribute. The administration said that soliciting donations for nonprofit enrollment efforts was well within the law and that the Bush administration had done the same thing in the lead-up to Medicare Part D's launch.[38]

The Obama administration didn't have the Boston Red Sox to help with enrollment (although, years later, Obama would get NBA stars Stephen Curry and LeBron James to do some promoting). But they did have lots of friends in Hollywood and, at the urging of actor Bradley Cooper, Obama agreed to appear on *Between Two Ferns,* a show that ran on the comedy website Funny or Die. The show was famous for host Zach Galifianakis insulting guests, and the White House played along; Galifianakis got to ask Obama whether the presidential library would be in Kenya and what he'd do when people stopped letting him win at basketball. Obama got to respond by dissing the third *Hangover* sequel, a recent Galifianakis movie that had bombed in the theaters. Along the way, he promoted HealthCare.gov.[39]

Some of the jokes landed better than others, but more than eleven million people watched the video in the first twenty-four hours, by far the most on Funny or Die's site. HealthCare.gov saw a surge too; traffic for the day was up 40 percent, officials said. By then, the numbers had been steadily improving, and watching enrollment numbers became a favorite pastime of wonks and journalists. Many followed through a website called ACA Signups, which Michigan-based web designer Charles Gaba started as a hobby, that turned out to be a better predictor of results than even the government's own data.[40]

With his eyes on the numbers, Gaba was a rare voice of optimism. Back in early February, he was one of the first people to predict that enrollment might actually hit the CBO projections or at least come very close. That optimism proved correct, though even Gaba had been overly conservative, because sign-up numbers exploded in the final week. People were lining up outside in-person enrollment centers, some waiting hours to get coverage, and jamming both phone lines and the website—which, by then, had an overflow function where people could leave their phone or email for a follow-up. The government pushed back the final deadline by a few days and, on the final night, made clear that anybody who got to the site by midnight was guaranteed a chance to purchase a plan.[41]

In mid-April, the White House announced the final sign-up numbers: more than eight million.

Detractors noted, correctly, that young people hadn't signed up in the proportions that the law's architects had hoped, which could mean insurers would end up with fewer healthy beneficiaries—forcing them, in coming years, to raise premiums. The plans people were buying frequently had high deductibles and narrow provider networks, issues that the new subscribers hadn't yet confronted because most of them didn't have serious claims yet. That would change with time.[42]

Still, while plenty of people were dealing with rate shock, plenty were also experiencing "premium joy"; the insurance available through the exchanges turned out to be cheaper than what they were paying before, usually because of the subsidies. Nobody had a definitive account of how many people ended up saving versus how many ended up paying more, but a survey from the Kaiser Foundation suggested more people were saving. And of course, even those paying more were getting insurance with more guarantees of coverage—plus there were many millions getting Medicaid, which was basically free.[43]

Back in October, Rush Limbaugh had declared that Americans were "not interested" in signing up, and as late as March, Speaker John Boehner was predicting that, on net, the number of people without insurance would rise because so many people had lost coverage. Rich Lowry, editor of *National Review*, had said the only people enrolling would be people who had insurance already. None of these forecasts turned out to be true.[44]

Obama got to announce the enrollment figures in the White House briefing room, where months before, in the bleakest moments of the HealthCare.gov crash, he and his team faced some of the toughest questioning of his presidency. Obama used the occasion to point out the many ways the program's detractors had been wrong—by, for example, predicting that the Affordable Care Act would lead to higher health care inflation (it hadn't) or that it would increase the deficit (it didn't). "This thing is working," he said.

Obama was relatively stoic during the prepared remarks, but got worked up (by his standards, anyway) during the question-and-answer period—when, after a few minutes, a reporter finally asked about the health care law. "Yes, let's talk about that," he said, steering the discussion to where he'd wanted it to be all along.

Obama spoke about a woman he'd met the day before, who finally had found coverage through the law. "This isn't an abstraction to her. She is saving her home. She is saving her business." And he attacked Republican state officials who still hadn't expanded their Medicaid programs "for no other reason than political spite. . . . That's wrong. It should stop. Those folks should be able to get health insurance like everybody else."

But mostly, Obama talked about the Republicans in Washington and his frustration that they remained singularly focused on repeal. "We've been having a political fight about this for five years," Obama said. "We need to move on to something else."[45]

The opposition had other ideas.

Twenty-three

Sabotage

1.

One of the most successful attacks on the Affordable Care Act started with Marco Rubio, the Republican senator from Florida.

Rubio, the son of Cuban immigrants, had worked his way up in politics from the very bottom, starting as a congressional intern in 1991, then winning elections to local office and the statehouse. At thirty-five, he became the second-youngest person ever to serve as Speaker of the Florida House. He had a natural, earnest charm that disarmed voters, along with an interest in policy that appealed to political professionals. He was also a former college football player. The Republican Party of Florida could not have created a more perfect specimen in a laboratory.[1]

As Speaker, Rubio battled the governor, Charlie Crist, who was also a Republican but frequently defied party orthodoxy. When Crist used his regulatory authority to tighten emission standards on cars, Rubio blasted them as "European-style big government mandates." In 2010, when Crist ran for Florida's open Senate seat, Rubio challenged him in the GOP primary. Crist was vulnerable because he had alienated the Tea Party by supporting Obama's economic stimulus. An attack ad from the Club for Growth showed video of Crist giving Obama a quick hug onstage during a presidential visit to Florida.[2]

Rubio promoted himself as the true conservative in the race, somebody who would fight Obama instead of embracing him. He won enthusiastic endorsements from Rush Limbaugh and blogger/provocateur Michelle Malkin and got a glowing cover profile in *National Review*. "If there is a face for the future of the Republican Party, it is Marco Rubio," Mike Huckabee, the minister and former Arkansas governor, told journalist Mark Leibovich. "He is our Barack Obama but with substance."[3]

In the summer of 2009, GOP primary polls had shown Crist ahead of Rubio by more than two to one. Ten months later, the polls had reversed, with Rubio getting 60 percent of support among Republican primary voters and Crist getting less than 30. Crist dropped out of the primary and announced he would run in the general election as an independent, which he did—splitting votes with Democratic candidate Kendrick Meek and allowing Rubio to win easily.

Rubio was a vocal critic of the legislation that became the Affordable Care Act, and in 2013, he started attacking a then obscure provision of the law: risk corridors, which insulated insurers from big losses in early years while they were figuring out how to price insurance in the new markets. The hope was that the program would be largely self-financing, with insurers making big profits paying into the program while insurers posting big losses would get money from it. But Rubio said the program would end up losing money and possibly give insurers incentives to underprice, to grab market share. He started calling it an "insurance company bailout," invoking a phrase that had been political poison ever since Bush and Obama had bailed out the banks in the 2008/09 financial crisis.[4]

In fact, risk corridors were not a novel or controversial concept. Medicare Part D had such a provision—and unlike the Affordable Care Act's version, which was set to last for only three years, Medicare Part D's was permanent. And while Rubio claimed that repealing the risk corridors would be good for consumers, the likely effect was to take away support that at least some insurers would need, forcing them to raise premiums or pull out of markets altogether.

Those nuances didn't get much consideration. And in yet another instance where the Affordable Care Act's drafting process left it vulnerable to attack, the risk corridor program had no dedicated funding, which meant it depended upon Congress approving an appropriation. In late 2014, a group of Republican lawmakers working on the must-pass year-end spending bill inserted a provision that would leave the program with almost no money.[5]

Andy Slavitt by this time had taken over CMS at the request of Sylvia Burwell, Sebelius's successor at HHS. Part of his job was meeting with lawmakers on Capitol Hill, and it hadn't taken him long to learn about the uniquely difficult politics of the Affordable Care Act.

If there was a problem with Medicare, something that needed attention from Congress, Republican offices were usually happy to hear him out and cooperate on fixes—even if, over the long run, they had designs on privatizing or cutting the program's spending. Their constituents depended on the program, after all. But that attitude didn't extend to the Affordable Care Act, whether because those lawmakers didn't think it mattered to enough constituents to warrant their cooperation or because the pressure to resist Obamacare at every opportunity was simply too overwhelming.

Throughout 2014, as it became clear Republicans were preparing to target the risk corridor funds, Slavitt and other officials warned that small insurers, in particular, might not survive. The danger was especially acute for state co-ops, which were a new, nonprofit style of insurance that had been the brainchild of Kent Conrad and were intended as a quasi-substitute for the public option. Co-ops looked like they would be most vital in rural areas, a point Slavitt made sure to emphasize, hoping Republicans might reconsider their position. They didn't.

Slavitt wasn't the only one GOP lawmakers were rebuffing. Insurance industry officials may not have loved the Affordable Care Act. But they preferred a stable system to an unstable one—and they certainly didn't want to lose those risk corridor payments. But Republicans they lobbied "just weren't interested in workability," one high-ranking insurance industry official said later. "The discussions at that point were all at a political level."[6]

In October, HHS was able to calculate precisely how big (or, more accurately, how small) the risk corridor payments would be. The job of informing smaller insurers fell to Mandy Cohen, a CMS official who was also an internal medicine physician. As a doctor, she said, she had learned long ago how to deliver bad news to patients and their families, including when death was imminent—and that, she knew, was likely the case for some of the fledgling insurers. She was not exaggerating. Twenty of the twenty-three co-ops operating nationally ultimately shut down, with executives and analysts repeatedly citing the risk corridor losses as a primary reason. Around CMS, it came to be known as "Sucktober."[7]

Outside Capitol Hill, the attack on risk corridors dismayed some conservatives who were looking past the Affordable Care Act to future policy debates—and the possibility that Republicans might someday decide, as they once believed, a universal coverage system based on private insurance made sense. "If you want insurers to participate more broadly in the individual market, you'll need to offer a carrot to offset the unavoidable uncertainties," the Manhattan Institute's Yevgeniy Feyman wrote in 2014. But mostly conservatives were thrilled that GOP leaders had found such an effective way to undermine the Affordable Care Act's new, still fledgling markets. Writing in *The Washington Post,* columnist Marc Thiessen listed off some of the insurer failures and then hailed Rubio for developing "a poison pill that is killing Obamacare from within."[8]

Statements like that were a big clue as to why the Affordable Care Act's trajectory seemed to be diverging from the trajectory of the Massachusetts reforms Democrats had seen as their model. The Massachusetts health care law had support from leaders in both parties, who in turn were standing shoulder to shoulder with community leaders, corporate officials, and representatives of the health care industry. Pretty much everybody wanted it to work. Nobody was rooting for failure.

The Affordable Care Act, by contrast, seemed to have more enemies than allies—not just in Washington but in the states, as well.

2.

One state where that happened was Tennessee—which, given its political profile, was not entirely predictable. The state's two U.S. senators, Lamar Alexander and Bob Corker, both had reputations as moderates, at least within the GOP caucus. Its governor, Bill Haslam, was a business-oriented Republican—the kind who, the Affordable Care Act's architects once imagined, was likely to implement the program faithfully because it would mean more money for his state and a relatively market-friendly way to get his residents health insurance.

The hunch seemed to be right in 2012 when Haslam announced that, despite his opposition to the Affordable Care Act, he was thinking about having the state run its own exchange. But the Tennessee political landscape by that point was changing in the same way that the national landscape was. The Tea Party found a footing there early, holding its 2010 national convention at the Gaylord Opryland convention hotel in Nashville. Its activists had helped elect a number of Republicans to the state legislature in 2010, giving the GOP a larger majority and an increasingly ornery right wing.[9]

The deadline to declare intentions about exchange management was in December 2012, and as the date approached, conservative activists and organizations started pressuring Haslam. At a rally on the steps of the capitol a few days before the deadline, a local radio host warned that "if Bill Haslam cannot say no, then it's time we get another governor."[10]

A few days later, Haslam said no.[11]

But the most important decision facing Tennessee, as in every state, was the decision whether to expand Medicaid eligibility. The state had a long, complex history with the program. In the early 1990s, Governor Ned McWherter got a special federal waiver to move more people into managed care, on the theory that it would hold down costs and let the state stretch its resources further. The new program, called TennCare, was supposed to increase coverage dramatically. But the program never fully delivered on its promises, and a decade later, Phil Bredesen, a business-oriented Democratic governor, oversaw a series of dramatic cuts that substantially increased the number of residents without insurance—in some cases, cutting off medically vulnerable people who suddenly had no way to pay for their medications.[12]

The Affordable Care Act's Medicaid expansion offered a chance to reverse that and realize TennCare's original coverage goal, only this time with Washington supplying most of the money. The idea had been a nonstarter with the legislature, and in early 2013, Haslam said he too was opposed. But in late 2014, he announced that he'd come up with a version that would work for Tennessee—one that would rely more heavily on private insurance and incentives for people to develop healthy behaviors, while still expanding coverage dramatically. "We made the decision in Tennessee nearly two years ago not to expand traditional Medicaid," Haslam said. "This is an alternative approach that forges a different path and is a unique Tennessee solution. Our approach is responsible and reasonable, and I truly believe that it can be a catalyst to fundamentally changing health care in Tennessee."[13]

The program he had in mind, with its various conservative twists, was a pretty far cry from what most liberals envisioned the Medicaid expansion would look like. But the Obama administration was actively working with Tennessee to make sure the proposal would fit the Medicaid program's legal requirements, because officials thought it was the best chance to reach hundreds of thousands of low-income Tennessee residents with no insurance.[14]

Back in Tennessee, some high-profile Democrats and their allies agreed. Among those praising Haslam were officials from the Tennessee Justice Center, the state's most prominent social justice advocacy group and a local labor federation. The top-ranking Democrat in the statehouse, Craig Fitzhugh, also committed his support. "The Governor and I have often disagreed on how best to approach this issue, but today I'm happy to stand with him working to get this passed," Fitzhugh said. "The road will no doubt be bumpy and there will be disagreements along the way, but our caucus will do all we can to assure more affordable, better quality health care for all Tennesseans."[15]

The idea seemed to be popular; one poll found supporters outnumbered opponents by roughly three to one. And back in Washington, both Alexander and Corker offered praise of their own. But inside the state legislature, lawmakers were a lot less enthusiastic (only a few showed up for Haslam's announcement), and conservative groups were downright hostile. The Beacon Center, a right-leaning think tank, attacked Haslam's effort "to expand Medicaid and the reach of Obamacare's tentacles into our state." An official from Tennessee's chapter of Americans for Prosperity said the group was "disappointed Governor Haslam has decided to try implementing more of ObamaCare in Tennessee, even as many of his colleagues in other states have held the line and protected their constituents from this disastrous law."[16]

Americans for Prosperity did more than criticize the proposal. It waged a campaign against it, including radio ads that portrayed a vote for expansion as a "vote for Obamacare" and Facebook posts featuring Obama's face. Lawmakers who voted for expansion, the group said, were "betraying Tennesseans." Americans for Prosperity also paid for a bus that transported activists from Knoxville to the statehouse in Nashville. "I'm skeptical of government-run programs," one of them told NBC News at a rally, though he made clear that he liked Medicare because it was "better" and he'd "paid into it my whole life."[17]

Haslam waged his own campaign on behalf of the expansion, sometimes emphasizing the moral imperative of helping the poor: "My faith doesn't allow me to walk on the other side of the road and ignore a need that can be met, particularly in this case when the need is Tennesseans who have life-threatening situations without access to medical care," he said. He also tried to defuse the association with Obamacare by circulating polling that showed the vast majority of Republican voters opposed the law but only a small fraction opposed Medicaid expansion.[18]

It wasn't enough. The proposal never got out of committee. Republican leaders said the program would end up costing the state too much money, even though funding would have come from a new assessment on hospitals rather than general funds. Some Democrats thought opposition had less to do with the merits of the expansion than the president whose law had made it an option. "Those who oppose it associate everything with President Obama," one Democrat in the state legislature said. "That's what has killed this." Eliot Fishman, an Obama administration official who had worked with Haslam's staff on the state's request, called the outcome "heartbreaking," especially given the painstaking effort to find a coverage model that would satisfy conservative objections. "It was externally driven, partisan hysteria that drove this," Fishman said.[19]

One resident who felt the consequences was Donnie Gene Rippy, a brickmason from a rural town northwest of Nashville, who broke bones in his back and several limbs when he fell off a roof—and who, after four surgeries, ended up with $60,000 in medical debt. He would likely have had no medical debt and gotten far better medical treatment if he'd simply lived fifty miles to the north, because that would have placed him inside the border of Kentucky, a state that had expanded Medicaid. "We're all in the United States, but yet you have some states that have the Medicaid part of it and some states decided not to take it," Rippy's partner told journalist Rachana Pradhan, who wrote about their story. "I just don't think that's fair."[20]

The contrast between Tennessee and Kentucky, two adjacent states with similar demographics and size, showed just how much difference the decision to expand Medicaid—or in Tennessee's case, not to expand Medicaid—could make. In 2013, the percentage of uninsured non-elderly adults was nearly the same in the two states: 21 percent for Kentucky, 20 percent for Tennessee. By 2015, the figure had fallen all the way to 8 percent in Kentucky, but only to 15 percent in Tennessee. The percentage of adults who went without care because of cost also fell by different rates in each state, with the most dramatic differences among low-income residents, according to research from the Commonwealth Fund.[21]

3.

At the time Tennessee's legislature rejected Haslam's proposal, about half the states still hadn't expanded Medicaid. Among the holdouts were the three biggest states in the South: Florida, Georgia, and Texas. Overall, the coverage gap of people who didn't have Medicaid because their state officials were blocking expansion was about three million, according to calculations by researchers at the Henry J. Kaiser Family Foundation.[22]

The coverage gap didn't get a lot of attention in the media. But the difficulties insurers were having in some markets did.

Before the Affordable Care Act took effect, Obama administration officials and their allies worried that the unpredictability of the new markets would scare away insurers. The fears proved unfounded. Insurers were excited about the opportunity to get new customers, and if anything, their premiums for the first year were coming in below expectations.

But in many states, the people signing up for coverage did not look like the actuaries had expected. Relatively speaking, there were fewer young people and more old people; fewer healthy people and more unhealthy people. Insurers responded by raising premiums. And while some quickly figured out how to manage the markets, others pulled out of states altogether. In some states, officials began to worry about the possibility of "bare" counties where literally no insurers might be offering coverage to people buying coverage on their own.

The market difficulties had a lot to do with the law's limitations—which, in turn, frequently reflected compromises the law's supporters had made to get their proposal through Congress. Democrats had reduced the mandate penalty to satisfy members and woo Republicans who thought it was too punitive, reducing the incentive for healthy people to remain uninsured. And the phaseout of assistance at higher incomes—a consequence of keeping outlays to under $1 trillion—meant that, especially as insurance prices rose, the cost of coverage would seem high, even staggering, to some middle-class people.

More generally, the whole premise of relying on competition to make health care more affordable was that insurers, seeking to win customers with low premiums, would use their leverage to drive down the prices that doctors, hospitals, and other providers of health care charged. This was supposed to be superior to the traditional method of simply having government set prices, which is what European national systems did but American politicians weren't willing to consider.

In practice, the way insurers got health care providers to accept lower prices was to play them off one another, threatening to include only those who agreed to low reimbursements. That simply wasn't possible in areas where one hospital system dominated the market. This was a frequent issue in rural parts of the country, because excluding the system would leave too many patients with no place to go. As one professor in Iowa noted, thinking about his own state, "If you go four hours east, you can carve up the providers in Chicago—in Iowa you can't do that. That makes it hard to keep costs down."[23]

The example wasn't hypothetical. In 2016, Iowa was among the states that had both rising premiums and fleeing insurers. Just 19 percent of the state's eligible population had signed up for coverage on the exchanges, according to Kaiser Foundation data. That was the lowest of any state.[24]

But that low enrollment wasn't simply a by-product of the Affordable Care Act's design deficiencies. It was also a consequence of actions that state leaders took—and didn't take. Terry Branstad, a Republican governor who after serving from 1983 to 1999 returned to office in 2011 as part of the Tea Party wave, had joined the lawsuit against the Affordable Care Act, rejected calls to create a state exchange, and spurned proposals for investing state resources in advertising and outreach. "We basically went into the ACA with an enormous lack of enthusiasm, because our governor didn't like it and didn't do a lot of things that he could have done to make it work better in Iowa," said Peter Fisher, research director at the Iowa Policy Project, a progressive-leaning watchdog group.[25]

Iowa was in particular trouble because an unusually large portion of the population remained in the old grandfathered plans, rather than signing up for the new exchanges. A big reason for that was the decision by Wellmark, Iowa's Blue Cross insurer, to stay out of the exchanges for the first few years and keep running its existing, profitable plans. It was one of only two Blue plans across the country to do so.

Wellmark was by far the state's most dominant insurer, and it was the one that maintained most of the grandfathered policies. Because it had such a trusted brand name, and the companies offering coverage on the exchanges were mostly new to the state, lots of subscribers figured they would just stay with the policy they had. They tended to be in relatively good health because people with preexisting conditions frequently couldn't get those Wellmark plans without rate hikes or big benefit exclusions—if they could get them at all. The people who had these plans were generally happy with them, because they were inexpensive and covered most care, although people who got severely ill could run into hidden gaps and limits. As Sarah Lueck, an Iowa native and analyst at the Center on Budget and Policy Priorities, noted, "For tens of thousands of Iowans, it's like the ACA never happened."[26]

One of the few insurance alternatives to lure customers successfully on

Iowa's exchange was its co-op, named CoOportunity. It was among the first to win federal approval, and with 120,000 subscribers spread across Iowa and Nebraska, it was the second-largest co-op in the country. But like every other Wellmark competitor, it was drawing customers in relatively worse health; the company said it had to finance twenty-one organ transplants in thirteen months, a high number for such a small group of people.[27]

CoOportunity, which quickly developed a reputation for strong customer service, had been counting on $66 million in risk corridor payments to help it get through its early difficulties—in the same way that venture capital would end up helping some for-profit insurers survive even larger losses. But it was slated to get only $7 million, because of the funding change Marco Rubio and his allies had secured. Days later, Iowa's insurance commissioner announced he was taking over the carrier and liquidating it because it had no way to meet its financial obligations.[28]

Although Wellmark had avoided selling policies on the exchanges, it did sell some policies that complied with the Affordable Care Act's regulations—which meant, among other things, those policies were available to people with preexisting conditions. But in 2016, Wellmark announced premium hikes of about 40 percent. The reason, the company said, was higher-than-expected utilization. Translation: Those policies were attracting people in worse health, just like CoOportunity's had.[29]

In a series of presentations to discuss the company's financial outlook, a Wellmark official mentioned one beneficiary in particular: a patient with a severe genetic disorder whose treatment cost up to $1 million a month. Those treatments, the official said, were one of the bigger reasons Wellmark had to raise premiums as much as it did. She later described the beneficiary in more detail, mentioning that it was a teenage boy with hemophilia. Tony Leys, health reporter for the *Des Moines Register,* wrote about it for a story that *USA Today* syndicated, and soon the tale of the $1 million–a-month boy with hemophilia was all over social media. Even *Teen Vogue* wrote about him.

The Wellmark executive didn't identify the boy or where he lived. But when a couple in Iowa read the story, they were nearly certain it was their child. He had a severe form of hemophilia, the kind that required treatment with a blood substitute—costing, yes, as much as a million dollars a month—because his body's immune system rejected standard transfusions. The condition was extremely painful. Blood would pool around joints and organs. As a baby and toddler, the boy would writhe in pain while his parents took turns holding him; as a teenager, he'd beg to be put under during acute episodes. The artificial blood products were a godsend, reducing both the frequency and severity of attacks, although they required daily infusions (through a permanent port on the boy's skin).

Paying for the medication was always a challenge. The parents had each turned down jobs to hold on to employer benefits when they had them, though the employer policies had limits of their own that the hemophilia treatments threatened to overwhelm. They thought about divorcing so that one of them could declare low income and go on Medicaid, but then the Affordable Care Act came along, offering a guarantee of coverage with no limits on benefits and subsidies for people with modest incomes.

They were precisely the sort of people whom the law was supposed to help, and they had peace of mind, finally. But now they felt like scapegoats for Iowa's market problems—which, however real, had a lot more to do with choices that government officials and the state's largest insurer had made. "I cried for two weeks," the boy's mother told me, after first making sure I would not reveal her family's identity. "Not only is he reading that he's the reason that people can't be insured, he's been reading people had to pay more money for insurance premiums just to take care of him. He's scared, and it's very upsetting."[30]

4.

If Tennessee and Iowa were case studies in how the Affordable Care Act wasn't supposed to turn out, California was a case study in how it was.

The state was an early and enthusiastic champion of the program and not simply because it was among the most reliably liberal states in the country. It had a long history of innovation on health care and using the government to expand coverage to the poor and medically vulnerable. Back in the 1990s, it was California officials who supplied the blueprint for what became the Clinton health care plan. Ten years later, it was Republican governor Arnold Schwarzenegger working with the Democratic state legislature to create their own version of the Massachusetts plan.

That effort fell apart because of arguments over financing, but the determination to reach for universal coverage remained, and when the Affordable Care Act became law, Schwarzenegger, in his last year as governor, proudly signed the law that made California the first to authorize its own exchange. His Democratic successor, Jerry Brown, picked up where Schwarzenegger left off and signed legislation authorizing Medicaid expansion.[31]

The expansion, which opened up enrollment for certain groups in 2011, was the single biggest reason that California's uninsured rate fell from about 17 percent to 7 percent, the largest decrease in the nation. And most of the remaining uninsured were undocumented residents who, by law, could not get either Medicaid or subsidized coverage. Among legal residents, only 3 percent were uninsured. And the coverage made a difference; subsequent studies showed that people who got coverage through California's Medicaid expansion were less likely to take out payday loans (a sign of accumulating debt) or face eviction because they couldn't keep up rent. Yet another study found that Medicaid enrollment reduced the out-of-pocket payments for low-income Californians.[32]

But the expansion's impact was perhaps most visible on the ground at federally funded community clinics like the St. John's Well Child & Family Center in Los Angeles. Its CEO, Jim Mangia, was a longtime health care activist who got his start, in the 1980s, on programs that provided treatment to AIDS patients in the Bay Area. In 1995, when Mangia took over St. John's, it had just one facility. By 2016, it had more than a dozen.

The growth had taken place gradually, and in the early 2000s, it was because of funding that came from President George W. Bush, who, although no fan of big government, had been enthusiastic about federal clinics going back to his days as Texas governor, where he had an up-close view of their work. The Affordable Care Act provided a new burst of support, thanks to the extra money Bernie Sanders had secured in exchange for his vote and the simple fact that, with Medicaid expansion, a much greater portion of St. John's patients had a form of insurance.

In addition to new facilities, the Affordable Care Act made it possible for St. John's to offer new services such as classes on diet and exercise and to open a produce market—an especially important addition in the neighborhoods that frequently lacked full-fledged grocery stores. "Obviously, we can't solve poverty in and of itself," Mangia said, "but we can impact on some of the conditions of poverty—and empower and educate our patients, so they can take control of their health."

St. John's also added mental health and addiction counselors and doubled down on its attempts to improve preventative measures; childhood vaccination rates for the patient population went up from 76 to 89 percent, while the cervical cancer screening rate increased from 40 to 88 percent. None of this was atypical; nationwide, clinic visits increased by 26 percent in the six years following the Affordable Care Act's enactment, with dental visits (another service many clinics provided) up 43 percent and behavioral health visits up 57 percent, according to data that the Commonwealth Fund compiled.[33]

Still, the showpiece for California's implementation of the Affordable Care Act was its exchange, Covered California, where premium growth was modest year after year and insurers for the most part were able to keep positive margins.[34]

California was among a handful of states that gave their exchanges the ability to negotiate directly with insurers and exclude those that didn't live up to their requirements. This "active purchaser" model was another carryover from Massachusetts. Among the ways California used it was to limit benefit design, so buyers had only a few choices. "If you are a consumer thinking about a silver product, you'll usually find six or seven silver products, and the difference will be that they have different doctors and maybe a different philosophy," said Peter Lee, who was CEO of the exchange. "What's not different is benefit design. Consumers aren't confused about what their co-pays will be, etc." Covered California also required that insurers pay for most outpatient care even for people who hadn't met their deductibles, so that even infrequent users of health care would see benefits to coverage.[35]

Restricting choice in this way seemed to run against the logic of competition, which had been a dominant thread in health care policy thinking for decades, going back to the 1970s, and had shaped the core design of the Affordable Care Act. But Lee and other officials at Covered California were familiar with research showing that too much choice was counterproductive. Most people didn't fully understand what terms like *coinsurance* actually meant (it's the percentage of costs people pay out of pocket after hitting a deductible). Even well-informed buyers were in no position to figure out the complexities of insurance benefits that insurers always buried in the fine print.[36]

"When I was selling plans before, if you were to look at the roster of all the companies, which are very similar to the companies in the market today, you might have had 100 different options that you could select," one broker working with Covered California explained. "We've really narrowed that down now, and there are lots of options for consumers based off the company, but there are less ways for them to make a bad decision."

As in most states, the most visible impact of the private insurance reforms was on the people who couldn't get decent coverage before. Maryann Hammers, a writer and editor who lived north of Los Angeles, was one of them.

For years, she'd carried the kind of insurance freelancers typically do: a policy with limited benefits. When exchange coverage became available, she switched and got the regular checkups she'd put off. In the course of an abdominal exam, a doctor felt a lump. She had ovarian cancer.

The coverage she had was hardly perfect. The policies all had relatively narrow networks of providers; when she had to switch policies, because one insurer had decided to drop out of the market, she had to change a bunch of her doctors. A data-entry error had created a problem in her electronic file that nobody seemed able to fix.

But even with the hassles, she said, the coverage was invaluable—not just because nobody could take away her insurance, but also because she knew it would cover the cost of her cancer treatments, which included several surgeries and rounds of chemotherapy. "Without the Affordable Care Act," she said, "I honestly don't know what I would have done."[37]

Lots of people felt the same way. But their stories never seemed to get much attention.

Twenty-four

Make Health Care Great Again

1.

Health care was a big issue in the 2014 midterms, although it was not the website saga or anything related to the Affordable Care Act preoccupying voters.

In early August, the World Health Organization declared an international health emergency because of an Ebola outbreak in Africa. The reports were ghastly. Symptoms included fever and intense gastrointestinal problems, followed by severe internal bleeding that frequently led to organ failure. Fatality rates were well above 50 percent. In late September, a Liberian man visiting family in Dallas, Texas, was diagnosed with the disease and died one week later, but not before infecting two of the health care workers treating him.

Obama had already dispatched American disease specialists and engineers to Africa to help treat and stop the pandemic at its source. But he declined to stop all international travel, despite repeated calls to do so. Maintaining an open flow of personnel and aid was too important, Obama said, echoing the consensus of public health experts. With careful screening at ports of entry plus quarantines for any domestic cases, Obama said, the United States would be okay.

Rand Paul, the ophthalmologist and Kentucky Republican senator, accused Obama of letting "political correctness" dictate public health policy. When Obama tried to reassure the public, Fox News host Jeanine Pirro said, incredulously, "You don't want us to panic? How about I don't want us to die!" And in New York, after the diagnosis of a case there, Donald

Trump fired off a tweet: "Ebola has been confirmed in NYC with officials frantically trying to find all of the people and things he had contact with. Obama's fault."[1]

The blowback was furious—and unjustified. Public health officials were able to isolate and treat the few Americans who got the virus; every single one who contracted Ebola on U.S. soil survived. It was a model of a successful crisis response—one that would look even better six years later, with the outbreak of another deadly virus.

None of this was clear to voters when they went to the polls in the first week of November 2014. Stories about Ebola filled the airwaves and fed a conservative narrative about Obama's failures, helping Republicans to pad their House majority and seize control of the Senate for the first time since 2006. The arrival of archconservatives like Tom Cotton of Arkansas and Ben Sasse of Nebraska only intensified the party's commitment to Obamacare repeal, which remained a central part of the GOP's agenda even though it had gotten much less attention than it had in previous campaigns.[2]

But some of the new Republicans had reservations—among them, Shelley Moore Capito, who had won the Senate seat in West Virginia. More than one hundred thousand of her constituents had already signed up for the law's Medicaid expansion; percentagewise, it was the third-largest increase in Medicaid enrollment nationwide. Although Capito had voted against the Affordable Care Act in 2009 and 2010, when she was serving in the House, and although she campaigned on a promise of repeal, she had pointedly declined to criticize the state legislature's decision to expand Medicaid—or to suggest that she would take away that coverage. "We are where we are now, and we have to figure out how to go forward," she said.[3]

After the election, she said she remained steadfast in her commitment to repeal, but wanted to "keep what works and get rid of what doesn't."[4]

2.

Mitch McConnell, who was about to become majority leader, knew that some of his caucus had mixed feelings. Right before the midterms, he had warned that passing full repeal would be difficult given the need for sixty votes in the Senate. Conservatives howled, calling that statement "surrender" because it didn't seem to allow for the possibility of using the reconciliation process, as the likes of Ted Cruz and his allies were demanding. (Heritage Action said moving a bill through reconciliation "signals a seriousness" about repeal.) An aide to McConnell said he was open to that approach.[5]

Over in the House, Boehner didn't seem especially eager to make Obamacare a priority yet again. Along with some other senior Republicans, he talked about repeal more and more as a political burden—requiring repeated votes so that members could show progress to their constituents while gumming up the works on other legislation because anything that even touched health care became a fight over supporting the president's health law. "It was just so clear that people weren't ready to let go of it, and it was just this present thing, all the time, that we needed to be doing," Brendan Buck, a former senior aide to Boehner, told me years later. "I think [leadership] would probably have been happy to give it the best fight and move on. But that was not where our members were, and they all needed to keep seeing us fighting on it."[6]

The situation was especially tough on Boehner because the debate over how to approach repeal was intertwined with a rapidly escalating fight about his leadership and the direction of the House Republican caucus more broadly.

Conservative activists had come away from the 2013 shutdown even more convinced that their problem was feckless leadership. A few months later, that sentiment created the season's biggest political upset when Eric Cantor, the number two ranking House Republican and potential successor to Boehner, lost a primary challenge to an economics professor named Dave Brat. A relative newcomer to politics, Brat had the backing of conservative activists associated with the Tea Party and Fox News host Laura Ingraham. It was enough to put him over the top even though he had raised just $231,000 for his campaign. Immigration, not health care, had been the dominant issue, but it was the broader message that mattered: Nobody in leadership was politically safe.[7]

Following the midterms, Boehner once again won his bid to be Speaker. But twenty-five GOP members voted against him, more than twice the number two years before. In January, at a secret meeting during the annual House Republican retreat, a group of conservatives agreed to form a Freedom Caucus whose goal was to push leadership—and the rest of the GOP caucus—to fight the administration more aggressively, including over the Affordable Care Act. In the summer, one of the Freedom Caucus's leaders, Congressman Mark Meadows of North Carolina, filed a motion to vacate the chair, an obscure parliamentary maneuver to oust the Speaker.[8]

Meadows didn't have the votes to make it happen. But it was another sign of how the caucus was changing, and by fall, Boehner had seen enough. Following an official visit to Washington by the pope—which Boehner, a devout Catholic, described as the pinnacle of his career—he announced that he was stepping down as Speaker and leaving Congress. Before he left, he brokered a compromise on repeal: The House would pass a reconciliation bill that left in place some of the law's key elements, including funding for the Medicaid expansion. Over in the Senate, that was fine with McConnell but not with his own increasingly antsy conservative wing. At the insistence of Cruz, Rubio, and several allies, who were threatening to withhold their votes, the Senate amended its bill so that it would wipe out every dollar that had gone to helping people get health insurance. The House went along with the new, more ambitious version and sent it to the president.[9]

Obama vetoed the bill, as expected, but the exercise of passing the bill gave Republicans a template for future action, because it required rulings from the Senate parliamentarian over what was permissible under the rules of reconciliation. Republicans learned, for example, that they could not defund Planned Parenthood completely, but they could dramatically reduce how much money it got. Republicans also got a preview of how Democrats would fight repeal. Obama's veto message cited statistics, which his economic advisers had extrapolated from Congressional Budget Office estimates, of repeal's likely consequences: 900,000 fewer people getting necessary care, 1.2 million more struggling with medical bills, and an additional 10,000 dying every year because they would lose the law's assistance and protections. "This legislation would cost millions of hardworking middle-class families the security of affordable health coverage they deserve," Obama wrote.[10]

Obama could say these things because as the Affordable Care Act took full effect, it was accomplishing its main goal: helping people to get insurance. By the first quarter of 2015, Gallup research found, the percentage of American adults without insurance had fallen to 11.9 percent, the lowest that the organization had ever recorded. Researchers were starting to pick up evidence the newly insured were better off, medically and financially. And in response, Republicans had passed a bill that repealed Obamacare without a replacement, wiping out those gains completely.[11]

It was a familiar pattern that dated back to the very first repeal bills in 2010. Republicans kept promising they were on the verge of coalescing around an alternative, something that would provide coverage as good or better than what the Affordable Care Act did. But it kept not happening.

One journalist, Jeffrey Young of *HuffPost*, started keeping informal track of these announcements by tweeting each of them with the phrase "Just in time!" He kept a running list of these tweets on a social media site, and by 2015, it already had more than fifty entries. "Any day now," Young wrote, "Republicans will agree on their Obamacare replacement. Any day now! Meanwhile, I'm getting a lot of mileage out of one dopey joke."[12]

3.

The problem for Republicans wasn't a lack of ideas per se. Policy experts like James Capretta and Yuval Levin of the American Enterprise Institute and Avik Roy, still with the Manhattan Institute, had written formal proposals. And a handful of Republicans in Congress had put together actual legislation.

One of them was Tom Price, a congressman from Georgia. A third-generation doctor with degrees from the University of Michigan, he had moved to the Atlanta suburbs after graduation in 1979 to "flee the cold" and join the prestigious orthopedic surgical residency program at Emory University. He stayed and established a private practice that, following a merger, became the largest orthopedics group in the state.[13]

Price first got involved with politics through the Georgia State Medical Association, because, like many doctors, he believed malpractice laws were capricious and overly punitive—forcing physicians to second-guess sound medical judgments, run unnecessary tests, and pay large sums of money either for liability insurance, unfair judgments, or both. As he started lobbying members in person, he realized many of them didn't really understand health policy. When a seat in the state senate opened up, he ran for it and won.[14]

Georgia has a citizen-legislator model, with limited sessions that allow lawmakers to keep their regular jobs, and for his first few years in office, Price was continuing to work on broken bones even as he was trying to work on Georgia's health care laws. But the confidence and meticulous attention to detail that had brought him success as a surgeon also propelled him into legislative leadership, until in 2002 he became the caucus leader right when Georgia Republicans captured the senate for the first time since Reconstruction. After his congressman, Johnny Isakson, decided one year later to run for U.S. Senate, Price ran for the open House seat and won.[15]

Price's interest in health insurance and payment dated back to the early 1990s and the debate over the Clinton plan. One of his first forays into politics, around the same time he was at the Georgia State Capitol talking about malpractice reform, was to meet Ira Magaziner and Hillary Clinton during a briefing on the plan. He got them to autograph a copy of the proposal and kept it as a souvenir. But he was also a committed, vocal opponent of their scheme, which perhaps was not surprising given his professional profile. Although the American Medical Association had warmed to the idea and many doctors, especially pediatricians and family doctors, were frequently loud proponents of universal coverage, specialists and surgeons in particular tended to be skeptical or downright hostile.[16]

Price was still interested in the subject, though, and after he got to Congress, he worked on some major health care proposals. In 2009, as Democrats were writing the legislation that became the Affordable Care Act, Price crafted an alternative he called the Empowering Patients First Act. Over the coming years, he introduced a new, slightly revised version with each new Congress, until by 2015 it was getting attention as a possible substitute for Obamacare.

Like so many GOP proposals, the bill had tax credits for buying private insurance and what conservatives described as protections for people with preexisting conditions. But the financial assistance was generally a lot smaller than what the Affordable Care Act made available, especially at lower incomes. Insurers could offer plans without coverage of prescriptions, mental health, or rehabilitative services, and with no limits on out-of-pocket expenses. The guarantee of insurance for people with preexisting conditions applied only to those who maintained "continuous coverage." For people who didn't, there would be "high-risk pools" offering minimal insurance as a stopgap.

The approach, Price said, would help people to get health care while preserving what he believed was best about American medicine—namely, its commitment to innovation and high-quality care. He believed both depended on a thriving private sector chasing profits with minimal government interference and patients having lots of flexibility over what kind of insurance they wanted to buy.

In a world in which the Affordable Care Act did not exist, passing and implementing the Price bill might have increased access and reduced the number of uninsured at the margins. But the Affordable Care Act existed, and whatever its pluses and minuses, it was providing coverage to something like twenty million people. Implementing Price's plan—in other words, using it to replace Obamacare, as he hoped Republicans would do—would have led to many fewer people with insurance and many more facing big medical bills.

The big reason for the coverage losses is that the Price bill anticipated less government spending; simply put, there'd be less help for people. But other factors mattered too. The guarantee for people who maintained continuous coverage, a common feature of Republican health plans, sounded good in theory. But it wouldn't help people whose insurance lapsed because they couldn't afford the premiums. And, with no more funding for Medicaid expansion, that safety net would be gone.

4.

Under most Republican proposals, including the Price bill and a proposal Orrin Hatch had introduced into the Senate, some people stood to save money because (if they were rich) their taxes would come down or (if they were relatively healthy) they would not be bearing as much of a financial burden for covering the sick. But by the very same token, people with preexisting conditions and those who developed severe medical problems after buying coverage were more likely to face large, sometimes crushing expenses, because they were more likely to face insurance company underwriting and because policies would have less comprehensive benefits. And many more people would be uninsured.

These sorts of trade-offs are inevitable in health care policy, and it's not hard to see why Republican officials might have been enthusiastic about legislation like the Price and Hatch bills, given their antipathy toward expensive, redistributive government programs. A significant number of voters might have felt the same way and, in 2015 and 2016, Republicans could have used their newly complete control of Congress the same way that Democrats had used theirs in 2007 and 2008—to forge a consensus around an approach, to educate their own members about the details, and to persuade the public that the upsides of their schemes outweighed the downsides.

But those sorts of conversations never went far, as a number of conserva-tive intellectuals and Republican officials told me later. "Everybody wanted to be on a replacement bill," one former GOP aide said. "Most members did not really know what that meant. . . . You got the sense that they never really cared what the policy was. They just needed to be on a bill for political purposes to say that they were for 'replace.'"[17]

"Obviously, it is the case that there were not enough conversations about 'replace,'" said Brian Blase, a health economist who worked on House and Senate Republican staff before later joining the Trump administration. "There was more work highlighting what in the ACA was not working well." Dean Rosen, a longtime senior aide to Senate Republicans who went on to become one of Washington's most influential health care lobbyists, said, "There was an intellectual simplicity or an intellectual laziness that for Republicans in health care passed for policy development. And I think that bit us in the ass when it came to repeal and replace."[18]

An internal debate would not have been easy, because on health care, the party broke into some pretty distinct factions. There were those who wanted what was either a downsized version of the Affordable Care Act or some other program that would help people get health insurance but on a smaller scale. There were those who wanted to push health care in a radically new direction, transforming existing government programs and maybe even employer insurance, to unleash competition and free-market forces. And then there were those who just wanted to get rid of the Affordable Care Act and didn't especially care what, if anything, took its place.

"The homework that hadn't been successful was the work to coalesce around a single plan, a single set of specific legislative items that could be supported by most Republicans," Price said. "Clearly, looking at the history of this issue, this has always been difficult for us because there are so many different perspectives on what should be done and what ought to be the role of the federal government in health care."[19]

A serious conversation about the Republican direction on health care would have required another kind of reckoning—on why the Massachusetts reform model, which a sizable chunk of the party and its supporters had found acceptable only a few years before, was now so far out of bounds. "What in the actual fuck happened on the Republican side?" Rodney Whitlock, the former Grassley aide, said to me later. "The Massachusetts plan, that was signed by a Republican Governor, Romney, and approved by a Republican administration, the Bush administration. . . . And the Heritage Foundation, they were up there on the dais, at the signing ceremony. This was the model. . . . What happened to Republican ideology that, by March 2010, it's anathema?"[20]

Working out these sorts of differences is what party leaders do when a goal is important to them and their members. But the reality about Republicans and health care, as Republicans and their supporters frequently admitted, was that the subject mattered to only a relatively few of them.

It was true in their extended networks of advisers, academics, and strategists—"There are about 30 times more people on the left that do health policy than on the right," Blase said, observing the same "wonk gap" that Cato's Michael Cannon had—and it was true on Capitol Hill. Unlike the Democrats, who had spent a century trying to establish universal coverage and believed it was an essential part of a just society, Republicans seemed more interested in the posture (fighting Obama and Obamacare) than the substance of health care itself. Even to the extent they were fighting for principles, most were reacting to Democratic proposals rather than trying to make changes of their own. "Republicans do taxes and national security," Brendan Buck said. "They don't do health care."[21]

Republicans in Congress had one last reason not to litigate health care in 2015 and 2016. A presidential campaign was underway. Many lawmakers figured they'd be taking cues from the party's eventual nominee—although, especially early in the cycle, few had any idea who that nominee would turn out to be.

5.

Most people remember Donald Trump's presidential campaign launch for his ride down the Trump Tower escalator and for his claim that Mexico was sending drug dealers and rapists across the border. But he also attacked the Affordable Care Act as a "big lie" and a "disaster" and talked about a doctor friend whose patients were struggling with their new insurance options. "We have to repeal Obamacare," Trump said.

It was not a new rallying cry for Trump. During his first formal stab at politics, a speech to the 2011 Conservative Political Action Conference while he was contemplating a 2012 presidential campaign, he had made a similar pledge. It was around that time he took control of his Twitter feed and began using it for political broadsides. The Affordable Care Act was a frequent target—at first, because of the damage Trump said it would do to business and the economy; later, because of the website crash and other launch problems. In November 2013, he tweeted: "Broken promises. A broken billion-dollar website. ObamaCare can't be fixed. Repeal!"[22]

Trump's tweets about the health care law had roughly the same level of accuracy as every other statement he made—which is to say, they were full of half-truths and outright non-truths. He recycled some of the brashest, most widely debunked lies of 2009 and 2010, tweeting that "ObamaCare gives free insurance to illegal immigrants" and that "ObamaCare does indeed ration care. Seniors are now restricted to 'comfort care' instead of brain surgery." When sign-ups hit the eight million mark in 2014, Trump tweeted, "The ObamaCare enrollment numbers are a lie. They will be 're-adjusted' by the White House at an opportune time, probably after '14 election."[23]

But by 2015, Trump was focusing more and more on rising premiums for people buying coverage on the exchanges. And although he frequently cited exaggerated figures, he had hit upon a real and politically potent development affecting many states. As insurers came to realize they had underpriced their products, because they expected more healthy people to sign up, they were raising premiums.[24]

Affordable Care Act defenders pointed out that adjustments like these in the first few years were to be expected—and that, absent GOP sabotage, premiums wouldn't be rising so quickly. Even with the hikes, advocates went on to say, subsidies protected the majority of buyers from feeling the impact directly. But middle- to upper-middle-class contractors and small business owners were unlikely to qualify for subsidies. They were a key Republican voting bloc and especially receptive to the story Trump told about Obamacare—that it was the product of big lies, told by elitist Democrats eager to spend the tax dollars of Americans on undocumented immigrants and other less deserving beneficiaries.

Trump was not the only Republican presidential candidate making these arguments about the Affordable Care Act. Every 2016 contender had committed to repeal; every one said it was based on lies. And with the lone exception of Ohio governor John Kasich, who had successfully pushed for Medicaid expansion by citing Scripture's commands to help the poor, every Republican agreed that the law had essentially no redeeming value.

But even as Trump was bashing Obamacare, he was going out of his way to say that he believed in universal coverage—a position, he boasted, that set him apart from traditional Republicans.

As incongruous as it sounded given Trump's background as a rapacious real estate developer, it was not an argument that Trump had stumbled upon recently. Back in 1999, Trump had told CNN's Larry King, "I'm conservative and even very conservative, but I'm quite liberal and getting much more liberal on health care and other things. I really say, what's the purpose of a country if you're not going to have defense and health care? If you can't take care of your sick in the country, forget it. It's all over, I mean it's no good. So I'm very liberal when it comes to health care. I believe in universal health care."[25]

The America We Deserve, the bestseller Trump published a year later, contained a similar claim. "We should not hear so many stories of families ruined by healthcare expenses. . . . With more than forty million Americans living day to day in the fear that an illness or injury will wipe out their savings or drag them into bankruptcy, how can we truly engage in the 'pursuit of happiness' as our Founders intended?" The book also praised Canada's single-payer system, and, while it did not endorse creating the same system in the United States, it called for a public-private hybrid that sounded an awful lot like the 1993/94 Clinton plan. (It also cited Stuart Butler of Heritage as an inspiration.)[26]

"[Trump] liked the idea of everybody having insurance," freelance writer Dave Shiflett, the book's ghostwriter, told me later. "He didn't sit around thinking about policy. I just think that, instinctively, he figured it was the right thing to do." And Trump continued to talk that way in the 2016 campaign, when he told Scott Pelley of *60 Minutes* that "everybody's got to be covered. This is an un-Republican thing for me to say. I am going to take care of everybody. I don't care if it costs me votes or not. Everybody's going to be taken care of much better than they're taken care of now."[27]

But if there was reason to think Trump genuinely liked the sound of being the president who would finally deliver great health insurance for everybody, there was no reason to think he understood—or cared—about the underlying concept of universal coverage, as a shared responsibility to take care of the vulnerable. Nor was there reason to take his statements as evidence of as seriously considered policy position, since as a candidate he hadn't produced anything remotely resembling a plan. The only firm commitment he made was to repeal—which, by itself, would move the country much further away from universal coverage by taking insurance away from tens of millions.

Eventually, the campaign published a list of seven brief bullet points, each one supporting a familiar conservative concept like allowing insurers to sell across state lines. It had no regulatory particulars, no dollar figures, no coverage estimates—in other words, it was not a campaign proposal in any meaningful sense. Journalists who pressed the campaign for details got a mixture of bombast, slogans, and nonsense. When journalist Dan Diamond wrote up a Q-and-A, he had to append a fact-checking note longer than the responses to document all the exaggerations and falsehoods.[28]

Trump's rivals noticed too. At a February 2016 debate in Houston, Cruz accused Trump of supporting "socialized medicine" while Rubio mocked Trump's lack of policy understanding. And if one of Cruz's old college debate judges had been scoring the exchanges, a befuddled Trump would have been the clear loser. He couldn't explain how universal coverage was consistent with conservative thinking (because in 2016, conservatives rejected the premise) or how his plans would help people get insurance (because he didn't have any plans). But Trump's candidacy kept rolling—right over Rubio's and, soon, Cruz's as well.

In the end, the dialogue about health care in the Republican primaries was just like the dialogue about health care in the Republican Congress. It was all about repeal, not replacement—and emotion, not policy. Nobody could match Trump.

6.

The debate over health care in the Democratic primaries could not have been more different. Hillary Clinton, eager to pick up her old signature issue, called for the creation of a public option and more generous subsidies that would reduce both premiums and out-of-pocket costs. If enacted, these and other policies would have turned the Affordable Care Act into a program more generous than even what the House had passed in 2009. The number of people without insurance would fall by up to 9.6 million, according to an estimate from the Commonwealth Fund and researchers at RAND. That still wouldn't be 100 percent coverage, but it would be getting close to the levels some European systems achieved. It was a bold agenda, although almost nobody noticed because her main rival was proposing something even bolder.[29]

That rival was Bernie Sanders, and his signature cause was still Medicare for All. Sanders appreciated the Affordable Care Act. He could see that many more people had insurance and knew that health care inflation had slowed down, arguably producing even more than the $2,500 savings Obama had promised. But it wasn't clear how much the Affordable Care Act's delivery reforms were responsible for that trend and, as Sanders kept pointing out, the U.S. still had the world's most expensive health care system, by far. Even many of the insured couldn't pay their bills or were struggling with insurance company bureaucracies, Sanders noted, to say nothing of the many millions who still had no coverage at all. He thought private insurers were, at best, a source of waste and, at worst, a menace to beneficiaries. Rather than shore up the existing system, he wanted to blow it up and put in place a single, government-run insurance program.[30]

Back in the 2008 presidential campaign, Medicare for All's champion, Ohio congressman Dennis Kucinich, was an afterthought to most voters. In 2016, Sanders was a legitimate challenger. And his long, lonely crusade for causes like Medicare for All had made him a hero to a growing constituency—a new generation of progressives who didn't have the political scars of the 1980s, '90s, and 2000s, and who were frustrated with the limitations of policies Democrats had enacted during those periods.

They didn't see the Affordable Care Act as a once-in-a-generation change, something that had required herculean political efforts simply to pass. They saw it as a heavily compromised, deeply flawed program that fell way short of what other countries had. When Sanders promised them a government-run system in which nobody would owe out-of-pocket expenses or have to deal with private insurance companies, they thought it sounded awfully good. The phrase "socialism" didn't faze them, and neither did the prospect of taking employer coverage away from people who liked it.

The debate in the Democratic primaries that followed was intense, although in a sense, the two candidates were arguing past one another. Sanders made the case that his system was better on the merits, because it would guarantee coverage for all, eliminate wasteful and frustrating insurance company bureaucracies, and, at least on paper, control costs more effectively. Clinton made the case that her vision was more feasible, because it wouldn't threaten people who were content with their existing insurance and because it wouldn't require deep, politically difficult cuts to the health care industry.

Clinton ultimately won the nomination, although her health care plan wasn't the reason. It didn't have a snappy slogan like "Medicare for All," it wasn't a simple concept, and it kept in place large elements of the existing system. To many progressives, Clinton's plan felt like just another instance of preemptive, self-destructive compromise.

In the general election, Clinton did her best to contrast her vision on health care with Trump's—which, she correctly noted, was the difference between somebody promising to build on the Affordable Care Act so that it reached more people and somebody determined to take it away. But insofar as health care got attention, it was usually in response to negative headlines, including an August announcement by Aetna that it was pulling out of eleven of the fifteen states where it still offered marketplace coverage.

Aetna said it was because of financial losses from a skewed risk pool; private correspondence, later published in *HuffPost,* suggested the company might have been trying to punish the Obama administration for scrutinizing a proposed merger with Humana. The nuances didn't make an impression. And while it's impossible to know what impact such developments had on the election, it's conceivable it shifted a small number of votes—which, in 2016, would have been enough to change the outcome.[31]

Twenty-five

The Boy Scout

1.

Paul Ryan never expected Donald Trump to become president, and he hadn't seemed especially excited about the prospect either. In December 2015, after Trump proposed blocking all Muslims from entering the country, Ryan condemned the proposal, telling reporters that it "is not what this party stands for and, more importantly, it's not what this country stands for." Even after Trump got a lock on the nomination, Ryan held out on his endorsement for a while.[1]

Ryan had become Speaker by this point, succeeding the embattled Boehner, and when he finally embraced Trump, in a June 2016 op-ed for his hometown *Janesville Gazette,* he said it was purely about their shared interest in advancing a Republican agenda. "It's no secret that he and I have our differences. I won't pretend otherwise." One day later, Trump attacked a judge who ruled against him in a civil case, saying the judge's Mexican American heritage biased him. Ryan called Trump's statement "unacceptable" and said it was "sort of like the textbook definition of a racist comment." In October, after release of the *Access Hollywood* tapes in which Trump had boasted of grabbing women "by the p***y," Paul convened a conference call and told fellow Republicans they should feel free to abandon the nominee, as journalists Anna Palmer and Jake Sherman later reported. "I am not going to defend Donald Trump," Ryan said.[2]

The antipathy made sense, given that it was hard to think of two men in Republican politics whose backgrounds or styles could have been more different. Ryan, a native midwesterner, took his Catholic faith seriously, by all accounts, and was devoted to his wife and three children. When Trump called him a "Boy Scout," Ryan assumed it was a compliment. His upward trajectory in politics—from intern to legislative aide to speechwriter and eventually congressman—was the product of effort, not celebrity. As a young staffer in Washington, D.C., during the 1990s, he had held down part-time jobs as a waiter and fitness trainer to make extra money. He had a knack for making connections with the right people (like a college professor who knew a member of Congress, and prominent Republicans he served at a Capitol Hill Tex-Mex restaurant), but he would win them over with his earnest, persistent enthusiasm for public policy.[3]

Ryan liked to think of himself as somebody who had gotten into politics to accomplish something—and, just in the last few years, that meant leavening his speeches with more talk about poverty and what he said Republicans could do to address it. He would frequently invoke the memory of a former mentor, Jack Kemp, the ex–NFL quarterback and congressman who went on to serve as secretary of Housing and Urban Development under President George H. W. Bush. Kemp was an early proponent of what later came to be known as "compassionate conservatism," championing initiatives like the creation of so-called Empowerment Zones, which sought to revitalize low-income neighborhoods by offering tax incentives for businesses to invest in them. It was under the auspices of the Jack Kemp Foundation that, in early 2016, Ryan cohosted a presidential forum on poverty with Tim Scott, the South Carolina senator who was the lone African American member of the GOP caucus.[4]

The focus on the plight and needs of low-income Americans was, in part, a response to the 2012 presidential campaign and the scrutiny that had come with Ryan's place on the GOP ticket. He had for years been describing the country as falling into two groups: "makers," who paid more in taxes than they received in government benefits, and "takers," who took in more than they paid. The country had too many takers and not enough makers, Ryan had argued, and Obama-backed policies like the Affordable Care Act were tipping the balance even more in that direction by directly subsidizing insurance for more lower- and middle-income people.

It was inefficient, and, worse still in Ryan's view, it was plain wrong. "It is not enough to say that President Obama's taxes are too big or the healthcare plan doesn't work for this or that policy reason," Ryan had said in 2009, during a speech in which he cited the teachings of libertarian writer

Ayn Rand. "It is the morality of what is occurring right now, and how it offends the morality of individuals working toward their own free will to produce, to achieve, to succeed, that is under attack."[5]

The sentiment was consistent with Ryan's record. The proposals he made while he was House Budget chairman, starting in 2010, envisioned dramatic cuts in programs like food assistance and Medicaid on which literally millions depended for their sustenance and, in some cases, their very lives. At the same time, the budgets proposed to cut taxes in ways that overwhelmingly benefited the wealthiest Americans. Robert Greenstein, who as head of the left-leaning Center on Budget and Policy Priorities was arguably Washington's most influential advocate on poverty issues, said that Ryan's agenda would produce "the largest redistribution of income from bottom to top in modern U.S. history" if enacted. Independent analyses suggested that description was not an exaggeration.[6]

Ryan, writing in his 2014 manifesto, *The Way Forward*, said that he belatedly understood why his rhetoric alienated so many Americans. "I soon realized that the phrase I'd been using implied a certain judgment about the group that receives government benefits—one that is in deep conflict with the American Idea." But if Ryan was rethinking his language, he wasn't rethinking his beliefs or his agenda. On the contrary, he remained as fixated as ever on containing or, better still, downsizing the welfare state. And for all his new talk about protecting society's most vulnerable members, their struggles with health care didn't seem to weigh heavily on his mind. The term "uninsured" appeared all of three times in his book, despite the many pages devoted to health policy.[7]

Ryan's other big justification for repeal was about the federal budget. He said that cutting spending was essential to reduce deficits. But while Ryan liked to call himself a fiscal hawk, and while the Washington press corps had frequently described him that way, he had a history of supporting measures that increased the deficit, just so long as the proposals came from Republicans. "The persistent belief in the existence of an authentic, deficit hawk Ryan not only sweeps aside the ugly particulars of his agenda," Jonathan Chait observed in *New York* magazine, "it also ignores, well, pretty much everything he has done in his entire career."[8]

The most clear-cut example of this was Ryan's 2003 vote in favor of Bush's Medicare drug benefit, which substantially increased deficits because it had no offsetting revenue or cuts. Ryan later said he was simply making a choice among his priorities—that the upside of nudging health care policy in the direction of private enterprise was bigger than the down-side of bigger deficits.

In 2016, when Ryan realized that Trump might be president, he cited similar moral calculus. Whatever his misgivings, Ryan said, the chance to enact a conservative agenda was too valuable to pass up—proclaiming, at a press conference the day after the election, "I'm very excited about our ability to work together."

2.

Twenty-four hours later, the two men met in Washington. As part of a photo op, Ryan walked Trump out to the building's west portico, offering the president-elect a glimpse of what he would see on January 20 when he took the oath of office. As Ryan explained what the inauguration edifice and viewing grounds would look like once construction crews were fin-ished, Trump looked to see if he could spot his new home. Ryan gestured toward the right, pointing out a cluster of trees at the other end of Penn-sylvania Avenue. The building behind them was the Treasury Department, Ryan explained, and right behind that was the White House.[9]

The ways of Washington were as unfamiliar to Trump as its street plan. A month later, when Ryan went to Trump Tower for that three-hour meeting on the agenda, a big chunk of the discussion was simply Ryan explaining the mechanics of passing legislation, especially when it came to budget reconciliation—the path that Republicans had decided, long ago, they would use for repeal. Trump took it all in, without much objection. Just as Ryan was willing to put aside his objections to Trump's behavior and campaign, Trump was willing to put aside his anger over Ryan's distancing during the campaign. On both substance and strategy, he was okay defer-ring to the Speaker.

Mitch McConnell was too. The Senate majority leader had never shown any particular interest in health care policy, except when it came to keeping his caucus unified against Obama's legislation. Insofar as he cared about issues, his priorities were primarily to pass a big tax cut and to put conser-vative judges on the bench. He was happy to let Ryan do the heavy lifting on repeal, move whatever legislation emerged quickly through the Senate, and then get on with other business.

Ryan, by contrast, really did care. And he was convinced that the key to success was speed. Trump would have maximum leverage immediately upon taking office, and Republicans, having voted for repeal so many times over the past few years, would eagerly support a chance to do it now that they had a president willing to sign the legislation. A delay in implementation—say, two years—would leave enough time to construct a replacement. And once the Affordable Care Act was off the books, the urgency of putting something else in its place would motivate at least some Democrats to work with GOP leaders on an alternative that conformed to conservative ideas about the proper role for government.

Ryan understood that repealing the law without a replacement carried risk, as both policy and politics, because it was impossible to be sure what kind of new system, if any, Congress would eventually create. But he thought the risk was worthwhile, given that constructing and then passing an alternative was sure to take a lot more time. Everybody had seen how much Democrats had struggled back in 2009, when their bill languished for months. The longer Republicans took to hash out their differences, the longer they would have to wait—and, potentially, the more political support they would lose—before working on a tax cut, which is what many members considered more important anyway.[10]

Not every Republican was so gung ho about Ryan's approach, however, and in December, GOP senators began airing their concerns publicly. None came right out and said they would vote against "repeal-and-delay" legislation, as it had come to be known, but Lamar Alexander of Tennessee, who was chairman of the HELP Committee, said "simultaneous" legislation made more sense. Susan Collins of Maine said, "A framework for what a replacement for the ACA would look like should accompany any repeal effort."[11]

Conservative policy experts also warned against trying to do repeal alone. Joe Antos and Jim Capretta said that insurers were likely to bail on the exchanges once repeal legislation passed. On paper, repeal legislation might not take effect for two or three years. In reality, they said, the program would collapse within the first year, creating chaos and leaving people without coverage.[12]

Ryan had tried to quell those concerns, telling the *Milwaukee Journal-Sentinel* in December that "clearly there will be a transition and a bridge so that no one is left out in the cold, so that no one is worse off." In early January, Vice President–elect Mike Pence backed the repeal-and-delay strategy in meetings with House and Senate Republicans.[13]

But inside the administration, the issue was not settled. Trump was constantly changing his mind, depending on who had spoken to him most recently, and he was getting calls all the time—from outside friends and advocates, as well as from individual members of Congress, all of whom seemed to have his personal mobile number. "We would make concrete decisions about what we were going to do, get presidential sign-off, and then within twenty-four hours, the decision would change," Tom Price, who served as HHS Secretary for most of Trump's first year, said to me later. "There was no consistency. You were always having to take the hill that you had taken the day before, the week before."[14]

With each passing day, opposition to repeal-and-delay spread. Initially, the skepticism had come mostly from relatively moderate Republican senators like Alexander, Collins, and Tennessee's Bob Corker. By January, it was coming from senators who were both closer to and more conservative than Trump, like Ron Johnson of Wisconsin and Tom Cotton of Arkansas. The loudest objections came from Rand Paul, the Kentucky senator, who on January 6 tweeted, "I just spoke to @realDonaldTrump and he fully supports my plan to replace Obamacare the same day we repeal it." Paul's objections were especially noteworthy, given his history of harsh rhetoric about the Affordable Care Act, and many colleagues wondered whether he secretly hoped for repeal to fail because Kentucky, like West Virginia, had such a large population of people getting insurance through the program.[15]

Paul and Trump spoke again two days later after Paul's tweet, and following that conversation, Trump and Ryan agreed to change course. Word got out in pieces—first with Trump telling Maggie Haberman of *The New York Times* that repeal and replacement will happen "very quickly or simultaneously, very shortly thereafter"; then with Ryan telling Capitol Hill reporters that "it is our goal to bring it all together concurrently"; and finally with Trump announcing at a Trump Tower press conference that "it will be essentially simultaneously. It will be various segments, you understand, but will most likely be on the same day or the same week, but probably the same day. Could be the same hour."[16]

The decision to take up replacement at the same time as repeal may have been the most pivotal strategic choice Republicans made in 2017. For the first time, the question wouldn't be whether the Affordable Care Act was good enough. The question would be whether the Affordable Care Act was better than the Republican alternative.

It was a debate that the law's architects had been waiting years to have—and that, in the very final weeks of the Obama presidency, they had done everything they could to start.

3.

By late 2016, most of the White House staffers who had worked on passing the Affordable Care Act were long since gone. Nancy-Ann DeParle was back in the private sector, at a private equity firm. Peter Orszag was too. Phil Schiliro was working on several outside projects and still working with Democrats. Rahm Emanuel was the mayor of Chicago.

But Jeanne Lambrew was determined to serve through the very last day of Obama's term. She had been among the administration's more polarizing figures, frustrating some colleagues who felt she was overly dogmatic or tried to control too much. But she inspired fierce loyalty among others and even critics conceded, as one told me, that "nobody worked harder and nobody cared more"—that in a city full of people trying desperately to grab power, she was always thinking about policy.[17]

Lambrew was also the administration's ultimate survivor, a bit like the law itself, and had been through its many near-death experiences. Following the *NFIB* oral arguments in 2012, when even supporters were pessimistic the law would survive, one of Lambrew's jobs was to draw up the plans for dismantling the program since the administration would have to manage that process within a fixed, relatively short time frame. It was a bit like a death row prisoner planning her own execution, only to be saved at the last minute when the governor—or, in this case, the chief justice—called with a reprieve.[18]

The chances of the Affordable Care Act surviving the Trump presidency seemed even smaller than its chances of surviving the Roberts court. On the first day after the election, when the White House felt like a morgue, spirits in the Domestic Policy Council and Office of Health Reform were especially low. Lambrew invited about a dozen staffers into her office and passed around some beers they kept in a refrigerator. She went around the room, asking if anybody thought the health care law would withstand the coming repeal effort. Nobody said yes—until, finally, it was Lambrew's turn. She said they were all wrong. A year from now, she predicted, it would still be on the books.[19]

Lambrew was thinking the exact same thing that Obama was. Republicans had talked up repeal and voted for it literally dozens of times. But those votes didn't have real-world consequences because they didn't control both chambers, and even when they did, they knew Obama was going to veto. Republicans never had to think through what it would really mean to take insurance away from a hotel housekeeper or office security guard on Medicaid—or to tell a working mom or dad that, yes, it was okay for an insurance company to deny coverage for their son or daughter's diabetes.

Now things were different. And although Republicans could try to adjust repeal legislation to soften its impact, every adjustment would come with its own trade-offs. Republicans would discover, quickly, that with each set of concessions came a new set of angry constituents or interest groups—and, eventually, a new set of anxious lawmakers.

The severity of the backlash would inevitably depend on whether the public understood repeal's consequences. Nobody was in a better position to educate voters on that subject than the outgoing president himself. Although the election felt in some ways like a referendum on his presidency, or at least what it represented, he remained among the most popular, most trusted leaders in the country—and he put that credibility to work. He gave a live, hour-long interview to Vox's Ezra Klein and Sarah Kliff, two of the most widely read and widely respected journalists on health care policy. He brought in stakeholders and advocates to the White House, urging them to speak out. And he met privately with Democrats on Capitol Hill.[20]

At every venue, Obama's message was the same: "Now is the time when Republicans have to go ahead and show their cards," he said in the Vox interview. "People need to be able to debate it, they need to be able to study it, the same way they did when we passed the Affordable Care Act. And let the American people gauge: Is this going to result in something better than what Obamacare has produced?"

"If they're so convinced they can do it better," Obama went on to say, "they shouldn't be afraid to make that presentation."[21]

Democratic leaders on Capitol Hill were already making versions of the same argument. There, too, most of the law's chief architects were gone. Baucus and Waxman had retired; Kennedy was dead. And in the Senate, the Democratic leader succeeding Reid, Chuck Schumer, had never been one of the Affordable Care Act's biggest fans.

Back in 2009, Schumer had been among those least enthusiastic about pursuing major health care reforms, given the political perils and likelihood that middle-class voters would feel like it wasn't about them. He was always looking to change the subject, frequently to jobs, and after Trump won the election, Schumer had made a big deal about the possibility of some kind of bipartisan infrastructure deal. But early on, Schumer adopted the same argument that Obama had put forward. If Republicans wanted to repeal the Affordable Care Act, Schumer said, they owed it to the country to explain what they intended to put in its place.

Former administration officials got to work as well. Neera Tanden, who had served with Sebelius at HHS before taking over as president of the Center for American Progress, sent out an email shortly after the election telling staff at the organization's advocacy arm that they were going to focus on defending the law—by highlighting what it accomplished and laying out the consequences of repeal. One of the very first efforts along those lines was a research brief cowritten by Topher Spiro, who had been on the HELP Committee staff in 2009 and 2010, showing that insurers were likely to abandon the new markets if repeal legislation passed, regardless of whether it officially had a two- or three-year delay on implementation. The brief, which appeared less than two weeks after Election Day, was an early version of the argument that conservative intellectuals like Joe Antos and Jim Capretta would later make to Republicans. Going forward, Spiro would be one of the loudest, most persistent repeal critics on Twitter.[22]

One of the few people who could rival Spiro's social media output was Andy Slavitt, who many people figured would head back to the health care industry once his term as administrator of Medicare and Medicaid was done. But having put in so much time to help rescue and then run the Affordable Care Act, Slavitt wasn't about to stand by while Republicans blew the whole thing up.

In the final weeks of his term, Slavitt had used his Twitter feed to become more vocal about the impact of the law, walking right up to the line of advocacy that, as the head of an agency, was off-limits. (Counterparts in the Trump administration would later cross that line with impunity.) The day Slavitt's tenure ended, he let loose, becoming a ubiquitous social media critic of repeal. And he did more than tweet. He began speaking around the country and working with some other administration veterans, including Lambrew (who had gone to work at the Century Foundation) and Chris Jennings (who, after his own stint in the Obama White House, was back to consulting). With the help of some liberal advocacy groups, they coordinated messaging and orchestrated a counter-offensive to stop repeal.[23]

They had regular phone calls and check-ins and brought in at least a dozen more former administration officials who were eager to pitch in. A familiar dynamic soon developed, according to one participant, with Lambrew doling out assignments and leaving one activist to ask, "She knows we don't work for her anymore, right?"[24]

Zeke Emanuel decided to undertake his own, much less public campaign to stop repeal. He had left the administration in 2011 and joined the faculty at the University of Pennsylvania, from where he had continued to write and do research—and to promote the various delivery reforms he, Bob Kocher, and Peter Orszag had pushed so hard for the Affordable Care Act to include. Of the ones that ended up in the bill, he was especially proud of the attempts at bundled payments. Early research suggested they were saving money and improving quality, just like they'd hoped, though that success had gotten much less attention than the experiments that were not panning out.

In the context of the administration's internal debates, Zeke had been among those more focused on controlling health care costs than making sure people had insurance. But in the context of the broader American political debate, he was still squarely on the side of universal coverage—and defending the Affordable Care Act. He also had an asset none of the law's other architects did: a direct line to Trump.

It had come from his brother Ari Emanuel, the Hollywood mega-agent who happened to be Trump's representative from his days starring on *The Apprentice* television show. At Ari's suggestion, Trump sought out Zeke's expertise following the election, reaching him by phone in December while Zeke was on the Acela high-speed train between Philadelphia and Washington. Zeke worried about who might overhear the conversation, given all the politicos and journalists who rode the Acela, so he went into the bathroom and started making his case. Repeal worked fine as a slogan, Zeke explained, but it made for lousy policy and ran contrary to Trump's promise of making sure everybody had insurance. Trump would end up owning whatever chaos and damage followed, Zeke said, and that was no way to launch a presidency.

Trump suggested Zeke come to the White House after the inauguration. Zeke said that would be too late, given all the decisions to be made during the transition, and secured an invitation to brief Trump in New York the following week. At the meeting, a gregarious Trump marveled at the achievements of the high-powered Emanuel brothers and talked about Zeke's academic pedigree. For all the disdain Trump heaped upon elites, he had a well-known fixation on intellectual credentials, especially Ivy League degrees—boasting constantly about his own from the Wharton School of the University of Pennsylvania (to which he'd transferred after two years at Fordham) and the high marks he claimed to have gotten there (subsequent media investigations suggested he hadn't).[25]

Zeke came with a presentation he deliberately kept to one page, because he knew Trump lacked patience for more, and picked up the argument he had started on the Acela; rather than focus on repeal, Zeke suggested, Trump should go after the pharmaceutical industry. He pointed out that Obama had tried and failed to curb prescription drug prices, playing to Trump's obsession with outperforming Obama. He also complimented Trump's children, hoping to ingratiate himself that way.

Zeke wasn't going rogue. He'd kept Schumer, Tanden, and other Democratic strategists apprised of his efforts, which they agreed was worth trying. Zeke was also pushing the line that, at the very least, Trump had to show the American people what replacement would look like—the same argument that Democrats were promoting and that Trump eventually adopted. Whether Zeke's lobbying influenced that decision, he certainly made an impression, and in 2017, Trump invited him back for another consultation.

That briefing took place in the Oval Office, several weeks after the inauguration, by which time the debate about legislation was well underway. It included a much larger group: Pence and Ryan, along with chief of staff Reince Priebus, strategist Steve Bannon, and several other aides. Tom Price was also there, as was Andrew Bremberg, a domestic policy adviser who was the White House point man on health reform. Zeke insisted some Democrats would work with Trump on modifications to the Affordable Care Act as long as Trump stopped trying to repeal the whole thing. Ryan said he didn't believe it. Zeke was outnumbered but holding his own and maybe then some. At one point, Bannon got Bremberg's attention and told him to speak up on behalf of repeal to move the conversation.[26]

Trump thanked Zeke for the visit and then got right back to the business of getting the Affordable Care Act off the books. If he was having misgivings about repeal or its potential impact, he wasn't showing them. But some other Republicans were.

4.

In 2016, Ryan had released an agenda for House Republicans called A Better Way that included an alternative to the Affordable Care Act. Like the Price and Hatch bills, it called for replacing the guarantee of coverage for preexisting conditions with the "continuous coverage" provision (which meant people whose coverage lapsed would no longer have the guarantee) plus high-risk pools (which had been famously and chronically underfunded in the past). It offered tax credits for buying insurance but offered less assistance than the Affordable Care Act.

Those changes, plus its call to transform Medicaid into a block grant—that is, a program where the federal government gave states predetermined sums of money, rather than letting the program's cost rise or fall with demand—meant that it was likely to have the same effect as every other major conservative plan. Government spending would come down, and some taxes would too. But many fewer people would have insurance, while the burden of medical bills would fall more squarely on the old and the sick.

Ryan and his top allies understood all of this. They were prepared to defend their approach on the merits by focusing on what they considered its upsides for everyday Americans. The unpopular individual mandate would be gone. Insurers could offer a wider variety of plans, including cheaper policies with thinner benefits that would appeal to younger and healthier people who figured they were unlikely to have major expenses. "We knew we were never going to compete on coverage," Brendan Buck, who in 2017 was a senior adviser to Ryan, told me afterward. "We always tried to make the argument we were going to get there on cost."[27]

But that was not the way Trump had talked about repeal.

In the campaign, Trump had promised universal coverage, emphasizing that he didn't care if that was an un-Republican way to talk. And he was still saying those things as president-elect. "We're going to have insurance for everybody," Trump said to Robert Costa of *The Washington Post*. "There was a philosophy in some circles that if you can't pay for it, you don't get it. That's not going to happen with us." He went on to say that Americans "can expect to have great health care. It will be in a much simplified form. Much less expensive and much better."[28]

A House aide later remembered the moment the interview went online, because the aide's phone was on vibrate and all the WTF messages from fellow staff were making the phone heat up. But House leaders were making big promises too. On the same day that Ryan had told reporters that replacing and repealing the law would happen "concurrently," Cathy McMorris Rodgers, a congresswoman from Washington who led the House Republican Conference, said, "No one who has coverage because of Obamacare today will lose that coverage. We're providing relief. We aren't going to pull the rug out from anyone."[29]

That line about not pulling the rug out from people was the new House Republican mantra, and although it was a more nuanced pledge than Trump's, it was still difficult to square with what Republicans were actually proposing to do. It was especially bold following the announcement that, through mid-December, more than 11.5 million people had signed up for 2017 coverage through the exchanges. That was up 300,000 from the previous year. It didn't look like the kind of imminent collapse that, according to Ryan and his allies, required Republicans to repeal the law swiftly.[30]

Anxiety over the distance between Republican promises and Republican policies spilled out into the open in late January, when Mike DeBonis of *The Washington Post* obtained an audio recording of a party retreat where GOP lawmakers peppered leaders with tough questions about the emerging plans.

"We're telling those people that we're not going to pull the rug out from under them," said Tom MacArthur, a House member from New Jersey, "and if we do this too fast, we are in fact going to pull the rug out from under them." Bill Cassidy, a Louisiana senator who was also a physician, wanted to know whether a replacement bill would continue to fund the Medicaid expansion that even many conservative-leaning states, including his, had embraced. The answer from Oregon congressman Greg Walden, chairman of Energy and Commerce, was, "These are decisions we haven't made yet."[31]

Other issues came up too. Republicans agreed that they wanted to replace the Affordable Care Act's subsidies for private insurance but couldn't agree on how. One big dispute was about whether to offer refundable tax credits or deductions. Deductions, useful only to people with income tax liabilities, would leave out the poor and some of the middle class; credits would reach everybody. But credits would cost the government a lot more, and they raised another issue as well. Many political professionals, including CBO analysts, considered credits a form of spending; as such, Republicans were determined to attach Hyde Amendment restrictions to them. But the parliamentarian was likely to rule that abortion language was not related to budget issues, making it impossible to include as part of a reconciliation bill.

The internal Republican debates sounded increasingly like the disputes that had bedeviled the Democrats when they wrote the Affordable Care Act. But Democrats had started working through these issues long before they had full control of the government. And then they took another year writing the legislation, in a process that, however politically painful, allowed a consensus to emerge.

GOP leaders had believed, going in, they had a similar consensus. "I think that there was a lack of appreciation on the part of all of us in the administration about how difficult this would be, because all Republicans had been publicly supportive of repeal for years," Tom Price said to me. "Mostly, we thought they would rally at the opportunity to do so." In reality, the Republicans "flat out were not ready," said Dean Rosen, who watched this all play out from the vantage point of his similarly dismayed clients. "They didn't do the heavy lifting or lay the deep intellectual groundwork that you had to lay in the years before." Instead, they were trying to put together legislation nearly from scratch—and trying to do so in a matter of weeks.[32]

They were also doing it in a highly centralized, tightly controlled process. Here, again, the contrast to 2009 was stark. Pelosi and Reid had let their committees of jurisdiction write the bills; the leaders took full control of the process only after the panels had approved legislation. In 2017, Ryan managed the process from the beginning. He was a veteran of the Budget Committee who had written health care proposals before, so it made some sense for him to take the lead. He had the experience plus the staff. And Ryan did work closely with the relevant committee chairmen. But as the legislation took shape, the leaders would share it on paper and in private rooms where the members couldn't take copies. Several complained that they didn't have an opportunity for real input, or that proposed changes didn't get a serious airing. "That was Paul's leadership style—he thought he was smarter than everybody," one particularly frustrated former GOP House member said later.[33]

At the end of February, Paul Demko of *Politico* got hold of a draft and wrote about it, prompting early squawking over the credit-versus-deduction debate. But House leaders still weren't ready to release it. That angered even some Republicans, most notably one on the other side of Capitol Hill. Senator Rand Paul started taking a portable office copy machine around the building in search of the secret House health care bill. It was a publicity stunt, and it worked perfectly, with reporters tagging along and Democrats cheering him on. Pelosi's office tweeted out a photo of dogs walking through the building, suggesting they could help sniff out the mystery legislation.[34]

One of the big GOP complaints about the Affordable Care Act had always been about the process. Republicans loved to say that Democrats had jammed it through Congress without due time for consideration and that the final vote on amendments took place under reconciliation rules, which required just fifty votes in the Senate. But the original Senate bill, which constituted the bulk of the final statute, had passed with sixty votes through regular order. Early versions of legislation were public for weeks before committee hearings, and no votes took place without formal, full CBO assessments. Lawmakers from both parties, as well as independent, outside analysts, had plenty of time to sort through the language and figure out what it actually meant.

That kind of scrutiny was precisely what Ryan's process was designed to avoid. But the haste and secrecy had consequences. When Ryan and the leaders finally unveiled their bill, relatively few members understood it well enough to answer critics. And those critics were everywhere. The nation's major hospital groups wrote a joint letter warning of "tremendous instability for those seeking affordable coverage" and "the loss of coverage for current [Medicaid] enrollees as well as cuts to a program that provides health care services for our most vulnerable populations, including children, the elderly and disabled." The American Medical Association, AARP, and a cluster of patient advocacy groups also came out against the bill.[35]

All these groups had backed the Affordable Care Act. Securing their support had been a major focus of reformers, because one of the big takeaways from the 1990s Clinton failure was the need to neutralize special interest opposition. It went a long way to explaining why the 2009/10 legislative process took so long and, especially given the concessions Democrats made to hospitals and drugmakers, why the program couldn't control costs more than it did. But it also meant that, in 2017, defending the Affordable Care Act's coverage gains was in the groups' self-interest.

The objections of health care organizations didn't stop Republicans from plowing ahead. The bill got approval from the Ways and Means Committee less than four days after leadership had introduced it—and, notably, before the CBO had finished its assessment. The most important committee in the House had signed off on what could be the most important legislation of the congressional term without a formal assessment of its most important effects.[36]

But the CBO score came a few days later. Once that happened, the debate was never the same.[37]

5.

Twenty-four million. That's how many more people would end up uninsured if the House bill became law, according to the CBO. And that was not the report's only devastating conclusion. The GOP bill redirected insurance subsidies, so that some older people would pay much more for their coverage, even as some younger people would pay much less.[38]

The assessment was not a surprise. Going back to late 2016 and the transition meetings about the 2017 GOP agenda, conservative experts and some senior Capitol Hill staff had warned about the potential for a devastating CBO score. Several administration officials brushed off the warnings, saying it was no big deal because nobody outside of the 202 area code cared about the CBO.[39]

Ryan's team and some of its allies were more prepared, figuring they could make the case that the CBO was overestimating the coverage loss. And their critique of the CBO had some merit. As the agency would later conclude, the individual mandate didn't ultimately matter as much as the projections suggested—a concession that, some former GOP officials noted angrily, came too late to help their cause.[40]

But the CBO's conventions had also been damaging to Democratic legislation back in 2009 and 2010. Dealing with the agency, which was scrupulously nonpartisan but whose predictions were subject to the inevitable uncertainties of its task, was something all lawmakers had to do. And whether the twenty-four-million figure was accurate, the gist of what the CBO was predicting was almost certainly correct. The House bill would take away insurance from a significant number of Americans who now depended on the Affordable Care Act for coverage. The only question was how many millions—and what would happen to them.

For years, these people had been an afterthought in mainstream media coverage. And in the conservative press, they were downright invisible, which may be one reason even those Republican leaders who had expected a rough CBO score figured their legislation could survive it. All GOP officials kept hearing from supporters and their media sources were stories about Obamacare's problems—the reports of rate shock and failing insurers, of people with five-digit deductibles and doctors they needed but couldn't see. Trump was especially prone to this, because of the raucous cheers his calls for repeal consistently generated at his rallies.[41]

The anger that Trump and other Republicans detected was real. The repeal cause wouldn't have gotten as far as it did without a substantial number of people who felt they were worse off. But there was a whole other side to the Obamacare story. It was about those people who benefited from the law and desperately wanted it to stay in place.

There were a lot of them. And with Obamacare on the brink of elimination, they spoke out.

Twenty-six

Thumbs-Down

1.

The groundswell started in early February 2017, while Ryan was still writing the bill. One of the first congressmen to confront it was Republican Gus Bilirakis, who was in his sixth term representing a conservative district north of Tampa, Florida. His town halls were frequently dull, poorly attended events. This one had two hundred people, packing the seats and lining the walls.

Some carried signs that said, "Obamacare Saves Lives," and one offered a personal testimonial. Evan Thornton, twenty-one, said that he had Marfan syndrome, a genetic and potentially life-threatening condition affecting connective tissue. "To take away the Affordable Care Act is taking away my freedom and justice," Thornton said, citing the law's protections for people with preexisting conditions. "It's taking away my life."[1]

Another town hall one week later attracted a similar crowd, and this time, a local family physician offered his perspective. "I used to have two or three self-pay patients a day, now I have maybe one every two weeks or so," Peter Riquetti said, recalling the days when many more patients had to pay their entire bills because they didn't have insurance. "Quite often the people who used to come were so sick I would have to send them to the hospital." One of the few attendees to defend repeal was a local Republican official, who said that "there's a provision in there [the Affordable Care Act] that anyone over the age of 74 has to go before what is effectively a death panel." Crowd members shouted, "Liar!" and drowned him out with boos.[2]

In Murfreesboro, Tennessee, GOP representative Diane Black heard from a teacher named Jessi Bohon. Bohon came armed with facts—like how the high-risk pools Republicans were proposing had historically offered inferior coverage and how Aetna, which had pulled out of Tennessee's insurance market, may have been using its exchange presence as leverage to get approval for the merger with Humana. But her main argument was about her faith. "As a Christian, my whole philosophy in life is, pull up the unfortunate," Bohon said. Without the Affordable Care Act, she warned, people with preexisting conditions would end up with inferior coverage or none at all. "That's the way it's been in the past," Bohon said. "And that's the way it will be again. So we are effectively punishing our sickest people."[3]

Videos from the Bilirakis and Black town halls went viral. So did clips from a Springdale, Arkansas, event with Senator Tom Cotton that filled a two-thousand-seat auditorium to capacity. Among those asking questions was Kati McFarland, a twenty-five-year-old with a genetic disorder, who said, "Without the coverage for preexisting conditions, I will die. That is not hyperbole, I will die." She wanted to know why Republicans didn't have a real replacement. Another woman said, "I could tell you three members of my family, including me, that would be dead, dead . . . if it was not for ACA." Her question for Cotton: "What kind of insurance do you have?" The audience roared.[4]

Cotton had expected the tough questions. He'd agreed to the event following protests at his district office and moved it to a larger venue when he realized how many people intended to show up. The protest organizers were from Ozark Indivisible, a local chapter of a grassroots organization with chapters forming all over the country as part of the broader backlash to Trump that had begun the day he won the presidency.

Indivisible was the brainchild of Leah Greenberg and Ezra Levin, twentysomething former congressional staffers who after the election published an online handbook on how to influence Congress and fight Trump's agenda through local activism. They brought to the exercise their expertise as former Capitol Hill aides who remembered the impact of the Tea Party backlash in the summer of 2009, when Lloyd Doggett (Levin's old boss) and Tom Perriello (Greenberg's old boss) each ran into protests against Democratic health care reforms. The progressive uprising of 2017 had started with the Women's March, whose crowds dwarfed Trump's inaugural, and then airport protests over Trump's ban on travel from seven Muslim-majority countries. The organizing that activists had done for those events left them with an infrastructure (email distribution lists, locations of congressional district offices) they then used to stage the health care demonstrations.[5]

The role of Indivisible, along with the Center for American Progress Action Fund and the newly established Protect Our Care, attracted the notice of Republican officials. "Protesting has become a profession now," White House press secretary Sean Spicer told *Fox and Friends*. "They have every right to do that, don't get me wrong. But I think we need to call it what it is. It's not these organic uprisings that we have seen over the last several decades. The Tea Party was a very organic movement. This has become a very paid, Astroturf-type movement."[6]

But the Astroturf accusation may have been even less true of the Resistance, as it was coming to be known, than it had been of the Tea Party. Indivisible operated on a shoestring budget for its first few months, subsisting entirely on online fundraising from small donations. And according to Levin, the organization never put out a call for people with personal stories. They just showed up on their own.[7]

These activists were also speaking for a much broader public. The Affordable Care Act had been underwater in the polls for most of its history, with more people disapproving than approving it. That changed in early 2017, as approval rose and disapproval fell, eventually pushing favorable opinion above 50 percent for the first time. And even before 2017, questions about repeal consistently showed majorities opposing it.[8]

The change in public opinion about the Affordable Care Act, however modest, was impossible to miss—and it wasn't because the program itself was suddenly performing more effectively. Coverage available through the exchanges still left many of the insured dealing with high out-of-pocket costs and impersonal, unresponsive insurance bureaucracies. Most of the town hall protesters actually acknowledged as much, saying they were all for improving the Affordable Care Act or, in some cases, replacing it with something like a single-payer plan. But what they saw and heard from Republicans was something very different: an effort to take the program away with nothing even resembling an adequate replacement.[9]

The underlying anger of the 2009 Tea Party protesters had been real, whether it was about perceptions of government overreach, a transfer of tax dollars to people they considered undeserving, or the fact that it was all happening at the behest of an African American president they believed to be illegitimate. They also thought Obama and the Democrats were lying about what the law would do—all the more so when, years later, it turned out some people couldn't keep their plans as he had so famously promised.

The Resistance protesters of 2017 were just as livid, for very different reasons. Trump had lost the popular vote by nearly three million, becoming president only because he happened to win just enough support in just the right states to capture the electoral college. That hardly seemed like a mandate for something as dramatic as repeal. And if some of the Affordable Care Act's selling points turned out to be exaggerated or dishonest, the program's overall effect was what Democrats had promised: Many millions got insurance. The effects of repeal, by contrast, would be the opposite of what Trump and Republicans promised. Many millions would lose insurance.

2.

The protests continued into March as Ryan and his lieutenants tried to get past what conservative journalist Rich Lowry had called the "worst rollout of any major piece of legislation in memory" and stitch together a majority coalition. They did so the way that legislators always do—by making deals, starting with an amendment to the legislation that would effectively save some counties in upstate New York and Long Island $2.3 billion they would otherwise spend on the state's Medicaid program. The provision applied only to those New York counties, whose representatives included GOP House members Chris Collins and John Faso. Critics, recalling all the controversy about Senator Ben Nelson and the Cornhusker Kickback back in 2009, started calling the Collins-Faso amendment the "Buffalo Bribe."[10]

Those wavering New York Republicans were part of the moderate Tuesday Group, whose members thought the bill's spending cuts and clawback of insurance rules went too far. They were the ones most alarmed by the CBO projections of massive coverage losses. Many also opposed cuts to Planned Parenthood, since they were abortion rights supporters.

But even as Ryan had to attend to those objections, he was also dealing with the Freedom Caucus and their allies in the conservative movement, who had started calling the bill "Obamacare 2.0." They wanted deeper spending cuts plus a more aggressive attack on the preexisting condition regulations that made insurance more expensive. "Our network has spent more money, more time and more years fighting Obamacare than anything else," said Tim Phillips, president of Americans for Prosperity. "And now with the finish line in sight, we cannot allow some folks to pull up and give up."[11]

Normally, the White House would broker some kind of compromise that could satisfy members of both factions, and Trump, who loved to brag about his negotiating skills, was eager to play that role. "We need a leader that wrote *The Art of the Deal*," he'd said in his 2015 announcement speech, referring to the bestseller that cemented his reputation as a corporate mastermind. But at least in the latter parts of his private-sector career, Trump had succeeded mostly because he was good at marketing his brand and himself, especially on NBC's *The Apprentice*.

Negotiating major legislation required attention to substance, not showmanship. In 2009 and 2010, Obama could close deals because he had a firm grasp on the details of legislation, how those details fit into the broader scheme of what he wanted to accomplish, and which parts would appeal to which member. Even as he was reminding Tennessee's Jim Cooper, a relatively conservative Democrat, of the bill's deficit reduction, he was emphasizing the coverage expansion to Dennis Kucinich, who favored Medicare for All. Especially at the end, when legislation was on the floor, Obama could also appeal to members' sense of higher purpose—by invoking the spirit of Harry Truman or, as he did in his final speech to the House Democratic caucus, reminding them that passing historic legislation was why most of them had come to Congress in the first place.

Trump could be charming in person, more than many outsiders realized. But he had no patience for the work required to grasp detail, expressed no firm commitments to what legislation should contain, and betrayed no sense of mission other than notching a victory—and, perhaps, undoing Obama's legacy. As a candidate, he hadn't gone through the exercise of developing a plan. As president, he made no visible effort to study GOP proposals, leaving everything to Paul Ryan. It showed in late March, as Trump was trying to lock up votes in the House. "He never talked policy," recalled Charlie Dent, the Pennsylvania Republican who was cochair of the Tuesday Group. "It was just, 'Let's get this thing done. Let's get a deal here.'"[13]

Sometimes Trump delivered that message politely, sometimes not. On March 23, he met at the White House with each of the factions. He kicked off the Tuesday Group meeting with a rant about some of the items on his mind, including the latest affront from MSNBC's Joe Scarborough and Mika Brzezinski. Then he started going around the table, one by one, and got to Dent, who was sitting on the opposite side next to Vice President Pence.[14]

Dent, having explained his objections to the bill in a similar meeting a few days before, said he hadn't changed his mind. When he started to talk about Medicaid, Trump cut him off: "If this bill goes down, I'm blaming you," Dent remembered Trump saying. "It's going to be your fault." Later in the meeting, Trump singled out Dent again. "Still a hard no?" When Dent nodded and started to talk, Trump turned his head in a different direction and said, "I don't want to hear it."[15]

Trump's meeting with the Freedom Caucus didn't yield votes, either, although it featured less hostility and followed a more convoluted set of negotiations. Earlier in the month, according to reporting in *Politico* and *The New York Times*, Mark Meadows and Ohio's Jim Jordan had reached out to Trump directly, saying they thought Ryan was not heeding their concerns. Trump signaled that he was willing to negotiate with them directly. But at a Capitol Hill meeting with the full House GOP caucus, Trump singled out Meadows in front of his peers, saying, "I'm gonna come after you" if the North Carolinian voted no.

Bannon, Pence, and other White House officials made a similar pitch at a meeting in the Eisenhower Executive Office Building, with Bannon telling members, "You have no choice but to vote for this bill." Bannon's posture was especially striking, because *Breitbart*, the publication he'd once led and to which he still had close ties, had originally attacked the House bill because it would raise premiums on older people—echoing Democrats, only with a specific focus on the voters who made up Trump's base. But, like Trump, he was now emphasizing the need for a win at all costs. And the harder he and the rest of the White House team leaned on the Freedom Caucus, the more defiant its members became.[16]

On the morning of Friday, March 24, the House leadership team was in the Speaker's office, preparing to pull the bill from the floor altogether because they knew it was going to fail. Then the White House called with a message: Keep at it. Priebus and Pence were meeting with the Freedom Caucus at the Capitol Hill Club, a swanky dining room across the street from the House office buildings. The feedback from members was positive; a majority was just within reach.

"We all looked at each other," one aide who was in the room recounted to me later. "We have the votes? That's news." Ryan and his lieutenants, majority leader Kevin McCarthy and whip Steve Scalise, spent the next ninety minutes on the phone, jackets off and cell phones in hand, reconstructing the whip list to see if they had missed anything. They hadn't. The votes just weren't there.[17]

This, too, was becoming a familiar experience, because White House officials would report positive vibes as commitments. "You didn't want to discourage them from going and trying to win over votes," one former congressional aide said about the White House legislative operation, "but they would come in and say, 'We think we need to get just three or four votes,' and we knew it was more like thirty."[18]

In the afternoon, Ryan went to the White House personally. He and Trump agreed to pull the vote, and in a somber press conference, an ashen-faced Ryan announced that "Obamacare is the law of the land. . . . We'll be living with Obamacare for the foreseeable future."[19]

3.

Mark Meadows was in many respects a prototype for the modern Republican lawmaker.

He grew up outside of Tampa, Florida, a self-described nerd who took up running and got into shape after a girl turned him down for a date. His father was a draftsman, his mother a nurse, and income was neither plentiful nor steady—an experience he later credited with shaping his worldview about the importance of individual initiative. "Growing up poor gave me a real appreciation for work," he said.[20]

Meadows moved to North Carolina after getting an associate of arts degree at the University of South Florida and marrying a high school acquaintance he had begun dating once they were both in college. They started a sandwich shop and sold it for a profit, after which he switched to real estate development and investment, and made a lot more money. He got involved in GOP politics as a financier and local party chair. When a veteran Blue Dog Democrat decided to retire rather than seek election from a newly gerrymandered seat, Meadows jumped into the race.[21]

The new district lines carved out a rural section surrounding Asheville that was in transition. It had the downscale remnants of abandoned textile factories and upscale retirement homes of Floridians and Georgians who had relocated to the Carolina mountains. In both cases, the population was overwhelmingly white and religiously observant—and staunchly Republican. Meadows won in a multicandidate primary by impressing key backers, including the local Tea Party, and espousing a mix of old-fashioned conservatism (invoking Reagan, promising "a hand up instead of a handout") and Obama-era stridency (warning about socialism and liberal judges threatening to honor sharia law). "We're going to take back our country," Meadows said at a campaign stop preserved on YouTube. "2012 is the time we are going to send Mr. Obama home to Kenya or wherever it is."[22]

Meadows had not even been in Congress one year when he first made an impact by helping to orchestrate the House's role in the Defund Obamacare shutdown. Two years later, by the time he had filed that motion to vacate against Boehner, Meadows was arguably one of the most influential members of the GOP caucus—which was no minor feat, given his ultra-brief tenure and lack of legislation to show for it. It helped that Meadows was a master communicator who had an endless appetite for chatting or texting with Capitol Hill reporters. More than most of his more senior colleagues, Meadows understood that the preferred currency of politics was headlines, not appropriations.[23]

Meadows also had a flair for drama. Following reports that he had been among the House members discussing a leadership coup in 2013, he went to Boehner and, literally, got on his knees to beg forgiveness. In 2017, House leaders groused that his opposition to the repeal bill was one part an objection over substance, one part an effort to grab attention yet again. If so, he succeeded—thanks in no small part to Trump, who a week after the canceled vote was still venting at Meadows and his group on Twitter: "The Freedom Caucus will hurt the entire Republican agenda if they don't get on the team, & fast. We must fight them, & Dems, in 2018!"[24]

Meadows's opposition to the repeal bill didn't seem to be hurting him at home (the local Tea Party group saluted his fight against "Ryancare") or in the conservative political universe (Michelle Malkin thanked the Freedom Caucus for "having our backs"). But Meadows was still thinking about ending Obamacare. On the Sunday after Ryan pulled the bill, Meadows told ABC's George Stephanopoulos that giving up on the effort was like giving up on then Patriots quarterback Tom Brady at halftime of the Super Bowl before a comeback win.[25]

It was a cryptic comment that revealed more than almost anybody understood at the time. Meadows had approached Dent about crafting a new compromise that could pass. Dent took the offer back to the Tuesday Group, which rejected the idea—in part, Dent later said, because many members sat on the committees of jurisdiction and thought they should leave any dealmaking to their chairmen. But one Tuesday Group member, Tom MacArthur of New Jersey, decided to work with Meadows directly. Vice President Pence also got involved, and Trump (mostly) held off attacking fellow Republicans on Twitter. Ryan dispatched a key policy adviser, Matt Hoffmann, to work out the details.[26]

The experience of failure turned out to be an effective motivator, as it had been for Democrats in 2009, and a deal started to take shape. The big Freedom Caucus demand was to scale back or, better still, eliminate the standards on benefits (i.e., the requirement that all plans include mental health, prescriptions, and so on) and pricing (i.e., the prohibition on charging more or less based on health risk). Meadows agreed to make it optional for states, since most of the moderates balking at that change came from more liberal parts of the country where officials were more likely to leave existing rules in place.[27]

Dent and other Tuesday Group members were furious at MacArthur for moving forward unilaterally and would later oust him from his leadership position. But once the Freedom Caucus as a whole endorsed the deal and conservative groups backed it, the White House and House leaders had momentum again. They picked up a key moderate, Michigan's Fred Upton, with some extra spending for high-risk pools and other measures for people with preexisting conditions. They won over a Florida Republican by tweaking the Medicaid funding formula for the state's nursing homes.[28]

Back in 2009, Ryan had said, "I don't think we should pass bills that we haven't read and don't know what they cost." Now, in 2017, he was calling a floor vote under precisely those circumstances, with legislative counsel still finalizing language and the CBO still running calculations. His members were right there with him. At a meeting of the caucus, Martha McSally, an Arizona Republican and former combat pilot, rallied her colleagues with a call to get this "fucking thing" done. A few hours later, they did, approving the bill 217–213.[29]

Trump was so elated that he invited Republicans who voted yes to the Rose Garden for a celebratory press conference. He praised House leaders and congratulated himself, as well: "Coming from a different world and only being a politician for a short period of time—how am I doing? Am I doing okay? I'm President. Hey, I'm President. Can you believe it? Right? I don't know, it's—I thought you needed a little bit more time. They always told me, more time. But we didn't."[30]

Trump also talked about the bill's impact, promising that it would mean lower premiums—which, in theory, it would, but mostly for younger and healthy people. That was because insurers in states using the new waivers would have fewer requirements on who or what they had to cover. In the meantime, people with serious medical needs were likely to have a harder time paying their bills. There was even a possibility that the bill, if passed, could weaken protections against catastrophic expenses for people with employer coverage.[31]

On top of that, there were the big cuts to Medicaid and private insurance subsidies, which were part of the original bill and unchanged by the Meadows-MacArthur amendment. When the CBO released its final assessment later in May, it came to virtually the same conclusion as before. Instead of "great health care for everybody," the CBO predicted, twenty-three million would lose coverage.[32]

Their fate now depended on the U.S. Senate.

4.

Mitch McConnell grew up in Alabama, Georgia, and Kentucky, which he would come to call home. The defining event of his childhood was a bout with polio that lasted from when he was two until he was four. The experience made him especially close with his mother, who had to care for him largely by herself because her husband, McConnell's father, was overseas serving in the military. As an adult, McConnell would say the experience instilled him with a sense of determination.

The polio's lasting physical effect was a weakness in one leg that caused a slight limp. It limited McConnell's ability in athletics, which he loved, so he channeled his competitive energy into politics—following it like a sport, even as a kid, and running for office regularly starting in high school. He lost some elections but won a few, as well, eventually becoming student council president at the University of Louisville, where he was an undergrad before getting a law degree at the University of Kentucky. He was introverted and slightly awkward, but he had a single-minded focus on winning that would become a trademark when he decided to make politics his career.

It was the 1960s, and Kentucky's transformation from Southern Democrat to Southern Republican was already underway. The question, as journalist Alec MacGillis wrote in a 2014 biography, "was not which party Mitch McConnell would sign up for. It was which kind of Republican he'd be." As a student and campaign worker, McConnell had been a vocal supporter of civil rights and opponent of the Vietnam War. His early patron and mentor, Senator John Sherman Cooper, was a moderate Republican from the Rockefeller wing of the party.[33]

But once McConnell got into elected office in the 1970s as a county leader and later as a U.S. senator, he started dropping liberal positions and picking up conservative ones on everything from abortion to labor law—drifting rightward with both Kentucky and the Republican Party, which people who knew McConnell said was no coincidence. As one of them later told *The New Yorker*'s Jane Mayer, when she searched for McConnell's core values, "You can look and look for something more in him, but it isn't there. I wish I could tell you that there is some secret thing that he really believes in, but he doesn't."[34]

McConnell became caucus leader in 2007, right when Republicans relinquished their majority, and it was in his role as a minority leader that he turned the practice of obstruction into an art form. He did so by uniting his party in opposition to Obama and doing as much as (and probably more than) any other individual to break traditional governing norms that encouraged cooperation. He had dramatically increased use of the filibuster to block legislation from getting votes, making it impossible for Democrats to pass legislation even when they had a majority on their side. Later, when he became majority leader, he refused even to hold confirmation hearings for Obama's choice to replace Supreme Court justice Antonin Scalia, who died in February 2016. McConnell said it was one of his proudest moments.[35]

McConnell's success at thwarting Obama and the Democrats cemented his reputation as a strategic savant. But passing legislation required a very different skill set from stopping it. He was more than happy to let the House sort out the contradictions and tensions of GOP dogma and, according to multiple reports, didn't expect Ryan and company to succeed. By the time they did, McConnell had a big problem on his hands.

Repeal had turned decidedly unpopular, in ways polls didn't fully capture. Until 2017, intensity had favored the law's critics. Now it favored supporters. They were showing up at town halls and, in one particularly poignant moment, on late-night television, when Jimmy Kimmel, the ABC host, gave an emotional monologue on his first show after taking paternity leave. His infant son had a congenital heart defect that required surgery shortly after birth. The experience made Kimmel think about his good fortune to have insurance and, then, the people who didn't.

"If your baby is going to die and it doesn't have to, it shouldn't matter how much money you make," Kimmel said, visibly tearing up. "I think that's something that whether you're a Republican or Democrat or something else, we all agree on that, right?"[36]

It was a sign that the repeal battle had broken out of the insular, confusing world of parliamentary tactics where McConnell did his best work, although the inside game was not going so well either. The House's rushed process drew criticism even from conservative Republican senators like South Carolina's Lindsey Graham. "A bill—finalized yesterday, has not been scored, amendments not allowed, and 3 hours final debate—should be viewed with caution," Graham tweeted. Other senators objected to the magnitude of the likely coverage losses. "Let's face it," said Orrin Hatch. "The House bill isn't going to pass over here."[37]

Objections from GOP senators were nothing new. It was Lamar Alexander and Rand Paul who, back in December and January, publicly called upon Trump and House leaders to drop the repeal-and-delay plan. And it was Tom Cotton who, in March, tweeted warnings that the "House healthcare bill can't pass Senate w/o major changes."[38]

But the public warnings didn't have a private counterpart. House Republican aides writing legislation were in constant contact with one another, but spoke to Senate staff only sporadically—and, even then, mostly to check on what was out of bounds under reconciliation rules. "They weren't trying to shape the policy," Emily Murry, a senior GOP aide on the Ways and Means Committee, told me. Trump administration officials weren't mediating either. It was yet another striking contrast to 2009 and 2010, when Democrats had standing conference calls for leadership and committee staff from both houses, usually with Nancy-Ann DeParle or Jeanne Lambrew on the line as well.[39]

The result for Democrats was a pair of bills that had the same basic structure and a group of lawmakers who, despite their institutional tensions, already understood each other's thinking and limits. Republican lawmakers in May 2017 were in a very different place. One house had passed a bill, another had not even started to work on one, and big, fundamental questions, like whether to alter Medicaid or how to keep preexisting condition protections, remained unanswered. "Looking back, we should have had more coordination and communication," Murry said. "We should have had weekly meetings, if not more, with the House, Senate, and administration."[40]

McConnell's solution was to construct a bill in the same way that Ryan had—by writing it himself. He created a thirteen-senator advisory group and made sure to include archconservatives Ted Cruz and Mike Lee (who were prone to giving him the same grief that the House Freedom Caucus has given Boehner and Ryan) as well as the more moderate Lamar Alexander and Orrin Hatch. The group did not include Susan Collins—or any women, for that matter. As the least conservative member of the caucus, Collins was the least likely to vote for the bill. Even so, her absence was conspicuous given her well-known interest in the issue and the fact that she'd been Maine's insurance commissioner for five years.[41]

Alexander and Hatch were chairmen of the HELP and Finance Committees, respectively, which meant they brought not just expertise to the task but their supporting staff, as well. But McConnell was bypassing the usual committee process altogether; the plan was to bring legislation straight to the floor. Even Paul Ryan had put his bill through committee markups, perfunctory though they were. "The extreme secrecy is a situation without precedent, at least in creating health law," wrote Julie Rovner, who had been covering health care since the 1980s. McConnell and his allies had been among those who accused Democrats of jamming the Affordable Care Act through Congress. But in 2009, Senate Democrats had twenty-two separate committee hearings on health care legislation, according to an analysis in *Vox*. Senate Republicans were going to have none.[42]

One goal was to shield legislation from too much public scrutiny before a vote. "We aren't stupid," an anonymous GOP aide told Axios. As in the House, however, that secrecy came at a price when McConnell unveiled the bill in late June, provoking a torrent of criticism from outside analysts, advocates, and organizations that most Republicans were unprepared or unwilling to rebut. Trump had told GOP senators that the House bill was too "mean" and, at the margins, McConnell's legislation was more generous than what Ryan and the House Republicans had produced. But it still shifted costs onto the old and the sick. It still envisioned less government spending to help people get insurance. Within forty-eight hours, the list of organizations in opposition read like a who's who of patient advocacy and medical groups: AARP, the Catholic Health Association, the American Cancer Society Cancer Action Network, just to name a few. When the CBO followed with its assessment, twenty-two million losing coverage, Republican senators defected en masse, starting with Collins.[43]

The numbers alone didn't convey the bill's full impact, because of a big change to Medicaid that was in both the House and Senate legislation. Instead of simply rolling back the Affordable Care Act's expansion of eligibility, Republicans were determined to change the funding formula for the entire program. The details were different in the two pieces of legislation, but each had the potential—and, many analysts would say, nearly certain likelihood—to reduce the services that Medicaid provided to the elderly, people with disabilities, or both. Those services included home aides and equipment that made it possible for people with severe mental or physical impairments to get jobs, go to college, and live independently.[44]

Republicans wanted these changes because they were a way to limit the growth of these programs and free up money for tax cuts, realizing two longtime conservative goals. But the provisions fired up disability advocates, including the group ADAPT (American Disabled for Attendant Programs Today), whose members made the journey to Washington and staged a Capitol Hill "die-in." Video of Capitol Police removing them exploded on social media and television news, dealing yet another political blow to the repeal effort.[45]

The specter of Medicaid cuts was especially troubling in states that were struggling with opioid addiction, because the program financed treatment in the low-income communities where the epidemic was hitting hardest. Among those states were Arkansas, Ohio, Pennsylvania, and West Virginia, which among them had five GOP senators. Kentucky was also on the list of states with a serious opioid problem, which some advocates thought might help explain the mixed feelings of McConnell and sometimes unpredictable opposition of Rand Paul—each of whom wanted to be against Obamacare but knew their state depended on it.[46]

McConnell had hoped to hold a vote before the July 4 recess, one week after making legislation public. But the bill was losing support, rather than gaining, and GOP senators like Wisconsin's Ron Johnson were openly questioning the rush. "We don't have enough information," Johnson said. "I don't have the feedback from constituencies who will not have had enough time to review the Senate bill. We should not be voting on this next week."[47]

Senate Democratic leaders, meanwhile, had responded to calls from Indivisible and its allies to withhold consent for routine business. That made it difficult for Republicans to hold a debate and vote, because without that consent, the Senate had to deal with all kinds of time-consuming procedural steps. McConnell relented and pushed the vote until after the recess.[48]

5.

McConnell found himself in the very same spot Ryan had occupied, torn between conservatives who said repeal didn't go far enough and (relative) moderates who said it went too far. And he wasn't getting much help from the White House. Three days after the postponement, Trump tweeted, "If Republican Senators are unable to pass what they are working on now, they should immediately REPEAL, and then REPLACE at a later date!" It was the option McConnell had preferred originally, back in January, that Trump ruled out at the behest of members who were no more likely to support it now than they had been back then.[49]

By this point, nobody seriously thought the legislation McConnell had constructed was good policy. It had obvious omissions that suggested sloppy draftsmanship, including one that Rodney Whitlock, the former Grassley aide, suggested on Twitter could create a death spiral. The politics seemed pretty dismal too, if the polls were right. And yet McConnell and the Republicans pushed ahead, which was a testimony to how powerful the drive to kill Obamacare was among Republicans in Congress—because they thought it was the right thing to do, because they thought their voters and financiers demanded it, because Trump was insisting upon it, or some other combination of reasons.[50]

Just getting to the voting stage was a challenge, because that took fifty votes, and both Collins and Lisa Murkowski, of Alaska, intended to vote no. This is where John McCain became part of the story. He had been in Arizona getting medical treatment for his newly diagnosed cancer; his return to the Senate had been a surprise. As protesters in the gallery shouted, "Kill the bill!" he provided the critical fiftieth aye on the motion to proceed, allowing the voting process to begin. It was a big win for McConnell, and everybody was paying so much attention to the impact that few dwelled on McCain's warnings about his unhappiness with the deliberative process, or lack thereof, that had produced the legislation.

McConnell's original hope was to pass his Senate bill, which he'd since modified—in part, by adding yet another amendment from Ted Cruz designed to weaken insurance rules and win over skeptical conservatives in the process. He'd also padded the bill with extra opioid treatment funds to assuage nervous Republican governors and to lock in Ohio's Rob Portman and West Virginia's Shelley Moore Capito. But the bill got just forty-three votes. Next McConnell tried a measure that was basically a version of repeal and delay. A similar bill had passed in 2015 with fifty-two votes. This one got just forty-five.[51]

The last option was "skinny repeal." On paper, all the bill would do was eliminate the individual mandate and requirements that employers contribute toward their workers' insurance. In practice, it was a vehicle to start a conference committee negotiation, where House and Senate leaders could work together on more substantial legislation. McConnell was able to get to forty-nine votes, which was no small thing, but he needed fifty—in other words, at least one from among Collins, McCain, and Murkowski.

Collins was not an option. She had made her objections clear and she was from Maine, a Democratic-leaning state. McConnell, sensitive to the needs of vulnerable members, gave her a pass. He made more of an effort to win over Murkowski, as did the White House. Interior secretary Ryan Zinke called both her and fellow Alaska senator Dan Sullivan to say that Murkowski's no vote could affect administration decisions on a series of projects important to the state.[52]

But Murkowski was uniquely positioned to resist intimidation. Back in 2010, after losing a primary battle to a Sarah Palin–backed Tea Party candidate, Murkowski ran as a write-in candidate and won. She owed nothing to McConnell, who had not backed her bid to keep her seniority after she lost the primary. She also had substantive concerns, especially when it came to abortion rights, which she supported, and what repeal would mean for Medicaid. About four in ten of the state's enrollees were Native Alaskans, and Murkowski had a close relationship with the tribes, whose support had been essential in her 2010 win.[53]

That left McCain, whose misgivings included a fear that the House would pick up the skinny repeal legislation, pass it as is, and be done with it. Paul Ryan spoke to him directly, promising a real conference committee negotiation, and McCain appeared alongside his old friend Lindsey Graham at a press conference to talk about the conversation. But at times, McCain seemed not to be paying attention to what Graham was saying. A former GOP aide who remembered watching later said, "I believe this is a guy who, during that press conference, talked himself into believing, 'This thing is so fucking stupid I've got to kill it. We've gotten so stupid here that we're doing this skinny repeal thing, but only to prove that we can pass something. And we are begging them never to pick it up, which we can't trust them to do, just so we can move on. And this is our process. Screw this, I'm going to just kill the whole thing.'"[54]

McCain bumped into Chris Murphy, Democratic senator from Connecticut, on his way to the Senate chamber—and told Murphy he was about to surprise a lot of people. He delivered a similar message to reporters outside the chamber: "Watch the show," he said. Still, most everybody thought the bill was going to pass, because McConnell would not have called a vote he didn't already know he would win. Few noticed that when Murkowski walked past a desk where McCain was sitting, he gestured a thumbs-down.[55]

A little while later, just after midnight, McCain spoke with Chuck Schumer and John Cornyn, the Texas Republican and chief deputy to McConnell. Schumer was grinning, Cornyn looked grim, and this time, the exchanges were right in the sight line of two congressional correspondents, who immediately tweeted what they saw. "I THINK WE HAVE NEWS!!!!" wrote Steven Dennis of Bloomberg. *HuffPost*'s Matt Fuller told followers, "All I can say right now is Chuck Schumer and John McCain had a conversation and Schumer left smiling."[56]

McConnell held the previous vote, originally scheduled for fifteen minutes, open for an hour just to buy some extra time. Intense lobbying of McCain followed by Pence (who was on the Senate floor) and then Rubio. It did not work. As Schumer gave his final remarks before the vote, decrying the rush and urging a no vote, McCain nodded along. He left the floor again—this time to take a call from the White House, according to subsequent reports—and then returned for the iconic thumbs-down.

The vote closed, the last effort at repeal legislation went down to defeat, and a dejected McConnell stepped forward with a message for his colleagues.

"It is time to move on."

6.

The repeal effort got the attention of a lot of people who had never focused on politics before. One of them was Elissa Slotkin, a former U.S. intelligence officer living in Holly, Michigan, a small town about an hour northwest of Detroit.

Slotkin had plenty of firsthand experience with medical bills, because as a child she watched her mother battle an aggressive form of breast cancer that ultimately required a double mastectomy. That diagnosis tagged her with a preexisting condition and made it impossible to find decent, affordable coverage—and at one point, her insurance lapsed altogether. She wasn't feeling well, went to a clinic, and got a diagnosis of ovarian cancer. Slotkin and her brother scrambled to pay her medical bills; at one point, Slotkin later remembered, she had to give a credit card number over the phone to a hospital, so her mother could get a scan. Slotkin and her fiancé accelerated their wedding and timed it so that her mother would be in between chemo regimens. She made it to the wedding, strong enough to deliver a toast and dance. Six months later, she died.[57]

Slotkin was an Iraq specialist, serving during both the Bush and Obama administrations. In 2017, she and her husband decided to leave Washington and go to Michigan to find work in the private sector. They were at home on the couch, Slotkin later remembered, when they saw television coverage of the Rose Garden ceremony where Trump was celebrating passage of the repeal bill with House Republicans. Slotkin had been following the legislation with growing anger, remembering her mother's struggles, and had started to entertain the idea of running for Congress. Then the camera panned to Trump's right, and there, just a few feet away, was Mike Bishop, the Republican congressman from her district, with a big grin. Slotkin said that she literally turned to her husband and said that was it. She was running.[58]

In the months that followed, as Slotkin geared up to launch a campaign, Republicans tried one more attempt at repeal—this time, a bill from Senators Bill Cassidy of Louisiana and Lindsey Graham of South Carolina. It failed too. At that point, Republicans quickly shifted their focus to a tax-cut bill, something they passed easily. It included a win of sorts on health care, because it effectively eliminated the individual mandate penalty by reducing it to zero. The provision that had caused so much debate and controversy, going back to the knock-down, drag-out fights of the 2008 Democratic primaries, was gone. Economists, including those at the CBO, predicted a sudden and serious deterioration in the insurance markets, but it never happened, offering some validation to critics who said the economists had overestimated its impact all along.[59]

But even with that legislative accomplishment, Republicans were in trouble politically, and a big reason was the backlash to repeal. The midterm campaign played out like an almost perfect inversion of 2010, with Democrats pounding Republican incumbents over the repeal votes and Republicans trying desperately to change the subject—and, when they couldn't, to lie about their records. In Arizona, Martha McSally, the House Republican who had exhorted her colleagues to "get this fucking thing done," proclaimed, "We cannot go back to where we were before Obamacare." In New Jersey, Tom MacArthur, the House Republican whose amendment had brought repeal back from the dead, said, "We are as committed to covering pre-existing conditions as they are."[60]

It was in Michigan, though, where the issue may have played the biggest role, in part because Slotkin was using it so effectively. A television advertisement featured grainy home video of her wedding, with her mother, head wrapped in a scarf, giving the toast. Then it went to Slotkin, walking on her family farm, talking about her mother's experience with medical bills—and the sight of Bishop at that Rose Garden event with Trump. "When I saw Congressman Bishop at the White House . . . something inside me broke," Slotkin said. "Mr. Bishop, that's dereliction of duty, and it's a fireable offense."[61]

Bishop defended himself the same way many other Republicans did—by talking about his wife, who had a medical condition of her own, and suggesting it proved he wouldn't have jeopardized anybody's access to care. But in interviews and debates, he had no answers when confronted with projections showing that the House bill, which he had supported and celebrated, would have left many millions without coverage. In 2016, riding the Trump wave, Bishop had won the district by seventeen points. In 2018, he lost to Slotkin by four.

And he had plenty of company. McSally, who was running for a U.S. Senate seat, lost an election she was supposed to win. MacArthur and a bunch of other incumbents lost their seats too. When it was all over, Republicans had relinquished their House majority, and although they lost fewer seats than the Democrats had in 2010, that was largely a by-product of the geographical advantage they had from gerrymandering. They had lost the national popular vote—that is, the total of all votes cast for House candidates—by nine points, which was a larger deficit than the Democrats had eight years before. It was evidence of how far the politics of health care had shifted, just like the success of ballot initiatives to approve Medicaid expansion in Idaho, Nebraska, and Utah, three deeply conservative states where the Republicans in power had blocked it.[62]

None of this meant that the Affordable Care Act was safe. The Trump administration still had tools for undermining it—and was already deploying them by, for example, slashing funds for advertising even though internal studies showed the advertising worked. Meanwhile, conservative officials from twenty states filed a lawsuit, claiming that, because the mandate was now zero, the whole law was suddenly unconstitutional. The lawsuit made no sense, as even conservative lawyers admitted, but a Republican-appointed district judge ruled in its favor and an appeals court panel—again, with two Republican appointees providing the majority—upheld its basic argument, putting the case on track to the Supreme Court.

It was a sign that the fights over health care in general and the Affordable Care Act in particular were destined to continue. But the most direct threat, of repeal by a Republican Congress with a Republican president ready to sign it, no longer existed—and, more importantly, the voters had rendered a definitive verdict.

There was plenty about the Affordable Care Act that Americans did not like. But they did not want to go back.

Conclusion

What Change Looks Like

1.

The architects of the Affordable Care Act hoped to commemorate their achievement with an event in Washington, D.C., on March 23, 2020, ten years after the bill signing. Barack Obama and Nancy Pelosi were both planning to attend; Sylvia Burwell, the former HHS Secretary, was going to host the event. Then COVID-19 struck and Washington shut down. Not for the first time, celebrating the law was on hold.

A few weeks before that, I visited the city to interview Obama at his office in a nondescript building near Georgetown. He was wearing a black long-sleeve button-down shirt, collar open, dark gray pants, and loafers. "I'm not even wearing any socks," he pointed out, calling that attire the "best part of not being president anymore." Suits were easy, he said; he never had to think much about what to wear. But he was always getting soup on his ties.

Our interview was supposed to go thirty minutes. It lasted fifty-five. I asked about his state of mind at key points in his career and the Affordable Care Act's lifetime—like January and August 2009, when he resisted advice to cut a quick deal on small-bore legislation, and during the January 2010 West Wing negotiations when House and Senate Democrats could barely stand to be in the same room.

On his substantive choices, Obama said once again how he would have pushed single-payer if starting from scratch and how the success of the Massachusetts reforms had gotten his attention. "I was never under an illusion that it would be the absolute optimal plan," he said. But the model seemed to be working there and had bipartisan buy-in, making it "an attractive option, a politically viable starter home from which you could then build." Then he talked about his disappointment that the bipartisan support never materialized—mentioning, unprompted, Jim DeMint's Waterloo line and some of the offers he made to Charles Grassley and even Mitch McConnell. "We got no take-up on any of that stuff," he said.

I asked him to identify his biggest mistake. "You mean besides HealthCare.gov?" he responded. "Still my most aggravating self-inflicted wound." But the regret looming large in his mind was a failure to anticipate the intensity of GOP opposition, not so much during the legislative battle as in the period afterward. He talked about the fights over large health care reforms in the past, like Medicare in 1965 and the drug benefit for seniors in 2003—when, once bills passed, "everybody moved on and tried to make it work." This time, Republicans didn't move on. Instead of shoring up his starter home, by fixing its problems and expanding it, Obama spent the rest of his presidency trying desperately to save it from destruction.

That struggle notwithstanding, Obama said, he was proud of what the law had achieved: "I meet people every single day who say, 'My son, who's twenty-eight, didn't have health insurance, and I persuaded him to get on the ACA once you passed it. He got a checkup for the first time since he graduated from college, and he had a tumor, and they caught it in time. And now he's doing fine, and he and his wife just had a baby. Thank you.'"

As we were wrapping up, I asked him about his line from the signing ceremony—that the law proved America can do big, complicated things. Had this experience shaken his faith? "No," he said quickly, "because it passed, and twenty million people got health insurance, and it's still there." Then he paused, opened his eyes a bit wider, and started again: "But I think what it does reveal is some major structural problems in our current political system that make it much harder to do big things than it used to be."[1]

2.

The next great debate over health care reform might not happen for many years. Or it might happen right away. It depends to some extent on what else is happening in politics—and how the Supreme Court rules on the new Obamacare case. But a debate will happen sooner or later, and when it does, two directions are possible.

One is to reverse course, to scale back the Affordable Care Act or eliminate it altogether. This remains the agenda of Republicans and their allies.

The idea is to cut back on the things conservatives instinctively oppose, so that taxes are lower, regulations are looser, and federal spending comes down. But for many, the objection to Obamacare also reflects a more basic rejection of universal coverage, which by definition means putting everybody into one system with a lot of redistribution—with contributions from healthy people financing the costs of the sick, and the wealthy paying extra to cover the poor.

Republicans want less of that redistribution or maybe none at all. And if they get their way someday, people who are healthy will save money, at least while they remain healthy, and people at higher incomes won't have to pay so much in taxes. But the burden of medical expenses will shift onto those who have more health problems and those who have less money, which is what every reputable projection about every serious Republican plan of the last ten years has shown.

Conservatives can make an intellectually honest case for this approach. It includes practical arguments (they think it works out better for the economy, encourages more medical innovation, and so on) and philosophical ones (they think redistribution is unjust and an infringement on liberty). Republicans could spend the next few years trying to translate this agenda into politically viable proposals, as some of them have been trying to do all along. But as conservative strategists and former GOP officials told me repeatedly, the party doesn't seem sufficiently interested—in health care or, for that matter, legislating more generally. The emphasis more and more is on stoking outrage and lining up Fox appearances, not on writing laws.

The alternative approach on health care is to continue the crusade for universal coverage that Democrats have been carrying on since the days of Roosevelt and Truman. It would mean finding some way to make sure everybody has insurance—as in 99 percent of the population, not just 92. It would mean improving benefits, so that everybody can afford to go to the doctor, or fill a prescription, or be admitted to the hospital without having to pay big out-of-pocket costs. Today, that's a problem even for many Americans with "good" coverage. Ideally, it would also mean a simpler system, one in which patients and providers weren't constantly fighting with insurance companies over billing and approvals, or shifting between plans and networks.[2]

The Affordable Care Act, like the Clinton plan before it, was an attempt to achieve the liberal end of universal coverage through a more conservative scheme that relied heavily on competition among private insurers. But the intellectual foundation for that calculation seems increasingly shaky, especially when it comes to controlling the cost of care. Although the law's delivery reforms have probably helped slow the rise in health care spending, overall competition among insurers hasn't pushed the system toward efficiency as much as the experts had hoped. Even many card-carrying economists schooled in the virtues of markets and hazards of government control now wonder whether it's time for the United States, like other developed nations, to set a global budget for health care, have the government regulate prices, or maybe do both of those things.

If the United States keeps moving in this direction, until everybody has coverage, it could end up with a single, government-run insurance program for everyone. It could also end up with a group of tightly regulated private plans, operating more like public utilities, in some kind of structured competition with each other. Or it could end up with some kind of hybrid, perhaps with a basic public plan and private supplementary policies. In short, it could end up with any of the varieties of national health insurance that exist in the most economically advanced countries around the world.

The version getting the most attention in American politics today is the single-payer proposal that Bernie Sanders and his followers have been promoting: Medicare for All. But the distinctions between versions of national health insurance aren't so important in the grand scheme of things. The reality is that any system that covers everybody with low out-of-pocket costs and some kind of government control over spending is going to look a lot more like Medicare for All than what the U.S. has now. That shouldn't scare anybody. Medicare for All is the same basic idea Harry Truman proposed in the 1940s, and it's in the DNA of Medicare, a program Americans cherish.

Moving to such a system, whether in one fell swoop or incrementally by building on the Affordable Care Act, would entail its own costs and complications—more, perhaps, than many of its champions realize. That's the nature of policy. The transition alone would be a massive challenge, given how much of the current medical ecosystem depends on existing financing arrangements. Advocates need to show that it's possible. They also need to convince Americans that they can guarantee better access without sacrificing quality, innovation, or convenience.

The case shouldn't be that hard to make, given how well the best systems abroad perform. But it will require a lot more work—by wonks and operatives, officials and activists—just like the last big health care reform effort did.[3]

3.

After taking office, Donald Trump famously declared that "nobody knew health care could be so complicated." That is not true. Democrats knew, and it is a big reason why the Affordable Care Act became law.

They had spent years working toward a consensus on what to propose and how to get it through Congress. They methodically built alliances with interest groups and stakeholders. They did the grinding, unglamorous work of policy making. When their opportunity came, they were ready to take advantage of it—although, even then, the political odds were against them.

One reason they made this effort was that they believed so deeply in the substance of what they were trying to do. It doesn't seem entirely coincidental that so many of the Democrats most responsible for the Affordable Care Act had defining, sometimes scarring personal experiences with the health care system, whether it was Obama or Nancy-Ann DeParle losing a mother to cancer and remembering her anxiety about medical bills. Or Jeanne Lambrew seeing her parents take care of the uninsured in their home. Or Andy Slavitt helping his best friend's widow pay off her husband's hospital debt. Or Zeke Emanuel watching patients die on the wards. Or Ted Kennedy talking—constantly—about the distraught parents he met back in the 1970s when taking Teddy Jr. for cancer treatments.

Health care reform also mattered to the Democrats because the underlying concept meshed with what the party has stood for since Roosevelt's day. At its core, universal health care is all about common strength in common vulnerability. It's a recognition that anybody can get sick or injured—that, by pooling resources together, everybody will be safe. It's the same exact concept as Social Security and Medicare, and why the party responsible for them has spent nearly a century trying to extend health care guarantees to the rest of the population.

The Affordable Care Act doesn't look a lot like those two programs. The mishmash of private and public insurance with its interlocking subsidies and regulations, the divided responsibility between federal and state governments—it's a whole other beast and nobody's ideal. But champions of universal coverage were willing to accept second-, third-, and fourth-best solutions because the specter of past failure loomed so large in their minds. That was particularly true for elected officials like John Dingell and Henry Waxman, and for many of their advisers, who figured that the 2009 reform push would likely be their last. "We had an opportunity of a generation," Nancy Pelosi told me. "We were not passing it by."[4]

Some of their choices may have been ill-advised. Maybe Obama and Harry Reid should have pushed Max Baucus harder, and maybe Baucus should have given up on the Gang of Six sooner. Maybe deficit reduction shouldn't have been such a priority, and maybe there were better places to spend capital than on the individual mandate. Maybe the health care industry deserved a little more hostility, and progressive supporters of reform a little more love.

But any second-guessing has to grapple with how difficult these decisions were in real-time. Obama and Reid gave Baucus leeway because they couldn't pass a bill without him. Reducing the deficit was essential to placate more conservative Democrats. The individual mandate secured favorable CBO scores. Neutralizing industry groups kept them from blocking legislation.

It's easy to imagine a substantially better version of the Affordable Care Act. It's hard to imagine a substantially better version of the Affordable Care Act getting through Congress, given the political environment that existed in 2009 and 2010. The best proof may be in the wafer-thin margins on final legislation. And without Obama's refusal to back off reform, without Reid's delicate orchestration of the caucus, without Pelosi's miracle work after Scott Brown's election, even those margins would have been out of reach.

History can help put the accomplishment in perspective. The only expansion of health insurance whose scale rivals the Affordable Care Act's is the creation of Medicare and Medicaid in 1965. But Johnson and his allies had larger congressional majorities, plus they were operating during a time when faith in government was a lot higher and deficits were much lower—and when legislating itself was a very different sort of exercise.

4.

Indeed, the Affordable Care Act is a case study in how policymaking works today, and the deep dysfunctions of American politics that will surely affect any similarly ambitious reform efforts in the future. Fighting climate change, reversing the trend toward greater economic inequality, making college more affordable again—really almost anything on today's progressive agenda, will run into the same obstacles that stood in the way of health care reform, before and after its enactment. If the champions of these causes hope to succeed, they need to learn from the Ten Year War and adapt.

The task starts with grasping the true nature of the opposition. The operating theory of the Affordable Care Act, both how to pass it and then how to implement it, was that adopting some conservative ideas would secure at least some buy-in from Republicans. But Republicans are more oppositional and more ideologically extreme than at any point in modern U.S. history. The transformation has been decades in the making, rooted in polarization that dates back to the 1960s and a conscious decision by conservatives around the same time to reject, rather than accommodate, the welfare state of the New Deal and Great Society.

It means that, at the national level, the party of Mark Meadows and Ted Cruz has no place for a modern-day version of John Chafee or John Heinz, or the version of Mitt Romney that was governor of Massachusetts. In the states, it means Republicans who don't adhere to strongly conservative policies do so at their own peril. And at both levels, it means that opposition will be as tribal as it is substantive, based less on the merits of arguments and more on who is making them. It's hard to escape the conclusion that for the most intense Obamacare critics, it was the "Obama" part more than the "care" they found so objectionable, whether because of partisan identity, race, or both.

That helps explain why repeal failed: in the end, even many Republican voters who said they hated the law didn't want to lose its benefits. It also helps explain why the party lost its House majority in 2018 and, maybe, why Trump lost his bid for reelection two years later.

Still, the political consequences for the GOP's strategy of all-out opposition, on health care and everything else, have been modest. Republicans have held the White House for three out of the last six presidential terms, despite winning the popular vote just once in that span. They've also held at least one house of Congress for most of that time, giving them an effective veto over policy, and they now dominate the judiciary as well. The biggest reason for this is the way that the small-state bias of the Senate and the electoral college, and to a lesser extent gerrymandering, presently give conservatives disproportionate influence over political outcomes.[5]

That reality doesn't simply make it harder for champions of progressive reforms to get power. It makes it harder for them to wield it. The ACA experience is proof. A Senate in which fifty members representing a clear majority of the population had the ability to pass legislation could have produced a much more ambitious health care bill, with more generous benefits, that likely would have been more popular. A House without so much gerrymandering and a presidency chosen by the popular, not electoral, vote might have remained under Democratic control—allowing them to make the kinds of adjustments and improvements that big programs historically got in their early years, but the Affordable Care Act didn't.

Going forward, progressives must either weaken such structural barriers to change or overwhelm them with grassroots energy. One of the most hopeful signs of recent years is the growth of a movement dedicated not only to electing leaders but also to pushing specific causes, including universal health care.

But some things about American politics haven't changed and one of them is the ambivalent, conflicted feelings of the public. Americans have a strong bias toward the status quo, even when they don't like it. On health care, they are wary of promises of new and better health insurance alternatives, especially when those come from a government that they still do not trust the way they did in the 1950s and 1960s. That reticence limited what Obama and his allies could accomplish, and it will surely limit the next generation of reformers, as well, quite possibly forcing them to make the very same kinds of compromises.

If so, it will be infuriating. Compromise frequently is. But it's easy to lose sight of what even heavily compromised reforms can achieve, and that's certainly true of the Affordable Care Act.

5.

One of the Affordable Care Act's legacies is the political one, which Republicans made clear in 2018 and 2020 every time they swore to protect people with preexisting conditions. Taking benefits away from people once they have them turns out to be nearly impossible, just as Bill Kristol predicted in his famous 1993 memo. Universal coverage does not yet exist in the U.S., but some of its principles now have wide acceptance. The boundaries of acceptable political conversation have changed, quite possibly forever.[6]

The Affordable Care Act's other legacy is the human one. And it is not ambiguous at this point. One major literature review from 2020, taking into account some of the most important studies on the topic, concluded that "the Affordable Care Act generated substantial, widespread improvements in protecting Americans against the financial risks of illness." That included fewer people racking up credit card debt or missing house payments; more people getting cancer screenings and maintenance care for their diabetes; and ultimately fewer people getting medical problems they could avoid. There's evidence of other benefits too, like more freedom to start businesses or take part-time jobs because insurance no longer depends on having a big, generous employer. Not everybody is better off, and certainly not everybody feels better off. But the improvements are tangible and significant.[7]

Probably nobody in America has looked at the law's effects more closely than the Kaiser Foundation's Larry Levitt, and probably nobody is more widely respected for his knowledge and intellectual honesty. "There are trade-offs in the ACA like in any big reform plan," he told me. "But the winners have certainly outnumbered the losers."[8]

Those winners aren't just statistics. They are real people. I know because I've met some of them.

There's the barista at a Michigan coffee shop who shattered several bones in his foot when he fell off a ladder but could pay his bills—and get back to work—because he had coverage through the state's Medicaid expansion.

There's the California girl with pulmonary stenosis, a congenital heart condition that requires frequent surgeries, plus ongoing screenings and medication. Her medical bills were approaching the lifetime benefit limits on her family's health insurance—until the Affordable Care Act declared those limits illegal.

And there's the twentysomething North Carolina community college student moonlighting as a busboy who nearly lost his arm in a car accident. He was on his mother's insurance, which she'd purchased through Health-Care.gov with the help of a federal subsidy. He got the care he needed and went back to school.[9]

The Affordable Care Act is a highly flawed, distressingly compromised, woefully incomplete attempt to establish a basic right that already exists in every other developed nation. It is also the most ambitious and significant piece of domestic legislation to pass in half a century—a big step in the direction of a more perfect union, and a more humane one as well.

It is not nearly good enough, and yet so much better than what came before it. In America, that is what change looks like.

Acknowledgments

This book was ten years in the making, or really more like twenty, and I have a lot of people to thank for it—starting with all the sources who have spent so many hours talking with me on the phone, meeting me in person, or corresponding via email. I am especially grateful to people who have opened up to me about their personal struggles with medical bills. They have taught me what I could not learn from reading reports and talking to experts; the real world always looks different and more complicated than the one in academic journals. They have also reminded me, constantly, of why these debates are so important. Real lives depend on their outcomes.

A number of journalists, scholars, and friends gave me advice or feedback on chapter drafts: Jonathan Chait, Matt Fuller, Tara Golshan, Ezra Klein, Ben Miller, Julie Rovner, Emma Sandoe, Michael Tomasky, Jeffrey Toobin, Joan Walsh, and Jason Zengerle. Shefali Luthra offered the expertise of a health care journalist young enough to have fresh eyes on what felt (to me) like recent history. I expect it won't be long before we'll be reading a book of hers. Mark Van Sumeren offered the perspective of somebody who had spent a professional lifetime in health care and cares deeply about making it work. Also he knows a ton about the University of Michigan football team. David Grann is quite simply the most talented wordsmith I know. He's also gifted at talking writers through their writerly mental crises, perhaps because he can relate.

A few other people who read large portions of the manuscript merit special acknowledgment, starting with Nora Caplan-Bricker, whose exquisite literary talents were obvious even when she was a young reporter working with me years ago. (I'm especially grateful for her help crafting visual descriptions, at which I am famously inept.) Adrianna McIntyre was an undergraduate at Michigan when I first met her. As of this writing, she's about to finish her doctorate and become a professor, specializing in health policy. The academic community is lucky to have her and so are her future students.

Over the years, I've come to rely on a small community of experts for story ideas, feedback and tutorials. Among them: Loren Adler, Drew Altman, David Anderson, Samantha Artigua, John Ayanian, Robert Blendon, Linda Blumberg, Thomas Buchmueller, Tsung-Mei Cheng, Sabrina Corlette, Cynthia Cox, Matthew Fiedler, Craig Garthwaite, John Holohan, Paula Lantz, Helen Levy, Sarah Lueck, Tricia Neuman, Len Nichols, Jonathan Oberlander, Karen Pollitz, Sara Rosenbaum, and Andy Schneider. I'm especially grateful to Edwin Park (of Georgetown), plus Aviva Aron-Dine and Judith Solomon (of the Center on Budget and Policy Priorities), who checked over sections of my analysis for policy accuracy. I also owe a debt to the late Uwe Reinhardt, the Princeton economist who had a special gift for accessible, frequently hilarious policy explication— and decided that an excellent use of that gift was to answer phone calls, respond to emails, and more generally tutor young reporters who kept pestering him.

One other person who deserves attention—and my eternal thanks—is the Kaiser Family Foundation's Larry Levitt. It would be difficult to exaggerate how much I've learned from him over the years, or how much I've benefited from his endless reservoirs of patience and good cheer. I know of no single person in health care whose expertise and thoughtfulness command more widespread respect, or whose integrity is more widely acknowledged. He hasn't been in government since his service during the Clinton administration, but his conversations with journalists and policy makers of all backgrounds have left an indelible mark on American health policy.

I am lucky to count Harold Pollack of the University of Chicago as both a mentor and a friend. When I read a new public policy study, he is frequently my first call, regardless of the subject, because chances are good he's already read it and everything else on the subject. He's also one of the kindest, most decent people you will encounter on the planet. (Relatedly, I am grateful to the University of Chicago's Center for Health Administration Studies for its financial support.)

My time covering health care spans my time at two publications, *The New Republic* and *HuffPost*. At each, I benefited from brilliant, supportive colleagues who helped me with my health care reporting—among them, Brian Beutler, Sarah Blustain, Hillary Frey, Ryan Grim, John Judis, Richard Just, Suzy Khimm, Rebecca Leber, Alec MacGillis, Kate Marsh, Rachel Morris, Kevin Robillard, Noam Scheiber, Peter Scoblic, Amanda Terkel, and Danny Vinik. Also the too-many-to-name interns and colleagues on editing desks whose work never gets the credit it deserves. I owe special thanks to Frank Foer, who as my editor at *The New Republic* assigned and then deftly stitched together a lengthy retrospective on the law right after its passage. That article, "How They Did It," was in many ways an early outline for what became Part II of this book.

At *HuffPost*, I'm especially grateful to Arianna Huffington (for bringing me on board), Sam Stein (for telling Arianna to bring me on board and also for reading a draft chapter of this book), Kate Sheppard (for being a great manager and even better human being), and my beat partner Jeffrey Young (for, among other things, reading a chapter). I admired his work from afar for many years. What I didn't know is that he's a terrific colleague too.

I worked with three talented undergraduate researchers—Mariana Boully Perez, Leah Graham, and Melanie Taylor—and with three meticulous fact-checkers—Ben Kalin, Hilary McClellen, and Isaac Scher. All six were diligent, resourceful, and beyond patient with a work process that was both halting and unpredictable. To be clear, any errors that remain in the text are mine and mine alone.

Kathy Robbins, my agent, met me when I was first getting my start in professional journalism and somehow saw my potential to write books when it wasn't obvious to a lot of people, including me. I am eternally grateful to her and her magnificent assistant, Janet Oshiro, not just for representing me but also for their editorial guidance and (much needed) encouragement. Having The Robbins Office as your agency is like having an extra publishing house on your side. And a cheerleading squad too.

Speaking of publishers, I am lucky that I landed at St. Martin's and more lucky, still, that I got to work with Tim Bartlett, who is as talented and wise an editor as everybody says. He saw the possibilities of this project from the very beginning. With the help of his assistant, Alice Pfeifer, and managing editor Alan Bradshaw, he somehow managed to see it through to completion even though the bulk of the writing and editing took place during a global pandemic that turned all of our lives upside down.

My mother-in-law, Carol Mainville, graciously agreed to read the entire manuscript, even though I am fairly certain this is not the kind of book she would normally pick up on her own. She is not a publishing professional; she's a physicist by training. But she did this for my last book and, as before, provided comments as insightful as any editor's.

My two boys, Tommy and Peter, were little kids when I wrote my first book. They're a lot older now, which means we don't sit on the floor playing with Legos or drawing pictures—and that I don't get to tuck them into bed, a ritual that always took thirty minutes because they knew exactly what questions would prompt a long explanation of history, the day's events, or my favorite movies. But they provide just as much joy because they are a lot of fun as young adults—and it turns out they are pretty good at editorial feedback too. I couldn't have done this without them, or without my wife, Amy, whose ridiculously full professional life over the last year has included not just managing her research and being a mentor to dozens of students, but also applying her (unrivaled) organizational skills to help coordinate the COVID-19 response at the University of Michigan. Somehow she still had time for me and the kids and put up with my writerly neuroses—which, trust me, is no small thing. Every day I remember how lucky I am that she is part of my life.

I suppose it goes without saying that nobody would be who they are without their parents and grandparents. And when I think about my writing on health care, I see their influence everywhere—whether it's an interest in medicine, which my grandfather practiced, or commitment to social justice, which my grandmother championed as a teacher and union activist. But it was the love and attention of my mother and father that equipped me with the skills and confidence to pursue journalism (a career neither of them knew much about) and take on big projects like this.

The final months of work on this book were difficult, because Mom, who had been battling illness for a long time, passed away. She was in a nursing home at the end, and I had spent a great deal of time with her there until COVID-19 made visiting impossible. Her mental abilities slipped but her memories did not; until the end, she lit up at mentions of family, especially her beloved grandchildren. I was so grateful for that, and for the kindness of those caring for her when we could not. It was a reminder of our common vulnerability, which has always been the animating spirit behind universal health care.

Mom supported universal coverage and politicians who fought for it, and I expect she would have liked this book for that reason. Of course, she would have liked it more because it was written by her son, whom she loved so much. She knew that I loved her too, though I'm not sure she appreciated how much I admired her belief that we can always make the world a better place. If this book does nothing else, I hope it captures some of that spirit.

Sources

The primary source for this book is my reporting on health care, and the politics of health care, for what works out to be the majority of my professional life, most of which I've spent at *The New Republic* and then *HuffPost*. But I also draw heavily on the works of other people—analysts, historians, and, especially, my fellow journalists.

That includes a number of authors who have written about the topics I take up here. It's not possible to write about the history of the American health care system without reading the work of sociologist (and my long-ago editor) Paul Starr, especially *The Social Transformation of American Medicine*. The same goes for the rest of what's become my canon on American health care: Ted Marmor's *The Politics of Medicare*, Jonathan Oberlander's *The Political Life of Medicare*, Jill Quadagno's *One Nation, Uninsured*, Rosemary Stevens's *In Sickness and in Wealth*, and Jacob Hacker's *The Divided Welfare State*. Essential histories of the Clinton health care plan specifically include *Boomerang* by Theda Skocpol, *The Road to Nowhere* by Jacob Hacker, and *The System* by Haynes Johnson and David Broder.

This is not the first book on the history of the Affordable Care Act. As my citations indicate, I read and learned enormously from several others: Steven Brill's *America's Bitter Pill* (which is especially good on the HealthCare.gov story), Lawrence Jacobs and Theda Skocpol's *Health Care Reform and American Politics* (which contextualizes the story with their considerable intellectual backgrounds), John McDonough's *Inside National Health Reform* (which among things includes a first-person perspective on the Massachusetts reforms), Tom Daschle's *Getting It Done* (which is part memoir on his time in the Obama administration), Richard Kirsch's *Fighting for Our Health* (which gives the perspective of an activist), Bryan Marshall and Bruce Wolpe's *The Committee: A Study of Policy, Power, Politics and Obama's Historic Legislative Agenda on Capitol Hill* (which is basically a day-by-day diary of the Energy and Commerce Committee), and Paul Starr's *Remedy and Reaction* (which puts the law in its historical context). *Landmark,* which the staff of *The Washington Post* published just weeks after the Affordable Care Act became law, remains a remarkably accurate and well-written account.

For insight on key characters, I was lucky to have several biographies, especially Molly Ball's *Pelosi,* Peter Canellos and the *Boston Globe* staff's *Last Lion,* Adam Clymer's *Edward M. Kennedy,* David Garrow's *Rising Star,* Edward Klein's *Ted Kennedy,* Nick Littlefield and David Nexon's *Lion of the Senate,* Alec MacGillis's *The Cynic,* and Richard Wolffe's *Renegade.* Much of what I know about Trump and the Republicans started with my reading the journalism of Tim Alberta (which he turned into his book *American Carnage*) and Jake Sherman and Anna Palmer (who then wrote *The Hill to Die On*). Jeffrey Toobin's *The Oath* is an invaluable resource on the Supreme Court.

Speaking of journalists, the health policy and health politics beat is full of some of the smartest and hardest-working people I know. The notes are full of their names, but I wanted to list some of them here, separately, because so much of what I know comes just from reading them every day: Reed Abelson, Stephanie Armour, Carrie Budoff Brown, Paige Winfield Cunningham, Paul Demko, Dan Diamond, Phil Galewitz, Abby Goodnough, Bob Herman, Matthew Holt, Joanne Kenen, Phil Klein, Kim Leonard, Noam Levey, Trudy Lieberman, Amy Lotven, Susannah Luthi, Shefali Luthra, Harris Meyer, Louise Norris, Charles Ornstein, Robert Pear, Rachana Pradhan, Jordan Rau, Elisabeth Rosenthal, Margot Sanger-Katz, Dylan Scott, Andrew Sprung, Zach Tracer, and Jon Walker.

Charles Gaba is not a journalist, but his blog is as indispensable as any publication. I'm lucky to work alongside one of the very best in the business, Jeffrey Young. One can't (and I didn't) follow the ACA story without following, word for word, the work of Ezra Klein and Sarah Kliff. The same goes for Julie Rovner, who has taught all of us how to do this right.

For the references below, I have not included citations to widely reported public events (like election results). For interviews, where I've had to rely on anonymous sources, I've tried to be specific about who is speaking, indicating both partisan affiliation and institutional position wherever possible. (An *aide* is somebody who works on Capitol Hill.) Although I listed only my primary sources for information, I have done my best to confirm facts with more than one source; when that was not possible, I at least checked with other sources to see if what I was hearing from one was plausible. Even so, I've tried to indicate throughout the text itself when I'm really leaning heavily on one person's recollections or perspectives.

Notes

Introduction

1. There are multiple ways of measuring the uninsured, and all showed record lows as of 2017. The official uninsured rate for the entire population, according to the U.S. Census Bureau, was 8.8 percent. Edward R. Berchick, Emily Hood, and Jessica C. Barnett, *Health Care Coverage in the United States: 2017* (Washington, DC: U.S. Census Bureau, September 12, 2018), https://www.census.gov/library/publications/2018/demo/p60-264.html.
2. Carl Hulse, "John McCain, Seeking Reelection, Releases Ad Against Likely Opponent," *New York Times*, May 18, 2016.
3. Senior Trump administration officials, Joe Lieberman, author interviews; Mark Salter, *The Luckiest Man: Life with John McCain* (New York: Simon and Schuster, 2020), Kindle edition, 527–533.
4. John McCain, *The Restless Wave* (New York: Simon & Schuster, 2018), 346–369.
5. For a breakdown of the scene in the Senate chamber on the night of the repeal vote, see David Mack, "Watch the Shocking Moment John McCain Killed the Republican Health Care Bill," *Buzzfeed*, July 28, 2017, https://www.buzzfeednews.com/article/davidmack/back-and-to-the -left; and "McCain's Dramatic 'Thumbs Down' on Health Care Bill," *PBS Frontline*, Season 2018, Episode 7, https://www.pbs.org/video/thumbs-down-6wiayp/.

Chapter 1: The Last Failure

1. Howard Markel, "69 Years Ago, a President Pitches His Idea for National Health Care," *PBS Newshour*, November 19, 2014, https://www.pbs.org/newshour/health/november-19-1945 -harry-truman-calls-national-health-insurance-program.
2. Haynes Johnson and David Broder, *The System: The American Way of Politics at the Breaking Point* (Boston: Little, Brown, 1996), 4–10.
3. Paul Starr, "What Happened to Health Care Reform?," *American Prospect*, winter 1995, 20–31; Carol Jouzatis, "On the Road Again: Clinton Sells His Plan," *Chicago Tribune*, September 24, 1993, D7; Clifford Krauss, "Congress Praises President's Plan But Is Wary of Taxes and Costs," *New York Times*, September 23, 1993, A20.
4. Karen Tumulty and Edwin Chen, "Mitchell Declares Health Reform Dead for Session," *Los Angeles Times*, September 27, 1994.
5. Adam Clymer, "National Health Program, President's Greatest Goal, Declared Dead in Congress," *New York Times*, September 27, 1994, A1; Henry J. Kaiser Family Foundation, "National Election Night Survey of Voters," press release, November 14, 1994, https://www.kff .org/health-costs/poll-finding/national-election-night-survey-of-voters-1994-2/.

Chapter 2: America's Path

1. "$6,000,000 Sought for New Hospital: The Gotham Is Projected for Persons of Moderate Means Who Do Not Want Charity," *New York Times*, October 3, 1929, 19.
2. "The Committee on the Costs of Medical Care," *Journal of the American Medical Association*, December 3, 1932.
3. This is still true today. See Bradley Sawyer and Gary Claxton, "How Do Health Expenditures Vary Across the Population?," Peterson-KFF Health System Tracker, January 16, 2019,

https://www.healthsystemtracker.org/chart-collection/health-expenditures-vary-across-population/#item-family-spending-also-is-concentrated-with-10-of-families-accounting-for-half-of-spending_2016.

4. For more on international health systems, see T. R. Reid, *The Healing of America* (New York: Penguin, 2009) and Ezekiel Emanuel, *Which Country Has the Best Health Care?* (New York: PublicAffairs, 2020).

5. Paul Starr, *The Social Transformation of American Medicine* (New York: Basic Books, 1982), 275–279; Jill Quadagno, *One Nation, Uninsured: Why the U.S. Has No National Health Insurance* (New York: Oxford University Press, 2005), 17–23; and the Committee on Economic Security, *Report on Health Insurance and Disability,* preliminary and unpublished draft, March 7, 1935, accessed at https://www.ssa.gov/history/reports/health.html.

6. Robert Cunningham III and Robert Cunningham Jr., *The Blues: A History of the Blue Cross and Blue Shield System* (Dekalb: Northern Illinois University Press, 1997), 3–6.

7. Ibid., 13–14.

8. Jacob Hacker, *The Divided Welfare State: The Battle over Public and Private Social Benefits in the United States* (Cambridge: Cambridge University Press, 2002), 212–243; Quadagno, *One Nation, Uninsured,* 25–76.

9. Hacker, *The Divided Welfare State,* 214.

10. Harry S. Truman, "Address at the Dedication of the Norfolk and Bull Shoals Dams," July 2, 1952, in *The Heart of Power: Health and Politics in the Oval Office,* David Blumenthal and James Morone (Berkeley: University of California Press, 2009), Kindle edition, locations 961–962, 5789–5790; Harry S. Truman, "Remarks at the National Health Assembly Dinner, Washington, D.C., May 1, 1948"; "Special Message to the Congress on the Nation's Health Needs, April 22, 1949"; Jonathan Oberlander, "Lessons from the Long and Winding Road to Medicare for All," *American Journal of Public Health,* November 2019, 1497–1500; Quadagno, *One Nation, Uninsured,* 17–47.

11. Herman Miles Somers and Anne Ramsey Somers, *Doctors, Patients and Health Insurance: The Organization and Financing of Medical Care* (Washington, DC: Brookings Institution, 1961), 308–316; Rosemary Stevens, *In Sickness and in Wealth,* 2nd ed. (Baltimore: Johns Hopkins University Press, 1999), 171–189; Cunningham and Cunningham, *The Blues,* 119; Hacker, *The Divided Welfare State,* 197–242.

12. Institute of Medicine, *Employment and Health Benefits: A Connection at Risk* (Washington, DC: National Academy Press, 1993), 66–69; "20,000,000 in Blue Cross: John R. Mannix Predicts Full Coverage," *New York Times,* January 14, 1946; Melissa A. Thomasson, "Early Evidence of an Adverse Selection Death Spiral? The Case of Blue Cross and Blue Shield," *Explorations in Economic History* 41 (2004): 313–328; J. F. Follmann Jr., "Experience Rating vs. Community Rating," *Journal of Insurance* 29, no. 3 (1962): 402–415; Oliver Dickerson, *Health Insurance,* 3rd ed., Irwin Series in Risk and Insurance (Homewood, IL: Irwin, 1968), 328–329; *Comparing Blue Cross and Blue Shield Plans with Commercial Insurers* (Washington, DC: General Accounting Office, July 11, 1986).

13. John F. Kennedy, "Address at a New York Rally in Support of the President's Program of Medical Care for the Aged, May 20, 1962," John F. Kennedy Presidential Library and Museum, https://www.jfklibrary.org/asset-viewer/archives/JFKWHA/1962/JFKWHA-096/JFKWHA-096.

14. Julian Zelizer, "How Medicare Was Made," *New Yorker,* February 15, 2015, https://www.newyorker.com/news/news-desk/medicare-made; W. J. Cohen, "Reflections on the Enactment of Medicare and Medicaid," *Health Care Financing Review,* suppl, December 1985: 3–11. For a more thorough look at Medicare's history, the two best sources are Theodore Marmor, *The Politics of Medicare* (Piscataway, NJ: Transaction Publishers, 1970) and Jonathan Oberlander, *The Political Life of Medicare* (Chicago: University of Chicago Press, 2003).

15. Zelizer, "How Medicare Was Made"; see also Joseph A. Califano Jr., "The Last Time We Reinvented Health Care," *Washington Post,* April 1, 1993.

16. Julie Rovner, "Kennedy's Lasting Devotion to Health Care for All," NPR, August 26, 2009, https://www.npr.org/templates/story/story.php?storyId=112242975; Committee on Finance, *National Health Insurance: Brief Outline of Pending Bills,* United States Senate Committee on Finance, 1974.

17. Blumenthal and Morone, *The Heart of Power,* location 2903; Harold M. Schmeck, "Nixon Sees Passage in '74 of a Health Insurance Plan," *New York Times,* February 6, 1974, 16.

18. The committee votes had been partisan, especially in the House. "Social Security History," Social Security Administration, https://www.ssa.gov/history/tally65.html; Catharine Richert, "Dean Claims Social Security and Medicare Were Passed Without Republican Support," PolitiFact, August 28, 2009, https://www.politifact.com/factchecks/2009/aug/28/howard -dean/dean-claims-social-security-and-medicare-were-pass/; Richard Nixon, "Special Message to the Congress Proposing a Comprehensive Health Insurance Plan," February 6, 1974.

19. David Nexon, author interview; Stuart Altman and David Shactman, *Power, Politics, and Universal Health Care* (Amherst, NY: Prometheus, 2011), Kindle edition; "Obama's Health Care Dilemma Evokes Memories of 1974," Kaiser Health News, September 3, 2009, https:// khn.org/stuart-altman/.

20. Richard Pearson, "Wilbur Mills Dies at 82," *Washington Post,* May 3, 1992; Matt Campbell, "One Night in the Tidal Basin: How a Stripper Doomed Health Care Reform in 1974," Blue Hog Report, November 21, 2013, https://www.bluehogreport.com/2013/11/21/one-night-in -the-tidal-basin-how-a-stripper-doomed-health-care-reform-in-1974/; Altman and Shact-man, *Power, Politics, and Universal Health Care;* Quadagno, *One Nation, Uninsured,* 114–132.

21. Matthew Green, "Back in the Day, Medicare Had Its Haters Too," KQED, August 3, 2015, https://www.kqed.org/lowdown/19169/50-years-ago-medicare-had-its-haters-too-and-we -never-did-awake-to-socialism; Jon Schwarz, "Medicare Celebrates Its 50th Birthday, Despite Ronald Reagan," *Intercept,* July 30, 2015, https://theintercept.com/2015/07/30/medicares -50th-birthday-lets-forget-ronald-reagans-insane-diatribe-trying-stop/; and Zelizer, "How Medicare Was Made."

22. For more on the creation and growth of "conservative infrastructure," see Michael Tomasky, *If We Can Keep It* (New York: W. W. Norton, 2019), 116–121; and, more generally, John Judis, *The Paradox of American Democracy* (New York: Routledge, 2001).

23. "Public Trust in Government: 1958–2019," Pew Research Center, April 11, 2019, https://www .pewresearch.org/politics/2019/04/11/public-trust-in-government-1958-2019/; for back-ground on the alienation of white voters from the Democratic Party in the 1970s and '80s, see Thomas Byrne Edsall and Mary D. Edsall, *Chain Reaction: The Impact of Race, Rights, and Taxes on American Politics* (New York: W. W. Norton, 1992) and E. J. Dionne Jr., *Why Americans Hate Politics* (New York: Simon & Schuster, 1991).

24. Spencer Rich, "Reagan Welfare Cuts Found to Worsen Families' Poverty," *Washington Post,* July 29, 1984; Susan Popkin, "Proposed Cuts to Public Housing Threaten a Repeat of the 1980s' Housing Crisis," Urban Institute, May 31, 2017, https://www.urban.org/urban-wire/proposed -cuts-public-housing-threaten-repeat-1980s-housing-crisis; "News Conference, August 12, 1986," Ronald Reagan Presidential Foundation & Institute, https://www.reaganfoundation.org /ronald-reagan/reagan-quotes-speeches/news-conference-1/; for more background on Rea-gan, the original welfare queen story, and its role in his campaign, see Josh Levin, *The Queen: The Forgotten Life Behind an American Myth* (Boston: Little, Brown, 2019).

25. John D. Rockefeller IV, "The Pepper Commission Report on Comprehensive Health Care," *New England Journal of Medicine,* October 4, 1990, 1005.

26. Thomas Rice et al., "The Medicare Catastrophic Coverage Act: A Post-Mortem," *Health Af-fairs,* fall 1990; Judith Feder and Chris Jennings, author interviews.

Chapter 3: A Right to Health Care

1. Don Phillips and Michael Specter, "Sen. Heinz Dies in Plane Crash," *Washington Post,* April 5, 1991; Pete Leffler, "Heinz Crash Report Raps Pilots' Judgment," *Morning Call,* September 18, 1991.

2. Tim Wirth, "Senator John Heinz Memorial Service," C-SPAN video, 1:19:23, April 12, 1991, https://www.c-span.org/video/?17526-1/senator-john-heinz-memorial-service, 39:45 mark.

3. Dan Balz, "Casey Names Wofford to Succeed Sen. Heinz," *Washington Post,* May 9, 1991; Mi-chael Decoursy Hinds, "In Pennsylvania Politics, It's a Season of Turmoil," *New York Times,* July 7, 1991.

4. Wofford was one of two aides who urged JFK to call Coretta Scott King while her husband was in Birmingham's jail. Many analysts have credited that call (and the relationship that fol-lowed) with helping give Kennedy the margins among African American voters he needed to

win the election. Steven Levingston, "John F. Kennedy, Martin Luther King Jr., and the Phone Call That Changed History," *Time,* June 20, 2017, https://time.com/4817240/martin-luther -king-john-kennedy-phone-call/.

5. Katharine Seelye, "The Democrats' Gunslinger Can Carve Another Notch," *Philadelphia Inquirer,* November 10, 1991.

6. Paul Begala, author interview; Harris Wofford, "Harris Wofford Oral History, Senator, Pennsylvania; CEO of the Corporation for National and Community Service (AmeriCorps)," Miller Center, November 2, 2017, https://millercenter.org/the-presidency/presidential-oral -histories/harris-wofford-oral-history-senator-pennsylvania-ceo.

7. Michael Decoursy Hinds, "Race for Senate Shows Big Split on Health Care," *New York Times,* October 31, 1991.

8. Paul Starr, author correspondence; Paul Starr, "The Middle Class and National Health Reform," *American Prospect,* summer 1991, 7; Starr, author correspondence.

9. Michael Decoursy Hinds, "The 1991 Election; Wofford Wins Senate Race, Turning Back Thornburgh; GOP Gains Edge in Trenton," *New York Times,* November 6, 1991.

10. The furloughed prisoner Willie Horton denied committing the rape; for more on his story, the ad, and its impact on the 1988 presidential campaign, see Beth Schwartzapfel and Bill Keller, "Willie Horton Revisited," Marshall Project, May 13, 2015, https://www.themarshallproject .org/2015/05/13/willie-horton-revisited; for more on the Democratic Party's electoral fortunes during the 1980s and the soul-searching it inspired, see E. J. Dionne Jr., *Why Americans Hate Politics* (New York: Simon & Schuster, 1991); among the movement's manifestos was a report by scholars William Galson and Elaine Kamarck called *The Politics of Evasion,* which made the case that it was not possible to win in national elections without repositioning the party; William Galson and Elaine Kamarck, *The Politics of Evasion: Democrats and the Presidency The Politics of Evasion: Democrats and the Presidency* (Washington, DC: Progressive Policy Institute, 1989), https://www.progressivepolicy.org/wp-content/uploads/2013/03/Politics_of _Evasion.pdf.

11. See Kenneth Baer, *Reinventing Democrats* (Lawrence: University Press of Kansas, 2000); and Lily Geismer, "Democrats and Neoliberalism," *Vox,* June 11, 2019, https://www.vox .com/polyarchy/2019/6/11/18660240/democrats-neoliberalism. Sometimes it was hard to tell how much of the New Democrats' political imperative was about bending to the antigovernment sentiment among disaffected white, working-class voters to avoid Reagan-style welfare attacks and how much was about bending to the wishes of the wealthy individuals and corporations who were underwriting New Democrat candidates and causes.

12. Elizabeth Kolbert, "The Governor: Clinton in Arkansas—A Special Report," *New York Times,* September 28, 1992, A1.

13. As the journalist Ron Fournier later observed, "State law did not require the governor's presence, but politics did: Clinton wanted to raise his national profile and reverse the Democratic Party's Soft-on-Crime Image." Ron Fournier, "The Time Bill Clinton and I Killed a Man," *Atlantic,* May 28, 2015, https://www.theatlantic.com/politics/archive/2015/05/the-time-bill -clinton-and-i-killed-a-man/460869/; Mitchell Locin, "Clinton Says He's a 'New Democrat,'" *Chicago Tribune,* October 22, 1992.

14. Paul Begala, author interview; Marc Lacey, "In New Hampshire, Clinton's Heart Is on His Sleeve," *New York Times,* January 12, 2001.

15. Robert Kerrey, "Why America Will Adopt Comprehensive Health Care Reform," *American Prospect,* summer 1991; E. Richard Brown, "Health USA: A National Health Program for the United States," *Journal of the American Medical Association,* January 22/29, 1992, 552.

16. Chris Jennings and Judy Feder, author interviews; see also Theda Skocpol, *Boomerang: Clinton's Health Security Effort and the Turn Against Government in U.S. Politics* (New York: W. W. Norton, 1996), 30–47.

17. Michael Weinstein, "The Bush-Clinton Health Reform," *New York Times,* October 10, 1992, 20.

18. See Jacob Hacker, *The Road to Nowhere* (Princeton, NJ: Princeton University Press, 1997); in that book, Hacker refers to Clinton's plan as a "liberal synthesis" of the Jackson Hole proposals and more traditional Democratic Party plans for universal coverage.

19. Gwen Ifill, "Clinton Proposes Making Employers Cover Health Care," *New York Times,* Sep-

tember 25, 1992, A1; David Lauter and Robert Rosenblatt, "Clinton Spells Out His Plan to Curb Health Care Costs," *Los Angeles Times*, September 25, 1992.

20. Jennings interview.

21. Begala interview; Ira Magaziner, "A New Order," *Brown Alumni Magazine,* 2014.

22. Haynes Johnson and David Broder, *The System: The American Way of Politics at the Breaking Point* (Boston: Little, Brown, 1996), 106; see also Magaziner, "A New Order."

23. Robert Pear, "Ending Its Secrecy, White House Lists Health-Care Panel," *New York Times,* March 27, 1993; Dana Priest and Michael Weisskopf, "Health Care Reform: The Collapse of a Quest," *Washington Post,* October 11, 1994.

24. Johnson and Broder, *The System*; Jennings, Len Nichols author interviews.

25. Jennings interview.

26. Adam Clymer, "Hillary Clinton, on Capitol Hill, Wins Raves, If Not a Health Plan," *New York Times,* September 29, 1993, A1.

27. Nichols, author interview.

Chapter 4: Harry and Louise

1. James Madison, *The Federalist,* no. 62, 1787.

2. Sarah Binder et al., "What Senators Need to Know About Filibuster Reform," Brookings Institution, December 10, 2010, https://www.brookings.edu/opinions/what-senators-need-to-know-about-filibuster-reform/; also see Thomas Geoghegan, "The Infernal Senate," *New Republic,* November 21, 1994, https://newrepublic.com/article/62471/the-infernal-senate.

3. Helen Dewar, "Shortcut for Health Care Plan Blocked: Obscure Byrd Rule in Senate Closes Budget 'Reconciliation' Route," *Washington Post,* March 14, 1993.

4. Other moderate Republican senators from 1993/94 included David Durenberger of Minnesota, Mark Hatfield and Bob Packwood of Oregon, James Jeffords of Vermont, and Arlen Specter of Pennsylvania; Adam Clymer, "John Chafee, Republican Senator and a Leading Voice of Bipartisanship, Dies at 77," *New York Times,* October 26, 1999, 10; Christine Ferguson, author interview.

5. Ferguson interview.

6. McKay Coppins, "The Man Who Broke Politics," *Atlantic,* November 2018, https://www.theatlantic.com/magazine/archive/2018/11/newt-gingrich-says-youre-welcome/570832/; the McConnell quote comes from Ann Devroy, "GOP Taking Joy in Obstructionism," *Washington Post,* October 7, 1994; see also James Salzer, "The Words of Newtspeak Transformed U.S. Politics," *Atlanta Journal-Constitution,* May 15, 2017, https://www.ajc.com/news/state--regional-govt--politics/the-words-newtspeak-transformed-politics/nfWIIkAqXknLToMHnsjTxI; and, more generally, Julian Zelizer, *Burning Down the House: Newt Gingrich, the Fall of a Speaker, and the Rise of the New Republican Party* (New York: Penguin, 2020).

7. Josh Marshall, "The 1993 Kristol Memo on Defeating Health Care Reform," Talking Points Memo, September 24, 2013, https://talkingpointsmemo.com/edblog/the-1993-kristol-memo-on-defeating-health-care-reform; Marshall got the memo online, via an upload from the website DailyKos; "William Kristol's 1993 Memo - Defeating President Clinton's Health Care Proposal | Medicare (United States) | Health Economics," Scribd, accessed September 22, 2020, https://www.scribd.com/document/12926608/William-Kristol-s-1993-Memo-Defeating-President-Clinton-s-Health-Care-Proposal.

8. Marshall, "Kristol Memo."

9. William Kristol, author interview.

10. Ronald Brownstein, "Dole's Hometown Folks Turn Out to Rally for 'Their Boy,'" *Los Angeles Times,* April 15, 1995.

11. Bernard Weinraub, "Dole, in Hospital Visit, Returns to Past," *New York Times,* January 7, 1988, A22; Timothy Clark, "The Clout of the 'New' Bob Dole," *New York Times,* December 12, 1982, 65.

12. Sheila Burke, author interview.

13. Ibid.

14. Robert Dole, "State of the Union Response," C-SPAN video, 12:48, January 25, 1994, https://www.c-span.org/video/?54051-1/state-union-response, 2:01 mark.

15. Paul Starr, "What Happened to Health Care Reform?," *American Prospect,* November 19, 2001, 20–31.
16. "'Harry and Louise' Health Care Advertisements," YouTube video, 2:46, posted by C-SPAN, July 20, 2009, https://www.youtube.com/watch?v=CwOX2P4s-Iw.
17. James Fallows, "A Triumph of Misinformation," *Atlantic,* January 1, 1995.
18. Pew Research Center, "Public Trust in Government: 1958–2019," April 11, 2019, https://www.people-press.org/2019/04/11/public-trust-in-government-1958-2019/.
19. Mickey Kaus, "No Exegesis," *New Republic,* May 8, 1995.
20. Fallows, "A Triumph of Misinformation."
21. Chip Kahn, author interview; Chris Jennings, author interview.
22. For two different views on this question, see Merrill Goozner, *The $800 Million Pill* (Berkeley: University of California Press, 2004) and Craig Garthwaite and Benedic Ippolito, "Drug Pricing Conversations Must Take the Cost of Innovation into Consideration," STAT, January 11, 2019, https://www.statnews.com/2019/01/11/drug-pricing-conversations-include-cost-innovation/; *Well-Healed: Inside Lobbying for Health Care Reform* (Washington, DC: Center for Public Integrity, 1994).
23. Robert Pear, "Health Care Tug-of-War Puts A.M.A. Under Strain," *New York Times,* August 5, 1994.
24. John Judis, "Abandoned Surgery," *American Prospect,* spring 1995, 65.
25. Thomas Friedman, "Adamant Unions Zero In on Clinton," *New York Times,* November 16, 1993; Haynes Johnson and David Broder, *The System: The American Way of Politics at the Breaking Point* (Boston: Little, Brown, 1996), 292.
26. Len Nichols and Larry Levitt, author interviews.
27. Jack Meyer, author interview; Meyer at the time was president of the Economic and Social Research Institute and a well-regarded expert on health care issues.
28. Nichols interview; Starr, "What Happened to Health Care Reform?"
29. Jennings interview. He recalled answering his mother sarcastically, saying, "Gee, Mom, I wish I had thought of that." She said she understood and they went to lunch, where they switched topics and started talking about her new grandchild, Chris's three-year-old son.
30. E. J. Dionne, *Why the Right Went Wrong: Conservatism: From Goldwater to Trump and Beyond* (New York: Simon & Schuster, 2016), 127–128. The defense of Medicare and Medicaid was part of a broader strategy, including opposition to proposed cuts in education and environmental programs that the administration dubbed M2E2.
31. Robert Blendon, Mollyann Brodie, and John Benson, "What Happened to Americans' Support for the Clinton Health Plan?," *Health Affairs,* summer 1995.

Chapter 5: The Freedom Trail

1. "Massachusetts Facts: Part Three," William Francis Galvin, Secretary of the Commonwealth of Massachusetts, accessed June 21, 2020, https://www.sec.state.ma.us/cis/cismaf/mf3.htm.
2. W. Mitt Romney and Brittany Karford Rogers, "Forty Years On," *BYU Magazine,* winter 2013.
3. Brian Mooney, "Romney and Health Care: In the Thick of History," *Boston Globe,* May 30, 2011, http://archive.boston.com/lifestyle/health/articles/2011/05/30/romney_and_health_care_in_the_thick_of_history/?page=full; Martha Bebinger, "Personal Responsibility: How Mitt Romney Embraced the Individual Mandate in Massachusetts Health Reform," *Health Affairs* 31, no. 9 (2012): 2105–2113.
4. Ryan Lizza, "Romney's Dilemma," *New Yorker,* May 30, 2011; John McDonough, *Inside National Health Reform* (Berkeley: University of California Press, 2012), 37–38.
5. "Romney's CEO Style Rankled Mass. Lawmakers," MassLive, August 2, 2012, https://www.masslive.com/politics/2012/08/gov_mitt_romneys_ceo_style_ran.html; Lizza, "Romney's Dilemma."
6. Neil Swidey, "The Lessons of the Father," *Boston Globe,* November 9, 2012; David Kirkpatrick, "For Romney, a Course Set Long Ago," *New York Times,* December 18, 2007; Benjamin Wallace-Wells, "George Romney for President, 1968," *New York,* May 18, 2012.
7. The friend was Eric Muirhead, from an interview I conducted with him in 2007 for a profile that included the other stories in this paragraph. See Jonathan Cohn, "Parent Trap," *New Republic,* July 7, 2007.

8. Eric Fehrnstrom, author interview. Fehrnstrom was a longtime Romney adviser.

9. On an evening in July 1969, Kennedy was the driver of a car that ran off one of the island's roads and into a pond. Kennedy swam to safety; his passenger, Mary Jo Kopechne, died. Kennedy did not report the incident until the next morning. He pled guilty to fleeing the scene, received a two-month suspended sentence, and called his actions "indefensible." For details on some of these stories, see Michael Kelly, "Ted Kennedy on the Rocks," *GQ*, February 1, 1990.

10. Sara Rimer, "Perfect 'Anti-Kennedy' Opposes the Senator," *New York Times,* October 25, 1994, A1; John Judis, "Stormin' Mormon," *New Republic,* November 7, 1994.

11. Joseph Newhouse, author interview; Joseph Newhouse, *Free for All? Lessons from the RAND Health Experiment* (Cambridge, MA: Harvard University Press, 1993); Michael Rich, "At 40, a Pioneering Health Care Experiment Remains Relevant," RAND blog, April 16, 2016, https://www.rand.org/blog/2016/04/at-40-a-pioneering-health-care-experiment-remains -relevant.html; Aviva Aron-Dine et al., "The RAND Health Insurance Experiment, Three Decades Later," *Journal of Economic Perspectives* 27, no. 1 (2014): 197–222; James Poterba and Lawrence Summers, "Public Economics and Public Policy: The Ideas and Influence of Martin Feldstein, 1939–2019," VoxEU, September 25, 2019, https://voxeu.org/article/ideas -and-influence-martin-feldstein-193902019; Martin Feldstein, "The Welfare Loss of Excess Health Insurance," *Journal of Political Economy* 81 (March/April 1973): 251–280, https://www .jstor.org/stable/1830513?seq=1; Sapna Maheshwari and Ben Casselman, "Martin Feldstein, 79, a Chief Economist Under Reagan, Dies," *New York Times,* June 12, 2019, https://www .nytimes.com/2019/06/12/us/martin-feldstein-dead.html.

12. Jonathan Gruber, author interview; see also Janet Currie and Jonathan Gruber, "Saving Babies: The Efficacy and Cost of Recent Changes in the Medicaid Eligibility of Pregnant Women," *Journal of Political Economy* 104, no. 6 (1996): 1263–1296; David Cutler and Jonathan Gruber, "Medicaid and Private Insurance: Evidence and Implications," *Health Affairs* 16, no. 1 (1997): 194–200.

13. Gruber and Chris Jennings, author interviews.

14. Gruber and Larry Levitt, author interviews. They eventually wrote a paper together: Jonathan Gruber and Larry Levitt, "Tax Subsidies for Health Insurance: Costs And Benefits," *Health Affairs,* January/February 2000; Robin Toner, "Bush's Approach to the Uninsured May Be Vulnerable in Its Details," *New York Times,* April 24, 2000; Gruber, Jennings, Levitt interviews.

15. Amy Lischko, author interview.

16. John McDonough, Andrew Dreyfuss, and Tim Murphy, author interviews.

17. Irene Wielawski, *Forging Consensus: The Path to Health Reform in Massachusetts,* Blue Cross Blue Shield Foundation of Massachusetts, July 2007, 14, https://www.bluecrossmafoundation .org/publication/forging-consensus-path-health-reform-massachusetts.

18. McDonough and Dreyfuss interviews.

19. McDonough interview; Dan Morgan, "States Clamor for Medicaid Funds," *Chicago Sun-Times,* October 24, 1994.

20. Gruber, Lischko, McDonough, and Murphy interviews; Mooney, "Romney and Health Care"; Lizza, "Romney's Dilemma."

21. Robert Draper, "The Mitt Romney That Might Have Been," *New York Times Magazine,* October 7, 2012; Wielawski, *Forging Consensus,* 20.

22. McDonough, *Inside National Health Reform,* 39.

23. Christine Ferguson, author interview; Lizza, "Romney's Dilemma."

24. Gruber interview; see also Peter Dizikes, "How Jonathan Gruber Became 'Mr. Mandate,'" *MIT News,* October 29, 2012, http://news.mit.edu/2012/profile-gruber-economics-mr -mandate-1029.

25. Gruber interview.

26. Gruber, Rick Tyler, author interviews, December 17, 2019; Tyler was an adviser to Gingrich. Brody Mullins and Janet Adamy, "Gingrich Applauded Romney's Health Plan," *Wall Street Journal,* December 27, 2011.

27. Edmund Haislmaier, *The Significance of Massachusetts Health Reform* (Washington, DC: Heritage Foundation, April 11, 2006), https://www.heritage.org/health-care-reform/report /the-significance-massachusetts-health-reform; Edmund Haislmaier and Nina Owcharenko, "The Massachusetts Approach: A New Way to Restructure State Health Insurance

Markets and Public Programs," *Health Affairs,* November/December 2006; David Broder, "For Romney, a Healthy Boost Insurance Plan an Asset for '08," *Washington Post,* April 30, 2006.

28. Jon Kingsdale, McDonough author interviews.

29. McDonough, Dreyfus interviews.

30. Kingsdale interview.

31. Blue Cross Blue Shield of Massachusetts Foundation, "Breast Cancer Survivor Jaclyn Michalos and Pitcher Tim Wakefield," Vimeo video, 0:46, posted 2011, https://vimeo.com /23865113; quoted in Jonathan Cohn, "Can the NBA Sell Obamacare to the American People?," *New Republic,* June 19, 2013, https://newrepublic.com/article/113547/can-nba-sell -obamacare-american-people.

32. McDonough interview; Lischko remembered feeling similar anxiety; Sharon Long and Karen Stockley, *Health Reform in Massachusetts: An Update on Insurance Coverage and Support for Reform as of Fall 2008* (Washington, DC: Urban Institute, September 2009), 3, https://www .urban.org/sites/default/files/publication/30646/411958-Health-Reform-in-Massachusetts -An-Update-on-Insurance-Coverage-and-Support-for-Reform-as-of-Fall--.PDF.

33. Trudy Lieberman, "Health Reform Lessons from Massachusetts, Part I: Critical Analysis Begins to Trickle In," *Columbia Journalism Review,* March 23, 2009, https://archives.cjr.org /campaign_desk/health_reform_lessons_from_mas.php; Trudy Lieberman, "Health Reform Lessons from Massachusetts, Part V: Finding Affordable Health Insurance," *Columbia Journalism Review,* August 5, 2009, https://archives.cjr.org/campaign_desk/health_reform _lessons_from_mas_4.php.

34. Michael Levenson, "Health Bill Signed Amid Hopes for $200b in Savings," *Boston Globe,* August 6, 2012, https://www.bostonglobe.com/metro/2012/08/06/governor-deval-patrick-signs -new-health-care-cost-measure-bill-builds-law-passed-when-gop-candidate-mitt-romney -was-governor/I9Voe8cHZOLZCmX7iyCeBO/story.html; "Charlie Baker's Health Care Bill Could Make a Real Difference," *Boston Globe,* October 26, 2019, https://www.bostonglobe .com/opinion/editorials/2019/10/26/charlie-baker-looks-for-health-care-revolution /diuzsAcySIO17MrNZiuCmN/story.html.

35. Benjamin D. Sommers, author interview; Benjamin D. Sommers, Sharon K. Long, and Katherine Baicker, "Changes in Mortality After Massachusetts Health Care Reform," *Annals of Internal Medicine* 162, no. 9 (2015): 668, https://doi.org/10.7326/l15-5085-2.

36. Haislmaier, *The Significance of Massachusetts Health Reform.*

37. "RomneyCare," *Wall Street Journal,* April 12, 2006.

38. Stephanie Ebbert, "Conservatives Split on Mandate and Business Fees," *Boston Globe,* April 13, 2006, http://www.boston.com/news/local/articles/2006/04/13/conservatives_split_on_mandate _and_business_fees/.

39. Jordan Rau, "State Health Plan Killed," *Los Angeles Times,* January 29, 2008; Anthony Wright, "Lessons from California," *American Prospect,* April 18, 2008, https://prospect.org/special -report/lessons-california/.

40. Kingsdale and McDonough, author interviews.

41. Gruber, Kingsdale, and Timothy Layton, author interviews. Layton is an economist at Harvard Medical School who studied the Connector. See also Louise Norris, "Massachusetts Health Insurance Marketplace: History and News of the State's Exchange," HealthInsurance .org, June 25, 2020, https://www.healthinsurance.org/massachusetts-state-health-insurance -exchange/.

42. Romney's ambivalence about universal benefits per se was one way he may have been different from his father, who thought more about solidarity. For more on this, see Robert Putnam with Shaylyn Romney Garrett, *The Upswing: How America Came Together a Century Ago and How We Can Do It Again* (New York: Simon and Schuster, 2020).

Chapter 6: Audacity

1. Barack Obama, "Remarks by Senator Barack Obama (D-IL) to the Families USA 2007 Conference," Vote Smart, January 25, 2007, https://votesmart.org/public-statement/292061 /remarks-by-senator-barack-obama-d-il-to-the-families-usa-2007-conference-topic-health

-care#.X2ue_5NKiqB; Marie Horrigan, "Obama Adopts Universal Health Care as Policy Theme," *New York Times*, January 25, 2007.

2. Jon Favreau and Dan Pfeiffer, author interviews.

3. Pfeiffer recalled that in the first few months, the organization was just trying to catch up with its more established rivals. "We were bolting the wings on the plane as it took off. We're trying to get an announcement together. We're trying to hire staff. We're getting office space—basically, all the things that Clinton and Edwards had been doing for the last two years, we were doing in the first three months of 2007." Pfeiffer interview; the Las Vegas forum has assumed almost legendary status in the story of Obama's evolution on health care. Among those who offered accounts were both Axelrod and Plouffe, in their memoirs. See David Axelrod, *Believer* (New York: Penguin, 2015), Kindle edition, 221–222; David Plouffe, *The Audacity to Win* (New York: Penguin, 2010), Kindle edition, 46–47. The SEIU posted a video of the event; "Health Care Forum: Barack Obama (1 of 3)," YouTube video, 9:34, posted by SEIU, March 29, 2007, https://www.youtube.com/watch?v=EbJCBP_2RvI. See also Karen Tumulty, "Obama's Health Care Learning Curve," *Time*, August 3, 2009, https://swampland.time.com/2009/08/03/obamas-health-care-learning-curve/.

4. Jonathan Cohn, "How They Did It," *New Republic*, May 21, 2010, https://newrepublic.com/article/75077/how-they-did-it; Plouffe, *The Audacity to Win*, 47.

5. Jeanne Lambrew, author interview.

6. "The period 1994–1998 was a time of record-low rates of growth in health insurance premiums and in the underlying medical expenses that are covered." Christopher Hogan, Paul B. Ginsburg, and Jon R. Gabel, "Tracking Health Care Costs: Inflation Returns," *Health Affairs*, 19, no. 6 (2000): 217, https://doi.org/10.1377/hlthaff.19.6.217.

7. David Hilzenrath, "Art Imitates Life When It Comes to Frustration with HMOs," *Washington Post*, February 10, 1998.

8. Alison Mitchell, "Two Clinton Aides Resign to Protest New Welfare Law," *New York Times*, September 12, 1996, A1.

9. Jonathan Cohn, "True Colors," *New Republic*, July 22, 1999; Jonathan Cohn, "Yuck Yuck," *New Republic*, November 6, 2000.

10. For the initial reports, see Institute of Medicine, *Coverage Matters: Insurance and Health Care* (Washington, DC: National Academy Press, 2001) and Institute of Medicine, *Care Without Coverage: Too Little, Too Late* (Washington, DC: National Academy Press, 2002). For an updated review, see Richard Kronick, "Health Insurance Coverage and Mortality Revisited," *Health Services Research* 44, no. 4 (2009): 1211–1231. For a skeptical perspective on the IOM reports and other large estimates of mortality effects, see Megan McArdle, "How Many People Die from Lack of Health Insurance?," *Atlantic*, February 11, 2010, https://www.theatlantic.com/business/archive/2010/02/how-many-people-die-from-lack-of-health-insurance/35820/; for a response, see Ezra Klein, "When Opinions on Health-Care Insurance Stop Being Polite and Start Getting Complicated," *Washington Post*, February 15, 2010, http://voices.washingtonpost.com/ezra-klein/2010/02/when_health-care_insurance_get.html#more.

11. Jack Meyer, author interview. The cost and coverage estimates came from the Lewin Group, an actuarial firm. For more information on the project, see M. B. Geisz, "Covering America Project Develops Proposals to Increase Health Insurance, but Finds Federal Money Tight," Robert Wood Johnson Foundation, November 1, 2006, https://www.rwjf.org/en/library/research/2006/11/covering-america-project-develops-proposals-to-increase-health-i.html.

12. Roger Lowenstein, "The Prophet of Pensions," *Los Angeles Times*, May 11, 2008.

13. Robert Fitch, "Big Labor's Big Secret," *New York Times*, December 28, 2005; for more on Stern and the SEIU in the early part of his tenure, see Chris Lehmann, "Andy Stern: The New Face of Labor," *Washingtonian*, March 1, 2010; Matt Bai, "The New Boss," *New York Times Magazine*, January 30, 2005; Steven Greenhouse, "A Union with Clout Stakes Its Claim on Politics," *New York Times*, October 30, 2007.

14. Andy Stern, author interview.

15. Ibid.; for more on the SEIU's role in promoting health care in the early 2000s, see "Anatomy of an Election Strategy: The Facts on SEIU's Role in Bringing Home a Victory for America's Working Families," P2004.Org, November 1, 2004, http://p2004.org/interestg/seiu110104pr

.html. Critics suggested the presence of health care workers skewed the union's priorities in favor of anything that would mean more jobs for its members. Stern and his allies responded that the large number of nurses among his members allowed them to speak to the issue with more authority—and more righteous indignation. The reason they were so passionate, Stern liked to say, was that they had a daily, up-close look at how much people suffered when they couldn't pay their medical bills.

16. For more on Dean's health care record and his 2004 presidential campaign, see Jonathan Cohn, "Invisible Man," *New Republic,* July 1, 2002, https://newrepublic.com/article/66351 /invisible-man-0.

17. Janny Scott, *A Singular Woman* (New York: Penguin, 2011), Kindle edition, 354; Janny Scott, "Obama's Young Mother Abroad," *New York Times Magazine,* April 20, 2011. See also David Maraniss, "The 44th President Was His Mother's Son," *Washington Post,* May 11, 2012; Todd Purdum, "Raising Obama," *Vanity Fair,* February 4, 2008.

18. Scott, *A Singular Woman.* See also Angie Drobnic Holan, "Obama's Mother Fought for Disability Coverage, Not Treatment, According to Book," PolitiFact, July 21, 2011, https://www .politifact.com/factchecks/2011/jul/21/barack-obama/obamas-mother-fought-disability -coverage-not-treat/.

19. Barack Obama, *Dreams from My Father: A Story of Race and Inheritance* (New York: Times Books, 1995).

20. Jeffrey Toobin, *The Oath: The Obama White House and the Supreme Court* (New York: Doubleday, 2012), 26; Philip M. Rubin, "Obama Named New Law Review President," *Harvard Crimson,* February 6, 1990.

21. Dan Morain, "Obama's Law Days Effective but Brief," *Los Angeles Times,* April 6, 2008.

22. Jack Van Der Slik, "Barack Obama - 1998 UIS Interview," YouTube video, 25:55, posted by "uistube," https://www.youtube.com/watch?v=42gbXMCbtAE, 5:20 mark; Barack Obama, author interview.

23. David Garrow, *Rising Star* (New York: William Morrow, 2017), Kindle edition; Obama interview.

24. Jonathan Cohn, "Medical History," *New Republic,* January 30, 2008, https://newrepublic.com /article/65704/medical-history.

25. Jim Duffett, author interview; Cohn, "Medical History."

26. Duffett interview; Edward McClelland, *Young Mr. Obama: Chicago and the Making of a Black President* (New York: Bloomsbury, 2010).

27. Duffett interview; Cohn, "Medical History."

28. Duffett interview.

29. Michael D. Shear and Ceci Connolly, "In Illinois, a Similar Health-Care Fight Tested Obama as State Senator," *Washington Post,* September 9, 2009; McClelland, *Young Mr. Obama;* Garrow, *Rising Star.*

30. *State of Illinois Adequate Health Care Task Force* (Chicago: Illinois Department of Public Health, 2007), http://www.idph.state.il.us/hcja/AHCTF%20Final%20Report%201.26.07.pdf and Public Act 093–0973, 2004, https://www.ilga.gov/legislation/publicacts/fulltext.asp ?name=093-0973&GA=093; Cohn, "Medical History"; Shear and Connolly, "In Illinois"; McClelland, *Young Mr. Obama;* Garrow, *Rising Star.*

31. Marwa Eltagouri, "Dr. Quentin Young, Chicago Activist for Civil Rights and Public Health, Dies at 92," *Chicago Tribune,* March 8, 2016, https://www.chicagotribune.com/news/ct-quentin -young-dead-20160308-story.html; Robert Zarr, "Statement in Memory of Dr. Quentin Young, 1923–2016," Physicians for a National Health Program, March 8, 2016, https://pnhp.org/news /statement-in-memory-of-dr-quentin-young-1923-2016/; "Barack Obama on Single Payer in 2003," Physicians for a National Health Program, June 4, 2008, http://www.pnhp.org/news/2008 /june/barack_obama_on_sing.php; Angie Drobnic Holan, "Obama Statements on Single-Payer Have Changed a Bit," PolitiFact, July 16, 2009, https://www.politifact.com/factchecks/2009/jul /16/barack-obama/obama-statements-single-payer-have-changed-bit/; Garrow, *Rising Star.*

32. Shear and Connolly, "In Illinois"; Garrow, *Rising Star.* Obama remembered Young well, describing him to me as a "sweet, sweet man." I also met Young once—at a Chicago event in 2007. I didn't take notes, but I recall him both expressing affection for Obama and disappointment that he didn't fight harder for single-payer.

33. Duffett interview.
34. Mark Leibovich, "The Speech That Made Obama," *New York Times Magazine*, July 27, 2016.
35. For more on Obama's 2004 Senate race, see Noam Scheiber, "Race Against History," *New Republic*, May 31, 2004; William Finnegan, "The Candidate," *New Yorker*, May 31, 2004; Laura Meckler, "The Capital's Unlikely Pals: Obama and Senate's 'Dr. No,'" *Wall Street Journal*, February 11, 2011, https://www.wsj.com/articles/SB100014240527487033133045761325813610 58672; Andrew Prokop, "Losing Obama's Favorite Republican," *New Yorker*, May 8, 2012, https://www.newyorker.com/news/news-desk/losing-obamas-favorite-republican; Angie Drobnic Holan, "Obama-Lugar Measure Included Weapons of Mass Destruction," PolitiFact, July 15, 2008, https://www.politifact.com/factchecks/2008/jul/15/barack-obama/obama-lugar -measure-included-weapons-of-mass-destr/.
36. Anna Galland, author interview. Galland was a senior leader at MoveOn from 2007 to 2019. See also Marc Andrew Eaton, "From the Seats to the Streets: MoveOn.org and the Mobilization of Online Progressive Activists," University of Colorado at Boulder, January 1, 2011, https:// scholar.colorado.edu/cgi/viewcontent.cgi?article=1004&context=socy_gradetds; David Karpf, "The MoveOn Effect: The Unexpected Transformation of American Political Advocacy," Harvard Kennedy School Ash Center for Democratic Governance and Innovation, April 3, 2013, https://ash.harvard.edu/event/moveon-effect-unexpected-transformation-american-political -advocacy; Matt Bai, "Profiting from the Pummeling," *New York Times*, September 23, 2007.
37. Richard Wolffe, *Renegade* (New York: Crown, 2009), Kindle edition, 43–58.
38. "Commencement Address: Barack Obama - Knox College," Knox College, July 18, 2013, https://www.knox.edu/news/president-obama-to-visit-knox-college-speak-on-economy /2005-commencement-address.
39. Karen Kornbluh, author correspondence; Wolffe, *Renegade*, 291–292; Tom Daschle, *Getting It Done* (New York: St. Martin's, 2010), Kindle edition, 70; David Cutler, author interview.
40. Chris Jennings, author interview.
41. Jeanne Lambrew, John D. Podesta, and Teresa L. Shaw, "Change in Challenging Times: A Plan for Extending and Improving Health Coverage," *Health Affairs* 24, suppl 1 (2005): W5-119–W5-132, https://doi.org/10.1377/hlthaff.w5.119. The paper was based on a proposal the three produced for the Center for American Progress.
42. Austan Goolsbee, author interview. Goolsbee also wrote about his concerns with single-payer for a column: Austan Goolsbee, "The Problem with Michael Moore's Policy Ideas," *Slate*, July 1, 2007, https://slate.com/technology/2007/07/the-problem-with-michael-moore -s-policy-ideas.html; Obama interview.
43. Obama, Jeffrey Liebman interviews. Liebman, a Harvard economist who joined the campaign in January 2007, told me "they had basically settled on the Massachusetts-style approach" when he arrived.
44. James Kvaal and Peter Harbage, memo to Senator John Edwards, "Health Issues and the Uninsured," April 18, 2006.
45. James Kvaal, author interview; James Kvaal and Peter Harbage, memo to Senator John Edwards, "Tomorrow's Health Care Call," January 12, 2007.
46. Paul Krugman, "Edwards Gets It Right," *New York Times*, February 7, 2007, https://www .nytimes.com/2007/02/09/opinion/09krugman.html.

Chapter 7: The Argument

1. Jacob Hacker, author interview.
2. Jacob Hacker, "Health Care for America: A Proposal for Guaranteed, Affordable Health Care for All Americans Building on Medicare and Employment-Based Insurance," Economic Policy Institute, January 16, 2007, https://www.epi.org/publication/bp180/; Helen Halpin and Peter Harbage, "The Origins and Demise of the Public Option," *Health Affairs* 29, no. 6 (2010): 1117–1124, https://doi.org/10.1377/hlthaff.2010.0363.
3. Hacker interview.
4. "Health System Reform," Atlantic Philanthropies, https://www.atlanticphilanthropies.org /subtheme/health-system-reform; Roger Hickey, quoted in Mark Schmitt, "The History of the Public Option," *American Prospect*, August 18, 2009, https://prospect.org/article/history -public-option./.

5. Halpin and Harbage, "The Origins and Demise of the Public Option."

6. Jeffrey Liebman, interview; Zaid Jilani, "Flashback: Obama Repeatedly Touted Public Option Before Refusing to Push for It in the Final Hours," ThinkProgress, December 22, 2009, https:// archive.thinkprogress.org/flashback-obama-repeatedly-touted-public-option-before-refusing -to-push-for-it-in-the-final-hours-380cbf31b6e0/; Kip Sullivan, "Bait and Switch: How the 'Public Option' Was Sold," PNHP, July 20, 2009, https://pnhp.org/2009/07/20/bait-and-switch -how-the-public-option-was-sold/; Tom Daschle, *Getting It Done* (New York: St. Martin's, 2010), Kindle edition, 74.

7. Obama campaign advisers, author interviews.

8. David Cutler, author interview; John McCormick, "Obama Defends Health Care Plan," *Chicago Tribune,* November 24, 2007; Dan Pfeiffer, author interview.

9. Gruber, Liebman author interviews.

10. Karen Tumulty, "Obama Channels Hillary on Health Care," *Time,* May 29, 2007, http:// content.time.com/time/nation/article/0,8599,1626105,00.html.

11. Ezra Klein, "A Lack of Audacity," *American Prospect,* May 30, 2007, https://prospect.org /article/lack-audacity/.

12. See Jonathan Cohn, "So, About That 15 Million Figure You've Been Hearing...," *New Republic,* December 3, 2007, https://newrepublic.com/article/38373/so-about-15-million-figure -you've-been-hearing and Jonathan Cohn, "Wading Pool," *New Republic,* May 28, 2007, https:// newrepublic.com/article/64506/wading-pool.

13. "Transcript: New Hampshire Democratic Presidential Candidates Debate," CNN, June 3, 2007, http://transcripts.cnn.com/TRANSCRIPTS/0706/03/se.01.html.

14. Patrick Healy, "Clinton Unveils Health Care Plan," *New York Times,* September 17, 2007, https://www.nytimes.com/2007/09/17/washington/17cnd-clinton.html.

15. "Clinton vs. Obama," FactCheck.Org, November 16, 2007, https://www.factcheck.org/2007 /11/clinton-vs-obama/; Ben Smith, "More Negative Mail," *Politico,* January 31, 2008, https:// www.politico.com/blogs/ben-smith/2008/01/more-negative-mail-005783.

16. Paul Krugman, "Obama Does Harry and Louise, Again," *New York Times,* February 1, 2008, https://krugman.blogs.nytimes.com/2008/02/01/obama-does-harry-and-louise-again/; Howard Wilkinson, "The Day Hillary Clinton Got Really, Really, Really Mad in Cincinnati," WVXU, July 27, 2018, https://www.wvxu.org/post/day-hillary-clinton-got-really-really-really-mad -cincinnati#stream/0.

17. Senior Obama campaign aides, author interviews; Jon Favreau, "Despairing the Debates," *Ringer,* September 23, 2016, https://www.theringer.com/2016/9/23/16041068/presidential -debates-are-not-on-the-level-b85266ea53fa; David Axelrod and Pfeiffer, author interviews.

18. Jonathan Oberlander, "The Partisan Divide—The McCain and Obama Plans for U.S. Health Care Reform," *New England Journal of Medicine* 359, no.8 (2008): 781–884, https://doi.org/10 .1056/nejmp0804659; Shweta Jha, "Studies Analyze Costs, Impact of Obama, McCain Health Care Plans," Commonwealth Fund, September 16, 2008, https://www.commonwealthfund.org /publications/newsletter-article/studies-analyze-costs-impact-obama-mccain-health-care-plans.

19. Angie Drobnic Holan, "Health Care Ad Is Right—Until the End," PolitiFact, October 3, 2008, https://www.politifact.com/factchecks/2008/oct/03/barack-obama/health-care-ad-is-right-- --until-the-end/; Maeve Reston and Seema Mehta, "Obama Attacks McCain Health Plan on Trail in Ads," *Los Angeles Times,* October 5, 2008, https://www.latimes.com/archives/la-xpm -2008-oct-05-na-campaign5-story.html.

20. Pfeiffer and Neera Tanden, author interviews.

21. John Nichols, "Obama v. McCain: 'Fundamental Difference' on Health Care," *Nation,* October 8, 2008, https://www.thenation.com/article/archive/obama-v-mccain-fundamental-difference -health-care/.

Chapter 8: Workhorses

1. Kevin Cullen, "Famine to Feast—Living the Dream," *Irish Times,* June 19, 2013, accessed July 14, 2020, https://www.irishtimes.com/culture/heritage/famine-to-feast-living-the-dream-1.1424566; David Bowen and Jim Manley, author interviews; "Senator Ted Kennedy 'Hideaway' Office," C-SPAN, November 11, 2013, accessed July 14, 2020, https://www.c-span.org/video/?c4475195 /senator-ted-kennedy-hideaway-office.

2. "Kennedy's 40 Year Push for Universal Coverage," WBUR, January 21, 2009, https://www .wbur.org/commonhealth/2009/01/21/kennedys-40-year-push-for-universal-coverage; Kennedy's incremental efforts for that Congress included bills on genetic nondiscrimination and mental health parity. "Kennedy, Enzi, Snowe Celebrate Passage of Genetic Information Nondiscrimination Act," U.S. Senate Committee on Health, Education, Labor, and Pensions, April 24, 2008, https://www.help.senate.gov/chair/newsroom/press/kennedy-enzi-snowe -celebrate-passage-of-genetic-information-nondiscrimination-act; Robert Pear, "House Approves Bill on Mental Health Parity," New York Times, March 6, 2008.

3. Bowen and David Nexon, author interviews.

4. Jeff Zeleny and Carl Hulse, "Kennedy Chooses Obama, Spurning Plea by Clintons," New York Times, January 28, 2008.

5. Karen Davis and Kristof Stremikis, "The Costs of Failure: Economic Consequences of Failure to Enact Nixon, Carter, and Clinton Health Reforms," Commonwealth Fund, December 21, 2009, https://www.commonwealthfund.org/blog/2009/costs-failure-economic -consequences-failure-enact-nixon-carter-and-clinton-health-reforms; Bowen interview.

6. Karen Tumulty, "Vicki Kennedy: The Woman Who Saved Ted," Time, August 26, 2009, https://time.com/time/politics/article/0,8599,1918905,00.html.

7. Staff of the Boston Globe, Last Lion: The Fall and Rise of Ted Kennedy, ed. Peter S. Canellos (New York: Simon & Schuster, 2009); Ted Kennedy, "EXCERPT: Ted Kennedy's 'True Compass,'" ABC News, September 10, 2009, https://abcnews.go.com/GMA/Books/excerpt-ted -kennedys-true-compass/story?id=8563422; Edward M. Klein, "The Lion and the Legacy," Vanity Fair, June 2009.

8. Nexon interview; Sally Jacobs, "Kennedy, His Children, and Cancer," Boston Globe, May 25, 2008, http://archive.boston.com/news/local/articles/2008/05/25/kennedy_his_children_and _cancer/?page=2.

9. David Rogers, "Kennedy Returns for Medicare Vote," Politico, July 9, 2008, https://www .politico.com/story/2008/07/kennedy-returns-for-medicare-vote-011638; Bowen interview.

10. Jon Ward, "'The Son of a Bitch Is Going to Run': Kennedy, Carter, and the Last Time a Powerful Politician Challenged an Incumbent President of Their Own Party," Vanity Fair, January 21, 2019, https://www.vanityfair.com/news/2019/01/the-last-time-a-powerful-politician -challenged-an-incumbent-president; Ted Kennedy, "1980 Democratic National Concession Address," speech, New York City, August 12, 1980.

11. Globe Staff, Last Lion; Ted Kennedy, "Transcript: Edward Kennedy's DNC speech," CNN, August 25, 2008, https://www.cnn.com/2008/POLITICS/08/25/kennedy.dnc.transcript/index.html.

12. David Brown, "For Medicare, an Inadequate Prescription," Washington Post, June 26, 2000; Sue Landry, "Many Elderly Americans Forced to Skip Medications," Tampa Bay Times, September 14, 2005, https://www.tampabay.com/archive/1998/12/26/many-elderly-americans -forced-to-skip-medications/.

13. "Gore Presses Advantage on Prescription Plan," Baltimore Sun, August 27, 2000; "No Deal on Prescription Benefit," CQ Almanac 2002, 58th ed. (Washington, DC: CQ-Roll Call Group, 2003), http://library.cqpress.com/cqalmanac/cqal02-236-10363-664020.

14. Robert Kuttner, "Bush's Troubling Medicare Plan," Boston Globe, September 10, 2000.

15. David Espo, "Medicare Deal Would Offer Equal Coverage," Associated Press, June 4, 2003, https://www.ourmidland.com/news/article/Medicare-Deal-Would-Offer-Equal-Coverage -7177650.php; Max Baucus, "Baucus Speaks on Bipartisan Medicare Framework," U.S. Senate Committee on Finance, June 5, 2003, https://www.finance.senate.gov/ranking-members -news/baucus-speaks-on-bipartisan-medicare-framework; David Nexon, "Senator Edward M. Kennedy: The Master Legislative Craftsman," Health Affairs 28, no. 1 (2009), https://www .healthaffairs.org/doi/full/10.1377/hlthaff.28.6.w1040.

16. Jack Anderson and Michael Binstein, "Scrounging for Swing Votes," Washington Post, May 2, 1993; Mike Dennison and Charles S. Johnson, "Controversy Aside, It's Been a Long Run for Max Baucus," Billings Gazette, February 9, 2014, https://billingsgazette.com/news/state-and -regional/govt-and-politics/controversy-aside-its-been-a-long-run-for-max-baucus/article _f8379aae-e082-5351-9259-a9c5e111c5c5.html.

17. Ari Berman, "K Street's Favorite Democrat," Nation, March 19, 2007; Jennifer McKee, "Baucus Staffers in Lobbyist Pipeline," Missoulian, April 13, 2008, https://missoulian.com/news/local

/baucus-staffers-in-lobbyist-pipeline/article_b7a30f9e-65b8-5fa7-b921-60a58087dbc7.html;
Kevin Zeese, "Max Baucus Should Not Be Deciding Health Care for America," PNHP, May 10,
2009, https://pnhp.org/news/max-baucus-should-not-be-deciding-health-care-for-america/.

18. Erin P. Billings, "Democrats Sit on Cash Piles," *Roll Call,* July 3, 2008, https://www.rollcall
.com/2008/07/03/democrats-sit-on-cash-piles/; Eric Alterman, "Grace Under Fire," *Rolling
Stone,* June 1, 1995; Max Baucus, author interview.

19. Robert Pear and Robin Toner, "Divided House Approves Expansion of Medicare," *New York
Times,* November 22, 2003; Ezra Klein, "The Sleeper of the Senate," *American Prospect,* October 23, 2008, https://prospect.org/features/sleeper-senate/.

20. Senior Democratic aide, author interview.

21. "Medicare Legislation Vote," C-SPAN video, 26:14, November 25, 2003, accessed July 19,
2020, https://www.c-span.org/video/?179290-1/medicare-legislation-vote.

22. Sarah Kliff, "Part D Was Less Popular Than Obamacare When It Launched," *Washington
Post,* June 21, 2013, https://www.washingtonpost.com/news/wonk/wp/2013/06/21/part-d
-was-less-popular-than-obamacare-when-it-launched/?arc404=true.

23. Liz Fowler and Jon Selib, author interviews.

24. Robert Pear and Robin Toner, "Medicare Plan Covering Drugs Backed by AARP," *New York
Times,* November 18, 2003; Robert Pear and Robin Toner, "A Final Push in Congress: The Overview; Sharply Split, House Passes Broad Medicare Overhaul; Forceful Lobbying by Bush," *New
York Times,* November 23, 2003, accessed July 18, 2020, https://www.nytimes.com/2003/11/23
/us/final-push-congress-overview-sharply-split-house-passes-broad-medicare-overhaul.html.

25. David Nexon and Nick Littlefield, *Lion of the Senate: When Ted Kennedy Rallied the Democrats in a GOP Congress* (New York: Simon & Schuster, 2015), 89; Bowen interview; Lee Da-
vidson, "Hatch, Kennedy Made Political Theater as 'Odd Couple,'" *Deseret News,* August 27,
2009, https://www.deseret.com/2009/8/27/20336963/hatch-kennedy-made-political-theater
-as-odd-couple#sen-edward-kennedy-d-mass-in-1970.

26. Kavita Patel, author interview.

27. Nexon interview.

28. Amy Sullivan, "Ted Kennedy's Quiet Catholic Faith," *Time,* August 27, 2009; Ted Kennedy,
"Maiden Speech," U.S. Senate, April 9, 1964, https://www.senate.gov/artandhistory/history
/common/image/CivilRightsFilibuster_MaidenSpeechTedKennedy.htm.

29. Democratic officials and senior aides, author interviews.

30. David Espo, "Congress Passes New Child Health Care Bill, Setting Up Another Veto Fight
with Bush," Seacoastonline.com, November 4, 2007, https://www.seacoastonline.com/article
/20071104/PARENTS/71102017.

31. Selib interview.

32. Fowler interview.

33. Max Baucus, "Prepare for Launch Health Reform Summit Opening Statement," speech,
Washington, D.C., June 16, 2008; "Fed Wary of Health Care Costs," CBS News, June 16, 2008,
https://www.cbsnews.com/news/fed-wary-of-health-care-costs/.

34. John McDonough, *Inside National Health Reform* (Berkeley: University of California Press,
2012), 63–64; Tom Price to Max Baucus, note, undated; Ezra Klein, "The 'Prepare for Launch'
Health Summit," *American Prospect,* June 16, 2008, https://prospect.org/article/prepare
-launch-health-summit./.

35. "Sen. Wyden Proposes Universal Health Plan," CBS News, December 2006, https://www
.cbsnews.com/news/sen-wyden-proposes-universal-health-plan/.

36. "Analysis of a Wyden/Bennett Health Insurance Proposal," Congressional Budget Office /
Joint Committee on Taxation, May 1, 2008, https://www.cbo.gov/publication/24777; Ezra
Klein, "Health Care's Odd Couple," *American Prospect,* February 15, 2008, https://prospect
.org/article/health-care-s-odd-couple/; Jonathan Cohn, "What's the One Thing Big Business
and the Left Have in Common?," *New York Times Magazine,* April 1, 2007.

37. Senior Democratic aides, author interviews; Drew Armstrong, "Wyden Pushes for Universal
Health Care Legislation," *CQ,* December 13, 2006.

38. Ron Pollack, author interview.

39. Tamar Lewin, "Hybrid Organization Serves as a Conductor for the Health Care Orchestra,"
New York Times, July 28, 1994.

40. Pollack interview; Lisa Wangsness, "Lobbies Backing Health Reforms," *Boston Globe,* December 3, 2008, http://archive.boston.com/news/nation/articles/2008/12/03/lobbies_backing_health_reforms/?page=1.

41. Pollack interview.

42. Michael Barbaro and Robert Pear, "Wal-Mart and a Union Unite, at Least on Health Policy," *New York Times,* February 7, 2007.

43. John McDonough and Pollack, author interviews; McDonough, *Inside National Health Reform,* 50–58.

44. McDonough interview; McDonough, *Inside National Health Reform,* 35–37.

45. Carrie Budoff Brown, "Who to Watch For in Debate over Care," *Politico,* May 3, 2009, https://www.politico.com/story/2009/05/who-to-watch-for-in-debate-over-care-021952; Mike Dennison, "Baucus Staffer Who Led Health Reform Drafting Moving to Obama Administration," *Billings Gazette,* July 13, 2010, https://billingsgazette.com/news/state-and-regional/montana/article_4a5924b4-8ed7-11df-93ce-001cc4c03286.html.

46. Fowler interview; Bowen, Fowler, Chris Jennings, and Jeanne Lambrew, author interviews; senior Democratic aides interviews.

47. Karen Tumulty, "Moving Forward on Health Care," *Time,* November 12, 2008, https://swampland.time.com/2008/11/12/moving-forward-on-health-care/.

48. "2009 Health Reform Plan," C-SPAN video, 37:28, November 12, 2008, https://www.c-span.org/video/?282373-1/2009-health-reform-plan.

49. Robert Pear, "Senator Takes Initiative on Health Care," *New York Times,* November 11, 2008, accessed July 20, 2020, https://www.nytimes.com/2008/11/12/washington/12health.html.

Chapter 9: Hard Things Are Hard

1. Robert Blendon, Tami Buhr, Tara Sussman, and John M. Benson, "Massachusetts Health Reform: A Public Perspective from Debate Through Implementation," *Health Affairs* 27, no. 1 (October 2008); Timothy Noah, "How Romneycare Killed Obamacare," *Slate,* January 20, 2010, https://slate.com/news-and-politics/2010/01/how-romneycare-killed-obamacare.html; Tim Dickinson, "The Coakley Cockup," *Rolling Stone,* January 19, 2010; James Kirchick, "Why Martha Coakley Lost Ted Kennedy's Senate Seat to Scott Brown Is No Big Mystery," *New York Daily News,* January 20, 2010; Jason Zengerle, "Who's to Blame for a Candidate Like Martha Coakley?," *New York Magazine,* January 17, 2010, https://nymag.com/intelligencer/2010/01/whos_to_blame_for_a_candidate.html; David Graham, "Six Explanations for Why Coakley Lost in Mass.," *Newsweek,* January 19, 2010, https://www.newsweek.com/six-explanations-why-coakley-lost-mass-70775; Tracey D. Samuelson, "Coakley Concedes Race: Five Lessons from Her Campaign," *Christian Science Monitor,* January 20, 2010, https://www.csmonitor.com/USA/Politics/2010/0120/Coakley-concedes-race-five-lessons-from-her-campaign.

2. Jim Messina, author interview.

3. "Democrats Conflicted on Next Steps for Health Care Reform," PBS, January 20, 2010, accessed September 15, 2020, https://www.pbs.org/newshour/health/among-democrats-conflicting-ideas-on-how-to-proceed-on-health-care-reform.

4. There have been multiple accounts of this meeting, including in my *New Republic* article from 2010. Here, I have based my description on multiple sources from within the administration. It lines up closely with the story that appeared in the *Washington Post* 2010 retrospective, which had the most detailed published version I found. Staff of *The Washington Post,* *Landmark: The Inside Story of America's New Health Care Law and What It Means for Us All* (New York: PublicAffairs, 2010), Kindle edition, 49–50.

5. Congressional Budget Office, H.R. 4872, Reconciliation Act of 2010 (Final Health Care Legislation), Washington, D.C., March 20, 2010, https://www.cbo.gov/publication/21351.

Chapter 10: Yes We Can

1. Danny Shea, "Juan Williams Tears Up: 'This Is America at Its Grandest' (VIDEO)," *HuffPost,* December 5, 2008, accessed September 15, 2020, https://www.huffpost.com/entry/juan-williams-tears-up-th_n_141242.

2. Jonathan Alter, *The Promise* (New York: Simon & Schuster, 2010), 38.

3. Senior Obama administration officials, author interviews.
4. Jeanne Lambrew, author interview; Katharine Whittemore, "The Maine Chance," *Amherst Magazine*, January 14, 2020, https://www.amherst.edu/amherst-story/magazine/issues/2020 -winter/the-maine-chance/; "Obituary: Costas T. Lambrew, MD, FACP, MACC," *Portland Press Herald*, December 15, 2019, https://www.pressherald.com/2019/12/15/obituarycostas -t-lambrew-md-facp-macc/.
5. Lambrew interview.
6. Tom Daschle, author interview; Alex Wayne and Drew Armstrong, "Obama Taps Daschle to Lead His Health Team," *CQ*, December 11, 2008, https://www.commonwealthfund.org /publications/newsletter-article/obama-taps-daschle-lead-his-health-team.
7. Paul West, "If Obama Wins the Election, Look for Tom Daschle Standing at His Side," *Baltimore Sun*, October 26, 2008, https://www.baltimoresun.com/news/bs-xpm-2008-10-26 -0810250066-story.html.
8. Carl Hulse and Jeff Zeleny, "Daschle Uses Senate Ties to Blaze Path for Obama," *New York Times*, February 5, 2008, https://www.nytimes.com/2008/02/05/us/politics/05daschle.html.
9. Daschle interview; Tom Daschle, *Getting It Done* (New York: St. Martin's, 2010), 61–63.
10. Noam Scheiber, *The Escape Artists* (New York: Simon & Schuster, 2011), 150–161; John H. Richardson, "How Peter Orszag's Budget Team Makes America Work," *Esquire*, February 1, 2010, https://www.esquire.com/news-politics/a6659/peter-orszag-1209/. The Orszag mentor was Princeton economist Alan Blinder.
11. Peter Orszag, author interview. See also Shannon Brownlee, *Overtreated: Why Too Much Medicine Is Making Us Sicker and Poorer* (New York: Bloomsbury USA, 2007), https://www .google.com/books/edition/Overtreated/ZjegAwAAQBAJ?hl=en&gbpv=1&dq=shannon+br ownlee+overtreated&printsec=frontcover; and, for an example of the Dartmouth work, see Elliott Fisher, David Goodman, Jonathan Skinner, and Kristen Bronner, "Health Care Spending, Quality, and Outcomes: More Isn't Always Better," *Dartmouth Atlas*, February 27, 2009, https://www.dartmouthatlas.org/downloads/reports/Spending_Brief_022709.pdf.
12. Ryan Lizza, "Money Talks," *New Yorker*, April 26, 2009, https://www.newyorker.com/magazine /2009/05/04/money-talks-4; Ezra Klein, "The Number-Cruncher-in-Chief," *American Prospect*, December 11, 2008, https://prospect.org/features/number-cruncher-in-chief/; Ben Smith, "Budget to Kick Off Health Care Rewrite," *Politico*, February 19, 2009, https://www.politico .com/story/2009/02/budget-to-kick-off-health-care-rewrite-019017; Andrea Seabrook, "Budget Chief Peter Orszag: Obama's 'Super-Nerd,'" NPR, April 6, 2009, https://www.npr.org /templates/story/story.php?storyId=102723682; Peter Orszag, "Time to Act on Health Care Costs," *Issues in Science and Technology* 24, no. 3 (Spring 2008), accessed September 15, 2020, https://issues.org/orszag/.
13. Dora Hughes, author interview; Paul Starr, *Remedy and Reaction: The Peculiar American Struggle Over Health Care Reform*, revised ed. (New Haven, CT: Yale University Press, 2013), 196.
14. Roger Simon, "The Legendary Rahm Emanuel," *Politico*, June 25, 2009, https://www.politico .com/story/2009/06/the-legendary-rahm-emanuel-024207; Peter Baker, "The Limits of Rahmism," *New York Times Magazine*, March 8, 2010.
15. In the early debates and throughout 2009/10, Rahm was a vocal skeptic of trying for comprehensive reform, according to multiple sources, although many of those same sources also commended Rahm's commitment to pursuing Obama's agenda, strategic misgivings notwithstanding. Here is how Rahm later described his position: "My own recommendation to President Obama was . . . he could push for universal coverage but in the drawer keep a plan to universalize some segments of the population." See Rahm Emanuel, "The ACA's Lessons for Future Health Reforms," in *The Trillion Dollar Revolution: How the Affordable Care Act Transformed Politics, Law, and Health Care in America*, ed. Ezekiel Emanuel and Abbe Gluck (New York: PublicAffairs, 2020), 326.
16. David Axelrod, author interview; Axelrod, *Believer* (New York: Penguin, 2015), Kindle edition, 370–372.
17. Phil Schiliro, author interview.
18. Senior Obama administration officials, author interviews. For more background on the economic crisis and the Obama administration's response, see Scheiber, *The Escape Artists*; David Dayen, *Chain of Title: How Three Ordinary Americans Uncovered Wall Street's Great*

Foreclosure Fraud (New York: The New Press, 2017); Timothy F. Geithner, *Stress Test: Reflections on Financial Crises* (New York: Crown, 2014); Alter, *The Promise*.

19. Senior Obama administration official interview; Alter and Daschle also note Biden's skepticism in their books.

20. Lambrew interview.

21. David Axelrod, in his book, remembered Jeanne Lambrew saying the president should pursue reform right away because he had promised to do so in the campaign—prompting Axelrod to snap back that he, not Lambrew, was on the campaign and remembered the promises and that Obama had not made such an exacting pledge. But it's not clear when that happened (Axelrod, *Believer*, 372). Some of the president's economic advisers later told me they thought Lambrew wasn't giving a candid assessment of what different budget projections showed. (Senior Obama administration officials, author interviews.)

22. Recollections from these meetings come primarily from multiple senior Obama administration officials. Prior accounts include Alter, *The Promise*, 114–115; and Daschle, *Getting It Done*, 62–63 and 110–117. For my contemporaneous account, see Jonathan Cohn, "Stayin' Alive," *New Republic*, April 1, 2009, https://newrepublic.com/article/68444/stayin-alive.

23. Senior Obama administration officials interviews; Daschle, *Getting It Done*, 117.

24. Senior Obama administration officials interviews.

25. Senior Obama administration official interview.

26. Axelrod and Dan Pfeiffer, author interviews.

27. Barack Obama, author interview.

Chapter 11: Party Lines

1. The Democratic Senate caucus at the start of 2009 included two members, Connecticut's Joe Lieberman and Vermont's Bernie Sanders, who were not formally members of the party but voted with it for majority leader and participated in meetings. As for the Senate back in Clinton's day, Democrats had fifty-seven at the start of his term. In the months that followed, Democrats lost four seats through special elections to fill vacancies and one switch, when Richard Shelby of Alabama decided to become a Republican. By Election Day 1994, the Democratic majority was down to fifty-three; Dana Milbank, "Mitch McConnell, the Man Who Broke America," *Washington Post*, April 7, 2017; Jane Mayer, "How Mitch McConnell Became Trump's Enabler-in-Chief," *New Yorker*, April 20, 2020; Fred Dews, "A Recent History of Senate Cloture Votes Taken to End Filibusters," Brookings Institution, November 21, 2013, https://www.brookings.edu/blog/brookings-now/2013/11/21/chart-a-recent-history-of-senate-cloture-votes-taken-to-end-filibusters/; Thomas E. Mann, "The Senate After Filibuster Reform," Reuters, November 25, 2013, http://blogs.reuters.com/great-debate/2013/11/25/the-senate-after-filibuster-reform/; Sarah A. Binder, "The History of the Filibuster," Brookings Institution, April 22, 2010, https://www.brookings.edu/testimonies/the-history-of-the-filibuster/; David Leonhardt, "Death to the Filibuster?," *New York Times*, February 26, 2019, https://www.nytimes.com/2019/02/26/opinion/filibuster-democrats-2020.html.

2. Peter Orszag, author interview.

3. Harry Reid, author interview; senior Obama administration officials and Democratic aides, author interviews.

4. Years later, Reid would join calls to end the filibuster. But in 2009, he said, the idea never came up (Reid interview).

5. Phil Schiliro, author interview.

6. Health team to Senator Baucus, internal memorandum, "Meeting on Health Reform with Senators Grassley, Kennedy, Enzi, Hatch, Rockefeller, Dodd," November 18, 2008; David Bowen and Liz Fowler, author interviews. Bowen was the one who told me about Hatch's outreach.

7. Fowler, "Notes from Member Meeting—Wednesday, December 18 @ 1:00 PM in S-219." Fowler said that her notes were nearly verbatim.

8. Noam Levey, "Taxes Plague Another Nominee," *Los Angeles Times*, January 31, 2009, https://www.latimes.com/archives/la-xpm-2009-jan-31-na-daschle31-story.html.

9. Jeff Zeleny, "Daschle Ends Bid for Post; Obama Concedes Mistake," *New York Times*, February 3, 2009, https://www.nytimes.com/2009/02/04/us/politics/04obama.html.

10. "Obama: 'I Screwed Up' in Daschle Withdrawal," NBCNews.com, February 3, 2009, https://www.nbcnews.com/id/wbna28994296; Schiliro interview.
11. Nancy-Ann DeParle, author interview; "Nancy-Ann Min DeParle," Tennessee Alumnus, accessed September 15, 2020, https://alumnus.tennessee.edu/100-distinguished-alumni/nancy-ann-min-deparle/; Michael Collins, "Health Care Healer," Knoxville News Sentinel, March 29, 2009, accessed September 15, 2020, http://archive.knoxnews.com/news/tennessee-native-overseeing-national-system-of-reform-ep-410217678-359494311.html/.
12. DeParle interview.
13. Ibid.
14. Ibid.; senior Obama administration officials interviews; Barack Obama, "A President Looks Back on His Toughest Fight," New Yorker, November 2, 2020, https://www.newyorker.com/magazine/2020/11/02/barack-obama-new-book-excerpt-promised-land-obamacare.
15. "White House Health Care Summit Closing," C-SPAN video, 57:42, March 4, 2009, accessed September 15, 2020, https://www.c-span.org/video/?284447-3/white-house-health-care-summit-closing.
16. Bowen and Liz Fowler, author interviews. For more details on the home, see Roland Flamini, "Inside Senator Edward M. Kennedy's House in Washington, D.C.," Architectural Digest, February 20, 2017, accessed September 15, 2020, https://www.architecturaldigest.com/story/senator-edward-m-kennedy-washington-dc-home.
17. Max Baucus, author interview.
18. Noam Scheiber, The Escape Artists: How Obama's Team Fumbled the Recovery (New York: Simon & Schuster, 2012).
19. Michael Grunwald, "The Party of No," Time, September 3, 2012, http://content.time.com/time/subscriber/article/0,33009,2122776-1,00.html.
20. Joshua Green, "Strict Obstructionist," Atlantic, January/February 2011, https://www.theatlantic.com/magazine/archive/2011/01/strict-obstructionist/308344/.
21. Senior Democratic aide, author interview.
22. Senior Obama administration official interview; see also Jonathan Cohn, "How They Did It," New Republic, May 20, 2010.
23. "Senate Session," C-SPAN video, 11:46:04, January 29, 2009, https://www.c-span.org/video/?283717-1/senate-session; Baucus interview.
24. Michael Zona, author correspondence. Zona was a Grassley spokesperson.

Chapter 12: House Rules

1. Cybele Bjorklund, author interview.
2. Debbie Curtis, author interview. Curtis was Stark's longtime adviser on health policy. See also Fortney H. "Pete" Stark Jr., "Pete's Life Story," Pete Stark Memorial, https://www.petestarkmemorial.com/pete-s-life-story and Katharine Q. Seelye, "Pete Stark, Fighter in Congress for Health Care, Dies at 88," New York Times, January 27, 2020, https://www.nytimes.com/2020/01/27/us/politics/pete-stark-dead.html.
3. Matt Schudel, "Pete Stark, Fiery California Congressman and Advocate of Universal Health Care, Dies at 88," Washington Post, January 15, 2020, https://www.washingtonpost.com/local/obituaries/pete-stark-fiery-california-congressman-and-advocate-of-universal-health-care-dies-at-88/2020/01/25/63a90284-3f91-11ea-8872-5df698785a4e_story.html.
4. Robert Pear, "Bill Passed by Panel Would Open Medicare to Millions of Uninsured People," New York Times, July 1, 1994.
5. David E. Rosenbaum, "For Once, Powerhouse Can't Produce the Votes," New York Times, July 2, 1994.
6. Bjorklund interview.
7. Joshua Green, "Henry Waxman Is Leaving Congress but Leaving Behind His Playbook," Bloomberg Businessweek, January 30, 2014 https://www.bloomberg.com/news/articles/2014-01-30/henry-waxman-is-leaving-congress-but-leaving-behind-his-playbook?sref=sGsy0HYh.
8. Jeffrey Goldberg, "Henry Waxman on How Faith Informs His Politics," Atlantic, August 25, 2009, https://www.theatlantic.com/international/archive/2009/08/henry-waxman-on-how-faith-informs-his-politics/22943/.
9. Richard Simon, "Rep. Henry Waxman to Retire from Congress," Los Angeles Times, Janu-

ary 30, 2014, https://www.latimes.com/politics/la-xpm-2014-jan-30-la-pn-henry-waxman
-retire-congress-20140130-story.html; Karen Tumulty, "Rep. Henry Waxman (D-Calif.) to
Retire at End of Congressional Session," *Washington Post,* January 30, 2014, https://www
.washingtonpost.com/politics/henry-waxman-to-retire/2014/01/30/c06485fa-892d-11e3
-833c-33098f9e5267_story.html.

10. Michael L. Stern, "Henry Waxman and the Tobacco Industry: A Case Study in Congressional
    Oversight," Constitution Project, https://archive.constitutionproject.org/wp-content/uploads
    /2017/05/Waxman.pdf; Jonathan Cohn, "Farewell to Henry Waxman, a Liberal Hero," *New
    Republic,* January 31, 2014, https://newrepublic.com/article/116418/henry-waxman-retiring
    -heres-why-well-miss-him.

11. Michael Hash, quoted in *Insights from the Top: An Oral History of Medicare and Medicaid*
    (Washington, DC: National Academy of Social Insurance, March 17, 2016), 139, https://
    www.nasi.org/sites/default/files/research/Insights_from_the_Top.pdf; *Rep. Henry A. Waxman's
    Record of Accomplishment* (Washington, DC: U.S. House of Representatives Committee
    on Energy and Commerce, December 2014), https://www.eenews.net/assets/2016/06/24
    /document_gw_10.pdf.

12. Christopher Beam, "Dingell Buried," *Slate,* November 20, 2008, https://slate.com/news-and
    -politics/2008/11/henry-waxman-s-victory-over-john-dingell-is-the-biggest-gift-obama
    -could-have-asked-for.html; Kate Sheppard, "Dingell Jangle," *Guardian,* November 21, 2008,
    accessed September 16, 2020, https://www.theguardian.com/commentisfree/cifamerica/2008
    /nov/21/climate-change-waxman-dingell; John M. Broder and Carl Hulse, "Behind House
    Struggle, Long and Tangled Roots," *New York Times,* November 22, 2008, https://www.nytimes
    .com/2008/11/23/us/politics/23waxman.html; Bradford Plumer, "Why The Dingell-Waxman
    Dispute Matters," *New Republic,* November 9, 2008, https://newrepublic.com/article/45918
    /why-the-dingell-waxman-dispute-matters; Josh Israel, "Dingell vs. Waxman—Are Their Pasts
    Prologue?," Center for Public Integrity, November 19, 2008, accessed September 16, 2020,
    https://publicintegrity.org/accountability/dingell-vs-waxman-are-their-pasts-prologue/.

13. Chris Jennings, Henry Waxman author interviews.

14. *House Committee Chairmen Miller, Waxman, and Rangel Pledge to Move Health Reform For-
    ward* (Washington, DC: U.S. House of Representatives Committee on Education and Labor,
    March 11, 2009), https://edlabor.house.gov/media/press-releases/house-committee-chairmen
    -miller-waxman-and-rangel-pledge-to-move-health-reform-forward; Alex Wayne, "House
    Panel Chairman Promise to Move Similar Health Care Overhaul Bills," *CQ,* March 11, 2009,
    https://www.commonwealthfund.org/publications/newsletter-article/house-panel-chairman
    -promise-move-similar-health-care-overhaul.

15. Cybele Bjorklund, "Leadership Meeting on Health Reform—Revised," memo to Charles
    Rangel, March 3, 2009; senior Obama administration officials and Democratic aides, author
    interviews.

16. David Bowen and Liz Fowler, author interviews.

17. Senior Obama administration officials and Democratic aides interviews.

18. Bjorklund, Curtis, and Kate Leone, author interviews. See also Nancy-Ann DeParle and
    Jeanne Lambrew, "Women's Importance in Enacting, Implementing and Defending the
    Affordable Care Act," Brookings Institution, September 2020, https://www.brookings.edu
    /essay/womens-importance-in-enacting-implementing-and-defending-the-affordable
    -care-act/.

19. Tom Daschle, *Getting It Done* (New York: St. Martin's, 2010), 97; Gene Sperling, author interview.

20. DeParle, senior Obama administration officials interviews.

21. Senior Obama administration officials interviews.

22. Atul Gawande, "The Cost Conundrum," *New Yorker,* May 25, 2009, https://www.newyorker
    .com/magazine/2009/06/01/the-cost-conundrum.

23. Robert Pear, "Health Care Spending Disparities Stir a Fight," *New York Times,* June 8, 2009,
    https://www.nytimes.com/2009/06/09/us/politics/09health.html?scp=4&sq=atul%20gawan
    de&st=cse.

24. Senior Obama administration officials, author interview.

25. *Focus on Health Reform* (Menlo Park, CA: Henry J. Kaiser Family Foundation, 2009), https://
    www.kff.org/wp-content/uploads/2013/01/healthreform_tri_full.pdf.

26. White House Office of the Press Secretary, "Letter from President Obama to Chairmen Edward M. Kennedy and Max Baucus," June 3, 2009, https://obamawhitehouse.archives.gov/the-press-office/letter-president-obama-chairmen-edward-m-kennedy-and-max-baucus; Budoff Brown, "Obama May Support Coverage Mandate," *Politico,* June 3, 2009, https://www.politico.com/story/2009/06/obama-may-support-coverage-mandate-023298.

27. Ezra Klein, "The House Agrees on Health Reform. Will the Senate?," *American Prospect,* March 13, 2009, https://prospect.org/article/house-agrees-health-reform.-will-senate/; Cybele Bjorklund, "Meeting of Tri-Committee Chairs," memo to Charles Rangel, March 3, 2009; senior Democratic aide interview; Steven Brill, *America's Bitter Pill: Money, Politics, Backroom Deals, and the Fight to Fix Our Broken Healthcare System* (New York: Random House, 2015); senior Democratic aides interviews.

28. Senior Democratic aide interview.

29. Molly Ball, *Pelosi* (New York: Henry Holt, 2020), Kindle edition, 177–178.

30. Senior Democratic aide, author interview.

31. Bryan W. Marshall and Bruce C. Wolpe, *The Committee: A Study of Policy, Power, Politics and Obama's Historic Legislative Agenda on Capitol Hill* (Ann Arbor: University of Michigan Press, 2018), Kindle edition, 59–60.

32. Waxman and senior Democratic aide, author interviews.

33. Waxman interview.

34. Waxman and senior Democratic aide interviews.

35. Waxman, senior Democratic aides, and Obama administration officials interviews.

Chapter 13: On the Bus

1. Robert Pear, "House's Author of Drug Benefit Joins Lobbyists," *New York Times,* December 16, 2004, https://www.nytimes.com/2004/12/16/politics/houses-author-of-drug-benefit-joins-lobbyists.html.

2. Michael Kirk, Jim Gilmore, and Mike Wiser, "Obama's Deal," PBS, April 13, 2010, https://www.pbs.org/wgbh/pages/frontline/obamasdeal/etc/script.html; Paul Blumenthal, "The Legacy of Billy Tauzin: The White House-PhRMA Deal," Sunlight Foundation, February 12, 2010, https://sunlightfoundation.com/2010/02/12/the-legacy-of-billy-tauzin-the-white-house-phrma-deal/.

3. Jon Selib, author interview.

4. Paul Blumenthal, "White House Visitor Logs Show Large Lobbyist Presence for Head of White House Health Office," Sunlight Foundation, February 25, 2010, https://sunlightfoundation.com/2010/02/25/white-house-visitor-logs-show-large-lobbyist-presence-for-head-of-white-house-health-office/; Jim Messina, author interview.

5. Senior Obama administration official Democratic aide, author interview; Washington Post Staff, *Landmark: The Inside Story of America's New Health Care Law and What It Means for Us All* (New York: Public Affairs, 2010), Kindle edition, 24.

6. Tom Hamburger, "Drug Industry Lobbyist Billy Tauzin to Resign," *Los Angeles Times,* February 12, 2010, https://www.latimes.com/archives/la-xpm-2010-feb-12-la-na-phrma12-2010feb12-story.html; Chris Frates and Carrie Budoff Brown, "Tauzin to Step Down from PhRMA," *Politico,* February 12, 2010, https://www.politico.com/story/2010/02/tauzin-to-step-down-from-phrma-032879.

7. See, for example, Lucette Lagnado, "Jeanette White Is Long Dead but Her Hospital Bill Lives On," *Wall Street Journal,* March 13, 2003; Lucette Lagnado, "Hospitals Try Extreme Measures to Collect Their Overdue Debts," *Wall Street Journal,* October 30, 2003; Jonathan Cohn, *Sick* (New York: HarperCollins, 2009), Kindle edition, 141–166.

8. John McDonough, *Inside Health Reform* (Berkeley: University of California Press, 2011), 77; senior Democratic strategist, author interview.

9. Selib interview; Drew Armstrong, "Health Insurers Gave $86 Million to Fight Health Law," Bloomberg, November 17, 2010, https://www.bloomberg.com/news/articles/2010-11-17/insurers-gave-u-s-chamber-86-million-used-to-oppose-obama-s-health-law; Ron Pollack, author interview.

10. Tom Hamburger, "Obama Gives Powerful Drug Lobby a Seat at Healthcare Table," *Los Angeles Times,* August 4, 2009, https://www.latimes.com/health/la-na-healthcare-pharma4

-2009aug04-story.html; Ryan Grim, "Internal Memo Confirms Big Giveaways in White House Deal with Big Pharma," *HuffPost*, September 13, 2009, https://www.huffpost.com /entry/internal-memo-confirms-bi_n_258285; Timothy Noah, "Obama's Biggest Health Reform Blunder," *Slate*, August 6, 2009, https://slate.com/news-and-politics/2009/08/how-big -pharma-s-billy-tauzin-conned-the-white-house-out-of-76-billion.html.

11. Kathy Ruffing and James R. Horney, "Downturn and Legacy of Bush Policies Drive Large Current Deficits," Center on Budget and Policy Priorities, October 10, 2012, https://www .cbpp.org/research/downturn-and-legacy-of-bush-policies-drive-large-current-deficits. On public opinion and there's a strong case that polling is relatively misleading and that, as Vanderbilt political scientist John Sides later to me, "I tend to think that the public's feelings about the effect of the ACA on the deficit—to the extent that they even thought about it or knew anything about it—would likely be rationalizations for attitudes about the ACA that they formed for other reasons." Sides, author correspondence.

12. Barack Obama, *The Audacity of Hope: Thoughts on Reclaiming the American Dream* (New York: Crown, 2006), Kindle edition, 183.

13. Toward the end of Obama's term, many (possibly most) left-of-center economists thought there was a strong case for more deficit spending in the short term. A smaller group on the left argued there was also a case for running bigger deficits indefinitely. The best-known advocate for this is Stephanie Kelton, a professor at the State University of New York at Stony Brook and former economist on the Senate Budget Committee Democratic staff, where she advised Vermont's Bernie Sanders. Stephanie Kelton, *The Deficit Myth: Modern Monetary Theory and the Birth of the People's Economy* (New York: PublicAffairs, 2020). The source for the meeting was a set of notes of a former senior Obama administration official.

14. Wilbur Mills, the Ways and Means chairman who had blocked the proposal for so many years, kept saying the program wouldn't pay for itself. Julian Zelizer, "How Medicare Was Made," *New Yorker*, February 15, 2015, https://www.newyorker.com/news/news-desk/medicare -made; Julian Zelizer, *Taxing America: Wilbur D. Mills, Congress, and the State, 1945–1975* (New York: Cambridge University Press, 1988), 244; Jonathan Cohn, "Obamacare, Medicare, and Baseball's Greatest Pitchers," *Yale Journal of Health Policy, Law, and Ethics* 15, no. 1 (2015), https://digitalcommons.law.yale.edu/cgi/viewcontent.cgi?article=1224&context=yjhple.

15. David Dayen, "Congress's Biggest Obstacle," *American Prospect*, January 28, 2020, https:// prospect.org/politics/congress-biggest-obstacle-congressional-budget-office/; Ezra Klein, "What Does the Congressional Budget Office Do?," *Washington Post*, September 7, 2009, http://voices.washingtonpost.com/ezra-klein/2009/09/what_does_the_congressional_bu .html; Jonathan Cohn, "Numbers Racket," *New Republic*, June 3, 2009, https://newrepublic .com/article/64725/numbers-racket.

16. Senior Obama administration official, author interview; Douglas Elmendorf, author interview.

17. Elmendorf interview.

18. Jeanne Sahadi, "Health Reform Bills Won't Reduce Costs," CNN, July 16, 2009, https:// money.cnn.com/2009/07/16/news/economy/health_care_reform/index.htm?postversion =2009071616; Robert Pear, "House Committee Approves Health Care Bill," *New York Times*, July 16, 2009, https://www.nytimes.com/2009/07/17/us/politics/17cbo.html; David Wessel, "Man Who Wounded Overhaul Effort Could Also Save It," *Wall Street Journal*, July 24, 2009, https:// www.wsj.com/articles/SB124829913479973605.

19. Senior Obama administration official interview; Ezra Klein, "The Congressional Budget Office vs. the White House," *Washington Post*, July 25, 2009, http://voices.washingtonpost.com /ezra-klein/2009/07/the_congressional_budget_offic_2.html; Peter Orszag, "CBO and IMAC," OMB Blog (preserved at the Obama White House online archive), July 25, 2009, https:// obamawhitehouse.archives.gov/omb/blog/09/07/25/CBOandIMAC/.

20. U.S. Library of Congress, Congressional Research Service, "The Tax Exclusion for Employer-Provided Health Insurance: Policy Issues Regarding the Repeal Debate, by Bob Lyke, RL34767 (2008)," https://www.everycrsreport.com/files/20081121_RL34767_902970b14cf5 c5056a020befbaaedeb2951b87fb.pdf; Jonathan Gruber, "The Tax Exclusion for Employer-Sponsored Health Insurance," *National Tax Journal* 64, no. 2 (2011), https://www.nber.org /papers/w15766.

21. Senior Obama administration official interview.

22. Elmendorf and senior Obama administration official interviews; Ryan Lizza, "The Obama Memos," *New Yorker*, January 23, 2012, https://www.newyorker.com/magazine/2012/01/30/the-obama-memos.

23. Senior Obama administration officials interviews; Noam Scheiber, *The Escape Artists: How Obama's Team Fumbled the Recovery* (New York: Simon & Schuster, 2012), 157.

24. David Leonhardt, "How a Tax Can Cut Health Costs," *New York Times,* September 29, 2009, https://www.nytimes.com/2009/09/30/business/economy/30leonhardt.html; Paul B. Ginsburg, "Employment-Based Health Benefits Under Universal Coverage," *Health Affairs* 27, no. 3 (2008), accessed September 19, 2020, https://www.healthaffairs.org/doi/full/10.1377/hlthaff.27.3.675.

25. For examples of this effect, see Robyn Tamblyn et al., "Adverse Events Associated with Prescription Drug Cost-Sharing Among Poor and Elderly Persons," *JAMA* 285, no. 4 (2001), https://jamanetwork.com/journals/jama/fullarticle/1108322; Vicki Fung et al., "Financial Barriers to Care Among Low-Income Children with Asthma Health Care Reform Implications," *JAMA* 168, no. 7 (2014), https://jamanetwork.com/journals/jamapediatrics/fullarticle/1872780; Dana P. Goldman, Geoffrey F. Joyce, and Yuhui Zheng, "Prescription Drug Cost Sharing: Associations with Medication and Medical Utilization and Spending and Health," *JAMA* 298, no. 1 (2007), https://www.ncbi.nlm.nih.gov/pmc/articles/PMC6375697/. For more discussion on the original RAND findings and their impact over the years, see Michael E. Chernew and Joseph P. Newhouse, "What Does the RAND Health Insurance Experiment Tell Us About the Impact of Patient Cost Sharing on Health Outcomes?," *American Journal of Managed Care*, July 15, 2008, https://www.ajmc.com/view/jul08-3414p412-414; Aviva Aron-Dine, Liran Einav, and Amy Finkelstein, "The RAND Health Insurance Experiment, Three Decades Later," *Journal of Economic Perspectives: A Journal of the American Economic Association* 27, no. 1 (2013), https://www.ncbi.nlm.nih.gov/pmc/articles/PMC3943162/#R9.

26. David M. Drucker, "Conrad Has Doubts About House, HELP Versions of Health Care Reform," *Roll Call,* July 16, 2009, https://www.rollcall.com/2009/07/16/conrad-has-doubts-about-house-help-versions-of-health-care-reform/.

27. Senior Democratic aide, author interview. See also "Conrad Cites Benefits of Higher Medicare Reimbursements," *Grand Forks Herald*, March 31, 2010, https://www.grandforksherald.com/news/2123418-conrad-cites-benefits-higher-medicare-reimbursements; Robert Pear, "Deep in Health Bill, Very Specific Beneficiaries," *New York Times,* December 20, 2009, https://www.nytimes.com/2009/12/21/health/policy/21healthcare.html/.

28. The Medicare drug program was an especially telling episode, because in the run-up to the vote, Trump administration officials had refused to circulate a cost estimate from another official accounting source, Medicare's in-house actuary. (One Bush official actually threatened the actuary with reprisals if he disobeyed.) See Jacob Weisberg, "Are Republicans Serious About Fixing Health Care? No, and Here's the Proof," *Slate,* December 12, 2009, https://slate.com/news-and-politics/2009/12/are-republicans-serious-about-health-care-no-and-here-s-the-proof.html; on Republican deficit hypocrisy more generally, see Jonathan Chait, *The Big Con: Crackpot Economics and the Fleecing of America,* reprint ed. (Boston: Mariner Books, 2008) and Paul Krugman, *Arguing with Zombies: Economics, Politics, and the Fight for a Better Future* (New York: W. W. Norton, 2020).

Chapter 14: Death Panels

1. "Frank Luntz Debate Focus Group Favors . . . Obama!," YouTube video, 3:08, posted by "johnny dollar," September 26, 2008, https://www.youtube.com/watch?v=i23rDuymLwk; Elizabeth Kolbert, "The Vocabulary of Votes; Frank Luntz," *New York Times Magazine*, March 26, 1995; Peter Kiefer, "GOP Pollster Frank Luntz Reveals Replicas of the Oval Office, Monica Lewinsky's Blue Dress in His L.A. Home," *Hollywood Reporter*, October 12, 2016, https://www.hollywoodreporter.com/news/gop-pollster-frank-luntz-reveals-replicas-oval-office-monica-lewinskys-blue-dress-his-la-home-photos-937141/.

2. Deborah Solomon, "The Wordsmith," *New York Times Magazine*, May 21, 2009; "NOW with Bill Moyers Transcript," PBS, July 2, 2004, https://www.pbs.org/now/transcript/transcript327_full.html; Ann Herold, "All the Presidents' Man," *Los Angeles Magazine*, June 13, 2013.

3. Molly Ball, "The Agony of Frank Luntz," *Atlantic*, January 6, 2014, accessed September 19, 2020, https://www.theatlantic.com/politics/archive/2014/01/the-agony-of-frank-luntz/282766/.

4. Mike Allen, "Luntz to GOP: Health Reform Is Popular," *Politico*, May 5, 2009, https://www.politico.com/story/2009/05/luntz-to-gop-health-reform-is-popular-022155; Igor Volsky, "Deconstructing Frank Luntz's Obstructionist Health Care Reform Memo," ThinkProgress, May 6, 2009, https://archive.thinkprogress.org/deconstructing-frank-luntzs-obstructionist-health-care-reform-memo-83e78d209e86/; Randy James, "How Republicans Should Talk About Health Care," *Time*, May 7, 2009, http://content.time.com/time/nation/article/0,8599,1896597,00.html.

5. David Welna, "Health Care Debate So Far: A War of Words," NPR, June 16, 2009, https://www.npr.org/templates/story/story.php?storyId=105451905; Arthur Delaney, "Luntz Health Care Talking Points Become GOP Message," *HuffPost*, June 14, 2009, https://www.huffpost.com/entry/luntz-health-care_n_203508.

6. Angie Drobnic Holan, "PolitiFact's Lie of the Year: 'Death Panels,'" PolitiFact, December 18, 2009, accessed September 20, 2020, https://www.politifact.com/article/2009/dec/18/politifact-lie-year-death-panels/; Trudy Lieberman, "Straight Talk, Part I," *Columbia Journalism Review*, August 13, 2009, https://archives.cjr.org/campaign_desk/straight_talk_part_i.php; Betsy McCaughey, "'End-of-Life Counselling': Death Panels Are Back," *New York Post*, July 12, 2015, https://nypost.com/2015/07/12/end-of-life-counselling-death-panels-are-back/; James Fallows, "Let's Stop This Before It Goes Any Further," *Atlantic*, February 12, 2009, https://www.theatlantic.com/technology/archive/2009/02/lets-stop-this-before-it-goes-any-further/555/; James Fallows, "I Was Wrong," *Atlantic*, August 13, 2009, https://www.theatlantic.com/technology/archive/2009/08/i-was-wrong/23254/; Justin Bank, "Palin vs. Obama: Death Panels," FactCheck.org, August 14, 2009, https://www.factcheck.org/2009/08/palin-vs-obama-death-panels/.

7. Ezra Klein, "Is the Government Going to Euthanize Your Grandmother? An Interview with Sen. Johnny Isakson," *Washington Post*, August 10, 2009, http://voices.washingtonpost.com/ezra-klein/2009/08/is_the_government_going_to_eut.html.

8. Glenn Thrush, "Obamacare Will Put Seniors 'to Death,' says Foxx," *Politico*, July 28, 2009, https://www.politico.com/blogs/on-congress/2009/07/obamacare-will-put-seniors-to-death-says-foxx-020247; Julie Rovner, "Kill Grandma? Debunking a Health Care Scare Tactic," Kaiser Health News, August 13, 2009, https://khn.org/news/npr-debunking-killing-grandma-claims/.

9. Jess Henig, "False Euthanasia Claims," FactCheck.org, July 29, 2009, https://www.factcheck.org/2009/07/false-euthanasia-claims/.

10. "A Multiple-Choice Living Will," *New York Times*, December 28, 1990; Linda L. Emanuel and Ezekiel J. Emanuel, "The Medical Directive: A New Comprehensive Advance Care Document," *JAMA* 261, no. 22 (1989); for more background on Zeke Emanuel, see Carrie Budoff Brown, "Health Care Zeke: The Other Emanuel," *Politico*, February 26, 2009, https://www.politico.com/story/2009/02/health-care-zeke-the-other-emanuel-019368; Charlotte Alter and Diane Tsai, "What Rahm, Zeke and Ari Emanuel Were Like Growing Up," *Time*, August 25, 2016, https://time.com/4464757/rahm-zeke-and-ari-emanuel-growing-up/; Sarah Auerbach, "Come for Dinner, Stay for Life," *Amherst Magazine*, summer 2009, https://www.amherst.edu/amherst-story/magazine/issues/2009summer/emanuel.

11. Zeke Emanuel, "Saving by the Bundle," *New York Times*, November 16, 2011, https://opinionator.blogs.nytimes.com/2011/11/16/saving-by-the-bundle/; Amol S. Navathe et al., "Spending and Quality After Three Years of Medicare's Voluntary Bundled Payment for Joint Replacement Surgery," *Health Affairs* 39, no. 1 (2020), https://www-healthaffairs-org.proxy.lib.umich.edu/doi/10.1377/hlthaff.2019.00466.

12. Michael Scherer, "Ezekiel Emanuel, Obama's 'Deadly Doctor,' Strikes Back," *Time*, August 12, 2009, http://content.time.com/time/nation/article/0,8599,1915835,00.html; Betsy McCaughey, "Deadly Doctors," *New York Post*, July 24, 2009, https://nypost.com/2009/07/24/deadly-doctors/.

13. Robert Farley, "Bachmann Says Obama Health Adviser Thinks Health Care Ought Not to Be Extended to the Disabled," PolitiFact, August 12, 2009, https://www.politifact.com/factchecks/2009/aug/12/michele-bachmann/bachmann-says-obama-health-adviser-thinks

-health-c/; Jim Rutenberg, "Bioethicist Becomes a Lightning Rod for Criticism," *New York Times,* August. 24, 2009, https://www.nytimes.com/2009/08/25/health/policy/25zeke.html.

14. Naftali Bendavid, "Emanuel's Brother Becomes a Target," *Wall Street Journal,* August 13, 2009, https://www.wsj.com/articles/SB125012376373527721.

15. Stuart Butler and Gail Wilensky, author interviews from 2009; first reported here: Jonathan Cohn, "Top Conservatives: Enough with the 'Death Panel' Lie," *New Republic,* August 18, 2009, https://newrepublic.com/article/51605/top-conservatives-enough-the-quotdeath-panelquot -lie; see also Jim Rutenberg and Gardiner Harris, "Conservatives See Need for Serious Health Debate," *New York Times,* September 2, 2009, https://www.nytimes.com/2009/09/03/health /policy/03conservatives.html.

16. The quotes from the 2011 article—Jonathan Cohn, "Second Opinion," *New Republic,* March 17, 2011, https://newrepublic.com/article/85323/wilensky-health-care-republicans—were consistent with her tone in 2009.

17. Ben Smith, "Health Reform Foes Plan Obama's 'Waterloo,'" *Politico,* July 17, 2009, https:// www.politico.com/blogs/ben-smith/2009/07/health-reform-foes-plan-obamas-waterloo -019961.

18. Brian Beutler, "DeMint Tries to Spin Away His Past Support for RomneyCare," Talking Points Memo, May 6, 2011, https://talkingpointsmemo.com/dc/demint-tries-to-spin-away-his-past -support-for-romneycare-video; Office of U.S. Senator Ron Wyden, "Bipartisan Blueprint for Health Reform: Ten Senate Leaders Say, 'Let's Fix Health Care Now,'" United States Senate, April 4, 2007, https://www.wyden.senate.gov/news/press-releases/bipartisan-blueprint -for-health-reformten-senate-leaders-say-lets-fix-health-care-nowsenators-of-both-parties -hope-to-work-with-the-president.

19. U.S. Senate, Health Care Freedom Act of 2009, S.1324, 111th Cong., 1st sess., introduced in Senate June 23, 2009, https://www.congress.gov/bill/111th-congress/senate-bill/1324/summary/.

20. Kate Zernike, "Tea Party Kingmaker Becomes Power unto Himself," *New York Times,* October 30, 2010; Pema Levy, "Is Jim DeMint the Most Hated Man in Washington?," *Politico,* March 3, 2014, https://www.politico.com/magazine/story/2014/03/jim-demint-the-most-hated-man -in-washington-104209; Kelefa Sanneh, "The Evolution of Jim DeMint," *New Yorker,* December 8, 2012; "DeMint Apologizes for Saying Unwed, Single Mothers Shouldn't Teach in Public Schools," WIS News 10, October 6, 2004, https://www.wistv.com/story/2394024/demint -apologizes-for-saying-unwed-single-mothers-shouldnt-teach-in-public-schools/.

21. Jim DeMint, *Saving Freedom: We Can Stop America's Slide into Socialism* (Nashville: Fidelis Books, 2009), 49; ibid., 50.

22. Peter J. Boyer, "Getting to No," *New Yorker,* September 21, 2009, https://www.newyorker.com /magazine/2009/09/28/getting-to-no.

23. Jane Mayer, "Covert Operations," *New Yorker,* August 23, 2010; Paul Starr, *Remedy and Reaction: The Peculiar American Struggle over Health Care Reform,* revised ed. (New Haven, CT: Yale University Press, 2013), 215.

24. Lee Fang, "Right-Wing Harassment Strategy Against Dems Detailed in Memo: 'Yell,' 'Stand Up and Shout Out,' 'Rattle Him,'" ThinkProgress, July 31, 2009, https://thinkprogress.org /right-wing-harassment-strategy-against-dems-detailed-in-memo-yell-stand-up-and-shout -out-rattle-him-94e9af741078/; Ian Urbina, "Beyond Beltway, Health Debate Turns Hostile," *New York Times,* August 7, 2009.

25. "Mike Sola Approaches Congressman Dingell at Town Hall," YouTube video, 4:04, posted by "ChrisUM11," August 8, 2009, https://www.youtube.com/watch?v=GJyMpAcLVV8&eurl =http%3A%2F%2Fwww.fightingforourhealth.com%2Fchapter%2F11%2Fvideos%2F&feature =player_embedded; Robert Draper, "John Dingell and the Tea Party," *Politico,* February 25, 2014, https://www.politico.com/magazine/story/2014/02/john-dingell-and-the-tea-party-103955.

26. Jonathan Oosting, "U.S. Rep. John Dingell Writes Letter to Mike Sola After Confrontation at Romulus Town Hall Meeting," MLive, August 14, 2009, https://www.mlive.com/news/detroit /2009/08/us_rep_john_dingell_writes_let.html; "Marcia E. Boehm," Temrowski & Sons, http://temrowski.tributes.com/obituary/show/Marcia-E.-Boehm-95571330.

27. Chris Savage, "Rep. Dingell Town Hall: A Teabagger Extravaganza," Daily Kos, August 7, 2009, https://www.dailykos.com/stories/2009/8/6/762925/-.

28. Anna Galland, author interview; Richard Kirsch, *Fighting for Our Health: The Epic Battle*

to Make Health Care a Right in the United States (New York: Rockefeller Institute Press, 2012), 208.

29. Amy Sherman, "Rick Scott 'Oversaw the Largest Medicare Fraud' in U.S. History, Florida Democratic Party Says," PolitiFact, March 3, 2014, https://www.politifact.com/factchecks /2014/mar/03/florida-democratic-party/rick-scott-rick-scott-oversaw-largest-medicare-fra/.

30. Savage, "Rep. Dingell Town Hall."

31. Ben McGrath, "The Movement," *New Yorker*, February 1, 2010.

32. Vanessa Williamson, Theda Skocpol, and John Coggin, "The Tea Party and the Remaking of Republican Conservatism," *Perspectives on Politics* 9, no. 1 (2011), https://scholar.harvard .edu/files/williamson/files/tea_party_pop_0.pdf.

33. Senior Democratic aides, author interviews.

34. In a memo to Obama, David Axelrod offered a gloomy synopsis of the souring public perspective and how, based on his reading, many voters were interpreting the program's overall cost as a sign reform was an unaffordable big government boondoggle. "Despite our best efforts to explain, many Americans are simply finding it too hard to square adding a trillion dollars as part of a strategy to cut costs," Axelrod wrote. "They suspect that this is about spending and taxing more to take care of someone else. And even if they see universal coverage as a laudable goal, they think it's irresponsible to undertake it now—a liberal indulgence we can't afford" (David Axelrod, *Believer* [New York: Penguin, 2015], 377).

35. Paul Waldman, "Yes, Opposition to Obamacare Is Tied Up with Race," *Washington Post*, May 23, 2014, https://www.washingtonpost.com/blogs/plum-line/wp/2014/05/23/yes-opposition -to-obamacare-is-tied-up-with-race/; Ashley Fantz, "Obama as Witch Doctor: Racist or Satirical?," CNN, September 17, 2009, https://www.cnn.com/2009/POLITICS/09/17/obama .witchdoctor.teaparty/.

36. Williamson, Skocpol, and Coggin, "The Tea Party"; Angie Maxwell, "How Southern Racism Found a Home in the Tea Party," *Vox*, July 7, 2016, https://www.vox.com/2016/7/7/12118872 /southern-racism-tea-party-trump.

37. Ezra Klein, "White Threat in a Browning America: How Demographic Change Is Fracturing Our Politics," *Vox*, July 30, 2018, https://www.vox.com/policy-and-politics/2018/7/30 /17505406/trump-obama-race-politics-immigration.

38. Michael Tesler, "The Spillover of Racialization into Health Care: How President Obama Polarized Public Opinion by Racial Attitudes and Race," *American Journal of Political Science* 56, no. 3 (2012): 690–704, https://onlinelibrary.wiley.com/doi/abs/10.1111/j.1540-5907.2011.00577 .x; Katherine T. McCabe, "The Persistence of Racialized Health Care Attitudes: Racial Attitudes Among White Adults and Identity Importance Among Black Adults," *Journal of Race, Ethnicity, and Politics* 4, no. 2 (2019): 378–398, https://www.cambridge.org/core/journals /journal-of-race-ethnicity-and-politics/article/persistence-of-racialized-health-care-attitudes -racial-attitudes-among-white-adults-and-identity-importance-among-black-adults/71AE14 950A86B01BA0FCC94B2B31BB16.

39. Axelrod, *Believer*, 379.

40. Linda Feldmann, "How Jim DeMint Did Obama a Favor," *Christian Science Monitor*, July 21, 2009, https://www.csmonitor.com/USA/Politics/2009/0721/how-jim-demint-did-obama-a -favor; "News Conference by the President," United States Office of the Press Secretary, July 22, 2009, accessed September 19, 2020, https://obamawhitehouse.archives.gov/realitycheck /the_press_office/News-Conference-by-the-President-July-22-2009; Jonathan Cohn, "Obama Has a Grown-up Talk with America (Gulp)," *New Republic*, July 22, 2009, https://newrepublic .com/article/51074/obama-has-grown-talk-america-gulp.

41. John R. Lott, "No Apology for Sergeant Crowley?," Fox News, July 27, 2009, https://www .foxnews.com/opinion/no-apology-for-sergeant-crowley; Katharine Q. Seelye, "Obama Wades into a Volatile Racial Issue," *New York Times*, July 23, 2009, https://www.nytimes.com /2009/07/23/us/23race.html.

42. "How One Scholar's Arrest Tainted the President's Image as a Racial Healer," *Washington Post*, April 22, 2016, https://www.washingtonpost.com/graphics/national/obama-legacy/henry-louis -gates-jr-arrest-controversy.html; Paul Steinhauser, "Poll: Did Obama's Reaction to Gates Arrest Hurt Him?," CNN, August 4, 2009, https://www.cnn.com/2009/POLITICS/08/04/obama.gates .poll/.

43. "Obama's Ratings Slide Across the Board," Pew Research Center, July 30, 2009, https://www
.pewresearch.org/politics/2009/07/30/obamas-ratings-slide-across-the-board/. For more on
public opinion during the 2009/10 debate, see Mollyann Brodie, Drew Altman, Claudia Deane
et al., "Liking the Pieces, Not the Package: Contradictions in Public Opinion During Health
Reform," *Health Affairs* 29, no. 6 (2010), https://www.healthaffairs.org/doi/pdf/10.1377/hlthaff
.2010.0434.

44. Senior Obama administration officials and Democratic aides, author interviews.

45. Senate Finance Staff, "All Possible HCR Votes," memorandum to Baucus, undated. (One of
the document's authors said it was from late spring, which would be consistent with the
fact that it lists Arlen Specter as a Democrat and the second Minnesota seat open. Specter
switched parties in late April, and Franken was declared the winner in late June); senior
Obama administration official interview.

46. Nancy DeParle, author interview.

47. David M. Drucker, "Hatch Withdraws from Bipartisan Health Talks," *Roll Call*, July 22, 2009,
https://www.rollcall.com/2009/07/22/hatch-withdraws-from-bipartisan-health-talks/; Ted
Barrett, "Hatch Shuts Door on Bipartisan Health Care Talks," CNN, July 22, 2009, https://web
.archive.org/web/20120229062444/https://politicalticker.blogs.cnn.com/2009/07/22/hatch
-shuts-door-on-bipartisan-health-care-talks/.

48. Senior Republican aide and senior Democratic aide, author interviews.

49. Senior Obama administration officials and Democratic aides interviews.

50. "Grassley Scolds Obama on Twitter," *Wall Street Journal*, June 7, 2009, https://www.wsj.com
/articles/SB124439441435992013; Shailagh Murray, "Sen. Grassley at Eye of Healthcare
Storm," *Los Angeles Times*, June 28, 2009, https://www.latimes.com/archives/la-xpm-2009
-jun-28-adna-grassley28-story.html.

51. Senior Republican aide interview; Jason Noble, "4 Other Times Grassley Has Faced Political Fire," *Des Moines Register*, April 3, 2016, https://www.desmoinesregister.com/story/news
/politics/2016/04/03/4-other-times-grassley-has-faced-political-fire/82523876/; "Alternate
History: A Grassley Primary Challenger," Bleeding Heartland, October 9, 2010, https://www
.bleedingheartland.com/2010/10/09/alternate-history-a-grassley-primary-challenger/; Tim
Alberta, "Kent Sorenson Was a Tea Party Hero. Then He Lost Everything," *Politico*, September 21, 2018, https://www.politico.com/magazine/story/2018/09/21/kent-sorenson-was
-a-tea-party-hero-then-he-lost-everything-220522; Jackie Calmes, "G.O.P. Senator Draws
Critics in Both Parties," *New York Times*, September 22, 2009, https://www.nytimes.com
/2009/09/23/us/politics/23scene.html.

52. Senior Republican aide interview; Starr, *Remedy and Reaction*, 211; Axelrod, *Believer*, 376.

53. Senior Obama administration official interview; senior Democratic aide and senior Republican aide interviews; senior Democratic aide interview.

54. DeParle interview; Tom Daschle, *Getting It Done* (New York: St. Martin's, 2010), 195; Steven
Brill, *America's Bitter Pill: Money, Politics, Backroom Deals, and the Fight to Fix Our Broken
Healthcare System* (New York: Random House, 2015), 145.

55. Multiple administration and Capitol Hill sources, author interviews. See also Starr, *Remedy
and Reaction*, 195. Here is how one senior Obama administration official put it: "Barack
Obama said, 'Chuck, if I give you everything you want, can you be for this bill?' And Grassley
said no. And you know, that was all about him being worried about a primary." Before that,
"Grassley told the president he wanted to work with Sen. Baucus on a truly bipartisan plan
that could get 65 or 70 votes in the Senate," according to spokesman Michael Zona.

56. Sam Stein, "Grassley Endorses 'Death Panel' Rumor: 'You Have Every Right to Fear,'" *Huff-
Post*, September 12, 2009, https://www.huffpost.com/entry/grassley-endorses-death-p_n
_257677; DeParle interview.

57. Senior Democratic aide interview.

58. DeParle, Phil Schiliro, and Kathleen Sebelius, author interviews.

59. The story of this meeting has been recounted in several places, including Jonathan Alter's
and Steven Brill's books as well as David Axelrod's memoir. It's also in my 2010 retrospective,
which drew on administration officials who were part of the conversation. The accounts are
consistent except for the exact wording of the "I feel lucky" quote. Schiliro seems to have
the clearest memory of it, so I have relied here on his version, which he also provided in a

PBS *Frontline* interview. "Phil Schiliro, Obama Adviser," PBS, January 17, 2017, accessed September 19, 2020, http://apps.frontline.org/divided-states-of-america-the-frontline-interviews/transcript/phil-schiliro.html.

60. Senior Obama administration official interview; first reported in Jonathan Cohn, "How They Did It," *New Republic,* May 20, 2010.

61. David Axelrod, author interview.

Chapter 15: Madam Speaker

1. Karen Tumulty, "Ted Kennedy's Health Bill," *Time,* July 15, 2009, https://swampland.time.com/2009/07/15/ted-kennedys-health-bill/.

2. Jeffrey Young, "Senate Panel Passes Health Reform Bill," *Hill,* July 15, 2009, https://thehill.com/homenews/senate/50280-senate-panel-passes-health-reform-bill; Ezra Klein, "The White House's Definition of Bipartisanship," *Washington Post,* July 15, 2009, http://voices.washingtonpost.com/ezra-klein/2009/07/the_white_houses_definition_of.html.

3. Senior Obama administration official, author interview.

4. Senior Obama administration officials, author interviews.

5. Jon Favreau, author interview.

6. Some conservatives said the system would still subsidize undocumented immigrants indirectly, by allowing them to buy private insurance—or a public option, if it became law as the House bill envisioned—through the new system. But even the House bill made clear that undocumented residents would not be eligible for government subsidies.

7. Angie Drobnic Holan, "Joe Wilson of South Carolina Said Obama Lied, but He Didn't," PolitiFact, September 9, 2009, https://www.politifact.com/factchecks/2009/sep/09/joe-wilson/joe-wilson-south-carolina-said-obama-lied-he-didnt/.

8. Senior Obama administration official interview.

9. Senior Democratic aide, author interview.

10. Ibid.

11. Senior Obama administration officials and Democratic aides, author interviews.

12. Drew Hammill, author interview. (Hammill was Pelosi's longtime aide.) For a thorough accounting of Pelosi's upbringing and then her career in politics, see Molly Ball, *Pelosi* (New York: Henry Holt, 2020); Karen Tumulty, "A Troublemaker with a Gavel," *Washington Post,* March 25, 2020, https://www.washingtonpost.com/opinions/2020/03/25/how-nancy-pelosis-unlikely-rise-turned-her-into-most-powerful-woman-us-history/?arc404=true; and senior Obama administration officials and Democratic aides interviews.

13. Clare Malone, "Even as a Freshman, Nancy Pelosi Was a Political Insider," *FiveThirtyEight,* January 31, 2019, https://fivethirtyeight.com/features/even-as-a-freshman-pelosi-was-a-political-insider/; David Dayen, "A Leader Without Leading," *American Prospect,* July 7, 2020, https://prospect.org/culture/books/nancy-pelosi-a-leader-without-leading/.

14. "Selected CBO Publications Related to Health Care Legislation, 2009–2010," Congressional Budget Office, December 2010, https://www.cbo.gov/sites/default/files/111th-congress-2009-2010/reports/12-23-selectedhealthcarepublications.pdf; Robert Pear, "Pelosi Backs Off Set Rates for Public Option," *New York Times,* October 28, 2009, https://www.nytimes.com/2009/10/29/health/policy/29health.html.

15. Faye Fiore and Richard Simon, "She Had to Leave Left Coast Behind," *Los Angeles Times,* November 9, 2009, https://www.latimes.com/archives/la-xpm-2009-nov-09-na-pelosi9-story.html.

16. Carl Hulse and Robert Pear, "Sweeping Health Care Plan Passes House," *New York Times,* November 7, 2009, https://www.nytimes.com/2009/11/08/health/policy/08health.html.

17. Alina Salganicoff, Laurie Sobel, and Amrutha Ramaswamy, "The Hyde Amendment and Coverage for Abortion Services," Kaiser Family Foundation, September 10, 2020, https://www.kff.org/womens-health-policy/issue-brief/the-hyde-amendment-and-coverage-for-abortion-services/.

18. Timothy Noah, "Don't Be Stupak," *Slate,* November 4, 2009, https://slate.com/news-and-politics/2009/11/abortion-foes-and-rep-bart-stupak-meddle-with-private-health-insurance.html.

19. *Washington Post* Staff, *Landmark: The Inside Story of America's New Health Care Law and What It Means for Us All* (New York: PublicAffairs, 2010), Kindle edition, 28.

20. Jennifer Steinhauer, "In Pelosi, Strong Catholic Faith and Abortion Rights Coexist," *New*

York Times, September 21, 2015, https://www.nytimes.com/2015/09/22/us/politics/in-pelosi -strong-catholic-faith-and-abortion-rights-coexist.html.

21. Timothy Jost, "The House Health Reform Bill: An Abortion Funding Ban and Other Late Changes," *Health Affairs*, November 9, 2009, https://www.healthaffairs.org/do/10.1377 /hblog20091109.002832/full/; Rachel Morris, "The Price of Health Reform: Abortion Rights?," *Mother Jones*, November 9, 2009, https://www.motherjones.com/politics/2009/11 /price-health-reform-abortion-rights/.

22. This account of Pelosi's meeting with the pro-choice causes is based on multiple published sources, including *The Washington Post*'s book *Landmark* and Ball's Pelosi biography, as well as author interviews with former Democratic staff and lawmakers for my 2010 *New Republic* retrospective. See also Patrick O'Connor and John Bresnahan, "Tears, Tempers Fly in Pelosi Campaign," *Politico*, November 8, 2009, https://www.politico.com/story/2009/11/tears -tempers-fly-in-pelosi-campaign-029305.

23. Ron Kind and senior Democratic aide, author interviews.

Chapter 16: March or Die

1. Max Baucus, "Baucus Opening Statement on Health Care Reform," YouTube video, 7:10, posted by "SenatorBaucus," September 22, 2009, https://www.youtube.com/watch?v=sUWJ1lIqidU.

2. Carrie Budoff Brown, "Baucus Releases Health Care Bill," *Politico*, September 16, 2009, https://www.politico.com/story/2009/09/baucus-releases-health-care-bill-027225; *Focus on Health Reform* (Menlo Park, CA: Henry J. Kaiser Family Foundation, 2009), https://www.kff .org/wp-content/uploads/2013/01/healthreform_tri_full.pdf.

3. Ben Smith, "Cadillac Tax," *Politico*, July 26, 2009, https://www.politico.com/blogs/ben-smith /2009/07/cadillac-tax-020192.

4. Jenny Gold, "'Cadillac' Insurance Plans Explained," Kaiser Health News, March 18, 2010, https://khn.org/news/cadillac-health-explainer-npr/.

5. John McDonough, *Inside National Health Reform* (Berkeley: University of California Press, 2012), 88.

6. Igor Volsky, "Insurance Industry Report Promises to Increase Premiums by 111% Under Health Reform," ThinkProgress, October 12, 2009, https://archive.thinkprogress.org /insurance-industry-report-promises-to-increase-premiums-by-111-under-health-reform -27ec40639b2e/; Jonathan Cohn, "Not All Bad," *New Republic*, October 21, 2009, https:// newrepublic.com/article/70403/not-all-bad; Lori Robertson, "The PricewaterhouseCoopers Premium Problem," FactCheck.org, October 13, 2009, https://www.factcheck.org/2009/10 /the-pricewaterhousecoopers-premium-problem/.

7. Robert Pear and David M. Herszenhorn, "Democrats Call Insurance Industry Report Flawed," *New York Times*, October 12, 2009, https://www.nytimes.com/2009/10/13/health/policy /13health.html; Carrie Budoff Brown, "Insurers Face Blowback After Report," *Politico*, October 12, 2009, https://www.politico.com/story/2009/10/insurers-face-blowback-after-report-028213.

8. Robert Pear and David M. Herszenhorn, "Republican's Vote Lifts a Health Bill, but Hurdles Remain," *New York Times*, October 13, 2009, https://www.nytimes.com/2009/10/14/health /policy/14health.html.

9. "Searchlight, Nevada Lives On," Legends of America, https://www.legendsofamerica.com/nv -searchlight/; K. J. Evanslas, "George Colton," *Las Vegas Review-Journal*, February 7, 1999, https://www.reviewjournal.com/news/george-colton/; Cecil Anderson, "A Look at Life in Searchlight, Nevada," KVVU TV, November 11, 2019, https://www.fox5vegas.com/news/local /a-look-at-life-in-searchlight-nevada/article_a62be0ac-04e7-11ea-a596-575b29707a36 .html; "A Little History," Searchlight Historical Museum, https://searchlightmuseum.org/os /history.html.

10. Josh Rosenblatt, "Harry Reid Returns to His Boxing Roots to Attack Trump," *Vice*, July 28, 2016, http://fightland.vice.com/blog/harry-reid-returns-to-his-boxing-roots-to-attack-trump; Harry Reid and Mark Warren, *The Good Fight: Hard Lessons from Searchlight to Washington* (New York: G. P. Putnam's Sons, 2008).

11. Benny Johnson, "7 Badass Things You Should Not Forget About Harry Reid," *BuzzFeed*, July 17, 2013, https://www.buzzfeednews.com/article/bennyjohnson/very-badass-things-you-should -not-forget-about-harry-reid; Harry Reid, author interview. He also talked about these experi-

ences in a conversation with the medical school dean at the University of Nevada–Las Vegas. See Barbara Atkinson, "Harry Reid's Health Care Legacy," University of Nevada–Las Vegas, June 19, 2019, https://www.unlv.edu/news/article/harry-reid-s-health-care-legacy.

12. Kate Leone, author interview.

13. Senior Democratic aide and Reid, author interviews.

14. Senior Democratic aides, author interviews; "Sen. Evan Bayh - Indiana, Top Industries 2003–2008," Center for Responsive Politics, https://www.opensecrets.org/members-of-congress/industries?cid=N00003762&cycle=2008&recs=0&type=C; Manu Raju, "Evan Bayh's Private Schedule Details Ties with Donors, Lobbyists," CNN, November 1, 2016, https://www.cnn.com/2016/10/31/politics/evan-bayh-indiana-senate/index.html; Dan Eggen and Ceci Connolly, "Medical Device Makers Court Unlikely Allies in Health Debate," *Washington Post,* October 18, 2009, https://www.washingtonpost.com/wp-dyn/content/article/2009/10/17/AR2009101700718.html; Max Baucus, "Letter Regarding Medical Device Tax," *New York Times,* September 16, 2009, https://www.nytimes.com/2009/09/16/health/policy/16prescriptions.text.html; Suzy Khimm, "Is Bayh Backing Off His Threat?," *New Republic,* October 29, 2009, https://newrepublic.com/article/70751/bayh-backing-his-threat; Alec MacGillis, "Um, About That Medical Device Tax . . . ," *New Republic,* September 28, 2012, accessed September 19, 2020, https://newrepublic.com/article/107878/why-evan-bayh-elizabeth-warren-and-others-are-wrong-about-medical-device-tax.

15. Senior Obama administration officials and senior Democratic aides, author interviews.

16. Sherrod Brown, author interview.

17. Senior Democratic aides interviews.

18. Richard Kirsch, *Fighting for Our Health: The Epic Battle to Make Health Care a Right in the United States* (New York: Rockefeller Institute Press, 2012), 304.

19. Carl Hulse and David Stout, "Democrats Hand Lieberman a Slap on the Wrist in Senate," *New York Times,* October 18, 2008, https://www.nytimes.com/2008/11/18/world/americas/18iht-congress.4.17937906.html.

20. Joe Lieberman, author interview; Glenn Thrush and Manu Raju, "Democrats Downplay Lieberman Threat," *Politico,* October 27, 2009, https://www.politico.com/story/2009/10/democrats-downplay-lieberman-threat-028817; Max Fisher, "Why Lieberman Is Making Democrats' Lives Miserable," *Atlantic,* December 14, 2009, https://www.theatlantic.com/politics/archive/2009/12/why-lieberman-is-making-democrats-lives-miserable/347266/.

21. Janet Hook and Noam Levey, "Reid Hopes to Sway Enough Senators on Public Option," *Los Angeles Times,* October 28, 2009, https://www.latimes.com/archives/la-xpm-2009-oct-28-na-healthcare-senate28-story.html; Brian Beutler, "Lieberman: Sure, I'd Filibuster a Health Care Reform Bill with a Public Option," Talking Points Memo, October 27, 2009, https://talkingpointsmemo.com/dc/lieberman-sure-i-d-filibuster-a-health-care-reform-bill-with-a-public-option; McDonough, *Inside National Health Reform,* 91.

22. Patrick O'Connor and Carrie Budoff Brown, "Reid: Dems Reach 'Broad Agreement,'" *Politico,* December 8, 2009, https://www.politico.com/story/2009/12/reid-dems-reach-broad-agreement-030371; Nick Baumann, "Joe Lieberman's Medicare Dodge," *Mother Jones,* December 3, 2009, https://www.motherjones.com/politics/2009/12/joe-liebermans-medicare-dodge/; Michael Scherer, "Joe Lieberman Says He Didn't Change on Medicare Buy-In, Things Did," *Time,* December 15, 2009, https://swampland.time.com/2009/12/15/joe-lieberman-says-he-didnt-change-mind-on-medicare-buy-in-things-did/; "Lieberman Supported Medicare Expansion," NBC News, December 14, 2009, accessed September 20, 2020, http://www.nbcnews.com/id/34420961/ns/politics-capitol_hill/t/lieberman-supported-medicare-expansion/#.X2bgsZNKjBJ.

23. David Drucker, "Lieberman Disputes Claim He Blindsided Reid," *Roll Call,* January 13, 2010, https://www.rollcall.com/2010/01/13/lieberman-disputes-claims-he-blindsided-reid/; Lieberman and Reid interviews. Lieberman reiterated to me his belief that he had made his objections known, though he allowed that there might have been some confusion over what he meant.

24. "Face the Nation - December 13, 2009, Transcript," CBS News, December 13, 2009.

25. David Bowen, Brown, and Leone, author interviews. *The Post's Landmark* also has a detailed account of the meeting in Reid's office, including Leone urging the senators not to give up. See *Washington Post* Staff, *Landmark: The Inside Story of America's New Health Care Law and What It Means for Us All* (New York: PublicAffairs, 2010), Kindle edition, 44.

26. Huma Khan and Jonathan Karl, "Howard Dean: Health Care Bill 'Bigger Bailout for the Insurance Industry Than AIG,'" ABC News, December 16, 2009, https://abcnews.go.com/GMA/HealthCare/howard-dean-health-care-bill-bigger-bailout-insurance/story?id=9349392.

27. Sheryl Gay Stolberg, "'Public Option' in Health Plan May Be Dropped," *New York Times,* August 17, 2009, https://www.nytimes.com/2009/08/18/health/policy/18talkshows.html; Craig Gordon, "Liberals: Why Didn't Obama Fight?," *Politico,* December 15, 2009, https://www.politico.com/story/2009/12/liberals-why-didnt-obama-fight-030648; Helen Halpin and Peter Harbage, "The Origins and Demise of the Public Option," *Health Affairs* 29, no. 6 (2010): 1117–1124, https://doi.org/10.1377/hlthaff.2010.0363; Barack Obama, "A President Looks Back on His Toughest Fight," *New Yorker,* November 2, 2002, https://www.newyorker.com/magazine/2020/11/02/barack-obama-new-book-excerpt-promised-land-obamacare.

28. Kenneth P. Vogel, "Health Firms Paid DeParle $5.8 Million," *Politico,* June 12, 2009, https://www.politico.com/story/2009/06/health-firms-paid-deparle-58-million-023688; Craig Gordon, "Liberals: Why Didn't Obama Fight?," *Politico,* December 15, 2009, https://www.politico.com/story/2009/12/liberals-why-didnt-obama-fight-030648; Jon Walker, "Really, Peter Orszag!?! Your Critics Have No Ideas for Controlling Cost?," *Shadowproof,* November 28, 2009, https://shadowproof.com/2009/11/28/really-peter-orszag-your-critics-have-no-ideas-for-controlling-cost/.

29. Chris Good, "MoveOn Raises $1 Million to Attack Lieberman . . . Plus: Lieberman as Obstinate Sock Puppet," *Atlantic,* December 17, 2009, https://www.theatlantic.com/politics/archive/2009/12/moveon-raises-1-million-to-attack-liebermanplus-lieberman-as-obstinate-sock-puppet/32264/; "Sock Puppet Lieberman Demands Pony in Exchange for Health Care Vote," *HuffPost,* December 17, 2009, https://www.huffpost.com/entry/sock-puppet-lieberman-dem_n_397463.

30. Brown interview.

31. Sanders remained reluctant to talk publicly about his mother's experience even years later, when he was running for president and his own strategists thought the story would resonate with voters. One of the few articles to discuss the story at length was in *The New York Times* by Sydney Ember, who had to rely heavily on interviews with his family and friends. Sydney Ember, "Bernie Sanders Went to Canada, and a Dream of 'Medicare for All' Flourished," *New York Times,* September 9, 2019, https://www.nytimes.com/2019/09/09/us/politics/bernie-sanders-health-care.html.

32. Olga Khazan, "The Stunning Rise of Single-Payer Health Care," *Atlantic,* November 21, 2019, https://www.theatlantic.com/health/archive/2019/11/why-people-support-medicare-all/602413/; "History of Single-Payer Legislation," Healthcare Now!, accessed September 20, 2020, https://www.healthcare-now.org/legislation/national-timeline/; Paul D. Wellstone and Ellen R. Shaffer, "The American Health Security Act—A Single-Payer Proposal," *New England Journal of Medicine* 328, May 1993, https://www.nejm.org/doi/full/10.1056/NEJM199305203282013.

33. *New York Times* Editorial Board, "Bernie Sanders, Senator from Vermont," *New York Times,* January 13, 2020, https://www.nytimes.com/interactive/2020/01/13/opinion/bernie-sanders-nytimes-interview.html; Nancy-Ann DeParle, author interview.

34. Ezra Klein, "Sen. Bernie Sanders: Health-Care Bill Could Spark 'a Revolution in Primary Health Care,'" *Washington Post,* December 30, 2009, http://voices.washingtonpost.com/ezra-klein/2009/12/sen_bernie_sanders_health_care.html.

35. Reid interview. See also "Single-Payer Health Care Plan Dies in Senate," NBC News, December 16, 2009, http://www.nbcnews.com/id/34446325/ns/politics-health_care_reform/t/single-payer-health-care-plan-dies-senate/#.X2bkbZNKjBJ.

36. Jeffrey Young and Michael O'Brien, "Nelson a 'No' on Health Reform Bill Pending Further Changes," *Hill,* December 17, 2009, https://thehill.com/blogs/blog-briefing-room/news/72767-nelson-a-no-on-health-bill-pending-further-changes.

37. Don Walton, "Nelson Welcomes Role as Swing Vote," *Lincoln Journal Star,* September 3, 2009, https://journalstar.com/news/local/govt-and-politics/nelson-welcomes-role-as-swing-vote/article_c5a5c8b2-9823-11de-8c15-001cc4c03286.html; Bowen Garrett, John Holahan, Allison Cook et al., "The Coverage and Cost Impacts of Expanding Medicaid," Kaiser Commission on Medicaid and the Uninsured, May 2009, https://www.kff.org/wp-content/uploads

/2013/01/7901.pdf; Susan Jaffe, "Coverage for Low-Income People," *Health Affairs*, July 24, 2009, https://www.healthaffairs.org/do/10.1377/hpb20090724.745708/full/.

38. Reid and Leone interviews. See also "Sen. Ben Nelson's Chronology," PBS, February 2010, https://www.pbs.org/wgbh/pages/frontline/obamasdeal/etc/cronnelson.html; Carrie Budoff Brown, "Ben Nelson's Medicaid Deal," *Politico*, December 19, 2009, https://www.politico.com/livepulse/1209/Ben_Nelsons_Medicaid_deal.html; Brian Montopoli, "Tallying the Health Care Bill's Giveaways," CBS News, December 21, 2009, https://www.cbsnews.com/news/tallying-the-health-care-bills-giveaways/.

39. Leone interview.

40. Manu Raju, "Nelson Tries to Repair Damage at Home," *Politico*, January 14, 2010, https://www.politico.com/story/2010/01/nelson-tries-to-repair-damage-at-home-031488; "Nelson: Medicaid Deal Can Help Other States," *Lincoln Journal Star*, December 22, 2009, https://journalstar.com/news/local/govt-and-politics/nelson-medicaid-deal-can-help-other-states/article_067a266c-ef5e-11de-a09f-001cc4c03286.html; Steve Jordon, "What Was the 'Cornhusker Kickback,' the Deal That Led to Nelson's Crucial ACA Vote?," *Omaha World-Herald*, July 20, 2017, https://omaha.com/livewellnebraska/obamacare/what-was-the-cornhusker-kickback-the-deal-that-led-to-nelson-s-crucial-aca-vote/article_a2eb3a1d-df14-513b-a141-c8695f6c258e.html.

41. Reid interview.

42. Aaron Blake, "Sen. Ben Nelson Won't Seek Reelection," *Washington Post*, December 27, 2011, https://www.washingtonpost.com/blogs/the-fix/post/sen-ben-nelson-wont-seek-reelection/2011/12/27/gIQAmDWnKP_blog.html.

43. Ron Elving, "More Kabuki Than Christmas in the Senate," NPR, December 21, 2009, https://www.npr.org/sections/watchingwashington/2009/12/more_kabuki_than_christmas_in.html.

44. Leone and Phil Schiliro interviews; Meredith Shiner, "Feingold Vote Advances Health Bill," *Politico*, December 17, 2009, https://www.politico.com/story/2009/12/eingold-vote-advances-health-bill-030773.

45. Leone interview.

46. *Washington Post* Staff, *Landmark*, 48.

47. Robert Pear, "Senate Passes Health Care Overhaul on Party-Line Vote," *New York Times*, December 24, 2009, https://www.nytimes.com/2009/12/25/health/policy/25health.html; Jeffrey Young, "Senate Passes Historic Healthcare Reform Legislation in 60–39 Vote," *Hill*, December 24, 2009, https://thehill.com/homenews/senate/73537-senate-passes-historic-healthcare-reform-bill-60-40.

48. "Presidential Remarks on Health Care Legislation Vote," C-SPAN video, 4:46, December 24, 2009, https://www.c-span.org/video/?290900-1/presidential-remarks-health-care-legislation-vote.

Chapter 17: A Big F***ing Deal

1. The House bill set the income threshold for Medicaid at 150 percent of the poverty line, not 130 percent as the Senate bill did. The House bill also offered more total financial assistance than the Senate bill, so that the average subsidy for an enrollee in 2019 would be $6,800 rather than $5,600. The subsidies were scaled to income in different ways, so that the House bill actually offered less help than the Senate bill did at higher income levels. But the House bill also offered more help with out-of-pocket costs and established a higher standard for minimum benefits.

2. Richard Kirsch, *Fighting for Our Health: The Epic Battle to Make Health Care a Right in the United States* (New York: Rockefeller Institute Press, 2012), 301–302.

3. Senior Obama administration officials and Democratic aides, author interviews; Molly Ball, *Pelosi* (New York: Henry Holt, 2020), Kindle edition, 188–189.

4. Liz Fowler, notes from conference call; Karen Nelson, author interview.

5. Senior Obama administration officials and Democratic aides interviews.

6. Ibid.; Kate Leone later remembered that "we stayed there and it was kind of weird, because it felt like you were in somebody else's house without the host." Kate Leone, author interview.

7. Barack Obama, author interview.

8. Jonathan Cohn, "How They Did It," *New Republic*, May 20, 2010; Debbie Curtis, author interview. She had also emailed as much to me at the time, while negotiations were going on.

"I really think the exchange thing has become a red herring," she said. I wrote about that email years later, when it offered insights into *King v. Burwell*, a lawsuit against the Affordable Care Act that had come before the Supreme Court. Jonathan Cohn, "One More Clue That the Obamacare Lawsuits Are Wrong," *New Republic,* July 29, 2014, https://newrepublic.com /article/118867/email-house-aide-undermines-halbig-lawsuit-obamacare-subsidies.

9. Senior Democratic aide, author interview.

10. Curtis interview.

11. It started as an email to me, when I asked for his assessment, and he allowed me to publish it verbatim as long as I identified him only as a "senior Democratic strategist." Jennings gave permission to use his name here. Jonathan Cohn, "The Abyss," *New Republic,* January 22, 2010, https://newrepublic.com/article/72685/the-abyss-0.

12. Ron Pollack, Jim Messina, author interviews.

13. Henry Waxman, author interview; David Axelrod, *Believer* (New York: Penguin, 2015), 385; senior Obama administration officials and Democratic aides interviews.

14. Tom Daschle, *Getting It Done* (New York: St. Martin's, 2010), 234; Karen Travers, "Exclusive: President Obama Says Voter Anger, Frustration Key to Republican Victory in Massachusetts Senate," ABC News, January 20, 2010, https://abcnews.go.com/Nightline/Politics/abc-news -george-stephanopoulos-exclusive-interview-president-obama/story?id=9611223.

15. Peter Baker and Carl Hulse, "Off Script, Obama and the G.O.P. Vent Politely," *New York Times,* January 29, 2010, https://www.nytimes.com/2010/01/30/us/politics/30obama.html.

16. Cohn, "How They Did It."

17. Carrie Budoff Brown, "The Obama Plan," *Politico,* February 22, 2010, https://www.politico .com/story/2010/02/the-obama-plan-033275; "Full Text: Obama's Health Care Proposal," Kaiser Health News, February 22, 2010, https://khn.org/news/obama-health-care-proposal/.

18. Senior Democratic aide interview; Cohn, "How They Did It."

19. Eleanor Clift, "Nancy Pelosi's Tireless Obamacare Push Vindicated by Supreme Court Ruling," *Daily Beast,* July 4, 2012, https://www.thedailybeast.com/nancy-pelosis-tireless -obamacare-push-vindicated-by-supreme-court-ruling.

20. Chris Murphy, author interview. Accounts of what Pelosi said at which meeting vary; some recall her making her declaration about moving forward at the second caucus meeting after the Scott Brown election, not the first. See Ball, *Pelosi,* 190.

21. Senior Obama administration officials and Democratic aides interviews; Jeffrey Young and Jonathan Cohn, "What the Obamacare Fight Says About Nancy Pelosi," *HuffPost,* November 27, 2018, https://www.huffpost.com/entry/nancy-pelosi-obamacare-leadership_n _5bfdc95de4b030172fa7f593.

22. Paul Krugman, "California Death Spiral," *New York Times,* February 18, 2010, accessed September 20, 2020, https://www.nytimes.com/2010/02/19/opinion/19krugman.html.

23. Senior Obama administration officials and Democratic aides interviews.

24. Senior Obama administration officials interviews. At one point, Pelosi also huddled with Nancy-Ann DeParle, Jeanne Lambrew, and Kathleen Sebelius to reiterate her opposition to Rahm's kids-only proposal.

25. Jay Newton-Small, "Health Care Clincher: The Importance of Being Stupak," *Time,* March 21, 2010, http://content.time.com/time/politics/article/0,8599,1973963,00.html.

26. "President Obama Rallies for Health Care," C-SPAN video, 0:23, May 31, 2013, https://www.c -span.org/video/?c4454328/president-obama-rallies-health-care; Sabrina Eaton, "Rep. Dennis Kucinich to Vote 'Yes' on Health Care: Video," Cleveland.com, March 17, 2010, https:// www.cleveland.com/open/2010/03/rep_dennis_kucinich_to_vote_xx.html.

27. Some conservatives later disputed the claims of homophobic and racial slurs, citing a YouTube video from the day that picked up no such rhetoric. But as a subsequent Associated Press report noted, the video was from a different time of day. A CNN producer actually heard the anti-gay slurs, and the other two members of Congress, Jim Clyburn of South Carolina and Emanuel Cleaver of Maryland, said that they, like Lewis, heard protesters using the N-word. See Sam Stein, "Tea Party Protests: 'Ni**er,' 'Fa**ot' Shouted at Members of Congress," *HuffPost,* May 20, 2010, https://www.huffpost.com/entry/tea-party-protests-nier-f_n_507116; Ted Barrett, Evan Glass, and Lesa Jansen, "Protesters Hurl Slurs and Spit at Democrats," CNN, March 20, 2010, https://web.archive.org/web/20161010170710/http://politicalticker

.blogs.cnn.com/2010/03/20/protesters-hurl-slurs-and-spit-at-democrats/; Jesse Washington, "Did Spit, Slurs Fly on Capitol Hill?," *Seattle Times,* April 13, 2010, https://www.seattletimes .com/nation-world/did-spit-slurs-fly-on-capitol-hill/. I was also on Capitol Hill that day. I did not hear anybody using such language; I did see Tea Party activists walking through the halls of congressional office buildings. Emotions were running high. Steve Brusk, "Pelosi to Use Historic Gavel to Preside over Vote," CNN, March 21, 2010, https://web.archive.org/web /20191013013008/http://politicalticker.blogs.cnn.com/2010/03/21/pelosi-to-use-historic -gavel-to-preside-over-reform/.

28. Senior Democratic administration official interview, plus my observations from the press gallery that night.

29. "House Session," C-SPAN video, 10:59:06, March 21, 2010, https://www.c-span.org/video /?292637-1/house-vote-health-care.

30. Senior Obama administration officials interviews; "Behind the Scenes: The Affordable Care Act," YouTube video, 8:52, posted by Obama White House, December 8, 2016, https://www .youtube.com/watch?v=SBBu5Fz4moc.

Chapter 18: The Last Stand

1. David Remnick, "Obama Reckons with a Trump Presidency," *New Yorker,* November 18, 2016, https://www.newyorker.com/magazine/2016/11/28/obama-reckons-with-a-trump -presidency; Julie Hirschfeld Davis, "Trump and Obama Hold Cordial 90-Minute Meeting in Oval Office," *New York Times,* November 10, 2016, https://www.nytimes.com/2016/11 /11/us/politics/white-house-transition-obama-trump.html; Lesley Stahl, "President-Elect Trump Speaks to a Divided Country," CBS News, November 13, 2016, https://www.cbsnews .com/news/60-minutes-donald-trump-family-melania-ivanka-lesley-stahl/; Monica Lang- ley and Gerard Baker, "Donald Trump, in Exclusive Interview, Tells WSJ He Is Willing to Keep Parts of Obama Health Law," *Wall Street Journal,* November 11, 2016, https://www .wsj.com/articles/donald-trump-willing-to-keep-parts-of-health-law-1478895339?ns =prod%2Faccounts-wsj.

2. A source familiar with the conversation, author interview; Tim Alberta, *American Carnage* (New York: HarperCollins, 2019), Kindle edition, 420; Rachel Bade, "Ryan: GOP Will Re- place Obamacare, Cut Taxes and Fund Wall by August," *Politico,* January 25, 2017, https:// www.politico.com/story/2017/01/republican-agenda-retreat-obamacare-wall-tax-cuts -234176.

3. Source familiar with the conversation interview.

Chapter 19: This Honorable Court

1. Jack Balkin, "The Health Care Mandate Is Clearly a Tax—and Therefore Constitutional," *At- lantic,* May 4, 2012, https://www.theatlantic.com/politics/archive/2012/05/the-health-care -mandate-is-clearly-a-tax-0151-and-therefore-constitutional/256706/; Jack Balkin, "From Off the Wall to On the Wall: How the Mandate Challenge Went Mainstream," *Atlantic,* June 4, 2012, https://www.theatlantic.com/national/archive/2012/06/from-off-the-wall-to-on-the -wall-how-the-mandate-challenge-went-mainstream/258040/.

2. James Ming Chen, "The Story of Wickard v. Filburn: Agriculture, Aggregation, and Com- merce," in *Constitutional Law Stories,* 2nd ed., ed. Michael C. Dorf (St. Paul, MN: Foundation Press, 2008), University of Louisville School of Law Legal Studies Research Paper Series No. 2008–40, September 15, 2008, https://papers.ssrn.com/sol3/papers.cfm?abstract_id=1268162.

3. Randy Barnett, "Commandeering the People: Why the Individual Health Insurance Mandate Is Unconstitutional," Georgetown Law Faculty Publications and Other Works, 2010, https:// scholarship.law.georgetown.edu/facpub/434/; Ilya Somin, "A Mandate for Mandates: Is the Individual Health Insurance Case a Slippery Slope?," *Law and Contemporary Problems* 75, no. 3 (2012): 75–106; Josh Blackman, *Unraveled* (New York: Cambridge University Press, 2016), 357; Andrew Koppelman, *The Tough Luck Constitution* (New York: Oxford University Press, 2013), 72–76.

4. Democrats could make an equally compelling case that the Bork appointment itself was a breach of convention, given its ideological intent. See E. J. Dionne, "Capitulating to the Right Won't End the Judicial Wars," *Washington Post,* September 23, 2010, https://www

.washingtonpost.com/opinions/capitulating-to-the-right-wont-end-the-judicial-wars/2020
/09/23/5402f378-fdd5-11ea-9ceb-061d646d9c67_story.html.

5. Lawrence Lessig, "Why Scalia Could Uphold Obamacare," *Atlantic*, April 13, 2012, https://
www.theatlantic.com/national/archive/2012/04/why-scalia-could-uphold-obamacare
/255791/.

6. Aaron Belkin and Sean McElwee, "Don't Be Fooled. Chief Justice John Roberts Is as Partisan as They Come," *New York Times*, October 7, 2019, https://www.nytimes.com/2019/10/07
/opinion/john-roberts-supreme-court.html.

7. Another prominent conservative lawyer, Paul Clement, represented states challenging the
Affordable Care Act and worked alongside Carvin; Michael Carvin, author interview.

8. Don Verrilli, author interview.

9. Verrilli and Joseph Palmore, author interviews.

10. Carvin interview.

11. I was in the chamber and saw all of them there.

12. Among the small handful of reporters to notice was Brian Beutler of Talking Points Memo.
"Roberts may have tipped his hand," Beutler wrote in his Monday dispatch. See Brian Beutler, "John Roberts May Have Tipped His Hand on 'Obamacare' Reasoning," Talking Points
Memo, March 26, 2012, https://talkingpointsmemo.com/dc/john-roberts-may-have-tipped
-his-hand-on-obamacare-reasoning.

13. Julie Hirschfeld Davis and Greg Stohr, "Republicans Tampered with Court Audio in Obama Attack Ad," Bloomberg, March 30, 2012, https://www.bloomberg.com/news/articles/2012–03–29
/republicans-tampered-with-court-audio-in-obama-attack-ad?sref=sGsy0HYh.

14. Palmore and Verrilli interviews.

15. Jan Crawford, "Roberts Switched Views to Uphold Health Care Law," CBS News, July 2,
2012, https://www.cbsnews.com/news/roberts-switched-views-to-uphold-health-care-law/;
Joan Biskupic, *The Chief* (New York: Basic Books, 2019), Kindle edition, 227–248; Jeffrey
Toobin, *The Oath* (New York: Doubleday, 2012), 272–293. Crawford's account, which appeared mere days after the decision, set off a frenzy of follow-up reporting and speculation
about what had happened. See Avik Roy, "Leaks Galore! More on the Inside Story of John
Roberts' Obamacare Supreme Court Flip-Flop," *Forbes*, July 5, 2012, https://www.forbes.com
/sites/aroy/2012/07/05/leaks-galore-more-on-the-inside-story-of-john-roberts-obamacare
-supreme-court-flip-flop/#3a4d1ed81177.

16. Jeffrey Rosen, "Roberts's Rules," *Atlantic*, January/February 2007, https://www.theatlantic
.com/magazine/archive/2007/01/robertss-rules/305559/.

17. A federal judge who ruled on one of the mandate lawsuits at the Circuit level made an important related point. He noted that, by striking down mandatory purchase requirements,
the courts would risk undermining attempts to "privatize the social safety net," which is what
many conservatives wanted to do. That judge was Brett Kavanaugh, whom Trump put on the
Supreme Court in 2018. See Kavanaugh, Dissenting Opinion, *Seven-Sky v. Holder*, 661 F. 3d
1 – Court of Appeals, Dist. of Columbia Circuit 2011.

18. George Will, "Liberals Put the Squeeze to Justice Roberts," *Washington Post*, May 25, 2012;
"Targeting John Roberts," *Wall Street Journal*, May 23, 2012.

19. Ramesh Ponnuru, author interview.

20. Verrilli interview.

21. Alexander Abad-Santos, "CNN Got the Supreme Court's Health Care Ruling Exactly Wrong," *Atlantic*, June 28, 2012, https://www.theatlantic.com/business/archive/2012/06/cnn-got-supreme
-courts-health-care-ruling-exactly-wrong/326465/.

22. Sara Rosenbaum and Timothy W. Westmoreland, "The Supreme Court's Surprising Decision
on the Medicaid Expansion: How Will the Federal Government and States Proceed?," *Health
Affairs*, August 2012, https://doi.org/10.1377/hlthaff.2012.0766.

23. Verrilli and Palmore interviews.

Chapter 20: The Anti-Universal Club

1. Michael Hiltzik, "David Koch's Real Legacy Is the Dark Money Network of Rich Right-
Wingers," *Los Angeles Times*, August 23, 2019, https://www.latimes.com/business/story
/2019-08-23/david-kochs-legacy-dark-money-network; Jane Mayer, "The Kochs v. Cato,"

New Yorker, March 1, 2012, https://www.newyorker.com/news/news-desk/the-kochs-vs -cato.

2. Michael Cannon, author interview; Michael Cannon, "The Anti-Universal Coverage Club Manifesto," Cato Institute, July 6, 2007, https://www.cato.org/blog/anti-universal-coverage -club-manifesto.

3. Cannon interview.

4. Michael Cannon, "Should Michigan Create a Health Insurance Exchange?," Mackinac Center for Public Policy, June 2011, https://www.mackinac.org/15237.

5. Cannon interview; Jonathan Adler, author correspondence.

6. "Who's in Charge? More Legal Challenges to the Patient Protection and Affordable Care Act," American Enterprise Institute, December 7, 2010, https://www.aei.org/press/whos-in -charge-more-legal-challenges-to-the-patient-protection-and-affordable-care-act/; "Who's in Charge? More Legal Challenges to the Patient Protection and Affordable Care Act," You-Tube video, 2:02:46, posted by American Enterprise Institute, March 11, 2014, https://www .youtube.com/watch?time_continue=4292&v=C7nRpJURvE4&feature=emb_logo.

7. Stephanie Armour, "The Lawyer Who Helped Spark This Week's Affordable Care Act Rul-ings," *Wall Street Journal,* July 24, 2014, https://www.wsj.com/articles/the-lawyer-who -helped-spark-this-weeks-affordable-care-act-rulings-1406231596.

8. Cannon interview.

9. Peter Suderman, "Watch Obamacare Architect Jonathan Gruber Admit in 2012 That Subsidies Were Limited to State-Run Exchanges (Updated with Another Admission)," *Reason,* July 24, 2014, https://reason.com/2014/07/24/watch-obamacare-architect-jonathan-grube-2/. I had my own small moment in this drama because of a comment I made on NPR's *Fresh Air* in early 2010; I was able to reconstruct my thinking from the time and actually found a contemporaneous email that suggested very strongly the Cannon-Adler theory was wrong. See Jonathan Cohn, "My Obamacare Truther Moment," *New Republic,* July 31, 2014, https:// newrepublic.com/article/118915/my-obamacare-truther-moment-what-i-told-terry-gross -about-exchanges; Jonathan Cohn, "One More Clue That the Obamacare Lawsuits Are Wrong," *New Republic,* July 29, 2014, https://newrepublic.com/article/118867/email-house -aide-undermines-halbig-lawsuit-obamacare-subsidies.

10. Timothy Jost, "Tax Credits in Federally Facilitated Exchanges Are Consistent with the Afford-able Care Act's Language and History," *Health Affairs,* July 19, 2012, https://www.healthaffairs .org/do/10.1377/hblog20120719.021337/full/; Jonathan Cohn, "The Legal Crusade to Un-dermine Obamacare—and Rewrite History," *New Republic,* December 5, 2012, https:// newrepublic.com/article/110770/legal-challenge-obamacare-insurance-exchanges-full-holes.

11. Sarah Kliff, "Congress Never Fought About Ending Tax Credits," *Vox,* July 26, 2014, https:// www.vox.com/2014/7/26/5937593/obamacare-halbig-gruber-tax-credits; Julie Rovner, "What Jon Gruber Says He Was Thinking," Facebook, July 25, 2014, https://www.facebook .com/julie.rovner/posts/10204540021609085.

12. Greg Sargent, "Senate Documents and Interviews Undercut 'Bombshell' Lawsuit Against Obamacare," *Washington Post,* July 29, 2014, https://www.washingtonpost.com/blogs/plum -line/wp/2014/07/29/senate-documents-and-interviews-undercut-bombshell-lawsuit -against-obamacare/.

13. Nicholas Bagley, "Hello, Justices? It's Reality Calling," *New York Times,* March 2, 2015.

14. Jonathan Cohn, "The Legal Crusade to Undermine Obamacare—and Rewrite History."

Chapter 21: Purification

1. Bill to Repeal the Patient Protection and Affordable Care Act, S.3152, 111th Cong. (2010).

2. "Johnson TV: 'Listening,'" YouTube video, 0:30, posted by Ron Johnson, September 27, 2010, https://www.youtube.com/watch?v=ZbIUW0qFCNM; Matthew Kaminski, "Tea Partier Beats Feingold," *Wall Street Journal,* October 8, 2010, https://blogs.wsj.com/ojelection/2010/11/02 /tea-partier-beats-feingold/; Jonathan Cohn, "Playing Offense on Health Care Reform," *New Republic,* October 1, 2010, https://newrepublic.com/article/78098/russ-feingold-campaign -ad-defends-health-care-reform.

3. Dave Umhoefer, "Ron Johnson Says Sen. Russ Feingold Cut Medicare by $523 Billion," PolitiFact, October 8, 2010, https://www.politifact.com/factchecks/2010/oct/08/ron-johnson

/ron-johnson-says-sen-russ-feingold-cut-medicare-52/; Mary Bottari, "Pants on Fire: The Whoppers of the 2010 Elections," PR Watch, November 15, 2010, https://www.prwatch.org /news/2010/11/9615/pants-fire-whoppers-2010-elections; Juliette Cubanski, Tricia Neuman, and Anthony Damico, "Closing the Medicare Part D Coverage Gap: Trends, Recent Changes, and What's Ahead," Henry J. Kaiser Family Foundation, August 21, 2018, https://www.kff.org /medicare/issue-brief/closing-the-medicare-part-d-coverage-gap-trends-recent-changes -and-whats-ahead/; Jim VandeHei, "The Wisconsin Race That Says It All," *Politico,* October 12, 2010, https://www.politico.com/story/2010/10/the-wisconsin-race-that-says-it-all-043444.

4. Andy Barr, "The GOP's No-Compromise Pledge," *Politico,* October 28, 2010, https://www .politico.com/story/2010/10/the-gops-no-compromise-pledge-044311; Glenn Thrush and Sarah Wheaton, "Boehner and Obama: Caught in a Bad Bromance," *Politico,* September 25, 2015, https://www.politico.com/story/2015/09/obama-boehner-bromance-214094.

5. "Fussbudget," *New Yorker,* August 6, 2012, https://www.newyorker.com/magazine/2012/08 /06/fussbudget.

6. Sheryl Gay Stolberg, "Roots of Bachmann's Ambition Begin at Home," *New York Times,* June 22, 2011, https://www.nytimes.com/2011/06/22/us/politics/22bachmann.html.

7. Ernest Luning, "Bachmann: 'Slit Our Wrists, Be Blood Brothers' to Beat Health Care Reform," *Colorado Independent,* September 31, 2009, https://www.coloradoindependent.com /2009/08/31/bachmann-slit-our-wrists-be-blood-brothers-to-beat-health-care-reform/.

8. Tim Alberta, *American Carnage* (New York: HarperCollins, 2019), Kindle edition, 84.

9. Stu Woo, "Overthrow a Sign of Tea-Party Clout," *Wall Street Journal,* May 10, 2010, https:// www.wsj.com/articles/SB10001424052748704307804575234541365605122.

10. Senior Republican aides, author interview.

11. Rodney Whitlock, author interview.

12. Noam Levey, "Many in GOP Who Oppose Health Insurance Requirement Used to Favor It," *Los Angeles Times,* May 28, 2011, https://www.latimes.com/health/la-xpm-2011-may-28-la -na-gop-insurance-mandate-20110529-story.html; Michael Cooper, "Conservatives Sowed Idea of Health Care Mandate, Only to Spurn It Later," *New York Times,* February 14, 2012, https://www.nytimes.com/2012/02/15/health/policy/health-care-mandate-was-first-backed -by-conservatives.html?referringSource=articleShare; "Obama's Running Mate," *Wall Street Journal,* May 12, 2011, https://www.wsj.com/articles/SB10001424052748703864204576317413439329644.

13. Jonathan Cohn, "Romney v. Romney," *New Republic,* May 12, 2011, https://newrepublic .com/article/88357/romney-obama-massachusetts-mandate-health-reform; Karen Tumulty, "Mitt Romney Defends His Health-Care Record," *Washington Post,* May 12, 2011, https:// www.washingtonpost.com/politics/mitt-romney-defends-his-health-care-record/2011/05 /12/AFNf9U1G_story.html.

14. Ryan Lizza, "Romney's Dilemma," *New Yorker,* https://www.newyorker.com/magazine/2011 /06/06/romneys-dilemma; Timothy Noah, "The $10,000 Question," *New Republic*, December 12, 2011, https://newrepublic.com/article/98448/the-10000-question; Emily Friedman, "Romney Book Changed to Remove Line About National Health Reform," ABC News, September 23, 2011, https://abcnews.go.com/blogs/politics/2011/09/romney-book-changed-to -remove-line-about-national-health-reform.

15. Lizza, "Romney's Dilemma."

16. Shushannah Walshe, "Rick Santorum Goes After Mitt Romney on Health Care: 'He Should Not Be the Nominee,'" ABC News, February 6, 2012, https://abcnews.go.com/blogs/politics /2012/02/rick-santorum-goes-after-mitt-romney-on-health-care-he-should-not-be-the -nominee; Alexander Burns, "Santorum Blitzes on Health Care," *Politico,* January 19, 2012, https://www.politico.com/blogs/burns-haberman/2012/01/santorum-blitzes-on-health-care -111571.

17. Timothy Noah, "Rick Santorum, Individual-Mandate Fraud," *New Republic,* January 27, 2012, https://newrepublic.com/article/100133/rick-santorum-individual-mandate-fraud; Pete Leffler, "Wofford Declines to Give Info to Voter's Guide," *Morning Call,* April 7, 1994, https:// www.mcall.com/news/mc-xpm-1994-04-07-2983594-story.html.

18. Michael Shear and Trip Gabriel, "Romney Faces Pressure from Right to Put Ryan on Ticket," *New York Times,* August 9, 2012, https://www.nytimes.com/2012/08/10/us/politics

/a-conservative-bid-for-paul-ryan-to-be-mitt-romneys-running-mate.html; "Romney's Pick of Ryan as His Running Mate Energizes Conservatives, Opponents," CNN, August 12, 2012, https://www.cnn.com/2012/08/11/politics/romney-ryan/index.html.

19. Donovan Slack, "Obama Campaign Launches Medicare Attack Against Romney-Ryan," *Politico*, August 13, 2012, https://www.politico.com/blogs/politico44/2012/08/obama-campaign-launches-medicare-attack-against-romney-ryan-131911.

20. Peter Baker, "Democrats Embrace Once Pejorative 'Obamacare' Tag," *New York Times*, August 3, 2012, https://www.nytimes.com/2012/08/04/health/policy/democrats-embrace-once-pejorative-obamacare-tag.html; Dan Pfeiffer, author interview.

21. Sabrina Siddiqui and Sam Stein, "John Boehner: Obamacare Is the Law of the Land," *HuffPost*, November 8, 2012, https://www.huffpost.com/entry/john-boehner-obamacare_n_2095172.

22. Senior Republican aide, author interview.

23. Molly Ball, "The Fall of the Heritage Foundation and the Death of Republican Ideas," *Atlantic*, September 25, 2013, https://www.theatlantic.com/politics/archive/2013/09/the-fall-of-the-heritage-foundation-and-the-death-of-republican-ideas/279955/; see also Stuart Butler and Peter Germanis, "Achieving a 'Leninist' Strategy," *Cato Journal* 3, no. 2 (fall 1983), https://www.cato.org/sites/cato.org/files/serials/files/cato-journal/1983/11/cj3n2-11.pdf.

24. Stuart Butler, author interview.

25. Stuart Butler, "Don't Blame Heritage for ObamaCare Mandate," Heritage Foundation, February 6, 2012, https://www.heritage.org/health-care-reform/commentary/dont-blame-heritage-obamacare-mandate; Avik Roy, "The Tortuous History of Conservatives and the Individual Mandate," *Forbes*, February 7, 2012, https://www.forbes.com/sites/theapothecary/2012/02/07/the-tortuous-conservative-history-of-the-individual-mandate/#126bf4b455fe; Ezra Klein, "Stuart Butler Explains His Change of Heart on the Individual Mandate," *Washington Post*, February 6, 2012, https://www.washingtonpost.com/blogs/ezra-klein/post/stuart-butler-explains-his-change-of-heart-on-the-individual-mandate/2011/08/25/gIQAnEDptQ_blog.html; Timothy Noah, "The Heritage Foundation Disowns Its Baby," MSNBC, August 21, 2013, http://www.msnbc.com/msnbc/the-heritage-foundation-disowns-its-baby; Brief of Amicus Curiae, the Heritage Foundation in Support of Plaintiffs-Appellees, *State of Florida, et al. v. United States Department of Health and Human Services, et al.*, U.S. Court of Appeals for the 11th Circuit, Nos. 11–11021 and 11–11067, filed May 11, 2011, https://www.dailysignal.com/wp-content/uploads/Heritage-Foundation-Amicus-Brief-05-11-11.pdf.

26. Robert Draper, "Will Obamacare Really Go Under the Knife?," *New York Times Magazine*, February 14, 2017, https://www.nytimes.com/2017/02/14/magazine/will-obamacare-really-go-under-the-knife.html.

27. Senior Republican interview; "Letter to Speaker Boehner and Leader Cantor 'Don't Muddy the Water,'" Heritage Action for America, March 15, 2012, https://heritageaction.com/blog/letter-to-speaker-boehner-and-leader-cantor-dont-muddy-the-water.

28. Charlie Dent, author interview.

29. Liz Halloran, "Tom Coburn, GOP Budget Hawk and Obama Friend, to Leave Senate," NPR, January 17, 2014, https://www.npr.org/sections/itsallpolitics/2014/01/17/263484054/tom-coburn-gop-budget-hawk-and-obama-friend-to-leave-senate; senior Republican aide interview.

30. Jake Silverstein, "Ted Cruz's Excellent Adventure," *Texas Monthly*, October 2012, https://www.texasmonthly.com/politics/ted-cruzs-excellent-adventure/; Rick Jervis, "Ted Cruz's Come-from-Behind 2012 Win Could Influence His Presidential Bid," *USA Today*, November 19, 2015, https://www.usatoday.com/story/news/politics/elections/2015/11/19/ted-cruz-senate-race-dewhurst/75934248/.

31. In the 1991 national competition, Cruz lost to a Yale team with future Obama adviser Austan Goolsbee. Emma Roller, "Ted Cruz Couldn't Help Himself from Taking the Shots," *Slate*, August 21, 2013, https://slate.com/news-and-politics/2013/08/ted-cruz-on-the-princeton-debate-circuit.html; Jason Zengerle, "Ted Cruz: The Distinguished Wacko Bird from Texas," *GQ*, September 23, 2013, https://www.gq.com/story/ted-cruz-republican-senator-october-2013.

32. Catherine Treyz, "Lindsey Graham Jokes About Murder of Ted Cruz," CNN, February 26, 2016, https://www.cnn.com/2016/02/26/politics/lindsey-graham-ted-cruz-dinner/.

33. Ali Vitali, "Cruz to GOP: 'How Do We Win This Fight? Don't Blink!,'" MSNBC, August 20, 2013, http://www.msnbc.com/msnbc/cruz-gop-how-do-we-win-fight-dont; "Hundreds in

Dallas Join Sen. Ted Cruz to Urge Congress to Stop Affordable Care Act," *Dallas News,* August 21, 2013, https://www.dallasnews.com/news/politics/2013/08/21/hundreds-in-dallas -join-sen-ted-cruz-to-urge-congress-to-stop-affordable-care-act/; Ashley Parker and Jonathan Martin, "Amid Talk of White House Run, Texas Senator Targets Obama's Health Plan," *New York Times,* August 20, 2013, https://www.nytimes.com/2013/08/21/us/politics/fueling -talk-of-a-2016-run-texas-senator-renounces-canadian-citizenship.html.

34. Senior Republican aide and Republican strategist, author interviews; senior Republican aide interview.

Chapter 22: Shock

1. I heard this story at the time from a White House official; a senior Obama administration official confirmed it many years later.

2. "HealthCare.gov: CMS Management of the Federal Marketplace: A Case Study," Office of Inspector General, February 2016, https://oig.hhs.gov/oei/reports/oei-06-14-00350.pdf; Robert Pear, Sharon LaFraniere, and Ian Austen, "From the Start, Signs of Trouble at Health Portal," *New York Times,* October 12, 2013; Sheryl Gay Stolberg and Michael Shear, "Inside the Race to Rescue a Health Care Site, and Obama," *New York Times,* November 13, 2013.

3. Maggie Fox, "Come Back in 2 Weeks: Even the Pros Struggle with New Health Exchanges," NBC News, October 23, 2013, https://www.nbcnews.com/healthmain/come-back-2-weeks -even-pros-struggle-new-health-exchanges-8C11443270; Lena Sun, "Maryland Struggling with Technological Problems with Online Insurance Exchange," *Washington Post,* November 19, 2013; Andrea Walker and Scott Dance, "Maryland Health Insurance Exchange Stumbles out of the Gate," *Baltimore Sun,* October 1, 2013.

4. Tom Cohen, "Contractors Blame Government for Obamacare Website Woes," CNN, October 25, 2013, https://www.cnn.com/2013/10/24/politics/congress-obamacare-website/index.html.

5. Amy Goldstein and Juliet Eilperin, "HealthCare.Gov: How Political Fear Was Pitted Against Technical Needs," *Washington Post,* November 2, 2013.

6. Senior Obama administration officials, author interviews.

7. Pear, LaFraniere, and Austen, "From the Start."

8. Goldstein and Eilperin, "HealthCare.Gov"; senior Obama administration official interview.

9. Medicaid considered whether a woman was pregnant to make sure its extra protections and services were already in place the moment a baby was born. The Affordable Care Act's subsidy formula didn't consider that. A newborn actually had to be born to trigger changes in the size of the tax credits. Kate Steadman, author interview, June 25, 2020. Steadman was an insurance specialist at HHS.

10. Bethany McLean, "Accounting for Obamacare: Inside the Company That Built Healthcare .Gov," *Vanity Fair,* December 23, 2013, https://www.vanityfair.com/news/politics/2013/12 /obamacare-website-cgi.

11. Pear, LaFraniere, and Austen, "From the Start"; "Patient Protection and Affordable Care Act: Status of CMS Efforts to Establish Federally Facilitated Health Insurance Exchanges," U.S. Government Accountability Office, no. GAO-13–601 (June), https://www.gao.gov/products /GAO-13-601; "HealthCare.Gov," OIG.

12. Eric Lipton, Ian Austen, and Sharon LaFraniere, "Tension and Flaws Before Health Website Crash," *New York Times,* November 22, 2013, https://www.nytimes.com/2013/11/23/us /politics/tension-and-woes-before-health-website-crash.html?pagewanted=2; Lena H. Sun and Scott Wilson, "Health Insurance Exchange Launched Despite Signs of Serious Problems," *Washington Post,* October 21, 2013, https://www.washingtonpost.com/national/health -science/health-insurance-exchange-launched-despite-signs-of-serious-problems/2013/10 /21/161a3500-3a85-11e3-b6a9-da62c264f40e_story.html; Steadman interview; senior Democratic state official, author interview.

13. Senior insurance industry official, author interview.

14. Louise Radnofsky, Christopher Weaver, and Timothy W. Martin, "Health Law Hits Late Snags as Rollout Approaches," *Wall Street Journal,* September 29, 2013, https://www.wsj.com /articles/health-law-hits-late-snags-as-rollout-approaches-1380497103.

15. "HealthCare.Gov," OIG.

16. Steven Brill, *America's Bitter Pill: Money, Politics, Backroom Deals, and the Fight to Fix Our Broken Healthcare System* (New York: Random House, 2015).

17. Rebecca Berg, "Hillary Clinton in 2007: 'If You Have a Plan You Like, You Keep It,'" *Washington Examiner*, November 14, 2013, https://www.washingtonexaminer.com/hillary-clinton-in-2007-if-you-have-a-plan-you-like-you-keep-it.

18. Larry Levitt, author interview.

19. Maggie Mahar, "Did President Obama 'Lie' When He Said 'If You Like the Policy You Have, You Can Keep It'? Context Is Everything," *Health Beat*, February 5, 2014, https://healthbeatblog.com/2014/02/did-president-obama-lie-when-he-said-if-you-like-the-policy-you-have-you-can-keep-it-context-is-everything/.

20. Jonathan Cohn, "Insurance Denied," *Self*, August 18, 2008, https://www.self.com/story/unable-to-buy-health-insurance; Julie Rovner, "Retroactive Cancellation Now Banned," Kaiser Health News, September 23, 2010, https://khn.org/news/npr-cancellation-banned/; the California stories, reported by Lisa Girion of the *Los Angeles Times*, got widespread attention and led to several state-level laws limiting or banning the rescission practice. Lisa Girion, "Doctors Balk at Request for Data," *Los Angeles Times*, February 12, 2008, https://www.latimes.com/business/la-fi-bluecross12feb12-story.html; Lisa Girion, "Health Insurer Tied Bonuses to Dropping Sick Policyholders," *Los Angeles Times*, November 9, 2007, https://www.latimes.com/business/la-fi-insure9nov09-story.html; Lisa Girion, "Insurer Cited in Policy Rescissions," *Los Angeles Times*, July 3, 2007, https://www.latimes.com/business/la-fi-insure3jul03-story.html; Trudy Lieberman, "Impressive Coverage at the LA Times," *Columbia Journalism Review*, February 20, 2008, https://archives.cjr.org/campaign_desk/impressive_coverage_at_the_la.php.

21. Marcy Wheeler, "'Affordable' Health Care," Emptywheel, December 27, 2009, https://www.emptywheel.net/2009/12/27/affordable-health-care/; Jon Walker, "The Fight for a Public Option Is the Fight for Affordability," Shadowproof, September 25, 2009, https://shadowproof.com/2009/09/25/the-fight-for-a-public-option-is-the-fight-for-affordiblity/. Wheeler and I had an online debate about this and, in retrospect, she was more right than I realized.

22. Timothy Jost, "Implementing Health Reform: Grandfathered Plans," *Health Affairs*, June 15, 2010, https://www.healthaffairs.org/do/10.1377/hblog20100615.005412/full/.

23. Ibid.; senior Obama administration officials interviews; Brill, *America's Bitter Pill*, 154, 208–214.

24. Jonathan Weisman and Robert Pear, "Cancellation of Health Care Plans Replaces Website Problems as Prime Target," *New York Times*, October 29, 2013, https://www.nytimes.com/2013/10/30/us/politics/cancellation-of-health-care-plans-replaces-website-problems-as-prime-target.html; Mike Dorning, "Obama Administration Under Fire for Individual Health Policy Cancellations," *Insurance Journal*, October 30, 2013, https://www.insurancejournal.com/news/national/2013/10/30/309752.htm.

25. Having reported extensively on the benefit gaps and other problems with non-group insurance, I failed to appreciate how many people liked the old policies; Robert Laszewski, "The (Not So) Affordable Care Act – Get Ready for Some Startling Rate Increases," Health Care Blog, December 5, 2012, https://thehealthcareblog.com/blog/2012/12/05/the-not-so-affordable-care-act-get-ready-for-some-startling-rate-increases/; Avik Roy, "Rate Shock: In California, Obamacare to Increase Individual Health Premiums by 64–146%," *Forbes*, May 30, 2013, https://www.forbes.com/sites/theapothecary/2013/05/30/rate-shock-in-california-obamacare-to-increase-individual-insurance-premiums-by-64–146/#6e12cf4e4df4.

26. Lisa Myers and Hannah Rappleye, "White House Knew Millions Could Not Keep Plans Under Obamacare," CNBC, October 29, 2013, https://www.cnbc.com/2013/10/29/white-house-knew-millions-could-not-keep-plans-under-obamacare.html; Angie Drobnic Holan, "PolitiFact - Lie of the Year: 'If You like Your Health Care Plan, You Can Keep It,'" PolitiFact, December 12, 2013, https://www.politifact.com/article/2013/dec/12/lie-year-if-you-like-your-health-care-plan-keep-it/.

27. Jonathan Allen and Jake Sherman, "Trust Frays Between Obama, Dems," *Politico*, November 14, 2013, https://www.politico.com/story/2013/11/trust-frayed-between-obama-dems-099897; Dan Balz and Peyton M. Craighill, "Health-Care Flaws Send Obama Ratings Tumbling," *Washington Post*, November 19, 2013, https://www.washingtonpost.com/politics/obamas-ratings-tumble-after-health-care-flaws/2013/11/18/c9cdbc2c-507c-11e3-9fe0-fd2ca728e67c

_story.html; Thomas Edsall, "The Obamacare Crisis," *New York Times*, November 19, 2013, https://www.nytimes.com/2013/11/20/opinion/edsall-the-obamacare-crisis.html.

28. Andy Slavitt, author interview. See also Eric Boodman, "Andy Slavitt Can't Stop: How a Health Care Wonk Became a Rabble-Rouser," STAT, May 25, 2017, https://www.statnews.com/2017/05/25/andy-slavitt-aca-town-halls/.

29. Slavitt interview.

30. Larry Buchanan, Guilbert Gates, Haeyoun Park, and Alicia Parlapiano, "How HealthCare .Gov Was Supposed to Work and How It Didn't," *New York Times*, December 2, 2013; "What Went Wrong with HealthCare.Gov: 10 Things to Know," Becker's Health IT, 2013, https://www.beckershospitalreview.com/healthcare-information-technology/what-went-wrong-with-healthcare-gov-10-things-to-know.html.

31. Phil Schiliro, author interview.

32. Chuck Todd, "Exclusive: Obama Personally Apologizes for Americans Losing Health Coverage," November 7, 2013, http://usnews.nbcnews.com/_news/2013/11/07/21352724-exclusive-obama-personally-apologizes-for-americans-losing-health-coverage?lite=; Roberta Rampton and Susan Cornwell, "An Apologetic Obama Unveils Fix on Health Law," Reuters, November 14, 2013, https://www.reuters.com/article/us-usa-healthcare-obama-plan/an-apologetic-obama-unveils-fix-on-health-law-idUSBRE9AD10520131114.

33. Juliet Eilperin, Amy Goldstein, and Lena H. Sun, "Obama Announces Change to Address Health Insurance Cancellations," *Washington Post*, November 14, 2013, https://www.washingtonpost.com/politics/obamato-to-announce-change-to-address-health-insurance-cancellations/2013/11/14/3be49d24-4d37-11e3-9890-a1e0997fb0c0_story.html.

34. Among those questioning the Obama administration's authority was Nicholas Bagley, the University of Michigan law professor who had been among the law's most vocal defenders during *King v. Burwell*. Nicholas Bagley, "President Obama Flouted Legal Norms to Implement Obamacare. Now Trump May Go Further," *Vox*, February 1, 2017, https://www.vox.com/the-big-idea/2017/2/1/14463904/obamacare-executive-power-trump-law.

35. Chad Terhune, "Some Health Insurance Gets Pricier as Obamacare Rolls Out," *Los Angeles Times*, October 26, 2013, https://www.latimes.com/business/la-fi-health-sticker-shock-20131027-story.html#axzz2j16CeysZ.

36. "Health Insurance Marketplace: January Enrollment Report," HHS, January 13, 2014, https://aspe.hhs.gov/system/files/pdf/177611/ib_2014jan_enrollment.pdf. For the Maryland story, see Joshua Sharfstein, *The Public Health Crisis Survival Guide: Leadership and Management in Trying Times* (New York: Oxford University Press, 2018).

37. Ron Pollack, author interview.

38. Sheila Hoag, Sean Orzol, and Cara Orfield, "Evaluation of Enroll America: An Implementation Assessment and Recommendations for Future Outreach Efforts," RWJF, July 28, 2014, https://www.rwjf.org/en/library/research/2014/07/evaluation-of-enroll-america.html; Anne Filipic, "After Nearly Six Years of Unprecedented Enrollment Success, Enroll America Is Ready to Pass the Torch," *HuffPost*, March 16, 2017, https://www.huffpost.com/entry/after-nearly-six-years-of-unprecedented-enrollment_b_58c9b302e4b0537abd956d9a; Ron Pollack, Anne Filipic, and Rachel Klein, "Securing the Enrollment of Uninsured Americans in Health Coverage," *Health Affairs*, May 3, 2013, https://www.healthaffairs.org/do/10.1377/hblog20130503.030625/full/.

39. Ashley Alman, "Obama Pushes Obamacare Enrollment on 'Between Two Ferns' with Zach Galifianakis," *HuffPost*, March 11, 2014, https://www.huffpost.com/entry/obama-between-two-ferns_n_4938804; Ian Crouch, "Obama Wins on 'Between Two Ferns,'" *New Yorker*, March 12, 2014, https://www.newyorker.com/culture/culture-desk/obama-wins-on-between-two-ferns; Matt Wilstein, "The One Joke Obama WH Wanted to Cut from 'Between Two Ferns,'" *Daily Beast*, September 25, 2019, https://www.thedailybeast.com/scott-aukerman-reveals-the-one-joke-obama-white-house-wanted-to-cut-from-between-two-ferns.

40. Jeff Yang, "'Between Two Ferns' Boosts Traffic to Obamacare Website—but Will It Last," *Wall Street Journal*, March 12, 2014, https://www.wsj.com/articles/BL-SEB-80280.

41. On Charles Gaba, see Jason Millman, "This Guy Knew When Obamacare Enrollment Would Hit 5M Before Anyone Else. Now He's Predicting 6.2M," *Washington Post*, March 19, 2014, https://www.washingtonpost.com/news/wonk/wp/2014/03/19/this-guy-knew-when-obamacare

-enrollment-would-hit-5m-before-anyone-else-now-hes-predicting-6-2m/; Charles Gaba, "My Ballpark QHP Predictions for January, February and March," ACA Signups, February 7, 2014, http://acasignups.net/14/02/07/my-ballpark-qhp-predictions-january-february-and -march. I wasn't as bold, but back in November 2013, following a dismal report on the first month of HealthCare.gov enrollment, I said there was still time to get the website working and that if it were fixed, enrollment would come close to targets. I got many things wrong about the Affordable Care Act; that was something I got right.

42. Sarah Kliff, "Obamacare's Narrow Networks Are Going to Make People Furious—but They Might Control Costs," *Washington Post,* January 13, 2014, https://www.washingtonpost .com/news/wonk/wp/2014/01/13/obamacares-narrow-networks-are-going-to-make-people -furious-but-they-might-control-costs/.

43. Jonathan Cohn, "Finally, We're Getting the Real Story on Obamacare Rate Shock," *New Re-public,* June 19, 2014, https://newrepublic.com/article/118250/obamacare-rate-shock-kaiser -survey-suggests-critics-exaggerated-story.

44. Sarah Kliff, "Predicted Obamacare Disasters That Never Happened," *Vox,* July 15, 2014, https://www.vox.com/2014/7/15/5898879/seven-predicted-obamacare-disasters-that-never -happened; Paul Krugman, "Zero for Six," *New York Times,* June 26, 2014, https://krugman .blogs.nytimes.com/2014/06/26/zero-for-six/; Arit John, "Pundit Accountability: The Best and Worst Obamacare Predictions," *Atlantic,* April 1, 2014, https://www.theatlantic.com /politics/archive/2014/04/pundit-accountability-the-best-and-worst-obamacare-predictions /359969/.

45. "President Obama Speaks to the Press," YouTube video, 31:25, posted by Obama White House, April 17, 2014, https://www.youtube.com/watch?v=1BTOvPwVtpo.

Chapter 23: Sabotage

1. Evan Osnos, "The Opportunist," *New Yorker,* November 30, 2015, https://www.newyorker .com/magazine/2015/11/30/the-opportunist.

2. Perry Bacon Jr., "In Florida House, Rubio Led a Conservative Revolt Against Fellow Repub-licans," NBC News, April 13, 2015, https://www.nbcnews.com/meet-the-press/florida-house -rubio-lead-conservative-revolt-against-fellow-republicans-n338736; Aaron Sharockman, "PolitiFact - Charlie Crist Says He Didn't Endorse Stimulus Bill," PolitiFact, November 5, 2009, https://www.politifact.com/factchecks/2009/nov/05/charlie-crist/charlie-crist-says-he -didnt-endorse-stimulus-bill/; Carol E. Lee, "When a Hug Becomes a Kiss of Death," *Politico,* November 17, 2009, https://www.politico.com/story/2009/11/when-a-hug-becomes-a-kiss -of-death-029519.

3. Mark Leibovich, "The First Senator from the Tea Party?," *New York Times Magazine,* January 6, 2010.

4. Marco Rubio, "Marco Rubio: No Bailouts for ObamaCare," *Wall Street Journal,* November 19, 2013, https://www.wsj.com/articles/no-bailouts-for-obamacare8217s-bumbling-1384815095.

5. Yuval Levin, "Rubio and the Risk Corridors," *National Review,* December 17, 2015, https:// www.nationalreview.com/corner/did-rubio-kill-obamacares-risk-corridors-yuval-levin/.

6. Senior insurance industry official, author interview.

7. Mandy Cohen and Andy Slavitt, author interviews; Sabrina Corlette, Sean Miskell, Julia Le-rche, and Justin Giovannelli, "Why Are Many CO-OPs Failing? How New Nonprofit Health Plans Have Responded to Market Competition," Commonwealth Fund, December 2015, https://www.commonwealthfund.org/publications/fund-reports/2015/dec/why-are-many -co-ops-failing-how-new-nonprofit-health-plans-have; Caitlin Owens, "Even If You Like Your Obamacare Co-Op Insurance, You Probably Can't Keep It," *Atlantic,* November 15, 2015, https://www.theatlantic.com/politics/archive/2015/11/even-if-you-like-your-obamacare-co -op-insurance-you-probably-cant-keep-it/452244/.

8. Yevgeniy Feyman, "Obamacare's Risk Corridors Won't Be a 'Bailout' of Insurers," *Forbes,* January 22, 2014, https://www.forbes.com/sites/theapothecary/2014/01/22/obamacares -risk-corridors-wont-be-a-bailout-of-insurers/#3ada6e8d64ca; Marc Thiessen, "How Marco Rubio Is Quietly Killing Obamacare," *Washington Post,* December 14, 2015, https://www .washingtonpost.com/opinions/how-marco-rubio-is-quietly-killing-obamacare/2015/12/14 /c706849a-a275-11e5-b53d-972e2751f433_story.html.

9. Kate Zernike, "Convention Is Trying to Harness Tea Party Spirit," *New York Times,* February 5, 2010, https://www.nytimes.com/2010/02/06/us/politics/06teaparty.html; Judson Phillips, "The Tea Party Ten Years Later," *Tennessee Star,* February 24, 2019, https://tennesseestar.com/2019/02/24/judson-phillips-commentary-the-tea-party-ten-years-later/; Nick Carey, "Tea Partiers Yearn for a 'Truly Red' Tennessee," Reuters, May 18, 2012, https://www.reuters.com/article/us-usa-politics-tennessee/tea-partiers-yearn-for-a-truly-red-tennessee-idUSBRE84H0UD20120518.

10. Andy Sher, "Tea Party Pressures Tennessee Gov. Bill Haslam," *Chattanooga Times Free Press,* December 6, 2012, https://www.timesfreepress.com/news/local/story/2012/dec/06/tea-party-pressures-tennessee-governor/94436/; "Tennessee Eagle Forum Newsletter," *Tennessee Eagle Forum,* December 6, 2012, https://www.votervoice.net/iframes/EAGLE/newsletters/12200.

11. Jeffrey Young, "Tennessee's GOP Governor Is Latest to Reject Obamacare Health Insurance Exchange," *HuffPost,* December 10, 2012, https://www.huffpost.com/entry/bill-haslam-obamacare_n_2272290?guccounter=1; Stephanie Mencimer, "Tea Party Trying to Kill Obamacare . . . by Friday," *Mother Jones,* December 11, 2012, https://www.motherjones.com/politics/2012/12/tea-partys-obamacare-hail-mary/. For a broader view of this issue, see David K. Jones, *Exchange Politics: Oppposing Obamacare in Battleground States* (New York: Oxford University Press, 2017).

12. Jonathan Cohn, *Sick* (New York: HarperCollins, 2009), Kindle edition, 115–140; Natalie Allison, " 'I did what had to be done': How Phil Bredesen's 'Painful' TennCare Cuts Play into US Senate Race," *Tennessean,* September 17, 2018, https://www.tennessean.com/story/news/politics/tn-elections/2018/09/18/phil-bredesen-tenncare-tennessee-us-senate-marsha-blackburn/1217149002/.

13. Cass Sisk and Tom Wilemon, "Tenn. Gov Won't Expand Medicaid to Cover Uninsured," *USA Today,* March 27, 2013, https://www.usatoday.com/story/news/nation/2013/03/27/tennessee-medicaid-health-care/2024599/#:~:text=%E2%80%94%20Tennessee%20will%20not%20expand%20its; Abby Goodnough, "Governor of Tennessee Joins Peers Refusing Medicaid Plan," *New York Times,* March 27, 2013, https://www.nytimes.com/2013/03/28/health/tennessee-governor-balks-at-medicaid-expansion.html; Richard Locker, "Tennessee's GOP Governor Unveils Alternative to Medicaid Expansion," Governing, December 16, 2014, https://www.governing.com/topics/health-human-services/tns-tennessee-medicaid-expansion.html; Rachana Pradhan, "Tennessee Tees Up Medicaid Expansion Battle," *Politico,* December 15, 2014, https://www.politico.com/story/2014/12/tennessee-medicaid-expansion-113577.

14. Rick Lyman, "Tennessee Governor Hesitates on Medicaid Expansion, Frustrating Many," *New York Times,* November 16, 2013, https://www.nytimes.com/2013/11/17/us/politics/tennessee-governor-hesitates-on-medicaid-expansion-frustrating-many.html; Jason Millman, "Three Republican Governors Have Now Endorsed the Medicaid Expansion Since the Midterms," *Washington Post,* December 15, 2014, https://www.washingtonpost.com/news/wonk/wp/2014/12/15/three-republican-governors-have-now-endorsed-the-medicaid-expansion-since-the-midterms/.

15. Emily Kubis, "Reactions to Medicaid Expansion Plan," *Nashville Post,* December 15, 2014, https://www.nashvillepost.com/home/article/20480618/reactions-to-medicaid-expansion-plan.

16. "63% of Tennesseans Support Medicaid Expansion," Tennessee Justice Center, https://www.tnjustice.org/tennesseans-support-medicaid-expansion-63-percent/; Andrea Zelinski and Emily Kubis, "Haslam to Call Special Session on Medicaid Expansion," *Nashville Post,* December 15, 2014, https://www.nashvillepost.com/home/article/20480644/haslam-to-call-special-session-on-medicaid-expansion; Kubis, "Reactions to Medicaid Expansion Plan"; Jeff Woods, "Obama Haters Waste No Time Opposing Haslam's Medicaid Plan," *Nashville Scene,* December 15, 2014, https://www.nashvillescene.com/news/pith-in-the-wind/article/13057296/obama-haters-waste-no-time-opposing-haslams-medicaid-plan.

17. "In Rebuke of Tennessee Governor, Koch Group Shows Its Power," NBC News, February 6, 2015, https://www.nbcnews.com/politics/elections/rebuke-tennessee-governor-koch-group-shows-its-power-n301031; Andy Sher, "Americans for Prosperity Aims for Tennessee Influence," *Tennessean,* May 5, 2015, https://www.tennessean.com/story/news/politics/2015/05/05/americans-prosperity-aims-tennessee-influence/26947607/; WBIR Staff, "Koch Brothers Group Relaunches Ads to Defeat Insure Tennessee," WBIR, March 31, 2015, https://www

.wbir.com/article/news/politics/koch-brothers-group-relaunches-ads-to-defeat-insure
-tennessee/311597540; Andy Sher, "Tennessee Governor's Medicaid Expansion Plan Fails
Again," Governing, April 1, 2015, https://www.governing.com/topics/health-human-services
/tns-tennessee-medicaid-expansion-fails-again.html.

18. David Plazas, "Haslam Counters Critics, Makes Case for Insure Tennessee," Tennessean,
February 2, 2015, https://www.tennessean.com/story/opinion/2015/02/02/haslam-counters
-critics-makes-case-insure-tn/22774731/.

19. "Tennessee Legislature Rejects Medicaid Expansion," Modern Healthcare, February 4,
2015, https://www.modernhealthcare.com/article/20150204/NEWS/302049940/tennessee
-legislature-rejects-medicaid-expansion; Steve Benen, "Paranoia Derails Medicaid Expansion in Tennessee," MSNBC, February 5, 2015, http://www.msnbc.com/rachel-maddow
-show/paranoia-derails-medicaid-expansion-tennessee; Eliot Fishman, author interview.

20. Rachana Pradhan, "The Wrong State to Have an Accident," Politico, July 13, 2013, https://
www.politico.com/agenda/story/2016/07/obamacare-equal-benefits-000163/.

21. Susan L. Hayes, Douglas McCarthy, David C. Radley, and Sara R. Collins, "Health Care Coverage and Access Rates in Kentucky Reflect the ACA's Successes," Commonwealth Fund,
March 17, 2017, https://www.commonwealthfund.org/blog/2017/health-care-coverage-and
-access-rates-kentucky-reflect-acas-successes.

22. "The Coverage Gap: Uninsured Poor Adults in States That Do Not Expand Medicaid – An
Update – Issue Brief – 8659–03," Kaiser Family Foundation, October 23, 2015, https://www
.kff.org/report-section/the-coverage-gap-uninsured-poor-adults-in-states-that-do-not
-expand-medicaid-an-update-issue-brief_/.

23. The professor was Brad Wright, a health policy scholar who at the time was on the faculty at
the University of Iowa. Jonathan Cohn, "An Iowa Teenager Didn't Wreck His State's Health
Care Market. Here's Who Did," HuffPost, October 29, 2017, https://www.huffpost.com/entry
/iowa-teenager-obamacare-scapegoat_n_59f4715de4b077d8dfc9dd70.

24. Data provided by the Kaiser Family Foundation, based on the Current Population Survey
for 2016.

25. Cohn, "An Iowa Teenager."

26. Clay Masters, "Health Insurance Startup Collapses In Iowa," NPR, January 14, 2015, https://
www.npr.org/sections/health-shots/2015/01/14/376792564/health-insurance-startup
-collapses-in-iowa; Cohn, "An Iowa Teenager"; Louise Norris, "Iowa Health Insurance
Marketplace: History and News of the State's Exchange: Obamacare Enrollment," Health
Insurance.Org, July 19, 2020, https://www.healthinsurance.org/iowa-state-health-insurance
-exchange/; Charles Gaba, "Iowa: *Approved* 2017 Avg. Rate Hikes: 30.1% (+ Some Rare
transitional Plan Data)," ACA Signups, August 30, 2016, http://acasignups.net/16/08/30
/iowa-approved-2017-avg-rate-hikes-301-some-rare-transitional-plan-data.

27. Joe Gardyasz, "CoOportunity Health Approved to Operate in Iowa," Business Record, March
28, 2013, https://businessrecord.com/Content/Finance---Insurance/Finance---Insurance
/Article/CoOportunity-Health-approved-to-operate-in-Iowa/171/833/57299; Abby Goodnough, "Health Care Success for Midwest Co-Op Proves Its Undoing," New York Times, February 16, 2015, https://www.nytimes.com/2015/02/17/us/success-proves-undoing-of-health
-insurance-co-op.html.

28. Michael Sparer and Lawrence D. Brown, "Why Did the ACA Co-Op Program Fail? Lessons
for the Health Reform Debate," Journal of Health Politics, Policy and Law 45, no. 5 (2020):
801–816, https://doi.org/10.1215/03616878-8543274; Clay Masters, "How a Health Insurance Co-Op Collapsed in Iowa," Governing, January 14, 2015, https://www.governing.com
/topics/health-human-services/how-a-health-insurance-startup-collapsed-in-iowa.html;
Trudy Lieberman, "Why Did CoOportunity Fail?," Columbia Journalism Review, January 19,
2015, https://archives.cjr.org/united_states_project/why_did_cooportunity_fail.php; Tony
Leys, "CoOportunity Health to Be Liquidated," Des Moines Register, January 23, 2015, https://
www.desmoinesregister.com/story/news/health/2015/01/23/iowa-liquidating-cooportunity
-health/22223393/; Timothy Jost, "Risk Corridor Payments, UnitedHealth, Cooperatives,
and the Marketplaces," Health Affairs, November 20, 2015, https://www.healthaffairs.org/do
/10.1377/hblog20151120.051894/full/; Steve Jordon, "CoOportunity Health Started in 2013
with Close to $150M in Federal Loans," Omaha.com, December 28, 2014, https://omaha

.com/livewellnebraska/cooportunity-health-started-in-2013-with-close-to-150m-in-federal-loans/article_2452180b-6854-5da8-a835-9d9430c7a5bb.html.

29. Tony Leys, "Wellmark Plans 38% to 43% Increases for Some Customers," *Des Moines Register,* May 12, 2016, https://www.desmoinesregister.com/story/news/health/2016/05/12/wellmark-plans-38-to-43-increases-some-customers/84277758/.

30. I was able to track down the family, after several weeks of searching, for an article that appeared in *HuffPost.* Cohn, "An Iowa Teenager."

31. Noam Levey, "So You Think Obamacare Is a Disaster? Here's How California Is Proving You Wrong," *Los Angeles Times,* October 7, 2016; Jonathan Cohn, "Trump Says Obamacare Is 'Imploding.' That's News to California," *HuffPost,* June 10, 2017, https://www.huffpost.com/entry/covered-california-obamacare_n_5936cf84e4b013c4816b639f; "Governor Brown Signs Historic Medi-Cal Expansion with the State Budget," Health Access, June 28, 2013, https://health-access.org/2013/06/governor-brown-signs-historic-medi-cal-expansion-with-the-state-budget/.

32. Xenia Shih Bion, "Researchers: Medicaid Expansion Equals Better Coverage, Better Outcomes," California Health Care Foundation, June 14, 2019, https://www.chcf.org/blog/researchers-medicaid-expansion-equals-better-coverage-better-outcomes/; Heidi Allen, Erica Eliason, Naomi Zewde, and Tal Gross, "Can Medicaid Expansion Prevent Housing Evictions?," *Health Affairs* 38, no.9 (2019): 1451–1457, https://doi.org/10.1377/hlthaff.2018.05071; Ezra Golberstein, Gilbert Gonzales, and Benjamin Sommers, "California's Early ACA Expansion Increased Coverage and Reduced Out-of-Pocket Spending for the State's Low-Income Population," *Health Affairs* 34 (10): 1688–1694, https://doi.org/10.1377/hlthaff.2015.0290.

33. Jonathan Cohn, "Congress Left Health Care for Millions of Poor People in the Lurch," *HuffPost,* February 4, 2018, https://www.huffpost.com/entry/community-health-center-fund-money_n_5a75174fe4b0905433b44227; Connie Lewis, Pamela Riley, and Melinda K. Abrams, "Care for Millions at Risk as Community Health Centers Go Over Funding Cliff," Commonwealth Fund, December 21, 2017, https://www.commonwealthfund.org/blog/2017/care-millions-risk-community-health-centers-lose-billions-funding.

34. John Bertko, Andrew Feher, and Jim Watkins, "Amid ACA Uncertainty, Covered California's Risk Profile Remains Stable," *Health Affairs,* May 15, 2017, https://www.healthaffairs.org/do/10.1377/hblog20170515.060064/full/.

35. Cohn, "Trump Says Obamacare Is 'Imploding.'"

36. Erin Taylor, Andrea Lopez, Ashley Muchow, Parisa Roshan, and Christine Eibner, *Consumer Decisionmaking in the Health Care Marketplace* (Santa Monica, CA: RAND, 2016), https://www.rand.org/content/dam/rand/pubs/research_reports/RR1500/RR1567/RAND_RR1567.pdf; Yaniv Hanoch, Thomas Rice, Janet Cummings, and Stacey Wood, "How Much Choice Is Too Much? The Case of the Medicare Prescription Drug Benefit," *Health Services Research* 44, no. 4 (2009): 1157–1168, https://doi.org/10.1111/j.1475-6773.2009.00981.x; Jason Abaluck and Jonathan Gruber, "Heterogeneity in Choice Inconsistencies Among the Elderly: Evidence from Prescription Drug Plan Choice," *American Economic Review* 101, no. 3 (2011): 377–381, https://doi.org/10.1257/aer.101.3.377.

37. Cohn, "Trump Says Obamacare Is 'Imploding.'"

Chapter 24: Make Health Care Great Again

1. Rebecca Kaplan, "Sen. Rand Paul Sounds Ebola Alarm," CBS News, October 1, 2014, https://www.cbsnews.com/news/sen-rand-paul-sounds-ebola-alarm/; Erik Wemple, "MSNBC's Chris Hayes Highlights Fox News's Extreme Coverage of Ebola," *Washington Post,* November 12, 2014, https://www.washingtonpost.com/blogs/erik-wemple/wp/2014/11/12/msnbcs-chris-hayes-highlights-fox-newss-extreme-coverage-of-ebola/; Donald Trump, Twitter post, October 23, 2014, 10:24 p.m., https://twitter.com/realdonaldtrump/status/525472979443273728?lang=en.

2. One tracking service found that Ebola was mentioned four thousand times on cable news in the last week before the election. Eric Boehlert, "When the Press Buried Obama for Ebola—and Two Americans Died," Press Run, July 30, 2020, https://pressrun.media/p/when-the-press-buried-obama-for-ebola; Jeremy Peters, "Cry of G.O.P. in Campaign: All Is Dismal," *New York Times,* October 9, 2014. Although it's impossible to know exactly what role the Ebola crisis

played in the midterms, surveys and subsequent academic studies suggested it helped Republican candidates. Alec Beall, Marlise K. Hofer, and Mark Schaller, "Infections and Elections," *Psychological Science* 27, no. 5 (2016): 595–605, https://doi.org/10.1177/0956797616628861; Tom Jacobs, "Ebola Fears Helped the GOP in 2014 Election," *Pacific Standard*, March 15, 2016, https://psmag.com/news/ebola-fears-helped-gop-in-2014-election; Steven Shepard, "Poll: Dems in Danger over Ebola," *Politico*, October 20, 2014, https://www.politico.com/story/2014/10/politico-poll-ebola-democrats-112017; Philip Rucker and Robert Costa, "Battle for the Senate: How the GOP Did It," *Washington Post*, November 5, 2014; Molly Ball, "The Republican Wave Sweeps the Midterm Elections," *Atlantic*, November 5, 2014, https://www.theatlantic.com/politics/archive/2014/11/republicans-sweep-the-midterm-elections/382394/.

3. Lisa Diehl, "W.V. in Top Tier of Medicaid Expansion," *Daily Yonder*, August 12, 2014, https://dailyyonder.com/wv-top-tier-medicaid-expansion/2014/08/12/.

4. Trip Gabriel, "West Virginia Democrats Face an Uneasy Time," *New York Times*, December 28, 2013; Greg Sargent, "A Good Question for Republicans About the Affordable Care Act," *Washington Post*, January 21, 2014, https://www.washingtonpost.com/blogs/plum-line/wp/2014/01/21/a-good-question-for-republicans-about-the-affordable-care-act/.

5. David Nather, "Ted Cruz out on a Limb on Obamacare Repeal," *Politico*, November 11, 2014, https://www.politico.com/story/2014/11/ted-cruz-obamacare-repeal-112791; "Cruz: Republicans Won Because US Wants Obamacare Repeal, No Amnesty," *Daily Signal*, November 5, 2014, https://www.dailysignal.com/2014/11/05/cruz-republicans-won-us-wants-obamacare-repeal-amnesty/.

6. Brendan Buck, author interview.

7. Jay Newton-Small, "Here's How Eric Cantor Lost," *Time*, June 10, 2014, https://time.com/2854761/eric-cantor-dave-brat-virginia/; Philip Bump, "David Brat Just Beat Eric Cantor. Who Is He?," *Washington Post*, June 10, 2014, https://www.washingtonpost.com/news/the-fix/wp/2014/06/10/david-brat-just-beat-eric-cantor-who-is-he/; Reid Epstein, "David Brat Pulls Off Cantor Upset Despite Raising Just $231,000," *Wall Street Journal*, June 11, 2014, https://www.wsj.com/articles/david-brat-beats-eric-cantor-despite-raising-just-231-000-1402455265.

8. Ryan Lizza, "The War Inside the Republican Party," *New Yorker*, December 14, 2015; Lauren French and Jake Sherman, "House Conservative Seeks Boehner's Ouster," *Politico*, July 28, 2015, https://www.politico.com/story/2015/07/house-conservative-john-boehner-ouster-120742.

9. Timothy Jost, "Senate Approves Reconciliation Bill Repealing Large Portions of ACA (Updated)," *Health Affairs*, December 4, 2015, https://www.healthaffairs.org/do/10.1377/hblog20151204.052111/full/.

10. Jennifer Haberkorn, "The Real Reason for the Obamacare Repeal," *Politico*, December 3, 2015, https://www.politico.com/story/2015/12/obamacare-repeal-real-reason-216409; "Budgetary and Economic Effects of Repealing the Affordable Care Act," CBO, 2015, https://www.cbo.gov/sites/default/files/114th-congress-2015-2016/reports/50252-effectsofacarepeal.pdf; Office of the Press Secretary, "Veto Message from the President—H.R. 3762," Obama White House, January 8, 2016, https://obamawhitehouse.archives.gov/the-press-office/2016/01/08/veto-message-president-hr-3762.

11. Jenna Levy, "In U.S., Uninsured Rate Dips to 11.9% in First Quarter," Gallup, April 13, 2015, https://news.gallup.com/poll/182348/uninsured-rate-dips-first-quarter.aspx; Samantha Artiga and Robin Rudowitz, "How Have State Medicaid Expansion Decisions Affected the Experiences of Low-Income Adults? Perspectives from Ohio, Arkansas, and Missouri," Kaiser Family Foundation, June 17, 2015, https://www.kff.org/medicaid/issue-brief/how-have-state-medicaid-expansion-decisions-affected-the-experiences-of-low-income-adults-perspectives-from-ohio-arkansas-and-missouri/.

12. Jeffrey Young, "Just in Time!," Wakelet, https://wakelet.com/wake/34004f5e-b297-4143-9ccd-9f9c97745fe0.

13. Melissa Nann Burke, "Trump's Pick for Health Chief Is a Lansing Native," *Detroit News*, November 29, 2016, https://www.detroitnews.com/story/news/local/michigan/2016/11/29/tom-price/94602446/.

14. Tom Price, author interview.

15. Ibid.; Greg Bluestein and Tamar Hallerman, "Tom Price: The Georgia Lawmaker Who Will

Lead Trump's Health Policy," *Atlanta Journal-Constitution,* January 12, 2017, https://www.ajc
.com/news/state--regional-govt--politics/tom-price-the-georgia-lawmaker-who-will-lead
-trump-health-policy/zuBYBN5nw4UmIehW4MnQ9I/; Heather Mongillo, "Rep. Tom Price
Talks Health Care, Jobs," *Eagle,* October 11, 2011, https://www.theeagleonline.com/article
/2011/10/rep-tom-price-talks-health-care-jobs; Áine Cain, "Trump's HHS Secretary Tom
Price Has Resigned—See How He Went from Surgeon to Capitol Hill," *Business Insider,* September 29, 2017, https://www.businessinsider.com/tom-price-secretary-health-and-human
-services-career-2017-9; Abby Goodnough, "Trump Health Secretary Pick's Longtime Foes:
Big Government and Insurance Companies," *New York Times,* January 16, 2017, https://www
.nytimes.com/2017/01/16/health/tom-price-health-secretary.html?mcubz=1.

16. Theories for why included the nature of their practices (generalists having more holistic
views of their patients' lives, specialists interacting with them more episodically), their inter-
actions with government (generalists seeing it as a source of coverage, specialists seeing it as
a source of interference), and financial situation (generalists frequently making less money
to be taken as taxes, specialists frequently having more medical debt to pay off). Jonathan
Cohn, "Rand Paul's Political Views Make Perfect Sense When You Look at His Medical
Background," *HuffPost,* April 8, 2015, https://www.huffpost.com/entry/rand-paul-doctor
_n_7027514; Greg Dworkin, "A Look at Doctors' Political Leanings by Specialty," Daily
Kos, February 22, 2015, https://www.dailykos.com/stories/2015/02/22/1365669/-A-look-at
-doctors-political-leanings-by-specialty; JAMA Network Journals, "Study Examines Political Contributions Made by Physicians," ScienceDaily, June 2, 2014, https://www.sciencedaily
.com/releases/2014/06/140602162652.htm.

17. Senior Republican aide, author interview.

18. Brian Blase and Dean Rosen, author interviews.

19. Price interview.

20. Rodney Whitlock, author interview.

21. Blase and Buck interviews.

22. "Donald Trump @ CPAC 2011," YouTube video, 13:59, posted by Gary Franchi, February 14,
2011, https://www.youtube.com/watch?v=PlT9fAkj0XU; Igor Bobic and Sam Stein, "How
CPAC Helped Launch Donald Trump's Political Career," *HuffPost,* February 22, 2017, https://
www.huffpost.com/entry/donald-trump-cpac_n_58adc0f4e4b03d80af7141cf; Democracy
in Action, "Feb. 10, 2011 Donald Trump at CPAC," P2012, February 2011, http://www.p2012
.org/photos11/cpac11/trump021011spt.html; Donald Trump, Twitter post, November 19,
2013, 4:38 p.m., https://twitter.com/realdonaldtrump/status/402913699242856448.

23. Donald Trump, Twitter post, February 28, 2012, 2:08 p.m., https://twitter.com/real
donaldtrump/status/174571702091644928; Donald Trump, Twitter post, November 28,
2011, 9:13 a.m., https://twitter.com/realdonaldtrump/status/141157735420006400; Donald
Trump, Twitter post, April 23, 2014, 3:43 p.m., https://twitter.com/realdonaldtrump/status
/459055101370712064.

24. Sarah Kliff, "Obamacare's Premiums Are Spiking. Does That Mean the Law Is Failing?," *Vox,*
October 26, 2016, https://www.vox.com/2016/10/26/13416428/obamacare-premiums-failing.

25. "Transcript: Donald Trump Announces Plans to Form Presidential Exploratory Committee," CNN.com, October 8, 1999, https://www.cnn.com/ALLPOLITICS/stories/1999/10/08
/trump.transcript/.

26. Dave Shiflett, *The America We Deserve* (New York: St. Martin's, 2000), Kindle edition, 216, 229.

27. Dave Shiflett, author interview; Aaron Blake, "Trump's Forbidden Love: Single-Payer Health
Care," *Washington Post,* May 5, 2017, https://www.washingtonpost.com/news/the-fix/wp
/2017/05/05/trumps-forbidden-love-singe-payer-health-care/.

28. Robert Pear and Maggie Haberman, "Donald Trump's Health Care Ideas Bewilder Republican Experts," *New York Times,* April 8, 2016, https://www.nytimes.com/2016/04/09/us
/politics/donald-trump-health-care.html; Dan Diamond, "Donald Trump Hates Obamacare
- So I Asked Him How He'd Replace It," *Forbes,* July 31, 2015, https://www.forbes.com
/sites/dandiamond/2015/07/31/donald-trump-hates-obamacare-so-i-asked-him-how-hed
-replace-it/#119523604e98.

29. Christine Eibner, Sarah Nowak, and Jodi Liu, "Hillary Clinton's Health Care Reform Proposals:

Anticipated Effects on Insurance Coverage, Out-of-Pocket Costs, and the Federal Deficit," Commonwealth Fund, September 23, 2016, https://www.commonwealthfund.org/publications/issue-briefs/2016/sep/hillary-clintons-health-care-reform-proposals-anticipated.

30. Jason Furman and Matt Fiedler, "The Economic Record of the Obama Administration: Reforming the Health Care System," White House Blog, the Obama White House Online Archive, December 13, 2016, https://obamawhitehouse.archives.gov/blog/2016/12/13/economic-record-obama-administration-reforming-health-care-system; Jonathan Cohn, "Bernie Sanders Releases Health Plan and It's Even More Ambitious Than You Thought," *HuffPost*, January 17, 2016, https://www.huffpost.com/entry/bernie-sanders-health-plan_n_569c3ddde4b0b4eb759ecf51.

31. Jonathan Cohn and Jeffrey Young, "Aetna CEO Threatened Obamacare Pullout If Feds Opposed Humana Merger," *HuffPost*, August 18, 2016, https://www.huffpost.com/entry/aetna-obamacare-pullout-humana-merger_n_57b3d747e4b04ff883996a13.

Chapter 25: The Boy Scout

1. Jay Newton-Small, "Speaker Paul Ryan Condemns Donald Trump's Ban on Muslims," *Time*, December 8, 2015, https://time.com/4140558/paul-ryan-donald-trump-muslims/; Eric Bradner, "Ryan: 'I'm Just Not Ready' to Back Trump," CNN, May 6, 2015, https://www.cnn.com/2016/05/05/politics/paul-ryan-donald-trump-gop-nominee/.

2. Paul Ryan, "Paul Ryan: Donald Trump Can Help Make Reality of Bold House Policy Agenda," *Janesville Gazette*, June 1, 2016, https://www.gazettextra.com/archives/paul-ryan-donald-trump-can-help-make-reality-of-bold-house-policy-agenda/article_293b0946-3341-53fd-8d16-f4ca2cf13531.html; Emmarie Huetteman and Maggie Haberman, "Speaker Paul Ryan, After an Awkward Courtship, Endorses Donald Trump," *New York Times*, June 2, 2016; Donovan Slack, "Paul Ryan Rips Trump Comments as 'Textbook Definition of Racist,'" *USA Today*, June 7, 2016, https://www.usatoday.com/story/news/politics/onpolitics/2016/06/07/paul-ryan-rips-trump-comments-textbook-definition-racist/85548042/; Emmarie Huetteman, "The Rocky Relationship of Donald Trump and Paul Ryan, a History," *New York Times*, https://www.nytimes.com/2016/08/04/us/politics/paul-ryan-donald-trump.html; Jake Sherman and Anna Palmer, *The Hill to Die On: The Battle for Congress and the Future of Trump's America* (New York: Broadway Books, 2019), 23.

3. Sherman and Palmer, *The Hill to Die On*, 30; Mark Leibovich, "This Is the Way Paul Ryan's Speakership Ends," *New York Times Magazine*, August 7, 2018; Jennifer Steinhauer and Jonathan Weisman, "Fast Rise Built with Discipline," *New York Times*, August 29, 2012; Tim Alberta, "The Tragedy of Paul Ryan," *Politico*, April 12, 2018, https://www.politico.com/magazine/story/2018/04/12/how-donald-trump-upended-paul-ryans-plans-217989; Tim Alberta, "Inside Trump's Feud with Paul Ryan," *Politico*, July 16, 2019, https://www.politico.com/magazine/story/2019/07/16/donald-trump-paul-ryan-feud-227360.

4. Michelle Cottle, "Can Paul Ryan Push Republicans to Prioritize Poverty?," *Atlantic*, January 14, 2016, https://www.theatlantic.com/politics/archive/2016/01/can-paul-ryan-move-his-party-to-prioritize-poverty/424101/.

5. Elspeth Reeve, "Audio Surfaces of Paul Ryan's Effusive Love of Ayn Rand," *Atlantic*, April 30, 2012, https://www.theatlantic.com/politics/archive/2012/04/audio-surfaces-paul-ryans-effusive-love-ayn-rand/328754/.

6. Robert Greenstein, "Greenstein on the Ryan Budget," Center on Budget and Policy Priorities, March 12, 2013, https://www.cbpp.org/blog/greenstein-on-the-ryan-budget-0.

7. Paul Ryan, *The Way Forward* (New York: Grand Central Publishing, 2014), Kindle edition, 142. Two of those references were in passages where he criticized the Affordable Care Act's expansion of Medicaid because, he said, "there was little difference between being on Medicaid and being uninsured" (Ryan, *The Way Forward*, 178). Although that was a popular argument in conservative circles at the time, the best available research suggested the very opposite that Medicaid had led to improvements in both finances and health. See Madeline Guth, Rachel Garfield, and Robin Rudowitz, "The Effects of Medicaid Expansion Under the ACA: Updated Findings from a Literature Review - Report," Kaiser Family Foundation, March 17, 2020, https://www.kff.org/report-section/the-effects-of-medicaid-expansion-under-the-aca-updated-findings-from-a-literature-review-report/.

8. Jonathan Chait, "The Legendary Paul Ryan," *New York,* April 27, 2012; Derek Thompson, "Paul Ryan's Sad Legacy," *Atlantic,* April 11, 2018, https://www.theatlantic.com/politics /archive/2018/04/paul-ryans-sad-legacy/557774/.

9. Senior Republican aide, author interview; "President-Elect Trump Viewing Inauguration Site," C-SPAN video, 2:54, November 10, 2016, https://www.c-span.org/video/?418429-101 /president-elect-trump-viewing-inauguration-site.

10. Senior Republican aides, author interviews. The tax cut was so important to Republicans and their supporters that some suggested taking up that legislation first, before health care. GOP leaders countered that repeal legislation would reduce CBO projections of future government revenue, making the budget impact of tax cuts look smaller—although the logic of that argument didn't make sense even to many budget experts. Kevin Drum, "Why Does Obamacare Repeal Have to Come Before Tax Cuts?," *Mother Jones,* April 13, 2017, https:// www.motherjones.com/kevin-drum/2017/04/why-does-obamacare-repeal-have-come-tax -cuts/; Howard Gleckman, "What Delaying Affordable Care Act Repeal Means for Tax Reform," Tax Policy Center, January 11, 2017, https://www.taxpolicycenter.org/taxvox/what -delaying-affordable-care-act-repeal-means-tax-reform.

11. Louise Radnofsky and Kristina Peterson, "Health-Law Backers Target Key Republican Lawmakers," *Wall Street Journal,* December 23, 2016; Nancy LeTourneau, "Chaos over Obamacare 'Repeal and Delay,'" *Washington Monthly,* December 6, 2016, https:// washingtonmonthly.com/2016/12/06/quick-takes-chaos-over-obamacare-repeal-and-delay/; Tierney Sneed, "Key GOP Senator: The Sooner We Come Up with ACA Replacement the Better," Talking Points Memo, December 6, 2016, https://talkingpointsmemo.com/dc/lamar -alexander-obamacare-sooner-the-better.

12. Joseph Antos and James Capretta, "The Problems with 'Repeal and Delay,'" *Health Affairs,* January 3, 2017, https://www.healthaffairs.org/do/10.1377/hblog20170103.058206/full/.

13. Craig Gilbert, "Paul Ryan: Obamacare Phaseout Will Leave 'No One Worse Off,'" *USA Today,* December 5, 2016, https://www.usatoday.com/story/news/politics/2016/12/05/paul-ryan -obamacare-phaseout-leave-no-one-worse-off/95002488/.

14. Tom Price, author interview; he said this was true throughout his time in the Trump administration.

15. M. J. Lee and Phil Mattingly, "Republicans Increasingly Worried About Obamacare Plan," CNN, January 10, 2017, https://www.cnn.com/2017/01/10/politics/republicans-unhappy -obamacare-strategy/index.html?sr=twpol011017republicans-unhappy-obamacare -strategy1137AMVODtopLink&linkId=33200438; Aaron Blake, "The GOP Has Officially Hit the 'Buyer's Remorse' Stage on Obamacare Repeal," *Washington Post,* January 10, 2017, https://www.washingtonpost.com/news/the-fix/wp/2017/01/06/the-gop-is-getting-skittish -on-repealing-obamacare-right-away-which-is-probably-smart/; Rand Paul, Twitter post, January 6, 2017, 9:25 p.m., https://twitter.com/RandPaul/status/817557831683608576.

16. Maggie Haberman and Robert Pear, "Trump Tells Congress to Repeal and Replace Health Care Law 'Very Quickly,'" *New York Times,* January 10, 2017, https://www.nytimes.com /2017/01/10/us/repeal-affordable-care-act-donald-trump.html; "Speaker Paul Ryan: GOP Will Work on Repealing, Replacing Health Law 'Concurrently,'" *Los Angeles Times,* January 10, 2017, https://www.latimes.com/nation/ct-paul-ryan-obamacare-repeal-20170110-story .html; Madeline Conway, "Trump Promises to Repeal and Replace Obamacare 'Essentially Simultaneously,'" *Politico,* January 11, 2017, https://www.politico.com/story/2017/01/trump -presser-obamacare-repeal-replace-233479.

17. Senior Obama administration officials, author interviews.

18. Jeanne Lambrew, author interview.

19. Lambrew and senior Obama administration official, author interviews.

20. Sarah Kliff and Ezra Klein, "Obama on Obamacare: Vox Interviews the President on January 6," *Vox,* December 30, 2016, https://www.vox.com/policy-and-politics/2016/12/30/14112224/vox -obama-interview; senior Obama administration official interview.

21. Jeff Stein, "Transcript: President Obama Talks to Vox About Obamacare's Future," *Vox,* January 6, 2017, https://www.vox.com/policy-and-politics/2017/1/6/14193334/obama-vox-interview -transcript.

22. Neera Tanden and Topher Spiro, author interviews; Topher Spiro and Thomas Huelskoetter, "Republican ACA Repeal Bill Would Unravel the Market Even Before It Goes into Effect," Center for American Progress, November 16, 2016, https://www.americanprogress.org/issues/healthcare/reports/2016/11/16/292394/republican-aca-repeal-bill-would-unravel-the-market-even-before-it-goes-into-effect/.

23. Andy Slavitt, author interview; Sam Brodey, "Andy Slavitt Already Saved Obamacare Once. Can He Do It Again?," *MinnPost*, March 23, 2017, https://www.minnpost.com/politics-policy/2017/03/andy-slavitt-already-saved-obamacare-once-can-he-do-it-again/; Juliet Eilperin, "A Cross-Country Bus Tour Aims to Help Save the Endangered Affordable Care Act," *Washington Post*, January 15, 2017, https://www.washingtonpost.com/national/health-science/a-cross-country-bus-tour-aims-to-help-save-the-endangered-affordable-care-act/2017/01/15/7fa1a71a-db3b-11e6-ad42-f3375f271c9c_story.html?utm_term=.d423e820e845; Eric Boodman, "Andy Slavitt Can't Stop: How a Health Care Wonk Became a Rabble-Rouser," STAT, May 25, 2017, https://www.statnews.com/2017/05/25/andy-slavitt-aca-town-halls/; Joanne Kenen and Dan Diamond, "Ex-Obamacare Boss Wants to Broker a Ceasefire in the Health Care Wars," *Politico*, January 23, 2017, https://www.politico.com/story/2017/01/obamacare-slavitt-repeal-replace-234017; Michael Shear and Robert Pear, "Former Obama Aides Lead Opposition to Health Care Repeal," *New York Times*, July 27, 2017, https://www.nytimes.com/2017/07/27/us/politics/obama-resist-health-care-repeal.html.

24. Former senior Obama administration official, author interview.

25. Ezekiel Emanuel, author interview. Trump, who transferred into Wharton after two years at Fordham, never made the dean's list and did not graduate with honors. A former admissions officer later said he met with Trump as a favor to Trump's brother, who was a friend; a book about Trump says this meeting helped him to get admission. Michael Kranish, "Trump Has Referred to His Wharton Degree as 'Super Genius Stuff.' An Admissions Officer Recalls It Differently," *Washington Post*, July 8, 2019, https://www.washingtonpost.com/politics/trump-who-often-boasts-of-his-wharton-degree-says-he-was-admitted-to-the-hardest-school-to-get-into-the-college-official-who-reviewed-his-application-recalls-it-differently/2019/07/08/0a4eb414-977a-11e9-830a-21b9b36b64ad_story.html; Dan Spinelli, "Why Penn Won't Talk About Donald Trump," *Politico*, November 6, 2016, https://www.politico.com/magazine/story/2016/11/donald-trump-2016-wharton-pennsylvania-214425; Jonathan Valania, "Fact-Checking All of the Mysteries Surrounding Donald Trump and Penn," *Philadelphia*, September 15, 2019, https://www.phillymag.com/news/2019/09/14/donald-trump-at-wharton-university-of-pennsylvania/.

26. Zeke Emanuel interview; Cliff Sims, *Team of Vipers* (New York: St. Martin's, 2019), Kindle edition, 118–119.

27. Brendan Buck interview.

28. Robert Costa and Amy Goldstein, "Trump Vows 'Insurance for Everybody' in Obamacare Replacement Plan," *Washington Post*, January 16, 2017, https://www.washingtonpost.com/politics/trump-vows-insurance-for-everybody-in-obamacare-replacement-plan/2017/01/15/5f2b1e18-db5d-11e6-ad42-f3375f271c9c_story.html.

29. Senior Republican aide interview.

30. Haberman and Pear, "Trump Tells Congress."

31. Mike DeBonis, "Behind Closed Doors, Republican Lawmakers Fret About How to Repeal Obamacare," *Washington Post*, January 27, 2017, https://www.washingtonpost.com/politics/behind-closed-doors-republican-lawmakers-fret-about-how-to-repeal-obamacare/2017/01/27/deabdafa-e491-11e6-a547-5fb9411d332c_story.html.

32. Price and Dean Rosen, author interviews.

33. Billy House and Arit John, "Republicans Hide New Obamacare Draft Under Shroud of Secrecy," Bloomberg, March 1, 2017, https://www.bloomberg.com/news/articles/2017-03-01/republicans-hide-latest-obamacare-draft-under-shroud-of-secrecy; Republican member of Congress, author interview.

34. Paul Demko, "Exclusive: Leaked GOP Obamacare Replacement Shrinks Subsidies, Medicaid Expansion," *Politico*, February 24, 2017, https://www.politico.com/story/2017/02/house-republicans-obamacare-repeal-package-235343; David Weigel, Sean Sullivan, and Mike DeBonis, "Conservative Groups and Lawmakers Demanding 'Full Repeal' Could Derail

Obamacare Rollback," *Washington Post,* March 2, 2017, https://www.washingtonpost.com/powerpost/conservative-groups-and-lawmakers-demanding-full-repeal-could-derail-obamacare-rollback/2017/03/02/0bf3f1a0-feaa-11e6-8ebe-6e0dbe4f2bca_story.html?itid=lk_inline_manual_18; House and John, "Republicans Hide New Obamacare Draft"; Amber Phillips, "Rand Paul, a Copy Machine and a 'Secret' Obamacare Bill," *Washington Post,* March 2, 2017, https://www.washingtonpost.com/news/the-fix/wp/2017/03/02/rand-paul-a-copy-machine-and-a-secret-obamacare-bill/.

35. America's Hospitals and Health Systems to Members of Congress, March 8, 2017, https://cdn2.vox-cdn.com/uploads/chorus_asset/file/8118041/HALO_Letter_to_House_AHCA_3-8-17.0.pdf; Sy Mukherjee, "These 3 Powerful Groups Are Slamming the GOP's Obamacare Replacement Plan," *Fortune,* March 8, 2017, https://fortune.com/2017/03/08/gop-healthcare-plan-aarp-ama-aha/.

36. Sarah Kliff, "Republicans' Rushed Health Bill Is Everything They Said They Hated About Obamacare," *Vox,* March 9, 2017, http://www.vox.com/policy-and-politics/2017/3/9/14867490/gop-obamacare-dead-of-night.

37. "American Health Care Act," CBO, March 13, 2017, https://www.cbo.gov/publication/52486; Jonathan Cohn, "Devastating CBO Report Exposes the Empty Promises of Obamacare Repeal," *HuffPost,* March 14, 2017, https://www.huffpost.com/entry/gop-health-care-plan_n_58c7de3be4b0428c7f1312a3; Sarah Kliff, "CBO Estimates 24 Million Lose Coverage Under GOP Plan. The Devastating Report, Explained," *Vox,* March 13, 2017, https://www.vox.com/2017/3/13/14912520/cbo-ahca-gop-plan.

38. Ibid.

39. Senior Republican aide and Republican strategist, author interviews.

40. Glenn Kessler, "The CBO's Shifting View on the Impact of the Obamacare Individual Mandate," *Washington Post,* February 26, 2019, https://www.washingtonpost.com/politics/2019/02/26/cbos-shifting-view-impact-obamacare-individual-mandate/.

41. One sign of this was something Trump said at the meeting with Zeke Emanuel, as Cliff Sims later recounted in his memoir. When Zeke suggested Trump work on a compromise, rather than repealing the law, Trump reminded him how popular the repeal slogan had been at rallies. "People hate it, doc. Honestly, you weren't out on the road in the campaign. People hate it—I mean hate it." Trump said that whenever he got to his signature line, that he was "going to repeal and replace the disaster known as Obamacare!" the crowd "would scream like nothing you've ever heard." Trump's depiction of the crowd reaction was accurate, but his crowds were not indicative of the country as a whole. Sims, *Team of Vipers,* 119.

Chapter 26: Thumbs-Down

1. Quincy Walters, "Obamacare Supporters Take Over Town Hall," WUSF Public Media, February 6, 2017, https://wusfnews.wusf.usf.edu/health-news-florida/2017-02-06/obamacare-supporters-take-over-town-hall.

2. "'We Need This Affordable Care Act': Voters Discuss Health Care at Florida Town Hall," YouTube video, 2:42, posted by *Washington Post,* May 11, 2017, https://www.youtube.com/watch?v=pBl9U49mb20; "Man to GOP Rep: 'Obamacare Saved My Daughter,'" YouTube video, 2:10, posted by CNN, February 11, 2017, https://www.youtube.com/watch?v=N3tLWf6LPBM; Sarah Kliff, "A GOP Official at a Town Hall Tried to Argue Obamacare Has Death Panels. It Did Not Go Well," *Vox,* February 12, 2017, https://www.vox.com/2017/2/12/14588086/death-panel-town-hall.

3. "Teacher's Town Hall Question Goes Viral," YouTube video, 2:58, posted by CNN, February 10, 2017, https://www.youtube.com/watch?v=H2qvE4uQHy4.

4. Mollie Reilly, "Angry Constituents Hammer Tom Cotton at Town Hall: 'Do Your Job,'" *HuffPost,* February 22, 2017, https://www.huffpost.com/entry/tom-cotton-town-hall-arkansas_n_58ae22e7e4b057efdce8e110; Emily Crockett, "Woman with Dying Husband Confronts Tom Cotton: 'What Kind of Insurance Do You Have?,'" *Vox,* February 22, 2017, https://www.vox.com/policy-and-politics/2017/2/22/14704812/tom-cotton-town-hall-angry-obamacare-insurance; Doug Thompson, "'I Will Die,' Springdale Woman Tells Cotton," Arkansas Online, February 23, 2017, https://www.arkansasonline.com/news/2017/feb/23/i-will-die-springdale-woman-tells-cotto/.

5. Leah Greenberg and Ezra Levin, *We Are Indivisible: A Blueprint for Democracy After Trump* (New York: Atria/One Signal, 2019), Kindle edition, 151; Ezra Levin, author interview.

6. David Weigel, "In Echoes of 2009, Republicans See 'Astroturf' in Democratic Protests," *Washington Post,* February 6, 2017, https://www.washingtonpost.com/news/post-politics/wp/2017/02/06/in-echoes-of-2009-republicans-see-astroturf-in-democratic-protests/.

7. Levin interview.

8. Mollyann Brodie, Elizabeth Hamel, Ashley Kirzinger, and Drew Altman, "The Past, Present, and Possible Future of Public Opinion on the ACA," *Health Affairs,* February 19, 2020, https://doi.org/10.1377/hlthaff.2019.01420.

9. Margot Sanger-Katz and Haeyoun Park, "Obamacare More Popular Than Ever, Now That It May Be Repealed," *New York Times,* February 1, 2017, https://www.nytimes.com/interactive/2017/02/01/us/politics/obamacare-approval-poll.html; Dhrumil Mehta, "Does Trying to Repeal Obamacare Actually Increase Its Appeal?," FiveThirtyEight, March 29, 2019, https://fivethirtyeight.com/features/does-trying-to-repeal-obamacare-actually-increase-its-appeal/; Adrianna McIntyre et al., "The Affordable Care Act's Missing Consensus," *Journal of Health Politics, Policy and Law,* October 2020, https://doi.org/10.1215/03616878-8543222.

10. Rich Lowry, "How the GOP Crackup Happens," *Politico,* March 15, 2017, https://www.politico.com/magazine/story/2017/03/how-the-gop-crackup-happens-214919; Matt Fuller and Jonathan Cohn, "GOP Health Care Bill Offers Upstate New York a Sweetheart Deal," *HuffPost,* March 20, 2017, https://www.huffpost.com/entry/new-york-sweetheart-deal-gop-health-care-bill_n_58d06f8de4b0ec9d29debda4; Jimmy Vielkind, "Health Care Bill's 'Buffalo Bribe' Detonates Across New York," *Politico,* March 21, 2017, https://www.politico.com/story/2017/03/health-care-new-york-medicaid-236328.

11. Jeremy Peters, "Patience Gone, Koch-Backed Groups Will Pressure G.O.P. on Health Repeal," *New York Times,* March 5, 2017, https://www.nytimes.com/2017/03/05/us/politics/koch-brothers-affordable-care-act.html; Fredreka Schouten, "Koch Groups Slam GOP Health Care Replacement Plan as 'Obamacare 2.0,'" *USA Today,* March 7, 2017, https://www.usatoday.com/story/news/politics/onpolitics/2017/03/07/charles-koch-david-koch-obamacare-repeal-opposition/98851754/.

12. Michael Kruse, "'He Pretty Much Gave In to Whatever They Asked For,'" *Politico,* June 1, 2018, https://www.politico.com/magazine/story/2018/06/01/donald-trump-deals-negotiation-art-of-deal-218584; John Cassidy, "Donald Trump's Business Failures Were Very Real," *New Yorker,* May 10, 2019, https://www.newyorker.com/news/our-columnists/donald-trumps-business-failures-were-very-real; Mike McIntire, Russ Buettner, and Susanne Craig, "How Reality-TV Fame Handed Trump a $427 Million Lifeline," *New York Times,* September 28, 2020.

13. Senior Trump administration officials and Republican aides, author interviews. Said Brian Blase, "There weren't a lot of people working on health care policy in the [Trump] campaign. I think President Trump had heard from Republicans for a long time, saying we have to repeal and replace Obamacare. He was supportive of repealing and replacing Obamacare and expected Congress to take the lead on the policy details. When he won, he just assumed that Congress was going to be able to deliver, because they had been talking about it forever"; Charlie Dent, author interview.

14. Julie Hirschfeld Davis, Thomas Kaplan, and Robert Pear, "Trump Warns House Republicans: Repeal Health Law or Lose Your Seats," *New York Times,* March 21, 2017, https://www.nytimes.com/2017/03/21/us/politics/house-republicans-health-care-donald-trump.html.

15. Dent interview. An account of this meeting also appears in the Cliff Sims memoir. The accounts are consistent except for some minor differences in dialogue. Sims recalls Trump telling Dent, "You're destroying your party," calling Dent "selfish," and saying, "I'm done with him" at the end. Cliff Sims, *Team of Vipers* (New York: St. Martin's, 2019), Kindle edition, 125.

16. Tim Alberta, *American Carnage* (New York: HarperCollins, 2019), Kindle edition, 436–437; Republican member of Congress, author interview. The quote from Steve Bannon was first reported by journalist Mike Allen, Axios, newsletter, March 25, 2017, https://www.axios.com/newsletters/axios-am-54b3f49b-5219-4565-8e8d-2264ef377fe4.html; Katie McHugh, "7 Reasons Why Obamacare 2.0 Is All But Guaranteed to Impose Crushing Costs on Voters, Hurt Trump's Base, and Hand Power Back to the Democrats," Breitbart, March 10, 2017, https://www.breitbart.com

/politics/2017/03/10/7-reasons-why-obamacare-2-0-is-all-but-guaranteed-to-impose-crushing
-costs-on-voters-hurt-trumps-base-and-hand-power-back-to-the-democrats/.

17. Senior Republican aides, author interviews.

18. Ibid.

19. "Speaker Ryan: 'ObamaCare Is the Law of the Land,'" C-SPAN video, 2:00, March 24, 2017, https://www.c-span.org/video/?c4663454/speaker-ryan-obamacare-law-land.

20. Caitlin Bowling, "Meadows Touts Rise as Self-Made Businessman," *Smoky Mountain News*, October 31, 2012, https://www.smokymountainnews.com/news/item/9204-meadows-touts-rise-as
-self-made-businessman; Brittney Parker, "Candidate Profiles Continue as Election Looms," *Macon County News*, October 18, 2012, https://web.archive.org/web/20150623051246/http://www
.maconnews.com/news/3796-candidate-profiles-continue-as-election-looms.

21. Steve Contorno, "As Trump Mulled Chief of Staff Pick, U.S. Rep. Mark Meadows's USF Degree Was Fixed on Wikipedia," *Tampa Bay Times*, December 18, 2018, https://www.tampabay
.com/florida-politics/buzz/2018/12/18/as-trump-mulled-chief-of-staff-pick-u-s-rep-mark
-meadowss-usf-degree-was-fixed-on-wikipedia/; Mark Barrett, "Mark Meadows Has Taken Chances in Rapid Rise to Power," *Asheville Citizen Times*, April 1, 2017, https://www.citizen
-times.com/story/news/local/2017/04/01/mark-meadows-has-taken-chances-rapid-rise
-power/99865648/.

22. He used the line on at least one more occasion. He also suggested that Hezbollah was involved in North Carolina's drug trade. Shira Tarlo, "More Mark Meadows Weirdness: Trump Defender Has Long History of Spreading Conspiracy Theories," *Salon*, February 28, 2019, https://www.salon.com/2019/02/28/more-mark-meadows-weirdness-trump-defender-has
-long-history-of-spreading-conspiracy-theories/.

23. Leigh Ann Caldwell, "Architect of the Brink: Meet the Man Behind the Government Shutdown," CNN, October 1, 2013, https://www.cnn.com/2013/09/27/politics/house-tea-party
/index.html.

24. Boehner told this story frequently and his chief of staff backed it up, calling it "the strangest behavior I had ever seen in Congress." See Lauren French and Jake Sherman, "House Conservative Seeks Boehner's Ouster," *Politico*, July 28, 2015, https://www.politico.com/story/2015/07
/house-conservative-john-boehner-ouster-120742; Alberta, *American Carnage*, 230; Donald Trump, Twitter post, March 30, 2017, 9:07 a.m., https://twitter.com/realDonaldTrump/status
/847435163143454723; Clare Foran, "Trump Threatens a 'Fight' Against the Freedom Caucus," *Atlantic*, March 30, 2017, https://www.theatlantic.com/politics/archive/2017/03/trump
-house-freedom-caucus-primary-challenge-fight/521307/.

25. "Thank You Mark Meadows for Standing Strong Against RyanCare," Asheville Tea Party, https://
ashevilleteaparty.org/thank-you-mark-meadows-for-standing-strong-against-ryancare/;
Michelle Malkin, Twitter post, March 24, 2017, 10:02 a.m., https://twitter.com/michellemalkin
/status/845274637021831168; "'This Week' Transcript 3-26-17: Sen. Chuck Schumer, Rep. Mark Meadows, Roger Stone, and Scott Pruitt," ABC News, March 26, 2017, https://abcnews.go.com
/Politics/week-transcript-26-17-sen-chuck-schumer-rep/story?id=46372022.

26. Dent interview; Tara Palmeri, "Inside Trump's Quiet Effort to Revive the Health Care Bill," *Politico*, April 26, 2017, https://www.politico.com/story/2017/04/26/trump-obamacare
-repeal-replace-237654.

27. Matt Fuller and Jonathan Cohn, "Some Republicans Think They May Have a Health Care Deal," *HuffPost*, April 19, 2017, https://www.huffpost.com/entry/republicans-health-care
-deal_n_58f819f7e4b0cb086d7df486?g39=.

28. Joe Williams, "Republicans Have No Deal on Obamacare Repeal but Talks Continue," *Roll Call*, April 20, 2017, https://www.rollcall.com/2017/04/20/republicans-have-no-deal-on-obamacare
-repeal-but-talks-continue/; "Repeal Obamacare Progress (MacArthur-Meadows Amendment)," Heritage Action for America, April 25, 2017, https://heritageaction.com/blog/repeal
-obamacare-progress-macarthur-meadows-amendment; Thomas Kaplan and Robert Pear, "With $8 Billion Deal on Health Bill, House G.O.P. Leader Says 'We Have Enough Votes,'" *New York Times*, May 3, 2017, https://www.nytimes.com/2017/05/03/us/politics/gop-eyes-8-billion
-addition-to-win-a-crucial-vote-to-the-latest-health-bill.html; Timothy Jost, "New $8 Billion for Those with Preexisting Conditions Appears to Boost AHCA; Critics Say Amount Is Too Low," *Health Affairs*, May 4, 2017, https://www.healthaffairs.org/do/10.1377/hblog20170504

.059954/full/; Susan Ferrechio, "How Nursing Home Beds Moved One Republican from 'No' to 'Yes' on Healthcare," *Washington Examiner*, May 4, 2017, https://www.washingtonexaminer.com/how-nursing-home-beds-moved-one-republican-from-no-to-yes-on-healthcare.

29. Dan Eggen, Twitter post, May 3, 2017, 8:07 p.m., https://twitter.com/DanEggenWPost/status/859922332604919809; Erica Werner, Twitter post, May 4, 2017, 10:25 a.m., https://twitter.com/ericawerner/status/860138281064943617; Timothy Jost, "House Passes AHCA: How It Happened, What It Would Do, And Its Uncertain Senate Future," *Health Affairs*, May 4, 2017, https://www.healthaffairs.org/do/10.1377/hblog20170504.059967/full/.

30. "Remarks by President Trump on Healthcare Vote in the House of Representatives," White House, May 4, 2017, https://www.whitehouse.gov/briefings-statements/remarks-president-trump-healthcare-vote-house-representatives/.

31. Sarah Lueck, "Eliminating Federal Protections for People with Health Conditions Would Mean Return to Dysfunctional Pre-ACA Individual Market," Center on Budget and Policy Priorities, May 3, 2017, https://www.cbpp.org/research/health/eliminating-federal-protections-for-people-with-health-conditions-would-mean-return; Aviva Aron-Dine, Edwin Park, and Jacob Leibenluft, "Amendment to House ACA Repeal Bill Guts Protections for People with Pre-Existing Conditions," Center on Budget and Policy Priorities, April 21, 2017, https://www.cbpp.org/research/health/amendment-to-house-aca-repeal-bill-guts-protections-for-people-with-pre-existing; Matthew Fiedler, "Allowing States to Define 'Essential Health Benefits' Could Weaken ACA Protections Against Catastrophic Costs for People with Employer Coverage Nationwide," Brookings Institution, May 2, 2017, https://www.brookings.edu/blog/usc-brookings-schaeffer-on-health-policy/2017/05/02/allowing-states-to-define-essential-health-benefits-could-weaken-aca-protections-against-catastrophic-costs-for-people-with-employer-coverage-nationwide/.

32. Sarah Kliff, "The Most Devastating Paragraph in the CBO Report," *Vox*, May 24, 2017, https://www.vox.com/policy-and-politics/2017/5/24/15688010/voxcare-cbo-report-ahca-devastating; "Cost Estimate: H.R. 1628 American Health Care Act of 2017," CBO, https://www.cbo.gov/system/files/115th-congress-2017-2018/costestimate/hr1628aspassed.pdf.

33. Alec MacGillis, *The Cynic: The Political Education of Mitch McConnell* (New York: Simon & Schuster, 2014), Kindle edition, 7.

34. Jane Mayer, "How Mitch McConnell Became Trump's Enabler-in-Chief," *New Yorker*, April 12, 2020.

35. Ibid. Also, Norm Ornstein and Thomas Mann have written extensively and authoritatively on McConnell's role in breaking congressional norms. Thomas Mann and Norm Ornstein, "How the Republicans Broke Congress," *New York Times*, December 2, 2017; Thomas Mann, E. J. Dionne, and Norm Ornstein, "How the GOP Prompted the Decay of Political Norms," *Atlantic*, September 19, 2017, https://www.theatlantic.com/politics/archive/2017/09/gop-decay-of-political-norms/540165/; Thomas Mann and Norman J. Ornstein, "The Republicans Waged a 3-Decade War on Government. They Got Trump," *Vox*, July 18, 2016, https://www.vox.com/2016/7/18/12210500/diagnosed-dysfunction-republican-party; Ron Elving, "What Happened with Merrick Garland in 2016 and Why It Matters Now," NPR, June 29, 2018, https://www.npr.org/2018/06/29/624467256/what-happened-with-merrick-garland-in-2016-and-why-it-matters-now.

36. Ed Mazza, "Tearful Jimmy Kimmel Breaks Down Revealing Newborn Son's Heart Surgery," *HuffPost*, May 2, 2017, https://www.huffpost.com/entry/jimmy-kimmel-baby-heart-surgery_n_590811f6e4b05c397681f094?ncid=inblnkushpmg00000009.

37. Sean Sullivan, Paige Winfield Cunningham, and Kelsey Snell, "While House Passes GOP Health-Care Bill, Senate Prepares to Do Its Own Thing," *Washington Post*, May 4, 2017, https://www.washingtonpost.com/powerpost/if-house-passes-gop-health-care-bill-a-steeper-climb-awaits-in-the-senate/2017/05/04/26a901da-30bd-11e7-8674-437ddb6e813e_story.html; Robert Pear, "13 Men, and No Women, Are Writing New G.O.P. Health Bill in Senate," *New York Times*, May 8, 2017, https://www.nytimes.com/2017/05/08/us/politics/women-health-care-senate.html.

38. Tom Cotton, Twitter post, March 9, 2017, 5:53 a.m., https://twitter.com/TomCottonAR/status/839791318020866048.

39. Emily Murry, author interview.

40. Ibid.

41. Pear, "13 Men."

42. Julie Rovner, "Veteran Health-Care Reporter: The Senate's Secrecy over Obamacare Repeal Has No Precedent," *Atlantic*, June 14, 2017, https://www.theatlantic.com/politics/archive/2017/06/the-senates-secrecy-over-health-care-was-decades-in-the-making/530337/; Sarah Kliff, "I've Covered Obamacare Since Day One. I've Never Seen Lying and Obstruction Like This," *Vox*, June 15, 2017, https://www.vox.com/health-care/2017/6/15/15807986/obamacare-lies-obstruction; Sarah Kliff, Garet Williams, and Carly Sitrin, "The GOP Health Effort Takes Secrecy to New Levels," *Vox*, July 25, 2017, https://www.vox.com/policy-and-politics/2017/7/25/15880262/republicans-health-hearings-repeal.

43. Caitlin Owens, "Senate GOP Won't Release Draft Health Care Bill," Axios, June 12, 2017, https://www.axios.com/senate-gop-wrapping-up-health-care-bill-but-wont-release-it-2440345281.html; Timothy Jost and Sara Rosenbaum, "Unpacking the Senate's Take on ACA Repeal and Replace," *Health Affairs*, June 23, 2017, https://www.healthaffairs.org/do/10.1377/hblog20170623.060756/full/; Sean Sullivan, Kelsey Snell, and Juliet Eilperin, "Senate GOP's Health Plan Debuts Amid Doubts," *Washington Post*, June 22, 2017, https://www.washingtonpost.com/powerpost/senate-gop-leaders-set-to-unveil-health-care-bill/2017/06/22/56dbe35c-5734-11e7-a204-ad706461fa4f_story.html; Jeffrey Young, "American Medical Association Slams Senate GOP Health Care Bill," *HuffPost*, June 26, 2017, https://www.huffpost.com/entry/american-medical-association-senate-health-care-bill_n_59514933e4b02734df2c5070; Nick Visser, "Sen. Susan Collins Comes Out Against Health Care Bill," *HuffPost*, June 26, 2017, https://www.huffpost.com/entry/susan-collins-no-health-care_n_59519143e4b02734df2cdc97.

44. Jonathan Cohn, "Cerebral Palsy Didn't Stop This College Junior. Obamacare Repeal Might," *HuffPost*, June 17, 2017, https://www.huffpost.com/entry/medicaid-cuts-disabilities_n_5941d2ade4b003d5948d133f.

45. Ryan Grenoble, "Police Haul Off Protesters, Some with Disabilities, from Mitch McConnell's Office," *HuffPost*, June 22, 2017, https://www.huffpost.com/entry/mitch-mcconnell-health-care-protest_n_594be412e4b0a3a837bdf1b7; Katie Reilly, "Disability Advocates Forcibly Removed from Senate Protest Say It Was Worth It," *Time*, June 23, 2017, https://time.com/4831386/disability-advocate-protest-gop-health-care-bill/.

46. Lisa Clemans-Cope, Dania Palanker, and Jane Wishner, "Repealing the ACA Could Worsen the Opioid Epidemic," *Health Affairs*, January 30, 2017, https://www.healthaffairs.org/do/10.1377/hblog20170130.058515/full/; Erin Schumaker and Igor Bobic, "What the GOP Health Bill Will Mean for Opioid Treatment," *HuffPost*, June 22, 2017, https://www.huffpost.com/entry/what-the-senate-gop-health-bill-will-mean-for-opioid-treatment_n_594aeb2ce4b0a3a837bcd1aa.

47. Sarah Kliff, "The Cruel Reality of High-Speed Health Care Legislating," *Vox*, June 26, 2017, https://www.vox.com/policy-and-politics/2017/6/26/15865598/senate-health-bill-fast-speed.

48. Jennifer Haberkorn, "Democrats to Halt Senate Business over Obamacare Repeal," *Politico*, June 19, 2017, https://www.politico.com/story/2017/06/19/democrats-stop-senate-business-obamacare-239715; Russell Berman, "The Democrats Stage a Senate Slowdown over Health Care," *Atlantic*, June 19, 2017, https://www.theatlantic.com/politics/archive/2017/06/the-democrats-stage-a-senate-slowdown-over-health-care/530817/.

49. Donald Trump, Twitter post, June 30, 2017, 6:37 a.m., https://twitter.com/realdonaldtrump/status/880737163247267840?lang=en.

50. Kliff, "The Cruel Reality of High-Speed Health Care Legislating."

51. Kelsey Snell, "Senate Passes Obamacare Repeal, Planned Parenthood Defunding Bill, Putting Republicans on Record," *Washington Post*, December 3, 2015, https://www.washingtonpost.com/news/powerpost/wp/2015/12/03/senate-passes-obamacare-repeal-planned-parenthood-defunding-bill-putting-republicans-on-record/; Alicia Parlapiano, Wilson Andrews, Jasmine C. Lee, and Rachel Shorey, "How Each Senator Voted on Obamacare Repeal Proposals," *New York Times*, July 25, 2017, https://www.nytimes.com/interactive/2017/07/25/us/politics/senate-votes-repeal-obamacare.html.

52. Erica Martinson, "Trump Administration Threatens Retribution Against Alaska over Mur-

kowski Health Votes," *Anchorage Daily News,* July 26, 2017, https://www.adn.com/politics /2017/07/26/trump-administration-signals-that-murkowskis-health-care-vote-could-have -energy-repercussions-for-alaska/.

53. Jeff Stein, "Why Alaska's Lisa Murkowski Isn't Afraid of Donald Trump," *Vox,* July 27, 2017, https://www.vox.com/policy-and-politics/2017/7/27/16030520/murkowski-republican -health-bill; "Any Version of Repeal Harms Alaska Natives," Families USA, July 2017, https:// familiesusa.org/wp-content/uploads/2017/07/FUSA_and_POCA_Alaska-Native-American _Factsheet_7-26-17revision.pdf; "Urging Congress to Protect Provisions That Benefit Tribes in Any Repeal of the Affordable Care Act," National Congress of American Indians, June 2017, http://www.ncai.org/resources/resolutions/urging-congress-to-protect-provisions-that -benefit-tribes-in-any-repeal-of-the-affordable-care-act.

54. Senior Trump administration officials and senior Republican strategist, author interviews.

55. Chris Murphy, author interview.

56. Steven Dennis, Twitter post, July 28, 2017, 12:10 a.m., https://twitter.com/StevenTDennis /status/890786555442282496; Matt Fuller, Twitter post, July 28, 2017, 12:08 a.m., https:// twitter.com/MEPFuller/status/890786101555675137.

57. Elissa Slotkin, author interview.

58. Ibid.; see also Lauren Gibbons, "Former U.S. Defense Official Elissa Slotkin announces Congressional Run," MLive, July 10, 2017, https://www.mlive.com/news/2017/07/former_us_defense _official_eli.html.

59. Sarah Kliff, "Republicans Killed the Obamacare Mandate. New Data Shows It Didn't Really Matter," *New York Times,* September 18, 2020, https://www.nytimes.com/2020/09/18/upshot /obamacare-mandate-republicans.html.

60. Simone Pathé, "He Helped Write the GOP's Health Care Bill. Now It's Catching Up with Him," *Roll Call,* October 29, 2018, https://www.rollcall.com/2018/10/29/he-helped-write-the-gops -health-care-bill-now-its-catching-up-with-him/; Jonathan Cohn, "Republicans Are Still Rewriting History on Pre-Existing Conditions," *HuffPost,* October 16, 2018, https://www.huffpost .com/entry/mcsally-republican-pre-existing-conditions_n_5bc62785e4b055bc947ade8a.

61. Jonathan Cohn, "Republicans Are Using Their Families to Defend Their Records on Health Care," *HuffPost,* October 9, 2018, https://www.huffpost.com/entry/pre-existing-conditions -obamacare-bishop-slotkin_n_5bbbad09e4b01470d0540f38.

62. Jonathan Cohn, "It's Not Just About Pre-Existing Conditions—Medicaid Is on the Ballot Too," *HuffPost,* November 5, 2018, https://www.huffpost.com/entry/medicaid-expansion -obamacare-midterms-republicans_n_5bde7aafe4b04367a87d340c.

Conclusion

1. Barack Obama, author interview.

2. U.S. Census Bureau, "Health Insurance Coverage in the United States: 2018," November 18, 2019.

3. For an overview of international systems and the merits of each, see Ezekiel Emanuel, *Which Country Has the Best Health Care?* (New York: PublicAffairs, 2020).

4. Nancy Pelosi, author interview.

5. As Ezra Klein wrote after the 2020 elections, "The fundamental feedback loop of politics— parties compete for public support, and if they fail the public, they are electorally punished, and so they change—is broken. But it's only broken for the Republican Party." Klein, "The Crisis Isn't Too Much Polarization. It's Too Little Democracy," *Vox,* November 12, 2020, https://www.vox .com/21561011/2020-election-joe-biden-donald-trump-electoral-college-vote-senate -democracy.

6. For more on the political effects of the Affordable Care Act, see Lawrence R. Jacobs and Suzanne Mettler, *Journal of Health Politics, Policy and Law,* August 2020, https://doi.org/10.1215/03616878 -8255505.

7. Sherry Glied, Sara Collins, and Saunders Lin, "Did The ACA Lower Americans' Financial Barriers To Health Care?" *Health Affairs,* March 2020, https://www.healthaffairs.org/doi/ abs/10.1377/hlthaff.2019.01448. See also Madeline Guth, Rachel Garfield, and Robin Rudowitz, "The Effects of Medicaid Expansion Under the ACA: Updated Findings from a Literature Review," Kaiser Family Foundation, March 2020, https://www.kff.org/report-section/the -effects-of-medicaid-expansion-under-the-aca-updated-findings-from-a-literature-review

-report/; Jacob Goldin, Ithai Z. Lurie, and Janet McCubbin, "Health Insurance and Mortality: Experimental Evidence from Taxpayer Outreach, Quarterly Journal of Economics," NBER, working paper No. 26533, December 2019, http://www.nber.org/papers/w26533; Anna L. Goldman, Danny McCormick, Jennifer S. Haas, and Benjamin Sommers, "Effects of the ACA's Health Insurance Marketplaces on the Previously Uninsured: A Quasi-Experimental Analysis," *Health Affairs,* April 2018, https://www.healthaffairs.org/doi/10.1377/hlthaff.2017 .1390; Hannah Archambault and Dean Baker, "Voluntary Part-Time Employment and the Affordable Care Act: What Do Workers Do with Their Extra Time?," Center for Economic and Policy Research, October 2018, https://cepr.net/images/stories/reports/atus-aca-2018 -10.pdf; Sara R. Collins, Munira Z. Gunja, Michelle M. Doty, and Sophie Beutel, "How the Affordable Care Act Has Improved Americans' Ability to Buy Health Insurance on Their Own," Issue Brief, Commonwealth Fund, February 2017, https://www.commonwealthfund .org/publications/issue-briefs/2017/feb/how-affordable-care-act-has-improved-americans -ability-buy.

8. Larry Levitt, author interview.

9. I told their stories in Jonathan Cohn, "This Is What Obamacare's Critics Won't Admit or Simply Don't Understand," *HuffPost,* February 18, 2017, https://www.huffpost.com/entry /obamacare-what-went-right-critics_n_58a725dce4b045cd34c11b4c and Jonathan Cohn, "It's Not Just About Pre-Existing Conditions—Medicaid Is on the Ballot Too," *HuffPost,* November 14, 2018, https://www.huffpost.com/entry/medicaid-expansion-obamacare -midterms-republicans_n_5bde7aafe4b04367a87d340c.

Index